Microsoft® Office 2007
Brief Edition

LABYRINTH
L E A R N I N G™

Microsoft Office 2007: Brief Edition
by Russel Stolins, Alec Fehl, Trisha Hakola,
Jill Murphy, and Pamela R. Toliver

Copyright © 2008 by Labyrinth Learning

LABYRINTH
L E A R N I N G™

Labyrinth Learning
PO Box 20820
El Sobrante, California 94803
800.522.9746
On the web at lablearning.com

President:
Brian Favro

Chief Operating Officer:
Ted Ricks

Acquisitions Editor:
Jason Favro

Series Editor:
Russel Stolins

Managing Editor:
Laura A. Lionello

Production Manager:
Rad Proctor

Indexing: Joanne Sprott

Cover Design:
Seventeenth Street Studios

Labyrinth Learning™ and the Labyrinth Learning logo are registered trademarks of Labyrinth Publications. Microsoft®, Outlook®, PowerPoint®, and Windows® are registered trademarks of Microsoft Corporation. Other product and company names mentioned herein may be the trademarks of their respective owners.

Screen shots reprinted with permission from Microsoft Corporation.

ITEM: 1-59136-149-4
ISBN-13: 978-1-59136-149-7

Manufactured in the United States of America.

10 9 8 7 6 5

Microsoft Office 2007
Brief Edition

Contents in Brief

UNIT 4 POWERPOINT 2007 AND ACCESS 2007

Table of Contents

UNIT 3 EXCEL 2007

Summary of Keyboard Shortcuts

Document Commands (All Applications)

Open	Ctrl + O
Print	Ctrl + P
Save	Ctrl + S
Select all	Ctrl + A

Editing Commands (All Applications)

Bold	Ctrl + B
Copy	Ctrl + C
Cut	Ctrl + X
Find	Ctrl + F
Italic	Ctrl + I
Paste	Ctrl + V
Redo/Repeat	Ctrl + Y
Replace	Ctrl + H
Show/Hide Ribbon	Ctrl + F1
Underline	Ctrl + U
Undo	Ctrl + Z

Access Commands

Move to last field in a record	Ctrl + End then Tab

Excel Commands

Autosum	Alt + =
Clear cell contents	Delete
Place a chart on its own sheet	F11
Select a column	Ctrl + Spacebar
Select a row	Shift + Spacebar
Show formulas	Ctrl + `

PowerPoint Commands

Advance a slide	Spacebar or →
Back up a slide	Backspace or ←

Word Commands

1.5 spacing	Ctrl + 1.5
Double spacing	Ctrl + 2
Insert date	Alt + Shift + D
Insert page break	Ctrl + Enter
New document	Ctrl + N
Single spacing	Ctrl + 1
Spelling & Grammar check	F7

Excel
ALT shift   2 words = 1 Column

Summary of Quick Reference Tables

Summary of New in Office 2007 Features

Preface

Microsoft® Office 2007: Brief Edition is an introduction to the Microsoft Office 2007 Suite. In Unit 1, students are introduced to the new Ribbon interface and review basic computer concepts and file management skills. In Unit 2, students work with Word 2007 basics. In Unit 3, students study Excel 2007 basics. And, in Unit 4, students create a PowerPoint 2007 presentation and learn to work with Access 2007 databases.

Labyrinth has been writing and publishing Microsoft Office courses for more than 10 years. We have expanded our book list to include other application programs, including Macromedia® Dreamweaver®, Intuit® QuickBooks®, digital photography, Adobe Photoshop Elements®, and more. Labyrinth has developed a unique instructional design that makes learning faster and easier for students at all skill levels. Teachers have found that the Labyrinth model provides effective learning for students in both self-paced and instructor-led environments. The material is carefully crafted and built around compelling case studies that demonstrate the relevance of the subject matter. Mastery of this subject matter is ensured through the use of multiple levels of carefully crafted exercises.

This course is also supported on the Labyrinth website with a comprehensive instructor support package that includes detailed lesson plans, PowerPoint presentations, a course syllabus, extensive test banks, and more.

We are grateful to the many teachers who have used Labyrinth titles and suggested improvements to us during the 10 years we have been writing and publishing books. *Microsoft Office 2007: Brief Edition* has benefited greatly from the reviewing and suggestions of Charles Barrett, City College of San Francisco (San Francisco, CA); Sue Gibson, Mid-East Career & Technology Center (Zanesville, OH); Susan Ieradi, Northern Essex Community College (Haverhill, MA); Debi Lorrain, UC Davis (Davis, CA); Cinthia Vera, Centinela Valley Adult School (Lawndale, CA); and Jeff West, Seattle Central Community College (Seattle, WA).

How This Book Is Organized

This book is organized according to the primary applications taught. This organization is designed to familiarize you with each application program and offers sufficient reinforcement so routine commands become second nature. Each unit ends with a series of unit-level Assessment exercises to further test students' knowledge.

Unit 1: Getting Started

These lessons prepare students to work with the Office 2007 applications. We begin with an introduction to Windows' new Ribbon interface. Topics discussed include contextual tabs, Live Preview, galleries, the Office menu, the Quick Access toolbar, and Help features. We then discuss file storage media, browsing files, and working with folders. By the end of this unit, students will be well-prepared for the remaining lessons in this course.

Unit 2: Word 2007

These lessons introduce word processing with Word 2007. We begin with a comprehensive look at the new Ribbon interface in Word and how to open, navigate in, and close documents. We then move on to the basic techniques for keying and editing documents, paying particular attention to business letters. In this unit, we also create and dynamically format memoranda and simple reports. We round out our Word discussion with a lesson on creating and working with tables.

Unit 3: Excel 2007

These lessons cover worksheet skills with Excel 2007. We begin with a comprehensive look at the new Ribbon interface in Excel and how to enter and edit entries, select cells and ranges, and clear cell contents. We also discuss how to print worksheets and worksheet selections. Next, we work with formulas and functions. Then, we discuss formatting with numbers, colors, and fills. We also modify the widths and heights of columns and rows and insert and delete columns, rows, and cells. We conclude the Excel unit by discussing charts.

Unit 4: PowerPoint 2007 and Access 2007

This unit begins with a lesson on PowerPoint 2007. Topics introduced include navigating in the program window; document themes; creating a presentation with bulleted lists, clip art, and animations; printing presentations; and techniques for delivering a slide show. In the Access 2007 portion of this unit, we begin by defining databases and exploring the Access environment. We also open, navigate, and close database objects; work with tabbed objects and tables; and view forms and reports. From there we move on to adding records and formatting datasheet layout, retrieving data and filtering records, previewing and printing data, and saving a database as a new file.

Appendix A

This appendix explains how to retrieve the student exercise files necessary for use with this book from the Labyrinth website and unzipping the files to a file storage location. Special attention is given to storing files on a USB flash drive. Complete the exercises in this appendix before beginning work on the lessons in this book.

Visual Conventions

This book uses many visual and typographic cues to guide you through the lessons. This page provides examples and describes the function of each cue.

`Type this text`   Anything you should type at the keyboard is printed in this typeface.

 TIP!   Tips, Notes, and Warnings are used throughout the text to draw attention to certain topics.

Command→
Command→
Command, etc.   This convention indicates how to give a command from the Ribbon. The commands are written: Ribbon Tab→Command Group→Command→ Sub-command.

FROM THE KEYBOARD
Ctrl+S to save   These margin notes indicate shortcut keys for executing a task described in the text.

 2007 new!   This icon indicates features that have changed dramatically from Office 2003 to Office 2007.

 QR▶   Quick Reference tables provide generic instructions for key tasks. Only perform these tasks if you are instructed to do so in an exercise.

 On the Web   This icon indicates the availability of a web-based simulation for an exercise or other online content. You many need to use a WebSim if your computer lab is not set up to support particular exercises.

    Hands-On exercises are introduced immediately after concept discussions. They provide detailed, step-by-step tutorials so you can master the skills presented.

    The Concepts Review section includes both true/false and multiple choice questions designed to gauge your understanding of concepts.

    Skill Builder exercises provide additional hands-on practice with moderate assistance.

    Assessment exercises test your skills by describing the correct results without providing specific instructions on how to achieve them.

About the Authors

Alec Fehl (BM, Music Production and Engineering, and MCSE, A+, NT-CIP, ACE, ACI certified) has been a technical trainer, computer consultant, and web application developer since 1999. After graduating from the prestigious Berklee College of Music in Boston, he set off for Los Angeles with the promise of being a rock star. After 10 years gigging in L.A., teaching middle school math, and auditioning for the Red Hot Chili Peppers (he didn't get the gig), he and his wife Jacqui moved to Asheville, North Carolina, where Alec now teaches computer classes at Asheville-Buncombe Technical Community College. Recently Alec was named 2007 Adjunct Teacher of the Year at AB-Tech Community College. Alec is author of Labyrinth's *Microsoft PowerPoint 2007: Comprehensive* and the upcoming *Web Page Design with HTML/XHTML: Essentials*.

Trish Hakola (BS, Biology) is an assistant principal for Poway Adult School in San Diego, CA. She has been using Excel since 1991 and teaching students to use the application since 1998. She earned her Bachelor of Science degree from Washington State University and has a Designated Subjects Vocational Education Teaching Credential from the state of California. In addition, she has a Certificate in Online Teaching from the University of California, San Diego (Extension). Currently, Trish is working on her Master's in Education Leadership at Point Loma Nazarene University. Trish serves as the President-Elect on the CAROCP (California Association of Regional Centers and Programs) Board for the counties of San Diego and Imperial. Trish is also the author of Labyrinth's *QuickBooks Pro 2004 and 2005: Comprehensive Course*, *QuickBooks Pro 2006: Essentials Course*, and *QuickBooks Pro 2007: Essentials*.

Jill Murphy (BS, Education) has twenty years of experience with the IBM Corporation in technical support, curriculum development, training trainers, and training management. Currently, Jill is an instructor for ExecuTrain of San Francisco, and she also focuses on instructional design and curriculum development. In her many years of training in the corporate environment, she has developed a deep understanding of adult learning principles and accelerated learning techniques. This experience has given her the background for writing effective training materials. Jill has authored and coauthored a number of books for Labyrinth, including *Microsoft Office Word 2003: Comprehensive Course* and *Microsoft Office 2003: Essentials Course*. When not writing or teaching, Jill enjoys practicing yoga and tai chi and taking long walks among the sycamore trees in her Mill Valley, CA neighborhood.

Russel Stolins (MA, Educational Technology) is an editor and best-selling author living in Santa Fe, New Mexico. He has been teaching adults about technology since 1982, including courses on desktop publishing, computer concepts, Microsoft Office applications, multimedia design, and the Internet. Russel's latest book is *Welcome to Photoshop Elements 4.0* (as co-author), published by Labyrinth in August 2006. His latest editing projects include *Welcome to Computers for ESL Students* and Series Editor for Labyrinth's Office 2007 series of books.

Pamela R. Toliver (BS, Business Teacher Education; MS, Industrial and Technical Education) has a wealth of teaching experience. After more than 15 years teaching business education and office management at the high school and university levels, she entered the corporate and executive training world and now has more that 12 years of experience teaching computer software in state and federal government agencies, large corporations, and training centers. She began teaching specialized proprietary software in 1993 and has worked with large agencies in systems analysis and design. She is a published author of college textbooks for computer applications and has developed and written more than fifty courseware training manuals for large corporations and law firms. Her experience also includes designing instructional and training programs for a variety of organizations. She is a certified expert in five major Microsoft Office programs and a certified IC3 expert. Pam and her husband have two grown children and one grandchild. They live in Fort Collins, Colorado.

Microsoft Office 2007
Brief Edition

Unit 1

Getting Started

In this unit, you will begin by working with Windows' new Ribbon interface. The Ribbon includes contextual tabs and galleries instead of the former menu bars, toolbars, and dialog boxes. In the first lesson of this unit, you will explore the Ribbon, use the new Office Menu button, customize the new Quick Access toolbar, and use the Help feature. In the second lesson of this unit, you will deal with file management issues. You will browse and open files using folder windows, copy and move files, create new folders, rename files and folder, and delete and restore files. This unit ends with a series of Assessment exercises.

Lesson 1: Introducing Basic Computer Concepts

Lesson 2: Working with Windows Programs

Unit 1 Assessments

LESSON 1

Working with the New Ribbon Interface

Office 2007 features a brand new interface that does away with the old conventions of menu bars, toolbars, task panes, and dialog boxes. These have been replaced by the Ribbon, Contextual Tabs, and Galleries. With this new task-based grouping of commands, users will easily and intuitively find the right command for their task. Additionally, the new uncluttered interface removes many of the distractions prevalent in previous versions of Office, allowing you to focus on your work. In this lesson, you will learn to use the Office Ribbon and other features of the new Office 2007 interface.

LESSON OBJECTIVES

After studying this lesson, you will be able to:

- Identify the major features of the new Office 2007 Ribbon interface
- Describe the functions of the new Office button
- Customize the Quick Access Toolbar
- Describe how to get help locating familiar commands on the new interface

Additional learning resources are available at labpub.com/learn/oe7b/

Case Study: Learning the Ribbon

Juanita has just purchased the new Office 2007 Suite. After installing the software, she creates a new blank document to try things out. She has heard about the new Office 2007 interface and is anxious to try the Ribbon and other new features. At first, it feels quite strange to work with a program that doesn't use menu bars. However, soon Juanita learns how to switch from one Ribbon tab to another to display the commands she needs. And, some new features such as Live Preview and the Gallery are quite intuitive immediately. Juanita also learns how to use online help to get information about upgrading from previous versions of a program to the new 2007 version.

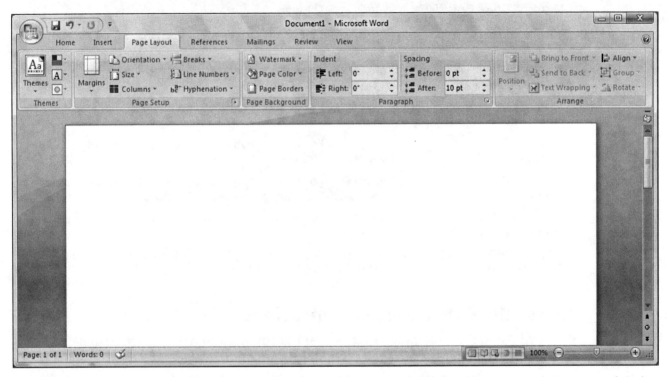

Like most Office 2007 Suite applications, Microsoft Office Word 2007 features a new interface. Many commands once accessed via the menu bar are now available on the Ribbon.

Introducing the Microsoft Office Suite Applications

The Microsoft Office 2007 Suite is not a single program. It is a suite of several programs, each aimed at accomplishing a specific task or creating a specific type of document. Microsoft offers eight different versions of the Microsoft Office 2007 Suite, each with a different collection of programs. The following table lists the programs included in each edition.

Version	Programs Included
Microsoft Office Basic 2007	Word, Excel, Outlook
Microsoft Office Home & Student 2007	Word, Excel, PowerPoint, OneNote
Microsoft Office Standard 2007	Word, Excel, PowerPoint, Outlook
Microsoft Office Small Business 2007	Word, Excel, PowerPoint, Publisher, Outlook with Business Contact Manager
Microsoft Office Professional 2007	Word, Excel, PowerPoint, Publisher, Outlook, Access, Outlook with Business Contact Manager
Microsoft Office Ultimate 2007	Word, Excel, PowerPoint, Publisher, Access, OneNote, Outlook with Business Contact Manager, InfoPath, Groove
Microsoft Office Professional Plus 2007	Word, Excel, PowerPoint, Publisher, Access, InfoPath, Communicator
Microsoft Office Enterprise 2007	Word, Excel, PowerPoint, Publisher, Outlook, Access, OneNote, InfoPath, Communicator, Groove

About the Office Suite Applications

- **Word:** Word is a word processing program. If you want to type a letter, term paper, shopping list, or create envelopes, Word is the program to use.

- **Excel:** Excel is a spreadsheet program, meaning its strength is in crunching numbers. Spreadsheets are great for analyzing numerical data and performing calculations. Many users mistake Excel for a database program and use it when Access would be better suited for their work.

- **PowerPoint:** PowerPoint is a presentation program. With it, you can create slide show presentations complete with animations, sound, and lecture notes.

- **Access:** Access is a database program. Use a database rather than a spreadsheet when you need to filter or sort your data based on changeable criteria, or when you have a lot of data to store.

- **Outlook:** At its most basic, Outlook is an email client. Use it to send and receive email. Outlook offers additional functionality, including a calendar to schedule appointments, an address book, and a to-do list.

- **OneNote:** OneNote is a digital notebook in which you can store typed and handwritten notes, audio and video clips, pictures, and scanned documents. It has a powerful search feature and allows you to share your notebook with other users.

Other Programs and Features

Office 2007 features several other programs and technologies, including Communicator (for real-time instant messaging), Groove (collaboration software), and Outlook with Business Contact Manager (which allows you to track customers and sales leads). When purchasing the Office 2007 Suite, you should pay particular attention to buy the edition that comes with the programs you need.

Working with the New Office 2007 Interface

Several Office 2007 Suite applications (but not all) introduce a new interface. This topic gives an overview of the most significant features of this interface.

Where'd They Go?—The Missing Menu Bars and Toolbars

Older versions of Microsoft Office, as well as most current software applications, rely on menu bars and toolbars to display available commands. Microsoft determined that because Office programs have so many options and commands, menu bars and toolbars were no longer an efficient way to display them. The old style menu bar and toolbars have been replaced by the Ribbon.

Microsoft has also reduced workspace clutter by removing task panes and dialog boxes wherever possible. The new Ribbon and Contextual Tab interfaces greatly simplify the grouping of commands and make it more intuitive to accomplish your tasks.

The Ribbon

The Ribbon, which has replaced the menu bar and toolbars, consists of several tabs. Each tab contains groupings of commands for similar tasks. The following illustration displays the Home tab as the active tab.

 NOTE! *These Ribbon examples are from Microsoft Word 2007. The Ribbon on other Office 2007 Suite applications will differ.*

Notice the seven default tabs: Home, Insert, Page Layout, References, Mailings, Review, and View. Click on a tab to reveal the available commands.

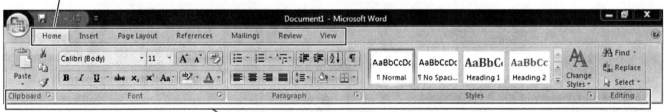

Home tab on the Word 2007 Ribbon

The Home tab contains commands split into several groups: Clipboard, Font, Paragraph, Styles, and Editing. Each group contains several icons and controls for a variety of tasks.

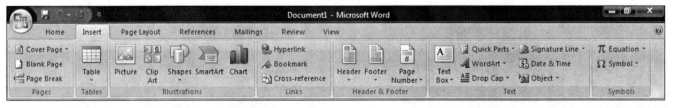

The Insert tab on the Word 2007 Ribbon displays an entirely new set of command groups and buttons.

Hands-On 1.1   **Explore a Ribbon**

In this exercise, you will view the Ribbon in Word and its various default tabs.

1. Launch Microsoft Word by clicking Start→All Programs→Microsoft Office→Microsoft Office Word 2007

   The Word program opens with a new blank document. Additionally, the Home tab is active. Take note of the different groupings of commands (Clipboard, Font, Paragraph, Styles, and Editing).

NOTE! *Depending on your screen size and resolution, the buttons on the Ribbon may not match the figures in the exercises exactly.*

2. Follow these steps to examine the Insert tab on the Ribbon:

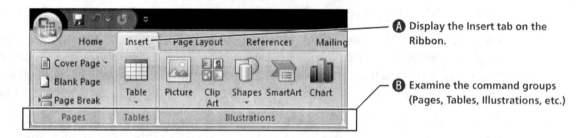

Ⓐ Display the Insert tab on the Ribbon.

Ⓑ Examine the command groups (Pages, Tables, Illustrations, etc.)

3. Continue clicking the remaining tabs and examining their command groups. When you are finished, click the Home tab.

   Leave Microsoft Word open.

Contextual Tabs

While the Word 2007 Ribbon displays only the seven default Tabs initially, other Tabs appear and disappear depending on what is selected on the document. For example, if a picture is selected, a Format tab will appear with commands applicable to formatting a picture. When the picture is deselected, the contextual Tab disappears.

The Word 2007 Ribbon displays the Format tab when you select a picture in the document.

Hands-On 1.2   View a Contextual Tab

In this exercise, you will view a contextual tab.

1. With Microsoft Word open and a new document on the screen, click anywhere on the blank white document. You should see your insertion point toward the top-left corner of the document.

2. Follow these steps to insert a table:

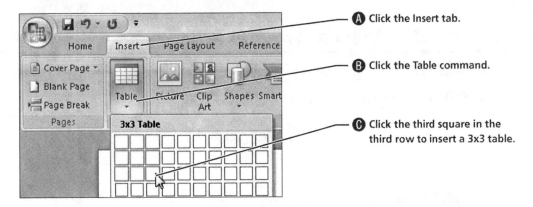

A Click the Insert tab.

B Click the Table command.

C Click the third square in the third row to insert a 3x3 table.

Two new Contextual Tabs (Design and Layout) appear at the right end of the Ribbon.

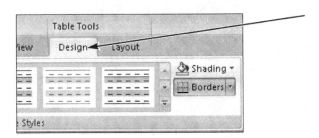

3. Click below the table. The additional tabs disappear. Click inside the table. The tabs reappear.
   Contextual tabs appear based on what you have selected on the page.

4. Click the Office [ ] button, and then click Close. When prompted to save changes, choose No.
   The document closes. Leave Microsoft Word open.

Live Preview

If you have ever changed the size or color of text only to decide the new color doesn't look so good and you change it back, you'll love Live Preview. Live Preview shows what your change will look like before you commit to it. For example, clicking on the Color menu and rolling your mouse over the various colors changes the text color on the page as you move your mouse, allowing you to preview all of your options before making a selection. And, Live Preview works with more than just text; it works anywhere you might make a formatting change, like table borders and shading.

 ## Hands-On 1.3   View a Live Preview

In this exercise, you will see a Live Preview of a command.

1. Follow these steps to create a new blank Word document:

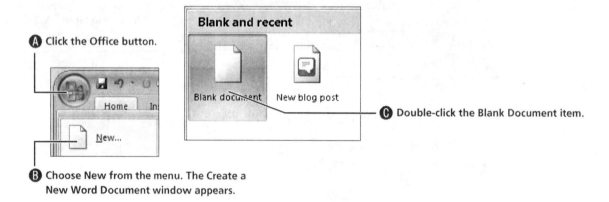

A new blank document appears.

2. Type the following text:
   This is an example of Live Preview.

3. Follow these steps to select a portion of the text:

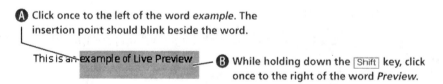

Word highlights the text between your two clicks. A floating formatting toolbar may appear after highlighting your text. Ignore it and continue formatting your text with the method in the next step.

4. Follow these steps to use Live Preview:

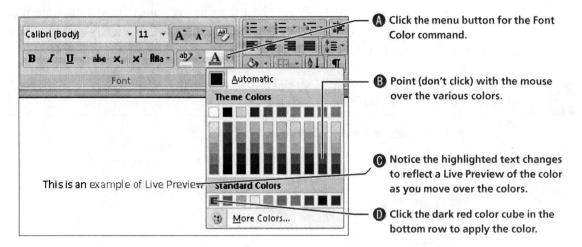

Ⓐ Click the menu button for the Font Color command.

Ⓑ Point (don't click) with the mouse over the various colors.

Ⓒ Notice the highlighted text changes to reflect a Live Preview of the color as you move over the colors.

Ⓓ Click the dark red color cube in the bottom row to apply the color.

5. Make sure that the text "example of Live Preview" is still selected, and then follow these steps to preview a new size:

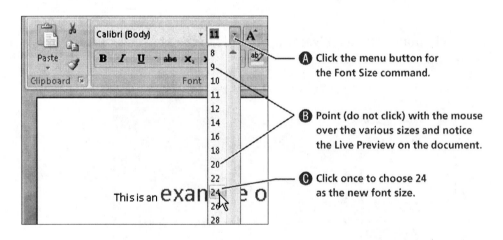

Ⓐ Click the menu button for the Font Size command.

Ⓑ Point (do not click) with the mouse over the various sizes and notice the Live Preview on the document.

Ⓒ Click once to choose 24 as the new font size.

Leave Microsoft Word open with the document still visible on the screen.

Galleries

Galleries make it easier to apply formatting or insert objects into a document by removing complex dialog boxes and their numerous options. Simply click on a command that offers gallery choices and you'll be presented with clear samples from which to choose.

 Hands-On 1.4   View a Gallery

In this exercise, you will view a sample gallery.

1. Click the Insert tab, and then click the Cover Page command.

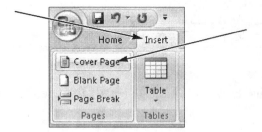

2. Scroll through the Gallery until you come to the Mod cover page. Click once on the Mod cover page gallery item.

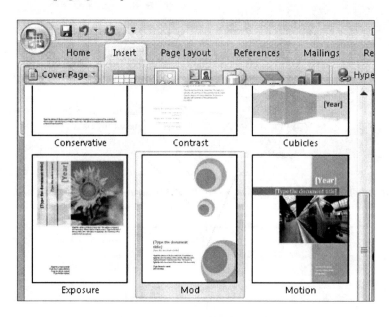

The Mod cover page is added to your document in a single click; you do not have to navigate through complex dialog boxes with numerous options.

Leave Microsoft Word open.

The Office Menu

 The menu bar has disappeared from the Office 2007 interface, but the new Office menu offers the basic commands you used to find under the *File* menu. Old favorites like New, Open, Close, and Exit are accessible through the Office menu.

Use these commands when you want to create new documents, open existing documents, or save open documents.

Use these commands when you are ready to output your document to a printer, send by email or fax, or apply other finishing options.

This button closes the active document.

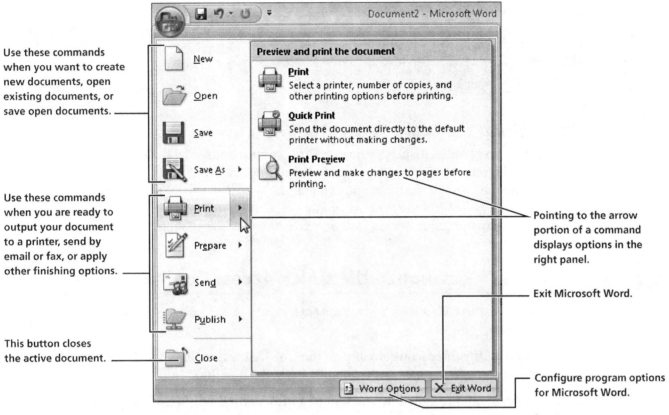

Pointing to the arrow portion of a command displays options in the right panel.

Exit Microsoft Word.

Configure program options for Microsoft Word.

Word's Office menu is typical of applications with the new interface.

Hands-On 1.5   Explore the Office Menu

In this exercise, you will navigate the Office menu. Some familiar commands from the File and Tools menus will be pointed out.

1. Click the Office button and examine the various commands available.
   Many options will be similar to those once found in the File menu of previous Word versions.

2. Point over the menu button for the Save As command, as shown at right.
   A list of options appears in the right panel. For example, you can save the document so it may be opened with previous versions of Word.

3. Point over the menu button for the Print command.
   Word displays options for printing or previewing the document.

4. Click anywhere on the document (or tap the [Esc] key twice) to close the Office menu without applying a command.
   Leave the Word window open.

The Quick Access Toolbar

The Quick Access toolbar offers just that: quick access to several commonly used commands. Rather than choosing the Print command from the Office menu, you can access the same print command with a single click on the Quick Access toolbar.

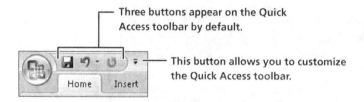

Three buttons appear on the Quick Access toolbar by default.

This button allows you to customize the Quick Access toolbar.

Customizing the Quick Access Toolbar

The Quick Access toolbar displays icons for three common tasks by default, but you can customize it by removing or adding icons to fit your needs. For example, if you find yourself changing the font size all the time, you can add the font size control to the Quick Access toolbar so it is available all the time without you having to activate the Home tab. You can also choose to display the Quick Access toolbar above or below the Ribbon.

 Hands-On 1.6   **Customize the Quick Access Toolbar**

In this exercise, you will add one useful command to the Quick Access toolbar. Then you will remove the added command.

1. Take note of the three icons already on the Quick Access toolbar. These are most likely the default buttons that appear on this toolbar when Office 2007 is first installed.

2. Click the Customize Quick Access Toolbar button, and then choose More Commands from the menu.

3. Follow these steps to add another command to the Quick Access toolbar:

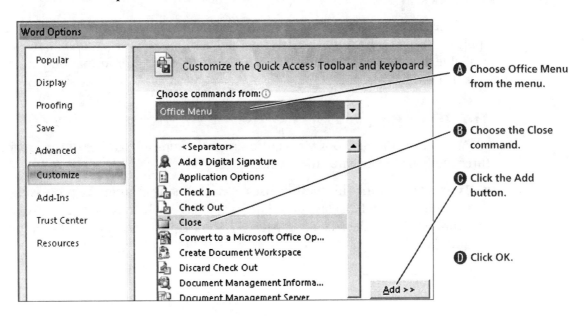

A Choose Office Menu from the menu.

B Choose the Close command.

C Click the Add button.

D Click OK.

Notice the new icon for the Close command at the right side of the Quick Access toolbar.

4. Click the Close button on the Quick Access toolbar, as shown at right, to close the current document. Choose No when prompted to save any changes.

5. As you did in step 1, click the small arrow to the right of the Quick Access toolbar, and then choose More Commands.

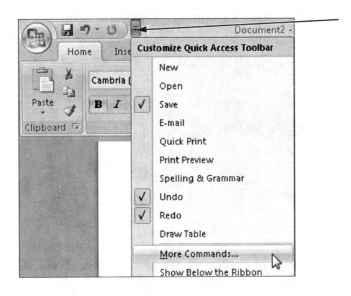

6. Click the Reset button at the bottom of the dialog box. Choose Yes when prompted to reset the toolbar to its defaults, and then click OK.
   Notice that the Quick Access toolbar has been reset to its default icons.

7. Click the Office button, and then choose Exit Word from the bottom of the menu. Choose No if you are prompted to save any changes.

Getting Help

All Office 2007 applications include excellent online help features. In fact, Office 2007 applications do not feature a printed manual at all. Any information you need is usually available directly from the Help box. Help searches look for information within your computer and also via the Internet.

The Help Box

You launch the Help box via a button near the top-right corner of the program. You have three methods to navigate online help:

- **Type a Question:** This method uses powerful natural language processing to interpret your question and display several items that are likely to contain the answer. Simply type your question in the box and tap Enter. The Help box displays a list of items related to your question.

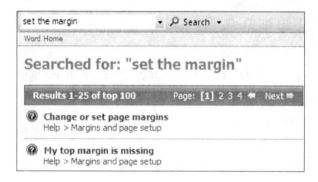

- **Browse Help:** Categorized lists display commonly performed tasks. Each category features a list of subcategories and individual items that give instructions to perform specific tasks.

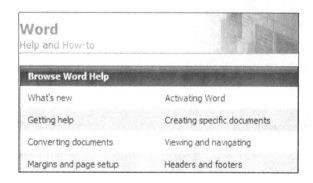

- **Search the Table of Contents:** The table of contents panel displays the complete online help content in a hierarchical format that you can expand and collapse. Browsing the table of contents can often be a good way to search when you're not quite certain of the feature name.

Concepts Review

1. Use the notes and the following illustration to identify parts of the Office 2007 interface:

   ■ Fill in the correct letter beside each feature of the new Office 2007 interface.

   ■ Place an "x" beside features that do not appear in the Office 2007 interface.

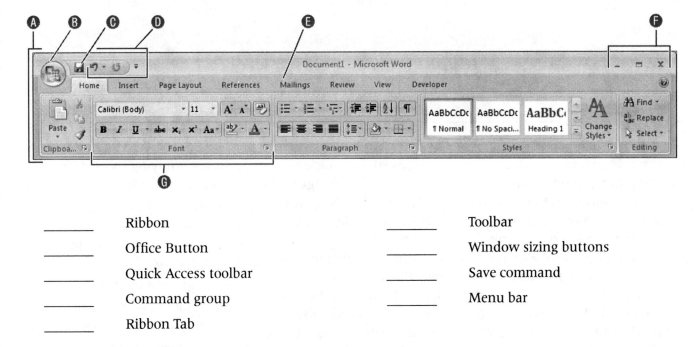

_____	Ribbon	_____	Toolbar
_____	Office Button	_____	Window sizing buttons
_____	Quick Access toolbar	_____	Save command
_____	Command group	_____	Menu bar
_____	Ribbon Tab		

2. The Office 🔲 menu is most similar to which menu in previous versions of Office Suite programs?

   a. Save menu

   b. Tools menu

   c. File menu

   d. None of the above

LESSON 2

Managing Computer Files

When you begin working with a computer, you will keep track of just a few files. But as your use of the computer grows, so will the number of files you must manage. After several months, you might have over a hundred files. After a year, you might have hundreds more. In this lesson, you will learn about Windows' extremely effective tool for managing files: folders. With folders, you can group related files together. You can even create folders inside of other folders.

As you learn how to use new features such as folders, you should take advantage of the excellent online Help system featured in Windows. Online Help makes it easy to find answers to many types of questions with three ways to search for the information you need. You will also learn about starting programs and adjusting the size of program windows.

LESSON OBJECTIVES

After studying this lesson, you will be able to:

- Browse files using folder windows
- Open files from a folder window
- Copy and move files
- Create new folders
- Delete and restore files using the Recycle Bin
- Rename files and folders

Case Study: Getting Organized

Chantal is taking four courses this term. As she goes over the syllabi, Chantal notices that three of her courses will require her to submit research papers. She decides to prepare for some of the research she must do. Chantal creates several folders on her computer to help her organize the files she will accumulate as she performs research for each paper. She creates a folder for each of her classes on the computer. Then she creates folders inside the class folders to further organize her files. For example, Final and Drafts folders for the word processor documents she will create. Chantal also creates a Research folder to hold the various files, web pages, and notes. She also creates a folder called Old Stuff for everything she thinks she doesn't need, but does not want to delete. She can delete the Old Stuff folder after the term project paper is completed.

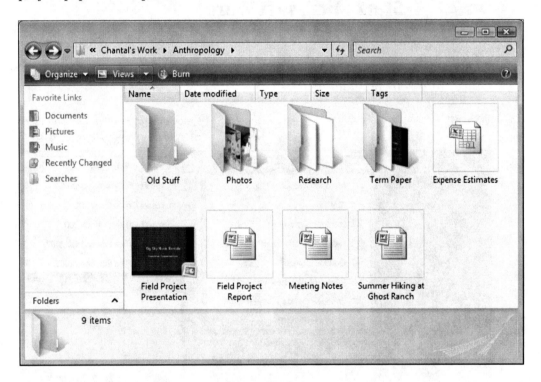

Starting Programs

You can start a program by clicking the Start button and choosing the desired program from the Programs menu. You can also start a program by double clicking a Desktop icon for the program (if a Desktop icon exists). For example, the Internet Explorer Web browser program typically has a Desktop icon. Also, you can launch some programs from the optional Quick Launch toolbar that is next to the Start button.

The Quick Launch toolbar lets you start programs with a single click.

 Hands-On 2.1   Start Microsoft Word

In this exercise, you will use the Start menu to launch the Microsoft Office Word program.

NOTE!

Win Vista instructions are on the next page.

1. Follow the steps below for the version of Windows you are running to open the Microsoft Office Word 2007 program:

Win XP

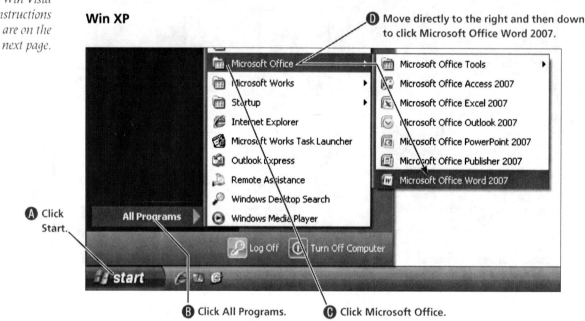

Ⓐ Click Start.

Ⓑ Click All Programs.

Ⓒ Click Microsoft Office.

Ⓓ Move directly to the right and then down to click Microsoft Office Word 2007.

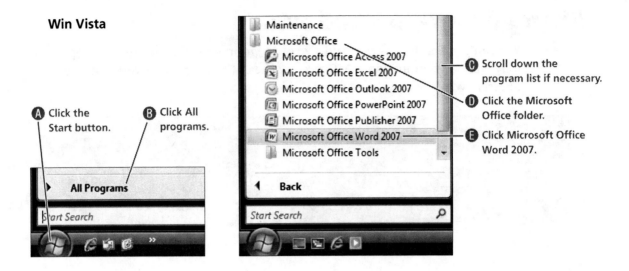

Win Vista

Ⓐ Click the Start button.

Ⓑ Click All programs.

Ⓒ Scroll down the program list if necessary.

Ⓓ Click the Microsoft Office folder.

Ⓔ Click Microsoft Office Word 2007.

The Word program window appears on the Desktop.

Elements of a Program Window

Every program runs in its own program window. Although the appearance of windows differ somewhat, the Word window is a good example of a typical Windows program. Since the controls in most program windows work similarly, once you have mastered a program such as Word or Excel, you are well on your way to mastering Windows programs in general. Take a few moments to look over the common features shown in the following illustration.

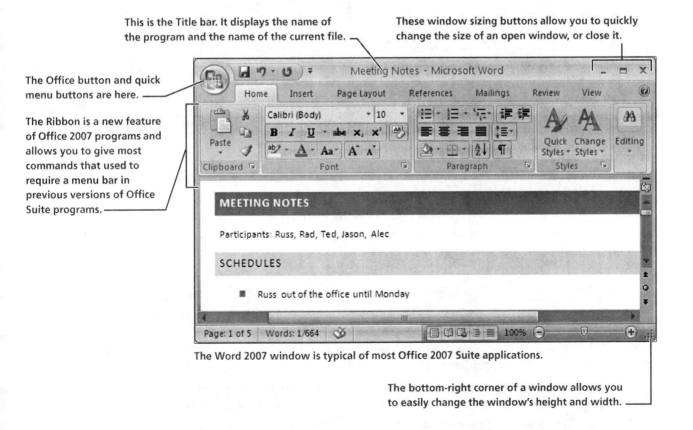

This is the Title bar. It displays the name of the program and the name of the current file.

These window sizing buttons allow you to quickly change the size of an open window, or close it.

The Office button and quick menu buttons are here.

The Ribbon is a new feature of Office 2007 programs and allows you to give most commands that used to require a menu bar in previous versions of Office Suite programs.

The Word 2007 window is typical of most Office 2007 Suite applications.

The bottom-right corner of a window allows you to easily change the window's height and width.

Sizing Program Windows

You can control the position and size of program windows on the Desktop. For example, you may want a program window to occupy the entire Desktop or you may want two or more program windows displayed side by side.

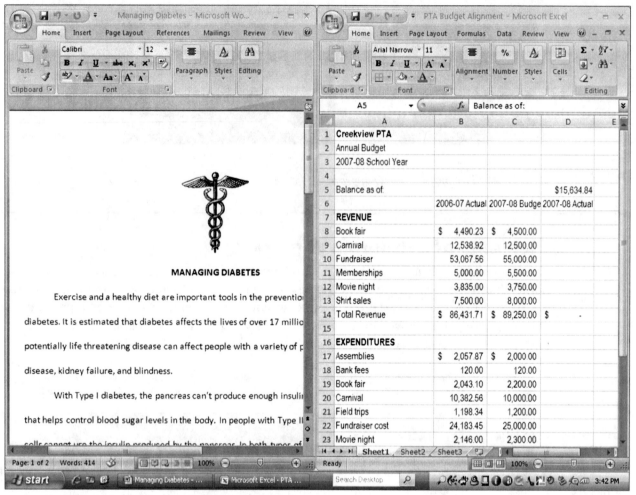

The Word 2007 and Excel 2007 program windows side by side

Quick-Sizing Buttons

Every program window displays quick-sizing buttons at the top right corner allowing users access to the most common window commands with a single click. The following table describes the function of each quick-sizing button.

Button	Description
— Minimize	Removes the program window from the Desktop but keeps the program running. Clicking the program button on the taskbar restores the program window.
☐ Maximize	Expands the program window until it covers the entire Desktop. Only the maximized program and the taskbar are visible.
❐ Restore	Restores a program window to the size it was set to before it was maximized. A restored window usually covers only a portion of the Desktop.
✕ Close	Closes a document window or exits a program.

Office 2007 Application Quick-Sizing Buttons

Some of the Office 2007 application programs introduce slightly different-looking quick-sizing buttons. Although their appearance is not identical with previous Windows programs, their function is.

Office 2007   Windows XP   Windows Vista

The Switching Restore and Maximize Buttons

The Maximize and Restore buttons never appear together. Instead, when either button is clicked, the window changes and displays the other button, as shown in the following example.

When you click   ...the middle button   When you click   ...the middle button
the Maximize   changes to the   the Restore   changes back to the
button here... ┐   Restore button. ┐   button... ┐   Maximize button. ┐

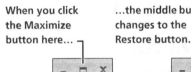      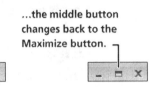

 Hands-On 2.2   Use the Quick-Sizing Buttons

In this exercise, you will practice using the Minimize, Maximize, Restore, and Close quick-sizing buttons.

1. Notice the Microsoft Word button near the Start button on the taskbar at the bottom of the screen.

   The button is recessed (pushed in) because Microsoft Word is the active program. A button appears on the taskbar for each running program.

2. Look at the top-right corner of the Microsoft Word window and notice the three quick-sizing buttons.
   If the window is already maximized, then the Restore button will be displayed in the center of the trio. If the last Microsoft Word user sized the window to cover just part of the Desktop, then the Maximize button will be displayed.

3. Choose the appropriate step:
   ■ If the middle quick-sizing button is the Maximize button, then click it.
   ■ If the middle quick-sizing button is the Restore button, then continue to step 4. (Do not click.)

   At this point, the Microsoft Word window is maximized. Only the Microsoft Word window, the taskbar, and the Start button should be visible. Since the Window is now maximized, the Restore button appears in the middle of the three quick-sizing buttons.

4. Click the Minimize button on the Microsoft Word window.
   The window vanishes, but the Word button is still visible on the taskbar.

5. Click the Microsoft Word button on the taskbar and the window reappears.

You can always restore a minimized window by clicking that program's button on the taskbar.

6. Click the Restore ▭ button, and the window will occupy only part of the Desktop. *Leave the Microsoft Word window open.*

Moving Program Windows

You can move a window on the Desktop to various screen locations by dragging on its title bar. The only time you cannot move a window is when it is maximized. You can tell when a window is maximized because it will have a Restore quick-sizing button.

Changing the Size of a Program Window

You can adjust the size and shape of an open window by dragging the window's borders. When you point to the border of a window that is restored (i.e., not maximized), a double arrow will appear. The arrows will point in the directions you can resize the window.

TIP! *You cannot change the size of a maximized window.*

Hands-On 2.3   Move and Size the Microsoft Word Window

In this exercise, you will move the Microsoft Word window to a different location on the Desktop and then change the size of the window.

1. Follow these steps to move the Microsoft Word window:

NOTE! *It's OK if your Word window has different dimensions than what is shown.*

You may not see the My Computer, My Network Places, or other icons on the Desktop depending on your computer's configuration.

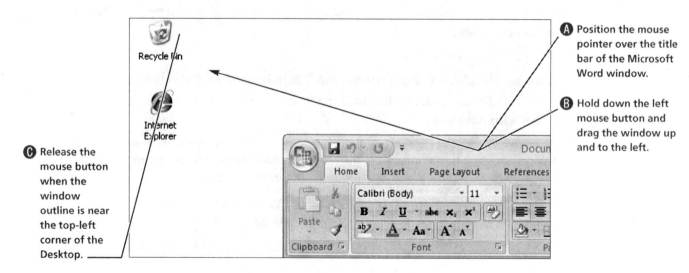

Ⓐ Position the mouse pointer over the title bar of the Microsoft Word window.

Ⓑ Hold down the left mouse button and drag the window up and to the left.

Ⓒ Release the mouse button when the window outline is near the top-left corner of the Desktop.

2. Drag on the title bar of the Microsoft Word window again, but this time drag down toward the bottom-right corner of the Desktop.

3. Drag the title bar once more to place the Microsoft Word window at the top-center of the Desktop.

4. Follow these steps to change the size of the Microsoft Word window:

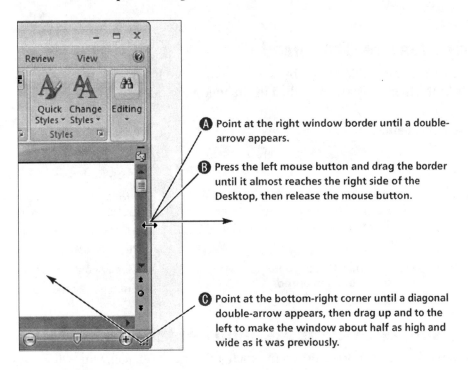

A Point at the right window border until a double-arrow appears.

B Press the left mouse button and drag the border until it almost reaches the right side of the Desktop, then release the mouse button.

C Point at the bottom-right corner until a diagonal double-arrow appears, then drag up and to the left to make the window about half as high and wide as it was previously.

5. Change only the height of the window by dragging the bottom border up or down.

6. Practice some more until you can place and size the Microsoft Word window at any desired location on the Desktop.
   This skill will be very useful when you run more than one program at once and need to arrange them on the Desktop so you can see the contents of one window as you work in a different window.

7. When you are finished, Maximize 🔲 the Microsoft Word window.
   It is often easier to work in a maximized window, because it covers any distracting elements that may be on the Desktop.

Browsing Through Files

In this lesson, you will learn how to organize the growing number of files that you can accumulate as you work with a computer. Besides your own files, there are hundreds or even thousands of files on the hard drive that run Windows and the application programs you use. Learning how all these files are organized will help you save time and find your own files more easily.

How Files Are Organized

Windows uses a flexible hierarchy that is common to most personal computers. The three levels in the hierarchy are described in the following table.

Level	Definition	Examples
Drive	This is a physical place where you store files.	■ An internal hard drive ■ A USB flash drive
Folder	This is an electronic location in which you store groups of related files. It is also possible to place folders inside of other folders.	■ A folder to store all of the files for an application program ■ A folder to store all of the letters you type for a project
File	This is a collection of computer data that has some common purpose.	■ A letter you've typed ■ A picture you've drawn

Browsing with Computer and Folder Windows

As you work with Windows programs such as Word and Excel, you will want to locate and open files you have created previously. Although you can open files from within an application program, sometimes it is more convenient to search directly through all of the files you have saved to a hard drive or floppy disk. This is the sort of task for which the My Computer window or a folder window is perfectly suited.

!**NOTE!** *Windows Vista calls this view Computer, not My Computer.*

The following illustrations describe the major features of the My Computer window. Take a moment to review these features before beginning Hands-On 2.4.

Win XP

The address bar displays the location you are currently browsing.

These panels contain links to display system task commands and other places you may wish to browse.

This panel displays details on whichever item you select in the right panel.

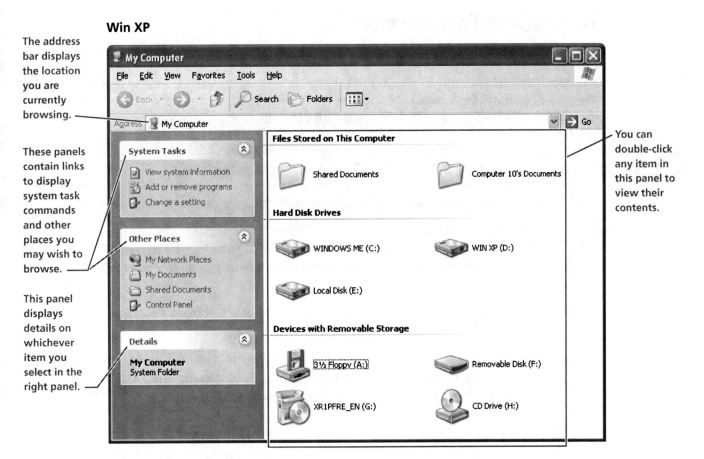

You can double-click any item in this panel to view their contents.

Win Vista

The address bar displays the location you are currently browsing.

The Search box allows you to search for files on your computer.

Forward and Back buttons help you navigate through the system.

These buttons help you perform common tasks.

These links jump you to collections of files on your computer.

Windows displays the various data storage drives. You can double-click any item in this panel to display their contents.

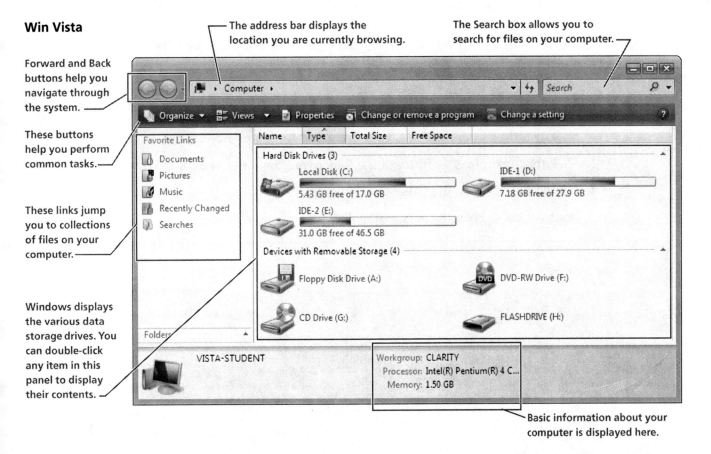

Basic information about your computer is displayed here.

Storing Your Exercise Files

Throughout this book you will be referred to files in a folder that corresponds to the lesson number you are studying (for example, "the Lesson 02 folder"). You can store your exercise files on various media such as a USB flash drive, the My Documents folder, or a network drive at a school or company. Appendix A, Storing Your Exercise Files, provides detailed instructions on downloading and unzipping the exercise files to your storage location.

 Hands-On 2.4   Open the My Documents Window

In this exercise, you will open the My Documents window and view the contents of your exercise folder.

Before You Begin: If you have not done so already, please turn to Downloading the Student Exercise Files section of Appendix A, Storing Your Exercise Files for instructions on how to retrieve the student exercise files for this book from the Labyrinth website and unzipping the files to your file storage location for use in this and future lessons.

1. Click Start→My Computer (Win XP) or Start→Computer (Win Vista).
   Windows displays the Computer folder.

2. Follow the appropriate step for your file storage location:
   - **USB Flash Drive:** Double-click the icon for your flash drive in the computer window. (It may or may not have a name similar to the figure to the right.)

   - **My Documents:** Double-click the [username's] Documents folder in the computer window. (It may or may not have a name similar to the figure to the right.)

⚠ **NOTE!** *Throughout this book, the My Documents folder shall also refer to the Documents folder in Windows Vista.*

   - **Floppy Disk:** Double-click the 3½ Floppy (A:) drive icon in the computer window.

   - **Any Other Location:** Ask your instructor for help if necessary.

3. Click the Maximize button if the folder window is not already maximized.

4. Double-click to open the Office 2007 Brief folder.

5. Double-click to open the Lesson 02 folder.

Opening Files

When you double-click on a file's icon, Windows launches the program used to create or edit that type of file and displays the file in the program window. This is a convenient way to start working with a file after you find it.

About Files

A file is a named collection of computer data. Users create files using application programs like Word and Excel. A typical hard disk drive has thousands of files stored on it. With most Windows programs, you use the Save command to save your work in a file. Users can choose various ways in which Windows displays files. In general, each file has a filename and an icon. The icon indicates what type of file you are viewing.

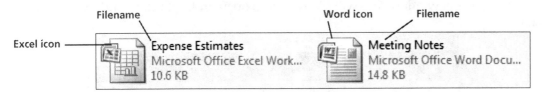

Files displayed in Windows XP in the Tile view

 Hands-On 2.5   Open and Close a Document File

In this exercise, you will open one of the files in the Lesson 02 folder.

Before You Begin: The Lesson 02 folder window should be open.

1. Examine the various files in the Lesson 02 window.
   Notice the files in the Lesson 02 folder display different icons. The icon is a visual cue as to which program will open the file.

2. Double-click the file named Meeting Notes, or click once to select the file and choose File→Open from the menu bar. (Or, the Open button from the Windows Vista menu bar.)
   Microsoft Word launches and displays the file in the program window.

3. Click the Office 🔘 button, and then choose Close from the menu to close the file and leave Microsoft Word running. Choose No if you are prompted to save changes.
   The Meeting Notes file closes, but the Microsoft Word program remains open.

4. Click the Close ☒ (XP)/ ☒ (Vista) button to close the Microsoft Word program window.
   The Lesson 02 folder and its contents should be visible. Leave the Lesson 02 window open.

Working with Folders

Folders are important tools for organizing files. You may have just a few files when you begin using a computer, but after a year or two you may have hundreds of files. What if you could only view your files in a single, long list? This would be similar to finding a book in a library that had only one long bookshelf. You could find the book eventually, but you would need to scan through many titles first.

Folder Hierarchy

Folders are organized into a hierarchy on each drive of a Windows system. Windows creates many folders when it is installed on the computer. You can create your own folders as well. The following illustration displays a common folder hierarchy on a Windows system. This is an example of an Exploring window. You will learn how to open an Exploring window later in this lesson.

This is the My Documents folder. It contains two folders and five files in this example.

The plus (+) sign beside the My Pictures folder indicates that there are additional folders inside it that are not displayed.

This is the computer's primary hard drive (C:).

This portable flash drive is plugged in to the computer's USB port.

This panel displays the contents of any drive or folder that is selected in the left panel.

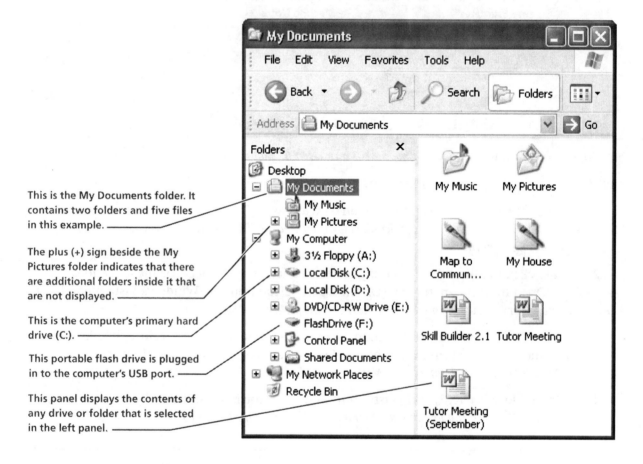

Creating Folders

You can create folders on a floppy disk, USB flash drive, or the hard drive whenever you need them. Folders can be created while you are viewing a drive in a My Computer or Exploring window. You can also create folders from the Save As dialog box of most Windows programs.

QUICK REFERENCE: CREATING A FOLDER

Task	Procedure
Create a folder from a window in Windows XP	■ Open a My Computer, My Documents, or any folder window. ■ Choose File→New→Folder from the menu bar. ■ Type a name for the new folder, and then tap the [Enter] key.
Create a folder from a window in Windows Vista	■ Open a Computer or Folder window. ■ Choose Organize→New Folder from the toolbar. ■ Type a name for the new folder, and then tap the [Enter] key.
Create a folder in the Save As dialog box of an application program	■ Choose File→Save As from the program's menu bar. ■ Click the Create New Folder 🗀 button near the top of the Save As window. ■ Type a name for the new folder, and then click OK.

Hands-On 2.6A   Create Folders (Win XP)

Win Vista Users: Skip this version of the exercise and perform the steps in Hands-On 2.6B on page 33.

In this exercise, you will create three folders in the Lesson 02 folder. Later in this lesson you will move and copy files into these folders.

Before You Begin: The Lesson 02 folder should still be open.

1. Follow these steps to create a new folder:

A Choose File→New→ Folder from the menu bar.

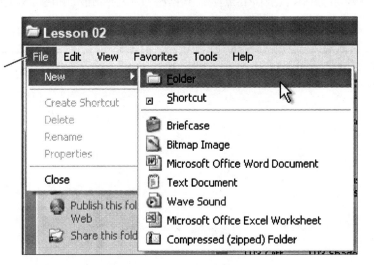

B Notice the new folder icon. The name is highlighted indicating you can immediately type a new name for the folder. ──────

C Type the name **Pictures** and tap the [Enter] key. ──────

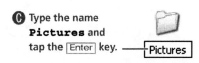

2. Double-click the Pictures folder icon to navigate to your new folder.

If your computer is configured to show the address bar at the top of folder windows, you will notice that the name of your new folder is displayed in the address bar, as well as in the title bar. This folder is empty now, but you will place files in it later.

The Pictures folder is considered a subfolder of the Lesson 02 folder. Conversely, the Lesson 02 folder is considered the parent folder of the Pictures folder.

3. Click the [Back] button in the toolbar to return to the Lesson 02 parent folder.

4. Click File→New→Folder to create a second subfolder within Lesson 02. Name it **Spreadsheets** and click a clear area in the window to deselect the folder and apply the name change.

5. Create a third subfolder named **Word Processing.** Your Lesson 02 folder should look similar to the following illustration:

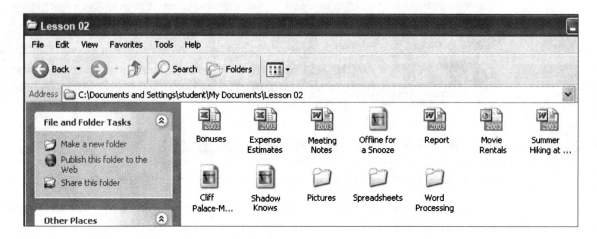

Leave the Lesson 02 window open.

Skip the Win Vista version of this exercise and continue reading Renaming Files and Folders section on page 34.

In this exercise, you will create three folders in the Lesson 02 folder. Later in this lesson you will move and copy files into these folders.

Before You Begin: The Lesson 02 folder should still be open.

1. Follow these steps to create a new folder:

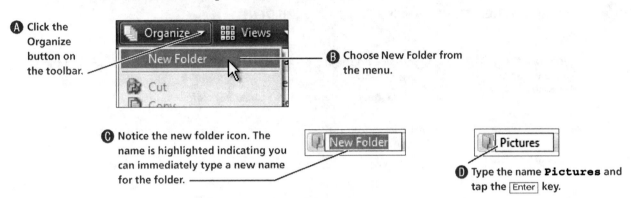

A Click the Organize button on the toolbar.

B Choose New Folder from the menu.

C Notice the new folder icon. The name is highlighted indicating you can immediately type a new name for the folder.

D Type the name **Pictures** and tap the Enter key.

2. Double-click the Pictures folder icon to navigate to your new folder.
   Notice that the name of your new folder is displayed in the address bar near the top of the folder window as shown in the following illustration. This folder is empty now, but you will place files in it later.

   The Pictures folder is considered a subfolder of the Lesson 02 folder. Conversely, the Lesson 02 folder is considered the parent folder of the Pictures folder.

3. Click the Back ⬅ button in the toolbar to return to the Lesson 02 parent folder.

4. Choose Organize→New Folder from the toolbar to create a second subfolder within Lesson 02. Name it **Spreadsheets** and tap the Enter key.

5. Create a third subfolder named **Word Processing**. Your Lesson 02 folder should look similar to the following illustration:

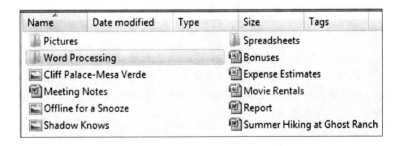

6. Choose Views→Medium Icons from the toolbar.
   Leave the Lesson 02 window open.

Renaming Files and Folders

Sometimes files are created with default names like Document1 or Workbook1. It is easy to rename a file when its icon displays in a folder window. Use any of the three methods described in the following Quick Reference table to rename a file or folder in a folder window. Whichever method you use, once the folder name is highlighted you can immediately type the new name and tap the Enter key.

QUICK REFERENCE: RENAMING FILES AND FOLDERS	
Task	**Procedure**
Rename a file or folder with the right-click method.	■ Right-click on the file or folder icon, and then choose Rename from the pop-up menu. ■ Type the new name, and then tap the Enter key.
Rename a file or folder with a keyboard shortcut.	■ Left-click once on the file or folder to select it, and then tap the F2 function key. ■ Type the new name, and then tap the Enter key.
Rename a file or folder with the click-pause method.	■ Left-click once on the filename under the icon. ■ Pause about one second, and then click on the filename again. ■ Type the new name, and then tap the Enter key.

Filename Extensions

Most Windows filenames have an extension that consists of three letters following a period at the end of the filename. Filename extensions identify the type of file you are working with and they allow Windows to launch the correct program when you double-click a file. For example, the *Bonuses* file is a spreadsheet document, so it has a filename extension of .xls. The .xls file extension tells Windows to launch Microsoft Excel when double-clicked. Windows application programs add an extension to any filename you type when you save a file. Most Windows systems hide the filename extension. But if your system is set to display it, you must type out the extension whenever you rename a file.

The filename ⎯⎯⎯⎯⎯⎯⎯   The extension. Most
                                        Windows systems are set
                                        to hide the extension.

Tutor Meeting.doc

WARNING! *You should not change the extension of a filename if it is visible when you rename a file. This causes Windows to lose track of which program created the file and will make it difficult to open the file in the future.*

Hands-On 2.7   Rename a File

In this exercise, you will rename files and folders using several methods.

1. Follow these steps to issue the Rename command with the right-click method.

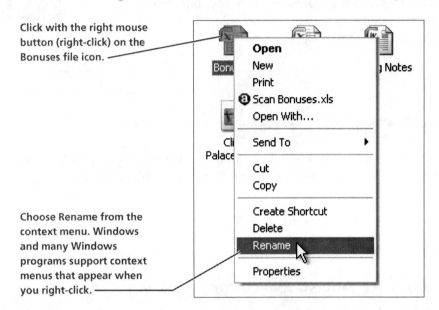

Click with the right mouse button (right-click) on the Bonuses file icon.

Open
New
Print
Scan Bonuses.xls
Open With...
Send To ▶
Cut
Copy
Create Shortcut
Delete
Rename
Properties

Choose Rename from the context menu. Windows and many Windows programs support context menus that appear when you right-click.

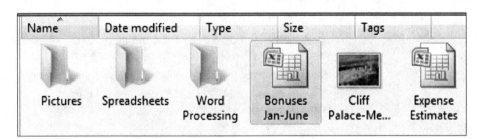

Name	Date modified	Type	Size	Tags

Pictures   Spreadsheets   Word Processing   Bonuses Jan-June   Cliff Palace-Me...   Expense Estimates

This context menu will look slightly different in Windows Vista, but the Rename option will still appear toward the bottom.

Windows highlights the filename for renaming. It may or may not display the three-letter file extension of .xls.

2. Examine the filename, and then follow the instructions that match the filename:

   ■ If the filename reads Bonuses, type **Bonuses Jan-June**, and then tap [Enter].

   ■ If the filename reads Bonuses.xls, type **Bonuses Jan-June.xls**, and then tap [Enter].

   The old name is deleted and replaced by the new name.

3. Click on a clear area of the window (the white part) to deselect the Bonuses Jan-June file.

4. Click once (do not right-click) on the Bonuses Jan-June filename (not the icon), pause one second, and then click again.
   The file name will be highlighted and ready for editing.

5. Tap the left arrow ⟵ key until the insertion point is blinking to the left of the B in Bonuses.
   The arrow keys allow you to move the insertion point without deleting any part of the filename.

6. Type **Company**, tap the ⟨Spacebar⟩ and then tap ⟨Enter⟩ so the new filename is Company Bonuses Jan-June.
   Leave the Lesson 02 window open.

Moving and Copying Files

Windows lets you move and copy files from one drive to another and from one folder to another. There are several techniques to move and copy files. In this lesson, you will learn two methods:

- Copy and paste: Copies files into a new location

- Cut and paste: Moves files to a new location

QUICK REFERENCE: MOVING AND COPYING FILES WITH CUT, COPY, AND PASTE

Task	Procedure

Copy files with Copy and Paste	■ Select the files to be copied.
	■ **Win XP:** Choose Edit→Copy from the menu bar.
	   Win Vista: Choose Organize→Copy from the toolbar.
	■ Navigate to the location in which the files are to be copied.
	■ **Win XP:** Choose Edit→Paste from the menu bar.
	   Win Vista: Choose Organize→Paste from the toolbar.

Move files with Cut and Paste	■ Select the files to be moved.
	■ **Win XP:** Choose Edit→Cut from the menu bar.
	   Win Vista: Choose Organize→Cut from the toolbar.
	■ Navigate to the location where the files are to be moved.
	■ **Win XP:** Choose Edit→Paste from the menu bar.
	   Win Vista: Choose Organize→Paste from the toolbar.

Selecting Multiple Files for Move and Copy Commands

You can move and copy a single file or dozens of files with the same command. Before you give the Cut or Copy command, select the file(s) you wish to be affected by the command. To select a single file, simply click on it. The two easiest methods of selecting multiple files are described in the following Quick Reference table. Combine these two techniques as your needs dictate.

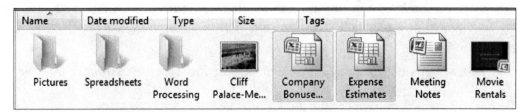

Name	Date modified	Type	Size	Tags

Pictures   Spreadsheets   Word Processing   Cliff Palace-Me...   Company Bonuse...   Expense Estimates   Meeting Notes   Movie Rentals

You can select nonconsecutive files for move and copy commands. In this example, only the Excel spreadsheet files are selected.

QUICK REFERENCE: SELECTING MULTIPLE FILES FOR COMMANDS

Task	Procedure
Ctrl +click technique to select several files	■ Click the first file you wish to select. ■ Press and hold the Ctrl key on the keyboard while you click any other files you wish to select. ■ Release the Ctrl key when you have made all of your selections.
Shift +click technique to select several files in a row	■ Click the first file you wish to select. ■ Press and hold the Shift key on the keyboard while you click the last file in the group that you wish to select, and then release the Shift key.
Deselect a selected file	■ Press and hold the Ctrl key on the keyboard while you click on the file you wish to deselect.

 Hands-On 2.8   Move and Copy Files

In this exercise, you will use Cut and Paste to move single files into one of your new folders. Then you will use Copy and Paste to copy files into another folder.

Move a File with Cut and Paste

1. With the Lesson 02 folder open, click once (do not double-click) to select the Company Bonuses Jan-June file.

2. Follow the step for your version of Windows:
   - **Win XP:** Choose Edit→Cut from the menu bar.
   - **Win Vista:** Choose Organize→Cut from the toolbar.

   Notice that the icon for the file you selected is "dimmed." This indicates that the file has been cut and will be moved when you give the Paste command.

3. Double-click to open the Spreadsheets folder.
   This navigates you to the empty Spreadsheets folder.

4. Follow the step for your version of Windows:
   - **Win XP:** Choose Edit→Paste from the menu bar.
   - **Win Vista:** Choose Organize→Paste from the toolbar.

   As the file is moved, it appears in the folder window.

5. Click the ⬅ Back / ⬅ button on the toolbar to return to the Lesson 02 parent folder.
   Notice that the Company Bonuses Jan-June file is no longer listed with the other files; it was moved to a different folder.

6. Repeat steps 1–5 to cut and paste (move) the file Expense Estimates into the Spreadsheets folder.

Copy Multiple Files

In this part of the exercise, you will use the Ctrl *key to select more than one file for the Copy and Paste commands.*

7. Click once (do not double-click) to select the Cliff Palace-Mesa Verde picture file.

8. Hold down the Ctrl key and keep it held down as you click once to select the other two image files:
   - Offline for a Snooze
   - Shadow Knows

9. Release the Ctrl key.
   The three image files are now selected for your next command. They remain selected even after you release the Ctrl *key.*

10. Follow the step for your version of Windows:
    - **Win XP:** Choose Edit→Copy from the menu bar.
    - **Win Vista:** Choose Organize→Copy from the toolbar.

11. Double-click to open the Pictures folder.

12. Follow the step for your version of Windows:
    - **Win XP:** Choose Edit→Paste from the menu bar.
    - **Win Vista:** Choose Organize→Paste from the toolbar.

    The files appear in the window as they are copied.

13. Click the ⬅ Back / ⬅ button on the toolbar to return to the Lesson 02 parent folder.
    Notice the three image files are still displayed in the Lesson 02 window as they were copied rather than moved.

    Leave the Lesson 02 window open.

Deleting Files and Folders

You can delete files and folders by selecting them and tapping the ⌈Delete⌉ key. When you delete a folder, any files inside that folder are deleted as well.

What Happens to Deleted Files?

Windows does not physically erase a deleted file from the hard drive. Instead, the file is placed in the Recycle Bin. The Recycle Bin holds the deleted files until you give a command to empty it, or until it runs out of the space allotted to store deleted files. If you delete files from the hard drive, you can recover them by opening the Recycle Bin, selecting the files you wish to recover, and then choosing File→Restore from the menu bar.

 WARNING! *Files and folders deleted from removable media such as floppy disks and USB flash drives or a network drive are not sent to the Recycle Bin! They are permanently deleted when you issue the delete command.*

 TIP! *Even files and folders emptied from the Recycle Bin can be recovered via special software. But this is a task for an expert, not a beginner.*

 Hands-On 2.9   Delete Files and a Folder

In this exercise, you will delete some of the files in the Lesson 02 subfolder. Then you will delete the Lesson 02 folder itself.

Delete Files

1. With the Lesson 02 window still open, double-click the Pictures folder.
   Windows displays the contents of the pictures folder.

2. Using the ⌈Ctrl⌉ key, select the three files in the right panel, and then tap the ⌈Delete⌉ key on the keyboard.
   Windows will probably display a prompt window asking you to confirm the delete command. This is a safeguard to protect against accidental deletions.

3. Choose Yes to confirm the deletion if a prompt window is visible.
   The files disappear from the right panel as they have been sent to the Recycle Bin. The Pictures folder is now empty.

 NOTE! *If you deleted the picture files from a USB flash or floppy drive, the files are not sent to the Recycle bin.*

4. Click the ⊙ Back / ⊙ button to return to the Lesson 02 parent folder.

Delete a Folder

5. Right-click the Pictures folder and choose Delete from the context menu. Choose Yes if Windows asks you to confirm the deletion.

   The Lesson 02 folder no longer shows the Pictures folder nested inside. The Pictures folder and its contents have been moved to the Recycle Bin. (Exception: the folder is not in the Recycle Bin if the files were deleted from a USB flash or floppy drive.)

6. Close ▣ / ▣ the Lesson 02 folder window if you use a USB flash drive or floppy disk to store your exercise files. Leave the window open if you store your files in the My Documents or Documents folder.

 NOTE! *Skip the rest of this exercise if you use a USB flash drive or a floppy disk as your file storage location. Files deleted from these types of storage location are not sent to the Recycle Bin.*

View Files in the Recycle Bin

Now you will view your files from within the Recycle Bin. Any file in the Recycle Bin can be restored (undeleted) back to the location from which it was deleted.

7. Minimize ▣ / ▣ the Lesson 02 folder.

8. Double-click the Recycle Bin icon on the Desktop.

   The Recycle Bin folder opens to show the contents of the Recycle Bin. Depending on the type of storage location from which you deleted the files, the three files deleted in step 2 may be visible.

9. Attempt to open the Cliff Palace-Mesa Verde file by double-clicking it.

   The file does not open. Instead a properties window opens. You are not able to open files if they are in the Recycle Bin.

10. Click the Cancel button at the bottom of the properties window to close it.

Restoring Files from the Recycle Bin

Files located in the Recycle Bin are permanently deleted from your computer only when you issue an Empty Recycle Bin command, or automatically on a First In First Out basis when the Recycle Bin runs out of space to keep deleted files. Depending on you computer's configuration, the Recycle Bin will be set to use a certain percentage of your hard drive's capacity. Once that limit is reached, the oldest files in the Recycle Bin are automatically and permanently deleted to make room.

Recycle Bin

Restoring Files

Files cannot be opened if they are located in the Recycle Bin. If you decide you need a file previously deleted, and it hasn't yet been permanently deleted from the Recycle Bin, you can restore the file to its original location by right-clicking the file and choosing Restore from the context menu. You can restore files using an Exploring window or the Recycle Bin icon directly on the Desktop.

QUICK REFERENCE: DELETING AND RESTORING FILES

Task	Procedure
Delete a file or folder	■ Select the file or folder in a folder window. You can select multiple files if you wish using the Ctrl and/or Shift keys. ■ Tap the Delete key on the keyboard, or right-click any selected file/folder, and then choose Delete from the context menu.
Restore an item from the Recycle Bin	■ Double-click the Recycle Bin on the Desktop. ■ Select the files and/or folders you wish to restore. ■ Click the Restore the Selected Items from the left panel of the Recycle Bin folder window.
Empty the Recycle Bin	■ Right-click the Recycle Bin icon. ■ Choose Empty Recycle Bin from the context menu. (Remember, this will permanently delete the contents of the Recycle Bin.)

Hands-On 2.10   Restore Files and Folders

In this exercise, you will restore the files and folders you deleted in the previous exercise.

Before You Begin: Skip this exercise if you use a USB flash drive or a floppy disk as your file storage location (see Appendix A).

1. If the Recycle Bin window is not already open, double-click the Recycle Bin icon on the Desktop.

2. Use Ctrl +click to select three files in the Recycle Bin:
   - Cliff Palace-Mesa Verde
   - Offline for a Snooze
   - Shadow Knows

   Your Recycle Bin may have more items, but we are only concerned with the files and folder deleted in the previous exercise.

3. Right-click any one of the three selected files, and then choose Restore from the context menu.
   The files and folder disappear from the right panel because they have been removed from the Recycle Bin and restored to their original locations.

4. Close ⊠ / ⊠ the Recycle Bin window.

5. If necessary click its button on the Windows taskbar to display the Lesson 02 folder.
   Notice that the Pictures folder has reappeared. It was re-created when you restored the three picture files that were deleted while inside it.

6. Double-click to open the Pictures folder.
   The three restored picture files should be visible.

7. Close ⊠ / ⊠ the Pictures folder window.
   The Windows Desktop is now empty.

Concepts Review

True/False Questions

1. You can change the location of a maximized window.   TRUE   FALSE

2. You can change the size of a maximized program window by dragging on the window borders.   TRUE   FALSE

3. You can use the Ctrl key to randomly select a group of files.   TRUE   FALSE

4. Folders can have subfolders within them.   TRUE   FALSE

5. You can use the Cut and Paste commands to move files.   TRUE   FALSE

6. Files deleted from a floppy disk or USB flash drive are sent to the Recycle Bin.   TRUE   FALSE

7. A quick way to open a file is to double-click on it in a folder window.   TRUE   FALSE

8. You cannot rename folders.   TRUE   FALSE

9. You must make a selection before you can give the cut or copy commands.   TRUE   FALSE

10. Files and folders stored in the Recycle Bin remain there unless you empty the Recycle Bin.   TRUE   FALSE

Multiple Choice Questions

1. Which of the following buttons restores a window?
   a. ×
   b. –
   c. ▭
   d. ▱

2. Which of the following buttons minimizes a window?
   a. ×
   b. –
   c. ▭
   d. ▱

3. Which of the following techniques is used to move a program window?
   a. Maximize the window and drag the title bar
   b. Restore the window and drag the title bar
   c. Minimize the window and drag the title bar
   d. Drag a corner-sizing handle

4. If one filename is already selected in a Folder window, which key can be used to select several more files by clicking just once?
   a. Ctrl key
   b. Shift key
   c. Alt key
   d. All of the above

Skill Builders

Skill Builder 2.1   Practice Sizing Program Windows

In this exercise, you will practice placing windows on the screen where you want them.

1. Follow the step for your version of Windows to Start Excel 2007:

    ■ **Win XP:** Choose Start→All Programs→Microsoft Office 2007→Microsoft Office Excel 2007.

    ■ **Win Vista:** Choose Start→Programs→Microsoft Office 2007→Microsoft Office Excel 2007.

2. Start the Word 2007 program.

3. If necessary, restore 🗗 the Word program window.
    Depending on how it was sized prior to being maximized, the Word window may still cover much of the screen, or only a small portion of it.

4. Follow these steps to change the location and size of the Word window.

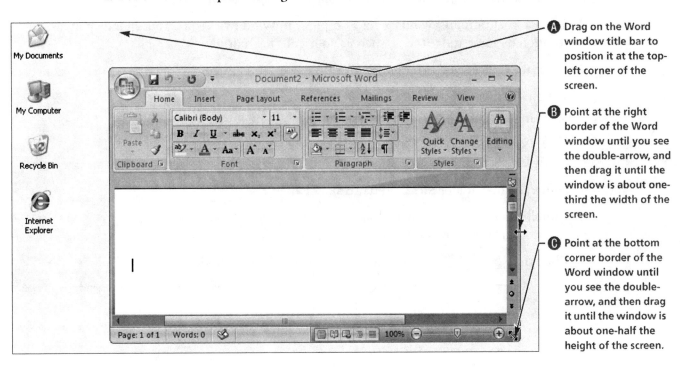

Ⓐ Drag on the Word window title bar to position it at the top-left corner of the screen.

Ⓑ Point at the right border of the Word window until you see the double-arrow, and then drag it until the window is about one-third the width of the screen.

Ⓒ Point at the bottom corner border of the Word window until you see the double-arrow, and then drag it until the window is about one-half the height of the screen.

5. Maximize 🗗 the Word window.

6. Restore 🗗 the Word window.
    The window returns to the size and location you set it to previously.

7. Click its button on the Windows taskbar to restore the Excel window.

8. Restore 🗗 the Excel window.
    You cannot change the borders of a maximized window.

9. Drag on the title bar to place the Excel window at the top-right corner of the screen.

10. Drag up and to the right on the bottom right corner of the Excel window to make it about half the height and half the width of the screen.

11. Drag down on the Excel window title bar to place the window in the bottom-right corner of the screen.
    Depending on the task you are working on, it can be quite useful to place a program window exactly where you need it.

12. Close [×] the program windows.

Skill Builder 2.2   Create a Folder

In this exercise, you will create a new folder in your file storage location.

1. Open a My Computer window (or Computer in Windows Vista), and then display the location of your student files, such as your USB flash drive.

2. Open the Office 2007 Brief folder, and then open the Lesson 02 folder.

3. Follow the step for your version of Windows to create a new folder:
   - **Win XP:** Choose File→New→Folder from the folder window menu bar.
   - **Win Vista:** Choose Organize→New Folder from the toolbar.

   A new folder appears. The generic folder name is already selected, ready for you to type the new name.

4. Name the new folder **Skill Builder 2.2**.

5. Double-click to open the new folder.
   The newly created folder is empty.

6. Click the [Back] / [←] button to return to the Lesson 02 folder.

Skill Builder 2.3   Copy and Delete Files

In this exercise, you will copy files to the new Skill Builder 2.2 folder, and then delete them.

Before You Begin: You must have completed Skill Builder 2.2. A folder window should be open to display the Lesson 02 folder on your file storage location. If this is the case, you can skip step 1.

1. If necessary, follow steps 1 and 2 of Skill Builder 2.2 to open a Folder window displaying the Lesson 02 folder.

Copy Files to a Folder

2. Using the [Ctrl] key, select the three Word document files.
   The files are selected for your next command.

3. Follow the step for your version of Windows:
   - **Win XP:** Choose Edit→Copy from the menu bar.
   - **Win Vista:** Choose Organize→Copy from the toolbar.

4. Double-click to open the Skill Builder 2.2 folder.

5. Follow the step for your version of Windows:
   - **Win XP:** Choose Edit→Paste from the menu bar.
   - **Win Vista:** Choose Organize→Paste from the toolbar.

   The three files you selected should appear in the folder.

6. Click the [◄ Back] / [◄] button to return to the Lesson 02 folder.

Delete Files

7. Using the [Ctrl] key, select the three Word files again, and then tap the [Delete] key on the keyboard. Chose Yes if Windows asks you to confirm the deletion.
   The three selected files disappear. If you deleted them from the Documents folder on the hard drive, these files are now in the Recycle Bin. However, if you deleted the files from a floppy or USB flash drive, they are effectively erased. (You would have to run special software to try to recover these files.)

Skill Builder 2.4   Move Files

In this exercise, you will move files from the new Skill Builder 2.2 folder back into the Lesson 02 folder.

Before You Begin: You must have completed Skill Builder 2.3. A folder window should be open to display the Lesson 02 folder on your file storage location. If this is the case, you can skip step 1.

1. If necessary, follow steps 1 and 2 of Skill Builder 2.2 to open a Folder window displaying the Lesson 02 folder.

2. Double-click to open the Skill Builder 2.2 folder.
   The folder displays the three files you copied in Skill Builder 2.3.

3. Using the [Ctrl] or [Shift] key, select the three Word document files.

4. Follow the step for your version of Windows:
   - **Win XP:** Choose Edit→Cut from the menu bar.
   - **Win Vista:** Choose Organize→Cut from the toolbar.

   The three files you selected appear dimmed, indicating that they have been cut for moving. They will stay in this folder until you give the Paste command.

5. Click the [← Back] / [←] button to return to the Lesson 02 folder.

6. Follow the step for your version of Windows:
   - **Win XP:** Choose Edit→Paste from the menu bar.
   - **Win Vista:** Choose Organize→Paste from the toolbar.

   The three moved files should appear in the folder.

7. Double-click to open the Skill Builder 2.2 folder.
   The folder is empty again since you have moved the files.

Delete a Folder

8. Click the [← Back] / [←] button to return to the Lesson 02 folder.

9. Select the Skill Builder 2.2 folder, and then tap the [Delete] key on the keyboard. Choose Yes if Windows asks you to confirm the deletion.
   Deleting a folder is just like deleting a file. If there had been any files within the folder, those would have been deleted as well.

Skill Builder 2.5   Create Multiple Folders

In this exercise, you will create four new folders in your file storage location. Three of these folders will be inside the first new folder.

Before You Begin: A folder window should be open to display the Lesson 02 folder in your file storage location. If this is the case, you can skip step 1.

1. If necessary, follow steps 1 and 2 of Skill Builder 2.2 to open a Folder window displaying the Lesson 02 folder.

2. Follow the step for your version of Windows to create a new folder:
   - **Win XP:** Choose File→New→Folder from the folder window menu bar.
   - **Win Vista:** Choose Organize→New Folder from the toolbar.

   A new folder appears. The generic folder name is already selected, ready for you to type the new name.

3. Name the new folder **Skill Builder 2.5**.

4. Double-click to open the new folder.
   The newly created folder is empty.

5. Give the new folder command again. Name the new folder **Document Files**.
   This new folder is created inside the Skill Builder 2.5 folder. Whenever you create a new folder, Windows creates it inside the folder you are currently viewing.

6. Give the new folder command again. Name the new folder **Spreadsheet Files**.

7. Create one more new folder named **Backup**.

8. Right-click (do not left-click) the Backup Folder name, and then choose Rename from the context menu.
   Windows highlights the current name, ready for you to type a new name or edit the existing name.

9. Rename the folder **Backup [Year]**. For example *Backup 2007*.
   You can rename a folder just as you would a file.

10. Click the ⬅ Back / ⬅ button to return to the Lesson 02 folder.

Unit 1 Assessments

Assessment 1.1   Configure Two Program Windows

In this exercise, you will manually arrange two program windows to appear on specific locations of the screen.

1. Start the Word Program.

2. If Word is maximized, click the Restore button to restore the window.

3. Drag on Word program window borders so that the Word window covers the left half of the Desktop.

4. Start the Excel Program. Make sure the Excel window is not maximized.

5. Drag on the Excel program window borders so that the Excel window covers the right half of the Desktop.

6. Get your instructor's initials when this task has been performed successfully. _____

7. Close ☒ the program windows.

Assessment 1.2   Create a Folder

In this exercise, you will create a new folder in your file storage location.

1. Open a Computer window, and then display the drive where your student files are located.

2. Open the Office 2007 Brief folder, and then open the Lesson 02 folder.

3. Create a new folder named **Assessment 1.2**.

Assessment 1.3   Copy Files to a Folder

In this exercise, you will copy word processor document files into a folder.

Before You Begin: A folder window should be open to display the Lesson 02 folder in your file storage location. If this is the case, you can skip step 1.

1. If necessary, open a Computer window, then open the Office 2007 Brief folder, and then open the Lesson 02 folder.

2. Select the Word files in the Lesson 02 folder and copy them into the Assessment 1.2 folder created in Assessment 1.2.

3. Return to viewing the Lesson 02 folder.

Assessment 1.4   Move Files to a Folder

In this exercise, you will move spreadsheet files into a folder.

Before You Begin: A folder window should be open to display the Lesson 02 folder in your file storage location. If this is the case, you can skip step 1.

1. If necessary, open a Computer window, then open the Office 2007 Brief folder, and then open the Lesson 02 folder.

2. Open the Spreadsheets folder, then select the Excel files in the folder, and then move them into the Assessment 1.2 folder created in Assessment 1.2.

 TIP! *You will need to use the Back button to return to the Lesson 02 folder in order to complete the command to move the files.*

3. Return to viewing the Lesson 02 folder.

Assessment 1.5   Create Multiple Folders

In this exercise, you will create a new folder in your file storage location.

Before You Begin: A folder window should be open to display the Lesson 02 folder in your file storage location. If this is the case, you can skip step 1.

1. If necessary, open a Computer window, then open the Office 2007 Brief folder, and then open the Lesson 02 folder.

2. Create a new folder named **Assessment 1.5**.

3. Create three new folders *inside* the Assessment 1.5 folder with the following names:
   - **Project Files**
   - **Backup Files**
   - **Recent Photos**

Unit 2

Word 2007

In this unit, you will practice using Word 2007 and many of its great features. You will begin by reviewing the new Ribbon interface in Word. You will then open, navigate through, and close Word documents. Once you're comfortable with these skills, you will move on to creating your own documents. Throughout these lessons, you will learn to create and enhance business letters, memoranda, and simple reports. In the last lesson of this unit, you will create, align, and format Word tables. This unit ends with a series of Assessment exercises.

Lesson 3: Working with Word Basics

Lesson 4: Creating and Editing Business Letters

Lesson 5: Creating a Memorandum and a Simple Report

Lesson 6: Working with Tables

Unit 2 Assessments

LESSON 3

Working with Word Basics

In this lesson, you will get an overview of Microsoft Office Word 2007. First you will learn to start Word, and then how to work with the Word interface. You will open and close documents, navigate through a multipage document, and work with Word Help. Finally, you will exit the Word program.

LESSON OBJECTIVES

After studying this lesson, you will be able to:

- Work with the Microsoft Word 2007 Ribbon interface
- Use the Quick Access toolbar and the Mini toolbar
- Open and close documents
- Navigate in a document
- Use Word Help

Case Study: Getting Oriented to Word 2007

Marissa Santos is studying to be a physician's assistant. In addition to her medical classes, she wants to take advantage of this opportunity to learn Microsoft Office Word 2007, so she can use it as a tool for working with her patients. She knows she'll need to use Word to take patient histories, maintain patient records, and so forth. She is currently researching diabetes for her nutrition class, and Word makes writing her research paper a snap.

MANAGING DIABETES

Exercise and a healthy diet are important tools in the prevention and management of diabetes. It is estimated that diabetes affects the lives of over 17 million Americans. This potentially life threatening disease can affect people with a variety of problems including heart disease, kidney failure, and blindness.

With Type I diabetes, the pancreas can't produce enough insulin. Insulin is a hormone that helps control blood sugar levels in the body. In people with Type II diabetes, the body's cells cannot use the insulin produced by the pancreas. In both types of diabetes, sugar builds up in the bloodstream. Without proper treatment, high blood sugar levels can damage the blood vessels and result in serious complications. If you have a family history that includes Type II diabetes, you have a risk of about 1 in 20 of contracting it yourself. However, both Type I and Type II diabetes can be managed and prevented through a combination of proper diet and exercise.

Starches and sugars (carbohydrates) can have a significant effect on blood sugar levels. Carbohydrates include breads, pasta, cereals, fruit, juices, and sweets. These foods have a considerable impact on blood sugar levels immediately after they are consumed. Blood sugar levels can get too high if more carbohydrates are consumed than the body can process. With proper carbohydrate management, such as spreading carbohydrate consumption throughout

Presenting Word 2007

Microsoft Office Word 2007 is a dynamic document-authoring program that lets you create and easily modify a variety of documents. Word provides tools to assist you in virtually every aspect of document creation. From desktop publishing to web publishing, Word has the right tool for the job. For these and many other reasons, Word is the most widely used word processing program in homes and businesses.

Starting Word

The method you use to start Word depends on whether you intend to create a new document or open an existing one. If you intend to create a new document, use one of the following methods to start Word:

- Click the **start** button, choose Microsoft Office from the All Programs menu, and then choose Microsoft Office Word 2007.

- Click the Microsoft Word 2007 **W** button on the quick launch toolbar located at the left edge of the taskbar. (This button may not appear on all computers.)

Use one of the following methods if you intend to open an existing Word document. Once the Word program starts, the desired document will open in a Word window.

- Navigate to the desired document using Windows Explorer or My Computer and double-click the document name.

- Click the **start** button and point to My Recent Documents. You can choose the desired document from the documents list, which displays the most recently used documents.

Hands-On 3.1   Start Word

In this exercise, you will experience starting Word, and you will examine the Word window.

1. If necessary, start your computer. The Windows Desktop appears.

2. Click the ***start*** button at the left edge of the taskbar, and choose All Programs, just above the Start button.

3. Choose Microsoft Office→Microsoft Office Word 2007 from the menu.

4. Make sure the Word window is maximized ⬜.
   The Word program loads and the document window shown in the following illustration appears. Don't be concerned if your document window looks a bit different from this example. The Word screen is customizable.

Ⓐ Microsoft Office button—This button leads to file management tasks, including opening, printing, and saving your work. The Office button also leads to the Word Options button, where you can change Word's default settings.

Ⓑ Quick Access toolbar—Frequently used commands appear here, and you can add your own favorites.

Ⓒ Title Bar—The name of your document appears here. You see a generic Documentx name until you save and name your document.

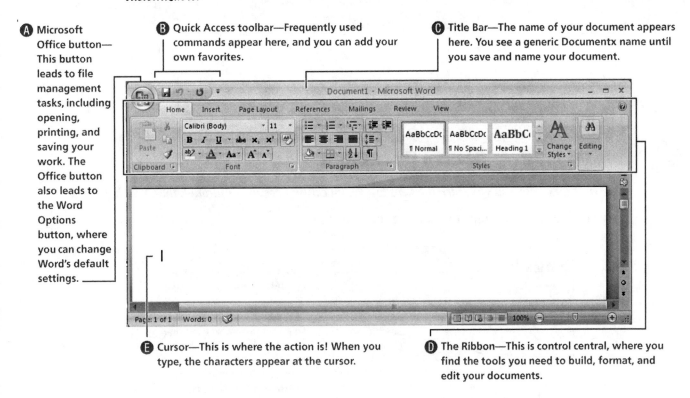

Ⓔ Cursor—This is where the action is! When you type, the characters appear at the cursor.

Ⓓ The Ribbon—This is control central, where you find the tools you need to build, format, and edit your documents.

Opening Documents

The Open command on the Office menu displays the Open dialog box, where you can navigate to a storage location and open previously saved documents. Once a document is open, you can edit or print it.

Opening Older Word Documents

If you open a document created in a previous version of Word, it opens in Compatibility Mode. The term appears in the Title Bar, as shown in the following illustration. Older Word documents do not understand the new features in Word 2007, so those features are limited or disabled.

 TIP! *When an older document is open, a Convert command is available on the Office menu, which you can use to upgrade the file and make the new features of Word 2007 available.*

 Hands-On 3.2   Open a Document

In this exercise, you will learn the steps to open an existing document through the Open dialog box.

1. Follow these steps to open the document:

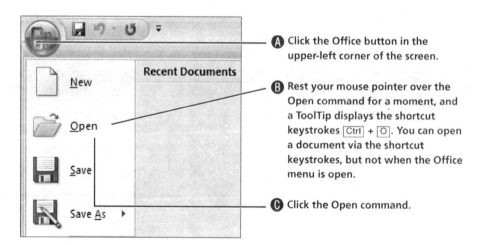

Ⓐ Click the Office button in the upper-left corner of the screen.

Ⓑ Rest your mouse pointer over the Open command for a moment, and a ToolTip displays the shortcut keystrokes Ctrl + O. You can open a document via the shortcut keystrokes, but not when the Office menu is open.

Ⓒ Click the Open command.

 NOTE! *Later in this lesson, the preceding steps will be written like this: Click Office [icon], and then choose Open from the menu.*

2. When the Open dialog box appears, follow these steps to open the Managing Diabetes document:

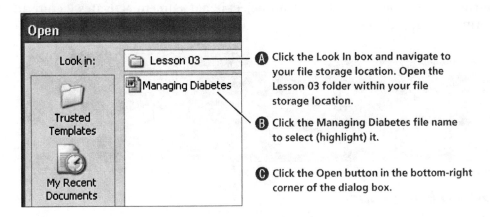

Ⓐ Click the Look In box and navigate to your file storage location. Open the Lesson 03 folder within your file storage location.

Ⓑ Click the Managing Diabetes file name to select (highlight) it.

Ⓒ Click the Open button in the bottom-right corner of the dialog box.

3. Make sure the Word window is maximized .

Working with the Word 2007 Interface

The band running across the top of the screen is the Ribbon. This is where you will find the tools for building, formatting, and editing your documents.

The Ribbon

The Ribbon consists of three primary areas: tabs, groups, and commands. The tabs include Home, Insert, Page Layout, and so on. A group houses related commands within a tab. Groups on the Home tab, for instance, include Clipboard, Font, Paragraph, Styles, and Editing. An example of a command in the Paragraph group is Increase Indent.

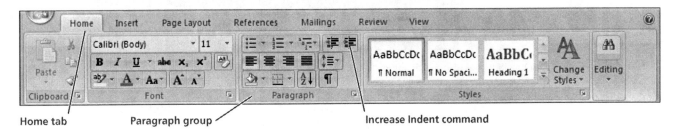

Home tab   Paragraph group   Increase Indent command

Be aware that the arrangement of the buttons on the Ribbon can vary, depending on your screen resolution and how the Word window is sized. Following are two examples of how the Paragraph group might appear on the Ribbon.

 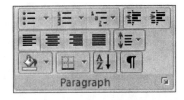

Contextual Tabs

Contextual tabs appear in context with the task you are performing. As shown in the following illustration, double-clicking a clip art object in a document activates Picture Tools, with the Format tab in the foreground.

Dialog Box Launcher

Some groups include a Dialog Box Launcher in the bottom-right corner of the group. This means that there are additional commands available for the group. Clicking the launcher opens the dialog box, or it may open a task pane, which, like a dialog box, houses additional commands related to the group.

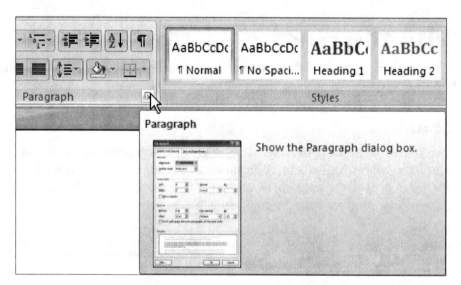

The dialog box launcher displays dialog or task panes boxes available for a given command.

Live Preview with Galleries

Live Preview shows what a formatting change looks like without actually applying the format. In the following example, selecting a block of text, and then hovering the mouse pointer over a font in the font gallery, previews how the text will look. Clicking the font name applies the font to the text.

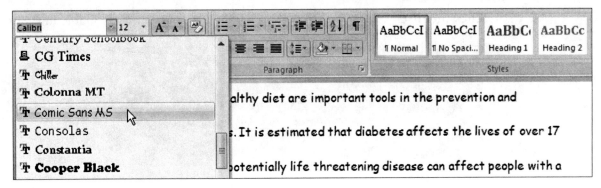

Live Preview of the Comic Sans MS Font

Hide the Ribbon

If you want more room to work, you can temporarily hide the Ribbon by double-clicking one of its tabs. This collapses the Ribbon, as shown in the following illustration.

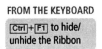

FROM THE KEYBOARD
Ctrl+F1 to hide/unhide the Ribbon

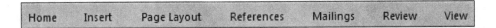

Clicking a tab, such as Home, redisplays the full Ribbon temporarily. It collapses again when you click in the document. If you want the Ribbon to remain open, right-click on the Ribbon and choose Minimize the Ribbon to turn off the feature.

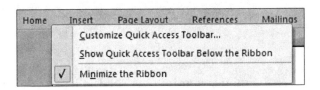

Hands-On 3.3   Work with the Ribbon

In this exercise, you will explore the various aspects of the Ribbon, including tabs, contextual tabs, the Dialog Box Launcher, and Live Preview. Finally, you'll hide and unhide the Ribbon.

Display the Insert Tab

1. Click the Insert tab on the Ribbon to display the commands available in that category.

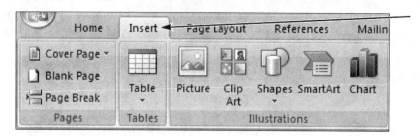

2. Take a moment to investigate some of the other tabs on the Ribbon, and then return to the Home tab.

Display Contextual Tabs and Use the Dialog Box Launcher

3. Double-click the clip art object at the top of your document to display the Picture Tools on the Ribbon.

Selection handles (small circles and squares) surround an object when you click it.

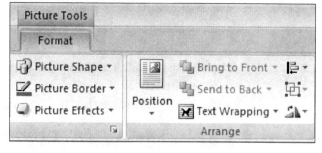

Picture Tools

4. Return to the Home tab, and hover the mouse pointer over the Dialog Box Launcher in the bottom-right corner of the Font group to display the ToolTip, as shown here.

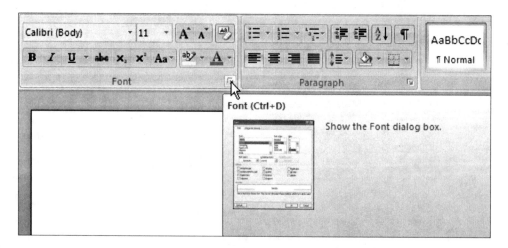

5. Click the launcher to open the Font dialog box.

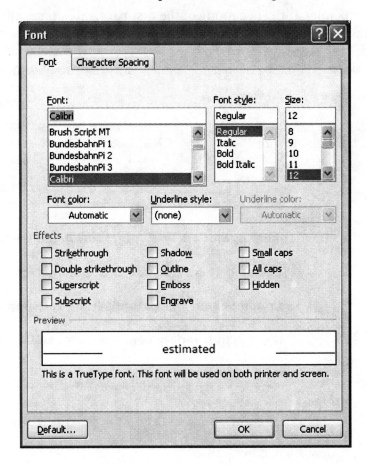

This dialog box provides additional tools for formatting text.

6. Click the Cancel button in the bottom-right corner to close the dialog box.

Use Live Preview

7. Position the mouse pointer at the beginning of the first paragraph, press and hold the mouse button, drag to the end of the paragraph to select (highlight) it, and then release the mouse button.

   If you notice a little toolbar fade in, you can ignore it for now. It will fade away on its own.

8. Follow these steps to use Live Preview:

Ⓐ Click the drop-down arrow on the Font list.

Ⓑ With the mouse pointer, drag the scroll box up to the top of the scroll bar.

Ⓒ Slide the mouse pointer up to Arial Black.

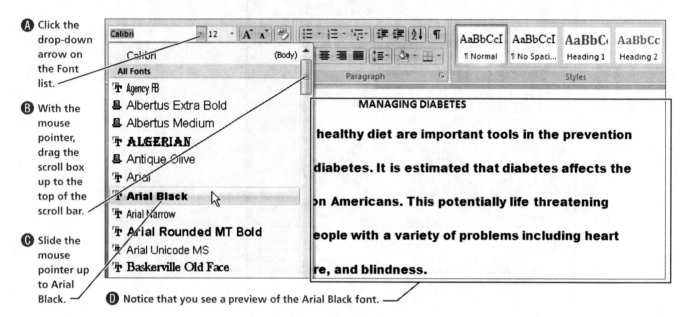

Ⓓ Notice that you see a preview of the Arial Black font.

9. Take a moment to preview a few other fonts.

10. Click anywhere in the document to close the font list, and deselect the highlighted text.

Hide/Unhide the Ribbon

11. Double-click the Home tab to hide the Ribbon.

12. Right-click the collapsed Ribbon and choose Minimize the Ribbon from the menu to turn off the feature.

The Quick Access Toolbar

The Quick Access toolbar in the upper-left corner of the screen contains frequently used commands. It is customizable and operates independently from the Ribbon.

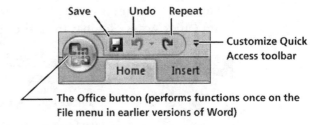

Save   Undo   Repeat

Customize Quick Access toolbar

The Office button (performs functions once on the File menu in earlier versions of Word)

Moving the Quick Access Toolbar

You can place the Quick Access toolbar in one of two positions on the screen. The default position is to the right of the Office button. Clicking the Customize Quick Access toolbar button at the right edge of the toolbar reveals a menu where you can choose Show Below the Ribbon.

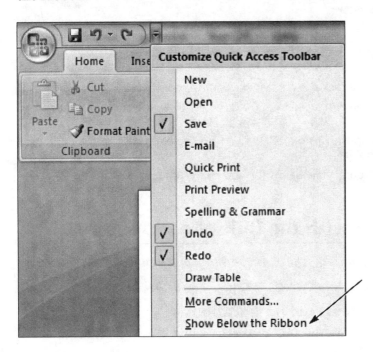

 TIP! *The Customize Quick Access Toolbar menu conveniently lists a series of frequently used commands that you can add to the toolbar by choosing them from the menu.*

Customizing the Quick Access Toolbar

You can add buttons to and remove them from the Quick Access toolbar to suit your needs. You might want to add commands you use regularly so they are always available.

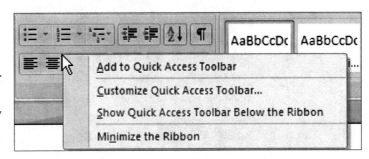

Right-click the Ribbon command you want to add (Center in this example), and choose Add to Quick Access Toolbar from the shortcut menu.

To remove a button from the Quick Access toolbar, right-click the button and choose Remove from Quick Access Toolbar from the shortcut menu.

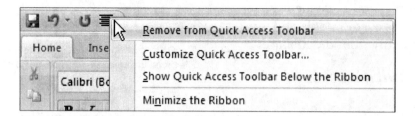

QUICK REFERENCE: WORKING WITH THE QUICK ACCESS TOOLBAR

Task	Procedure
Add a button to the toolbar	■ Right-click the button you want to add. ■ Choose Add to Quick Access Toolbar from the menu.
Remove a button from the toolbar	■ Right-click the button you want to remove. ■ Choose Remove from Quick Access Toolbar from the shortcut menu.
Change the location of the toolbar	■ Click the Customize Quick Access Toolbar button at the right edge of the toolbar. ■ Choose Show Below (or Above) the Ribbon.

Hands-On 3.4   Work with the Quick Access Toolbar

In this exercise, you will reposition the Quick Access toolbar, and then you will customize it by adding and removing buttons.

Change the Quick Access Toolbar Location

1. Follow these steps to move the Quick Access toolbar below the Ribbon:

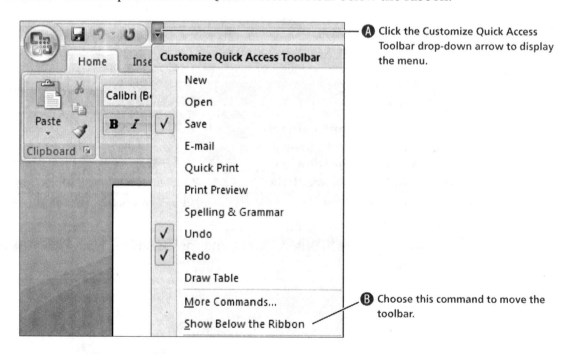

Ⓐ Click the Customize Quick Access Toolbar drop-down arrow to display the menu.

Ⓑ Choose this command to move the toolbar.

The toolbar appears below the Ribbon at the left edge of the window. Now you will return it to its original position.

2. Click the drop-down arrow at the right edge of the Quick Access toolbar again, and this time choose Show Above the Ribbon.

Add a Button to the Quick Access Toolbar

3. Make sure that the Home tab is in the foreground, and then follow these steps to add the Bullets button to the toolbar:

Ⓐ Right-click the Bullets button in the Paragraph group to display the shortcut menu.

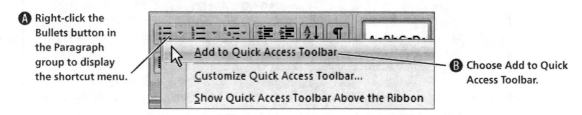

Ⓑ Choose Add to Quick Access Toolbar.

The Bullets button now appears on the toolbar.

Remove a Button from the Quick Access Toolbar

4. Right-click the Bullets ⬚ button on the Quick Access toolbar and choose the Remove from Quick Access Toolbar command.

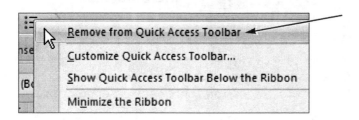

The button disappears from the Quick Access toolbar.

The Mini Toolbar

There's another toolbar in Word, and it contains frequently used formatting commands. When you select (highlight) text, the Mini toolbar fades in. After a pause, it fades away. Make it reappear by right-clicking the selected text.

In the following example, clicking the Bold **B** button on the Mini toolbar applies the Bold feature to the selected text.

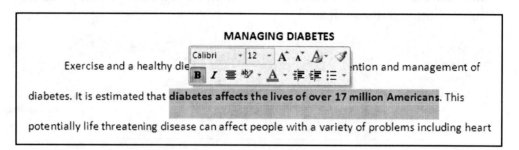

![Hands-On icon] Hands-On 3.5 **Use the Mini Toolbar**

In this exercise, you will use the Mini toolbar to format text.

1. Follow these steps to italicize a word:

Ⓐ Double-click the word *Exercise* at the start of the paragraph to select (highlight) it.

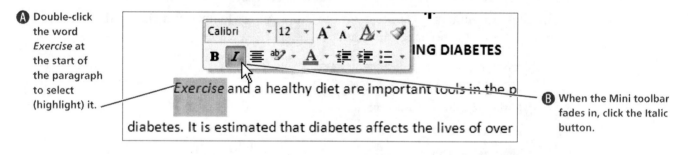

Ⓑ When the Mini toolbar fades in, click the Italic button.

⚠ **NOTE!** *If this timid little toolbar disappears, right-click the highlighted text and it will reappear.*

2. Click anywhere in the document to deselect the text and view the formatted word.
You will get more practice with this toolbar in Lesson 5, Creating a Memorandum and a Simple Report.

Navigating in a Word Document

If you are working in a multipage document, it is helpful to know about various techniques for moving through a document. You can navigate using the scroll bar located at the right side of the screen, or you can use keystrokes.

Navigating with the Scroll Bar

The scroll bar lets you browse through documents; however, it does not move the cursor. After scrolling, you must click in the document to reposition the cursor. The following illustration shows the components of the scroll bar.

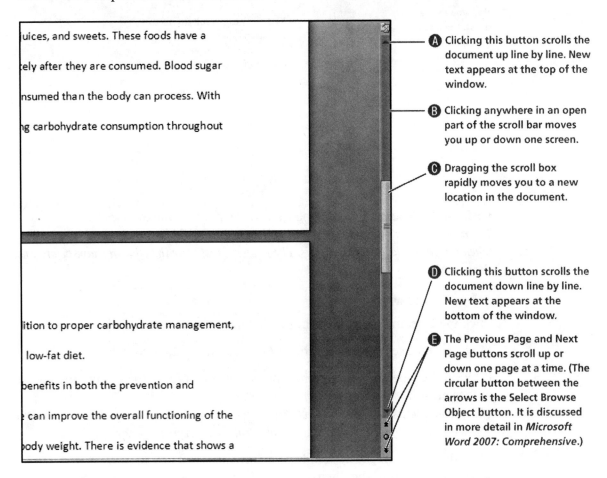

A Clicking this button scrolls the document up line by line. New text appears at the top of the window.

B Clicking anywhere in an open part of the scroll bar moves you up or down one screen.

C Dragging the scroll box rapidly moves you to a new location in the document.

D Clicking this button scrolls the document down line by line. New text appears at the bottom of the window.

E The Previous Page and Next Page buttons scroll up or down one page at a time. (The circular button between the arrows is the Select Browse Object button. It is discussed in more detail in *Microsoft Word 2007: Comprehensive*.)

In this exercise, you will use the scroll bar to practice moving through a document, and then you will position the cursor.

Scroll in the Document

1. Follow these steps to scroll in the document:

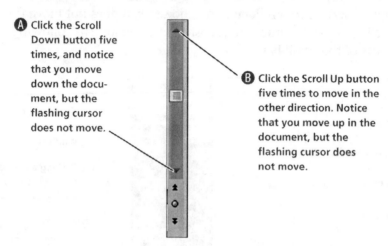

A Click the Scroll Down button five times, and notice that you move down the document, but the flashing cursor does not move.

B Click the Scroll Up button five times to move in the other direction. Notice that you move up in the document, but the flashing cursor does not move.

2. Position the I-beam I mouse pointer in the body of the document.
   The mouse pointer looks like an I-beam when it's inside the document, and it looks like a white arrow when it is in the document margins. The pointer must have the I-beam shape before you can reposition the cursor.

Position the Cursor

3. Click the I-beam I anywhere in the document to position the blinking cursor.

4. Move the mouse pointer into the left margin area. The white arrow shape is now visible.

5. Position the I-beam I in the first line of the body of the document, and click the left mouse button.
   The cursor appears just where you clicked. If the background is highlighted, you accidentally selected the text. Deselect by clicking the mouse pointer in the document background.

6. Click the open part of the scroll bar below the scroll box to move down one screen, as shown in the illustration to the right.

Use the Scroll Box and the Next Page/Previous Page Buttons

7. Drag the scroll box to the bottom of the scroll bar with the mouse pointer.

8. Click the I-beam I at the end of the text to position it on the last page.

9. Drag the scroll box to the top of the scroll bar, and click the I-beam I in front of the first word of the first paragraph.

10. Click the Next Page button to move to the top of page 2.
    The cursor moves with you when you use the Next Page and Previous Page buttons.

11. Click the Previous Page button to move to the top of page 1.

Navigating with the Keyboard

Whether you use the mouse or the keyboard to navigate through a document is a matter of personal preference. Navigating with the keyboard always moves the cursor, so it will be with you when you arrive at your destination.

The following Quick Reference table provides keystrokes for moving quickly through a document.

QUICK REFERENCE: NAVIGATING WITH THE KEYBOARD			
Press	**To Move**	**Press**	**To Move**
→	One character to the right	Page Down	Down one screen
←	One character to the left	Page Up	Up one screen
Ctrl + →	One word to the right	Ctrl + End	To the end of the document
Ctrl + ←	One word to the left	Ctrl + Home	To the beginning of the document
↓	Down one line	End	To the end of the line
↑	Up one line	Home	To the beginning of the line

 Hands-On 3.7   Use the Keyboard to Navigate

In this exercise, you will use the keyboard to practice moving through a document.

Use the Arrow Keys

1. Click the I-beam Ⅰ in the middle of the first line of the first paragraph.

2. Tap the right arrow → and left arrow ← keys a few times to move to the right and left, one character at a time.

3. Tap the down arrow ↓ and up arrow ↑ keys a few times to move down, one row at a time.

Use Additional Keys

4. Hold down the Ctrl key and keep it down, then tap the Home key to move to the beginning of the document. Release the Ctrl key.

5. Use the arrow keys to position the cursor in the middle of the first line of the first paragraph.

6. Hold down the Ctrl key and keep it down, then tap the left arrow ← key a few times to move to the left, one word at a time. Release the Ctrl key.

7. Hold down the Ctrl key and keep it down, then tap the right arrow → key several times to move to the right, one word at a time. Release the Ctrl key.

8. Tap the Home key to move to the beginning of the line.

9. Tap the End key to move to the end of the line.

10. Spend a few moments navigating with the keyboard. Refer to the preceding Quick Reference table for some additional keystrokes.

Closing Documents

You close a file by clicking the Office button and choosing the Close command from the menu. If you haven't saved your document, Word will prompt you to save it.

 Hands-On 3.8   Close the Document

In this exercise, you will close a file.

1. Click the Office button, and then choose Close from the menu.

2. When Word asks you if you want to save the changes, click No.

3. If a blank document is open on the screen, use the same technique to close it.
   The document window always has this appearance when all documents are closed.

Starting a New Blank Document

FROM THE KEYBOARD

Ctrl + N to start a new document

When all documents are closed, you can click the Office button, and then choose the New command from the menu to open a new blank document.

 Hands-On 3.9   Start a New Document

In this exercise, you will open a new blank document. There should not be any documents in the Word window at this time.

1. Click the Office button, and then choose New from the menu.

2. When the New Document dialog box appears, click the Create button in the bottom-right corner to display the new document.
   Now you will close the new document and try using the shortcut keystrokes to start another new document.

3. Click the Office button, and then choose Close from the menu.

4. Hold down the Ctrl key and tap the N on your keyboard to open a new document.

5. Leave this document open.

Getting Help in Word 2007

 The Microsoft Office Word Help button appears in the upper-right corner of the Word screen. Clicking the Help button opens the Word Help window where you can browse through the Table of Contents, click links to access a variety of topics, or type a term in the search box and let the system find the answer for you.

Hands-On 3.10 Use Word Help

In this exercise you will practice working with several Help techniques.

1. Click the Help button in the upper-right corner of the Word window.

2. Follow these steps for an overview of Word Help:

A Some of these toolbar buttons are like ones you may already be familiar with from using a web browser. Click the mouse pointer on the top frame of the Word Help window to activate it, and then hover the mouse pointer over buttons to see Tool Tips describing their purpose.

B Type **printing** in the Search box, and then click the Search button to display related topics.

C Look through the Table of Contents by clicking the Formatting book icon to display the topics in the group.

D Click Set Tab Stops to display the topic in the right pane.

E Scroll through the topic.

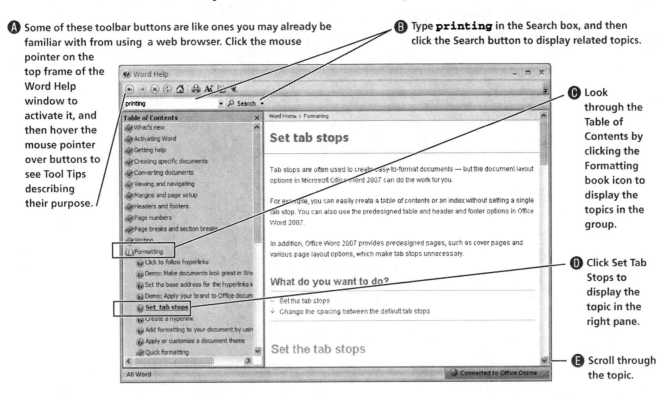

3. Click the Close button in the upper-right corner of the Word Help window.

Exiting from Word

Clicking the Office button and then clicking the ✕ Exit Word button closes the Word application. It's important to exit Word in an orderly fashion. Turning off your computer before exiting Word could cause you to lose data.

 Hands-On 3.11   Exit from Word

In this exercise, you will practice exiting from Word. Since the blank document on the screen has not been modified, you won't bother saving it.

1. Click the Office button.

2. Click the ✕ Exit Word button in the bottom-right corner of the window.

3. If Word prompts you to save changes, click No.
   Word closes and the Windows Desktop appears.

Concepts Review

True/False Questions

1. The cursor automatically repositions when you scroll through a document using the scroll bars. TRUE FALSE

2. The Mini toolbar appears in the upper-left corner of the Word screen. TRUE FALSE

3. A Dialog Box Launcher leads to additional commands for a group on the Ribbon. TRUE FALSE

4. The band running across the top of the Word screen is known as the Ribbon. TRUE FALSE

5. Tapping the Home key always moves the cursor to the top of the document. TRUE FALSE

6. Contextual tabs appear in context with the task you are performing. TRUE FALSE

7. The Page Down key on your keyboard moves you down though a document one page at a time. TRUE FALSE

8. If you open a document created in a previous version of Word, the term Compatibility Mode appears in the title bar. TRUE FALSE

9. The Quick Access toolbar works in conjunction with the Ribbon; therefore, it is not customizable. TRUE FALSE

10. Tabs on the Ribbon, such as the Home tab, are divided into command groups. TRUE FALSE

Multiple Choice Questions

1. Which of the following terms does not relate to the Ribbon?
   a. Contextual tabs
   b. Undo
   c. Dialog Box Launcher
   d. Galleries

2. Which of the following commands is correct regarding keyboard navigation?
   a. Alt + → moves the cursor one word to the right.
   b. Ctrl + End moves the cursor to the end of the document.
   c. Home moves the cursor to the beginning of the previous paragraph.
   d. Alt + End moves the cursor to the end of the line.

3. Word provides the capability to view what formatting changes would look like without actually applying the format. That feature is known as _____.
   a. Formatting Ribbon
   b. Contextual tabs
   c. Print Preview
   d. Live Preview

4. Which of the following statements is correct regarding the Mini Toolbar?
   a. It's located on the Home tab of the Ribbon.
   b. It is customizable.
   c. It appears when you select text.
   d. You hold down the Ctrl key and tap M to display it.

Skill Builders

Skill Builder 3.1   Identify Elements of the Word 2007 Window

In this exercise, you will practice using correct terminology with parts of the Word screen. It's important to use the right terms when talking about the Word application. If, for example, you need to discuss an issue with people in your IT department, they can help you faster if they are clear on what you are talking about.

1. Start Word 2007.

2. Using the table to the right of the illustration, write in the correct terms for items A through E.

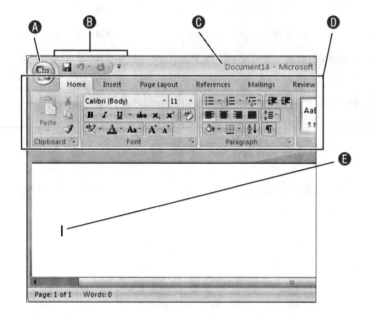

LETTER	TERM
A	_____
B	_____
C	_____
D	_____
E	_____

Skill Builder 3.2   Use Word Help

In this exercise, you will work with the Word Help window to find information that can assist you as you work.

1. Click the Microsoft Office Word Help  button in the upper-right corner of the Word window.

Use the Table of Contents

Now you'll review opening a file.

2. Using the following illustration as a guide, click the book icon to the left of File Management in the Table of Contents to reveal the items in that topic. Then scroll down and click the Open a File link to display the topic in the right side of the window.

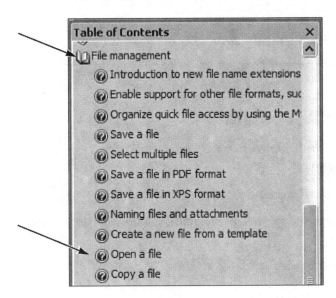

3. Click the Word Home link at the top of the right-hand pane to return to the Browse Word Help pane.

4. Click the Getting Help link in the right pane of the Word Help window.

5. Click the Work with the Help Window link in the right pane.

6. Scroll down to see the major topics that are covered.
   In the next lesson, you will learn to select (highlight) text. As a preview, you will search for the Select Text topic and read a little about it in advance.

Search for Help

7. Follow these steps to locate the Select Text topic:

Ⓐ Click the I-beam in this box, located in the upper-left corner of the Word Help window, and type **select text.**

Ⓑ Click the Search button.

8. Click the Select Text link on the right side of the Word Help window to view the topic.

9. Scroll down and take a moment to read the first few entries under Select Text by Using the Mouse.

10. Click the Close ⊠ button in the upper-right corner of the Word Help window.

Skill Builder 3.3   Navigate in a Document

In this exercise, you will use a letter that an exchange student in Paris wrote to his friend. It's a long letter, so it will provide good practice for navigating.

1. Click the Office 🗔 button, and choose Open from the menu.

2. When the Open dialog box appears, if necessary, navigate to your file storage location, and then open the Lesson 03 folder.

3. Double-click to open the file named sb-Exchange Student.

Navigate with the Scroll Bar

4. Click the Next Page ⬇ button at the bottom of the scroll bar to move to the top of page 2.

5. Click the scroll bar below the scroll box to move down one screen.

6. Drag the scroll box to the top of the scroll bar, and click the cursor at the beginning of the document.

7. Click the Scroll Down ⬇ button, and hold the mouse button down to scroll quickly through the document.

8. Click the Previous Page button ⬆ enough times to return to the top of the document.

Navigate with the Keyboard

9. Tap the down arrow ⬇ key twice to move to the beginning of the first paragraph.

10. Tap the End key to move the cursor to the end of the line.

11. Tap the Home key to move to the beginning of the line.

12. Tap Ctrl + End to place the cursor at the end of the document.

13. Tap Ctrl + Home to move to the top of the document.

14. If you press and hold the arrow keys, they quickly move the cursor through the document. Press and hold the ⬇ key long enough to move to the beginning of the second paragraph.

15. Hold down the Ctrl key and tap the → key three times to move to the right, one word at a time.

16. Please leave this document open for the next exercise.

Skill Builder 3.4   Work with the Quick Access Toolbar

In this exercise, you will move the Quick Access toolbar below the Ribbon, and you will customize the toolbar by adding a button to it.

Before You Begin: The sb-Exchange Student document should be open in Word.

1. Follow these steps to move the Quick Access toolbar:

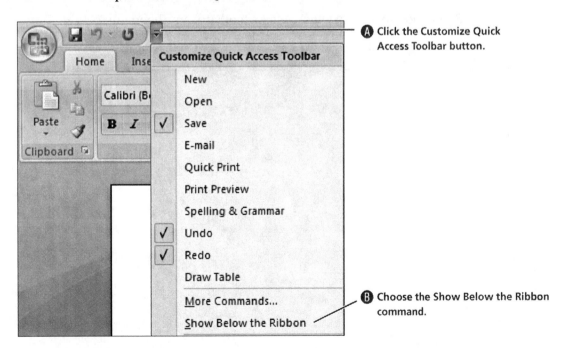

Ⓐ Click the Customize Quick Access Toolbar button.

Ⓑ Choose the Show Below the Ribbon command.

Now you will return the toolbar to its original position.

2. Click the drop-down arrow at the right edge of the toolbar, and choose Show Above the Ribbon from the menu.
   Next you'll add a button to the Quick Access toolbar.

3. Make sure you're on the Home tab. If not, click the tab to bring it to the foreground.

4. Follow these steps to add the Clear Formatting  button to the toolbar:

A Right-click the Clear Formatting button in the Font group.

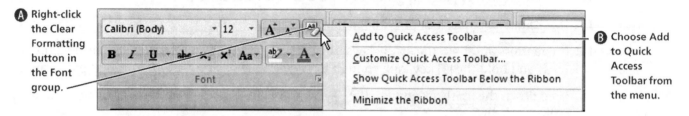

B Choose Add to Quick Access Toolbar from the menu.

5. The button now appears on the toolbar, as shown here.

6. Ask your instructor to inspect your work and initial here to verify the placement of the Clear Formatting button on the toolbar. _____
   Next you will remove the button you just added to the toolbar.

7. Place the mouse pointer over the Clear Formatting  button on the Quick Access toolbar and click the right mouse button.

8. Choose Remove from Quick Access toolbar from the menu.

9. Close the document; if you are asked to save your changes, choose Yes.

LESSON 4

Creating and Editing Business Letters

In this lesson, you will create business letters while learning proper business document formatting. You will also learn fundamental techniques of entering and editing text, copying and moving text, and saving and printing documents. In addition, you will learn to use Word's AutoCorrect tool to insert frequently used text.

LESSON OBJECTIVES

After studying this lesson, you will be able to:

- Type a professional business letter
- Save a document
- Select and edit text
- Use the AutoCorrect feature
- Copy and move text
- Print a document

Case Study: Taking Care with Business Letters

Terrel Richardson just landed his first job as a medical assistant in the Cardiology Department at St. Mary's Hospital. He is working for Dr. Wright, a cardiologist in the Electrophysiology Lab. A primary care physician is referring one of his patients to the lab for an ablation procedure. Dr. Wright asked Terrel to prepare a standard letter for patients orienting them to the department and providing information about the procedure.

Terrel starts by referring to his business writing class textbook to ensure that he formats the letter correctly for a good first impression and a professional appearance.

February 10, 2007

Ms. Suzanne Frost
813 Sunnyside Avenue
Harbor Hills, CA 99999

Dear Ms. Frost:

Dr. Vijay Singh referred you to us for a consultation in the Electrophysiology Department at St. Mary's Hospital to discuss an ablation procedure. Catheter ablation is a non-surgical technique that destroys (ablates) parts of the abnormal electrical pathway that is causing your arrhythmia (abnormal heart rhythm).

I have enclosed information for your review regarding this procedure. After reading the booklets, please contact our office at your earliest convenience so we can discuss your options.

Sincerely,

Terrel Richardson
Medical Assistant
Electrophysiology Department

tr
Enclosures (2)
cc: Dr. Marjorie Wright

Defining Typical Business Letter Styles

There are several acceptable styles of business letters. The styles discussed in this text include block, modified block standard format, and modified block indented paragraphs. All business letters contain the same or similar elements, but with varied formatting. The following styles are described in this section:

- Block Style

- Modified Block Style—Standard Format

- Modified Block Style—Indented Paragraphs

Block Style

The following illustration outlines the parts of the block style business letter.

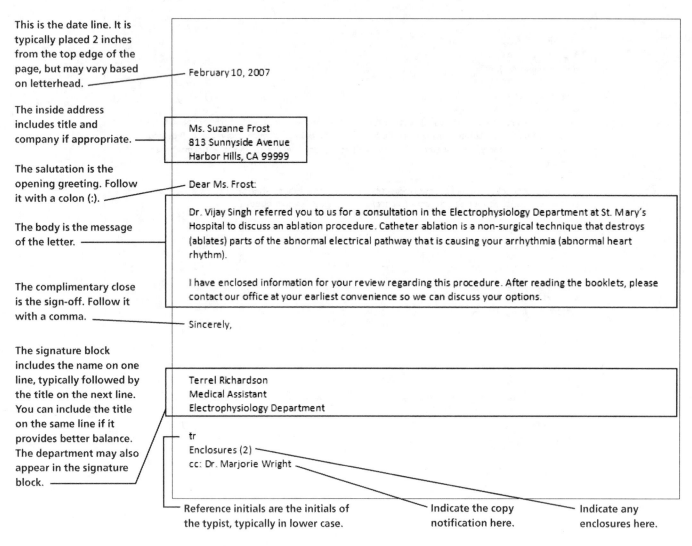

This is the date line. It is typically placed 2 inches from the top edge of the page, but may vary based on letterhead.

February 10, 2007

The inside address includes title and company if appropriate.

Ms. Suzanne Frost
813 Sunnyside Avenue
Harbor Hills, CA 99999

The salutation is the opening greeting. Follow it with a colon (:).

Dear Ms. Frost:

The body is the message of the letter.

Dr. Vijay Singh referred you to us for a consultation in the Electrophysiology Department at St. Mary's Hospital to discuss an ablation procedure. Catheter ablation is a non-surgical technique that destroys (ablates) parts of the abnormal electrical pathway that is causing your arrhythmia (abnormal heart rhythm).

I have enclosed information for your review regarding this procedure. After reading the booklets, please contact our office at your earliest convenience so we can discuss your options.

The complimentary close is the sign-off. Follow it with a comma.

Sincerely,

The signature block includes the name on one line, typically followed by the title on the next line. You can include the title on the same line if it provides better balance. The department may also appear in the signature block.

Terrel Richardson
Medical Assistant
Electrophysiology Department

tr
Enclosures (2)
cc: Dr. Marjorie Wright

Reference initials are the initials of the typist, typically in lower case.

Indicate the copy notification here.

Indicate any enclosures here.

Modified Block Style—Standard Format

The following illustration outlines the differences in the standard modified block style business letter from the block style business letter.

The date line, the complimentary close, and the signature block begin at the center of the page. All other lines begin at the left margin.

February 10, 2007

Ms. Suzanne Frost
813 Sunnyside Avenue
Harbor Hills, CA 99999

Dear Ms. Frost:

Dr. Vijay Singh referred you to us for a consultation in the Electrophysiology Department at St. Mary's Hospital to discuss an ablation procedure. Catheter ablation is a non-surgical technique that destroys (ablates) parts of the abnormal electrical pathway that is causing your arrhythmia (abnormal heart rhythm).

I have enclosed information for your review regarding this procedure. After reading the booklets, please contact our office at your earliest convenience so we can discuss your options.

Sincerely,

Terrel Richardson
Medical Assistant
Electrophysiology Department

tr
Enclosures (2)
cc: Dr. Marjorie Wright

Modified Block Style—Indented Paragraphs

The following illustration shows the modified block style business letter with indented paragraphs.

This format is the same as the Modified Block Style—Standard Format, except the first lines of the body paragraphs are indented one-half inch. ——

February 10, 2007

Ms. Suzanne Frost
813 Sunnyside Avenue
Harbor Hills, CA 99999

Dear Ms. Frost:

———— Dr. Vijay Singh referred you to us for a consultation in the Electrophysiology Department at St. Mary's Hospital to discuss an ablation procedure. Catheter ablation is a non-surgical technique that destroys (ablates) parts of the abnormal electrical pathway that is causing your arrhythmia (abnormal heart rhythm).

———— I have enclosed information for your review regarding this procedure. After reading the booklets, please contact our office at your earliest convenience so we can discuss your options.

Sincerely,

Terrel Richardson
Medical Assistant
Electrophysiology Department

tr
Enclosures (2)
cc: Dr. Marjorie Wright

Inserting Text

You always insert text into a Word document at the flashing cursor. Therefore, you must position the cursor at the desired location before typing.

AutoComplete

Word's AutoComplete feature does some of your typing for you. It recognizes certain words and phrases, such as names of months and names of days, and offers to complete them for you, as shown here.

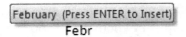

As you begin typing the month Febr, AutoComplete offers to finish typing it out.

You accept AutoComplete suggestions by tapping [Enter]. If you choose to ignore the suggestion, just keep typing, and the suggestion will disappear.

Using the Enter Key

You use [Enter] to begin a new paragraph or to insert blank lines in a document. Word considers anything that ends by tapping [Enter] to be a paragraph. Thus, short lines such as a date line, an inside address, or even blank lines themselves are considered paragraphs.

Tapping [Enter] inserts a paragraph ¶ symbol in a document. These symbols are visible when you display formatting marks.

Showing Formatting Marks

The Show/Hide ¶ button in the Paragraph group of the Home tab shows or hides formatting marks. Although they appear on the screen, you will not see them in the printed document. Marks include dots representing spaces between words, paragraph symbols that appear when you tap [Enter], and arrows that represent tabs.

Viewing these characters can be important when editing a document. You may need to see the nonprinting characters to determine whether the space between two words was created with the [Spacebar] or [Tab]. The following illustrations show the location of the Show/Hide button and the characters that appear when you tap the [Spacebar], the [Enter] key, or the [Tab].

Show/Hide button

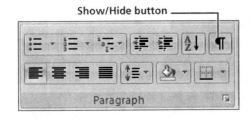

These symbols are para-graph marks. They appear whenever you tap [Enter].

The dots between words are inserted when you tap the [Spacebar].

Tabs are represented by small arrows.

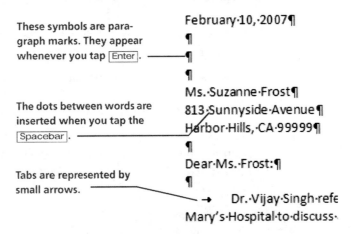

February·10,·2007¶
¶
¶
¶
Ms.·Suzanne·Frost¶
813·Sunnyside·Avenue¶
Harbor·Hills,·CA·99999¶
¶
Dear·Ms.·Frost:¶
¶
→ Dr.·Vijay·Singh·refe
Mary's·Hospital·to·discuss·

Spacing in Letters

Word 2007 introduces a new default line spacing. Rather than a default of single spacing, which has been the standard for word processors from the beginning, Word 2007 introduces 1.15 line spacing. This additional space can make your documents easier to read. The new spacing also includes an extra 10 points of space at the end of paragraphs. (That's a little over an eighth of an inch.) Rather than tapping [Enter] twice at the end of a paragraph, just tap [Enter] once, and Word adds the extra spacing.

Apply Traditional Spacing Using the Line Spacing Button

When writing letters, a traditional, more compact look (without the additional spacing) is still considered appropriate. Therefore, when you begin a letter, you may wish to switch to single (1.0) spacing and remove the extra space after paragraphs by choosing the options shown in the following figure.

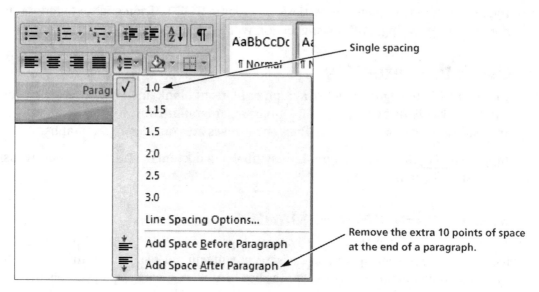

Apply these settings when you wish to type a more compact, traditional letter.

Apply Traditional Spacing Using the No Spacing Style

An alternative to using the Line Spacing button to achieve traditional spacing is to apply the No Spacing style located in the Styles group of the Home tab on the Ribbon, as shown here.

When you begin a new document, click the No Spacing icon on the Ribbon to achieve traditional spacing. The concept of Word's Styles feature is covered in detail in *Microsoft Word 2007: Comprehensive*.

 TIP! *The exercises in this lesson use the Line Spacing button to set traditional spacing; however, feel free to use this alternate method instead if you prefer.*

Word Wrap

If you continue typing after the cursor reaches the end of a line, Word automatically wraps the cursor to the beginning of the next line. If you let Word Wrap format your paragraph initially, the paragraph will also reformat correctly as you insert or delete text.

 Hands-On 4.1   Type a Letter

In this exercise, you will display formatting marks, adjust spacing, use AutoComplete, work with the Enter *key, and let Word Wrap do its job.*

Display Nonprinting Characters and Modify Line Spacing

1. Start Word. Make sure the Word window is maximized ▢.

2. Choose Home→Paragraph→Show/Hide ¶ from the Ribbon, as shown to the right. *New documents contain a paragraph symbol; you won't see it if you don't turn on the Show/Hide feature. Paragraph symbols carry formatting in them. For a new document, formatting includes default spacing of 1.15 lines and extra space at the end of a paragraph.*

   In the next step, you'll select (highlight) the paragraph symbol and reformat it, changing the default line spacing to 1.0 and removing additional space after a paragraph.

3. Position the I-beam I left of the paragraph symbol, press and hold the mouse button, drag to the right to select (highlight)the paragraph symbol, and then release the mouse button.

4. Follow these steps to reformat the paragraph symbol:

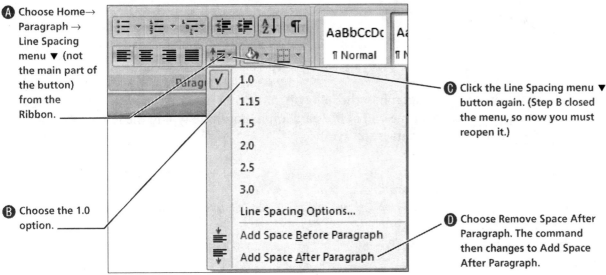

Ⓐ Choose Home→ Paragraph → Line Spacing menu ▼ (not the main part of the button) from the Ribbon.

Ⓑ Choose the 1.0 option.

Ⓒ Click the Line Spacing menu ▼ button again. (Step B closed the menu, so now you must reopen it.)

Ⓓ Choose Remove Space After Paragraph. The command then changes to Add Space After Paragraph.

Turn On the Ruler and Type the Letter

5. Click the View Ruler ⬚ button at the top of the vertical scroll bar to display the ruler.

6. Tap [Enter] six times to place the cursor 2 inches from the top of the page (at approximately the 1 inch mark on the vertical ruler).

7. Start typing **Febr,** but stop when AutoComplete displays a pop-up tip.
   AutoComplete suggests the word it thinks you are typing and offers to complete it.

8. Tap [Enter] to automatically insert February into the letter.

9. Finish typing the date as **February 10, 2007.**

10. Continue typing the letter as shown in the following illustration, tapping [Enter] wherever you see a paragraph symbol. If you catch a typo, you can tap the [Backspace] key enough times to remove the error, and then continue typing.

¶
¶
¶
¶
¶
¶
February·10,·2007¶
¶
¶
¶
Ms.·Suzanne·Frost¶
813·Sunnyside·Avenue¶
Harbor·Hills,·CA·99999¶
¶
Dear·Ms.·Frost:¶
¶
¶

11. Type the first body paragraph in the following illustration. Let Word Wrap do its thing, and then tap [Enter] twice at the end of the paragraph. Continue typing the letter, tapping [Enter] where you see a paragraph symbol.

⚠ **NOTE!** *If you see a wavy red line, that is Word's way of telling you that a word might be misspelled. If a term is not in Word's dictionary, it is marked as a possible error, even if it is spelled correctly. Wavy green lines indicate possible grammar errors. Ignore red and green wavy lines for now. You'll learn more about them in the next lesson.*

Dear Ms. Frost:¶

¶

Dr. Vijay Singh has referred you to us for a consultation in the Electrophysiology Department at St. Mary's Hospital to discuss an ablation procedure. Catheter ablation is a non-surgical technique that destroys parts of the abnormal electrical pathway that is causing your arrhythmia. ¶

¶

Enclosed please find informational materials for your review regarding this procedure. After reading the booklets, please contact our office ASAP so that we can discuss your options.¶

¶

Yours truly,¶

¶

¶

¶

Terrel Richardson¶

Medical Assistant¶

Electrophysiology Department¶

¶

¶

12. Choose Home→Paragraph→Show/Hide 🔳 to turn off formatting marks.

TIP! *Feel free to turn the Show/Hide feature on or off as you see fit throughout this course.*

Saving Your Work

It's important to save your documents frequently! Power outages and accidents can result in lost data. Documents are saved to storage locations such as hard drives and USB flash drives.

The Save Command

There are three primary commands used to save Word documents:

FROM THE KEYBOARD
Ctrl+S to save

■ The Save 🔳 button on the Quick Access toolbar

■ The Office 🔳→Save command

■ The Office 🔳→Save As command

When you save a document for the first time, the Save As dialog box appears. The following illustration describes significant features of the Save As dialog box.

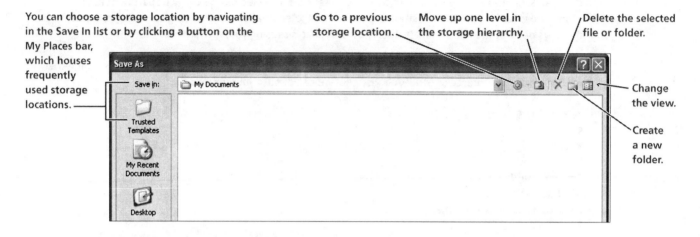

You can choose a storage location by navigating in the Save In list or by clicking a button on the My Places bar, which houses frequently used storage locations.

Go to a previous storage location.

Move up one level in the storage hierarchy.

Delete the selected file or folder.

Change the view.

Create a new folder.

Save Compared to Save As

While the Save and Save As commands are quite similar, each has a specific use. If the document was never saved, Word displays the Save As dialog box, where you specify the name and storage location of the document. If the document was previously saved, choosing the save command again replaces the prior version with the edited one, without displaying the Save As dialog box.

Word's DOCX File Format

A file format is a technique for saving computer data. Previous versions of Word saved documents in the *doc* format. Word 2007 introduces a new file format: *docx*. This is important because users of earlier versions of Word may not be able to read Word files in the new docx file format without installing special software.

 TIP! *Users can download a* compatibility pack *from the Microsoft website. This allows users of previous versions of Word to open, edit, save, and create files in the new docx file format.*

Hands-On 4.2   Save the Letter

In this exercise, you will save the letter you created in the previous exercise.

1. Click the Save 💾 button on the Quick Access toolbar. Word displays the Save As dialog box, since this is the first time you are saving this document. Once the file is named, this button will simply save the current version of the file over the old version.

2. Follow these steps to save the letter:
   Keep in mind that your dialog box may contain more files than shown here.

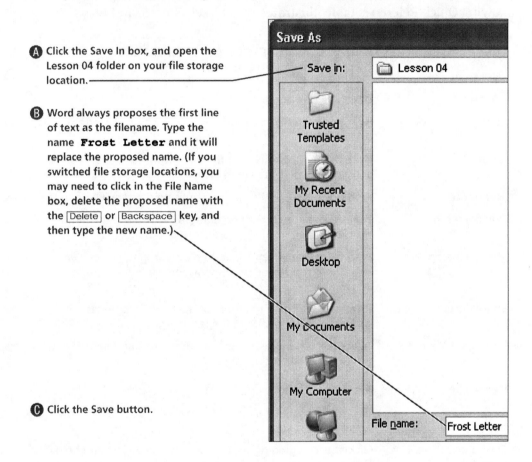

Ⓐ Click the Save In box, and open the Lesson 04 folder on your file storage location.

Ⓑ Word always proposes the first line of text as the filename. Type the name **Frost Letter** and it will replace the proposed name. (If you switched file storage locations, you may need to click in the File Name box, delete the proposed name with the Delete or Backspace key, and then type the new name.)

Ⓒ Click the Save button.

3. Leave the file open for the next exercise.

Selecting Text

You must select (highlight) text if you wish to perform some action on it. Suppose you want to delete an entire line. You would select the line first, and then tap Delete.

Selection Techniques

Word provides many selection techniques; some use the mouse, and some use the keyboard. Beginners may find the mouse difficult to control; keyboard techniques tend to provide greater control. Use the keyboard techniques if you have difficulty controlling the mouse. Deselect text by clicking in the white background of the document or by tapping an arrow key. The following Quick Reference table illustrates various selection techniques.

QUICK REFERENCE: WORKING WITH SELECTION TECHNIQUES	
Item to be Selected	**Mouse Technique**
One word	Double-click the word.
Continuous block of text	Press and hold the left mouse button while dragging the I-beam over the desired text.
A line	Place the mouse pointer in the margin to the left of the line. Click when the pointer is shaped like an arrow.
A sentence	Hold down Ctrl and click the mouse pointer anywhere in the sentence.
One paragraph	Triple-click anywhere in the paragraph, or place the mouse pointer in the margin to the left of the paragraph and double-click.
Multiple paragraphs	Drag the I-beam over the desired paragraphs, or position the mouse pointer in the left margin and drag up or down when the pointer is shaped like an arrow.
Entire document	Triple-click in the left margin, or make sure no text is selected and then press and hold Ctrl and click in the left margin.
Nonadjacent areas	Select the first block of text, and then press and hold Ctrl while dragging over additional blocks of text.
Item to be Selected	**Keyboard Technique**
One word	Click at the beginning of the word, and then press and hold Shift+Ctrl while tapping →.
Continuous block of text	Click at the beginning of the text, and then press and hold Shift while tapping any arrow key. You can also click at the beginning of the text, press and hold Shift, and click at the end of the phrase.
A line	Press Shift+End to select from the cursor to the end of the line. Press Shift+Home to select from the cursor to the beginning of the line.
Entire document	Press Ctrl+A to execute the Select All command, or press Ctrl and click in the left margin.

Hands-On 4.3 Select Text

In this exercise, you will practice various selection techniques using the letter you just created. Selecting text causes the Mini toolbar to fade in. You can ignore it for now. You'll learn to use it to format text in Lesson 5, Creating a Memorandum and a Simple Report.

Select Using the Left Margin

1. Follow these steps to select text using the left margin:

A Point outside the margin of the first line until the mouse pointer tilts slightly to the right, as shown here.

B Click once to select the entire line.

Ms. Suzanne Frost
813 Sunnyside Avenue
Harbor Hills, CA 99999

C Make sure the pointer tilts to the right, and then click once to select this line. (Notice that the previously selected line is no longer selected.)

Dear Ms. Frost:

Dr. Vijay Singh has referred you to us for consultation in the Electrophysiology Department at St. Mary's Hospital to discuss an ablation procedure. Catheter ablation is a non-surgical technique that destroys parts of the abnormal electrical pathway that is causing your arrhythmia.

D Select this paragraph by double-clicking in front of it, using the white selection arrow.

2. Making sure the mouse pointer tilts to the right 𝄡, drag down the left margin. Be sure to press and hold the left mouse button as you drag. Then, click in the body of the document to deselect the text.

3. Move the mouse pointer back to the margin so it is tilting to the right 𝄡 and outside the margin, then triple-click anywhere in the left margin.
Word selects the entire document.

4. Click once anywhere in the body of the document to deselect it.

Select Words

5. Point on any word with the I-beam I, and then double-click to select it.

6. Double-click a different word, and notice that the previous word is deselected.

Nonadjacent Selections

You can also select multiple locations within a document.

7. Double-click to select one word.

8. With one word selected, press and hold the [Ctrl] key while you double-click to select another word, and then release the [Ctrl] key.
Both selections are active. You can select as many nonadjacent areas of a document as desired using this technique. This can be quite useful when formatting documents.

Drag to Select

9. Follow these steps to drag and select a block of text:

A Position the I-beam here, just in front of *Dr. Vijay Singh....* Make sure the I-beam is visible, not the right-tilting arrow.

B Press and hold down the mouse button, and then drag to the right until the phrase *Dr. Vijay Singh has referred you to us for a consultation* is selected.

I‐Dr. Vijay Singh has referred you to us for a consultation in the Hospital to discuss an ablation procedure. Catheter ablation is parts of the abnormal electrical pathway that is causing your a

C Release the mouse button; the text remains selected.

Editing Text

Word offers many tools for editing documents, allowing you to insert and delete text and undo and redo work.

Insert and Delete Text

When you insert text in Word, existing text moves to the right as you type. You must position the cursor before you begin typing.

Use [Backspace] and [Delete] to remove text. The [Backspace] key deletes *back* to the left of the cursor. The [Delete] key removes characters to the *right* of the cursor. You can also remove an entire block of text by selecting it, and then tapping [Delete] or [Backspace].

Use Undo and Redo

FROM THE KEYBOARD
[Ctrl]+[Z] to undo the last action

Word's Undo button lets you reverse your last editing or formatting change(s). You can reverse simple actions such as accidental text deletions, or you can reverse more complex actions, such as margin changes.

The Redo button reverses Undo. Use Redo when you undo an action and then change your mind.

The Undo menu ▼ button (see figure at right) displays a list of recent changes. You can undo multiple actions by dragging the mouse pointer over the desired items in the list. However, you must undo changes in the order in which they appear on the list.

Hands-On 4.4   Insert and Delete Text and Use Undo and Redo

In this exercise, you will insert and delete text. You will delete characters using both the [Backspace] *and* [Delete] *keys, and you will select and delete blocks of text. You will also use the Undo and Redo buttons on the Quick Access toolbar.*

1. In the first line of the first paragraph, double-click the word *has*, as shown to the right, and then tap [Delete] to remove the word.

   Dear Ms. Frost:

   Dr. Vijay Singh has referred Mary's Hospital to discuss a

2. Click with the I-beam (not the right-tilted arrow) at the beginning of the third line of the first paragraph, and type **(ablates),** and then tap the [Spacebar].

3. Position the cursor at the end of the first paragraph between *arrhythmia* and the period at the end of the sentence.

4. Tap the [Spacebar], and type **(abnormal heart rhythm).**

5. Drag to select the first three words of the second paragraph as shown, and then type **I have enclosed** to replace the selected text.

   Enclosed please find informational
   Booklets, please contact our office

6. Click with the I-beam after the next word, *informational*, and tap [Backspace] twice to change the word to *information*.

7. Double-click the next word, *materials*, and tap [Delete] to remove it.

8. In the next line, double-click *ASAP,* and type **at your earliest convenience,** in its place.

9. In the same line, double-click *that* and tap [Delete].

10. Move the mouse pointer into the margin to the left of *Yours truly.* Remember, the mouse pointer is a white arrow when it's in the left margin.

11. Click once to select the line, and then type **Sincerely,** in its place.

Use Undo and Redo

12. You've decided that you prefer *Yours truly,* so click the Undo button on the Quick Access toolbar to return to *Yours truly.*

13. Well, maybe *Sincerely* is better after all. Click the Redo button on the Quick Access toolbar to return to *Sincerely.*

Save Your Changes

14. Click the Save button on the Quick Access toolbar to save your changes.

15. Leave the document open for the next exercise.

Working with AutoCorrect

AutoCorrect is predefined text used for automatically correcting common spelling and capitalization errors. You may have noticed AutoCorrect changing the spelling of certain words while working through this course.

Word's AutoCorrect feature corrects more than spelling errors. For example, you could set up AutoCorrect to insert the phrase *as soon as possible* whenever you type *asap* and tap the Spacebar. AutoCorrect will also capitalize a word it thinks is the beginning of a sentence.

 Hands-On 4.5   Use AutoCorrect

In this exercise, you will type some terms that AutoCorrect will fix for you.

1. Tap Ctrl + End to move the cursor to the end of the document.

2. If necessary, tap Enter a few times to provide some space to practice.

3. Type the word **teh** and tap the Spacebar.
   AutoCorrect corrects the mistake and capitalizes the word because it thinks it is the first word of a sentence.

4. Type the word **adn** and tap the Spacebar.

5. Now select and Delete the words you were just practicing with.

AutoCorrect Options Smart Tag

Word uses smart tags, small buttons that pop up automatically, to provide menus of options that are in context with what you are doing at the time. One of those smart tags is the AutoCorrect Options smart tag.

If Word automatically corrects something that you don't want corrected, a smart tag option allows you to undo the change. For example, when Word automatically capitalizes the first C in the cc: line, you can quickly undo the capitalization, as shown here.

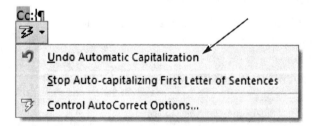

 TIP! *You will see many smart tags as you work. If you do not want to use a smart tag, you can ignore it and it will disappear on its own.*

Hands-On 4.6   Use the AutoCorrect Smart Tag

In this exercise, you will use the AutoCorrect Options smart tags.

1. Choose Home→Paragraph→Show/Hide ¶ to display formatting marks.
   The reference initials should appear on the second blank line following the signature block. Make sure two paragraph symbols appear, as shown here.

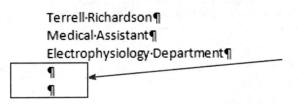

2. If necessary, position the cursor and use Enter to create the blank line(s).

3. Position the cursor next to the second paragraph symbol, and type **tr** as the reference initials, and then tap Enter.
   Notice what happened. Autocorrect capitalized the T, and it should not be capitalized.

4. Position the mouse pointer over the T, and you should see a small blue rectangle just below the T. Then drag down a little, and the AutoCorrect Options screen tip appears.

5. Click the AutoCorrect Options smart tag to display the menu shown below. (This is a delicate mouse move, so you may need to try it a couple of times.)

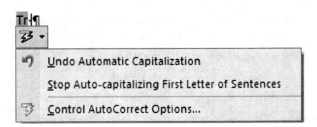

6. Choose Undo Automatic Capitalization from the menu.
   Notice that Word marks the initials with a wavy red line, indicating it's a possible spelling error. You can just ignore it.

7. Make sure the cursor is on the blank line below the initials. Then type the enclosures notification, **Enclosures (2),** and tap Enter.

8. Save 🖫 the document and leave it open for the next exercise.

Setting AutoCorrect Options

To open the AutoCorrect dialog box, choose Office 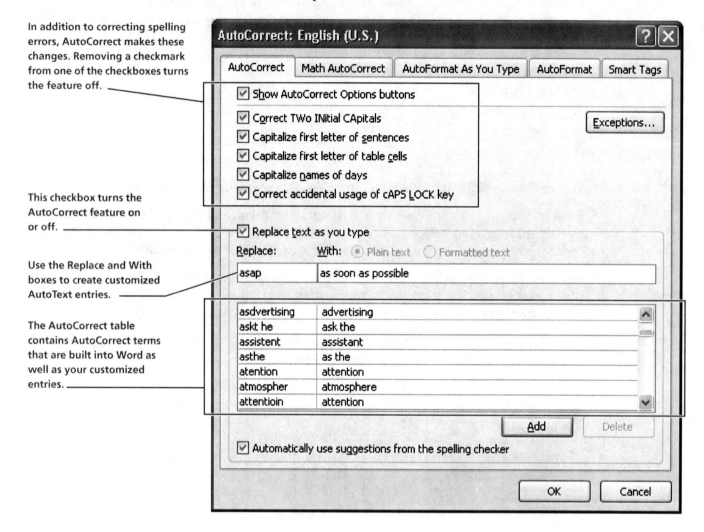, and then click the Word Options button to display the Word Options window. Choose Proofing from the menu on the left, and then click the AutoCorrect Options button.

In addition to correcting spelling errors, AutoCorrect makes these changes. Removing a checkmark from one of the checkboxes turns the feature off.

This checkbox turns the AutoCorrect feature on or off.

Use the Replace and With boxes to create customized AutoText entries.

The AutoCorrect table contains AutoCorrect terms that are built into Word as well as your customized entries.

Customizing AutoCorrect

Word's AutoCorrect feature also lets you automatically insert customized text and special characters, and it is useful for replacing abbreviations with full phrases. For example you could set up AutoCorrect to insert the phrase *as soon as possible* whenever you type *asap*.

!TIP! *You can also customize AutoCorrect by deleting default entries that come installed with Word.*

Hands-On 4.7   **Create a Custom AutoCorrect Entry**

In this exercise, you will create a custom AutoCorrect entry. It's now time for the copy notification, and you plan to copy Dr. Wright. Since you work for her, you know you'll need to type her name frequently, so it's a perfect candidate for a custom AutoCorrect entry.

1. Click the Office ![button] button, and then click the Word Options button in the bottom-right corner of the window.

2. When the Word Options window opens, follow these steps to display the AutoCorrect dialog box:

Ⓐ Choose the Proofing category.

Ⓑ Click the AutoCorrect Options button.

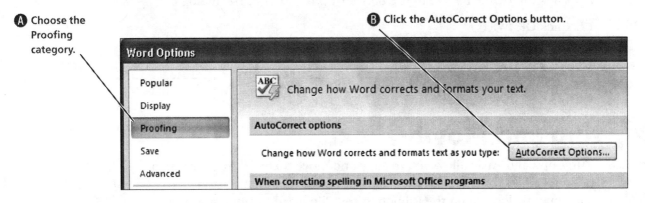

3. When the AutoCorrect dialog box appears, follow these steps to add a custom AutoCorrect entry:

Ⓐ Type **dw** in the Replace box.

Ⓑ Type **Dr. Marjorie Wright** in the With box.

Ⓒ Click the Add button.

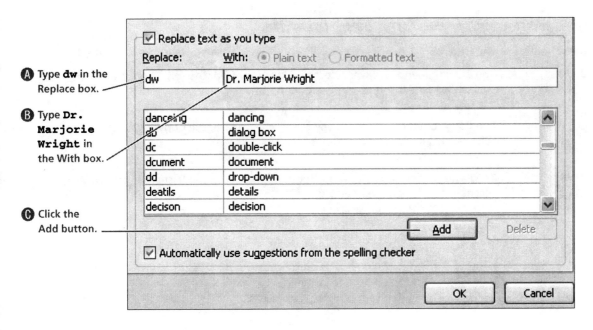

4. Click OK twice.

5. Type **cc:** and tap the ⌨Spacebar.

6. Use the AutoCorrect Options smart tag to undo the automatic capitalization.
   Now you can try out the new AutoCorrect item you added in Step 3.

7. Type **dw** and tap ⌨Enter to automatically type the doctor's name.

Delete the Custom AutoCorrect Entry

You can easily remove AutoCorrect entries, whether they are new custom entries you added or default entries you did not create originally.

8. Click the Office button, and then click the Word Options button in the bottom-right corner of the window.

9. Choose Proofing from the menu, and then click the AutoCorrect Options button in the right-hand pane.

10. Type **dw** in the Replace box, which scrolls the list to Dr. Marjorie Wright.

11. Click the Delete button in the bottom-right corner of the dialog box.

12. Click OK twice.

13. Save 🖫 the letter and leave it open for the next exercise.

Copying and Moving Text

FROM THE KEYBOARD
Ctrl + C to copy
Ctrl + X to cut
Ctrl + V to paste

Cut, Copy, and Paste allow you to copy and move text within a document or between documents. The Cut, Copy, and Paste commands are conveniently located on the Ribbon in the Clipboard command group at the left side of the Home tab.

The following table describes these commands.

QR

QUICK REFERENCE: USING CUT, COPY, AND PASTE		
Command	**Description**	**How to Issue the Command**
Cut	The Cut command removes selected text from its original location and places it in the Clipboard.	Click the Cut ✂ button.
Copy	The Copy command places a copy of selected text in the Clipboard, but it also leaves the text in the original location.	Click the Copy 📋 button.
Paste	The Paste command pastes the most recently cut or copied text into the document at the cursor location.	Click the Paste 📋 button.

Hands-On 4.8   Use Cut, Copy, and Paste

In this exercise, you will move and copy information and work with the Clipboard.

1. If necessary, choose Home→Paragraph→Show/Hide 🔳 from the Ribbon to display the formatting marks.

2. Position the mouse pointer in the margin to the left of the date, and then click once to select the line.

3. Choose Home→Clipboard→Copy 🔳 from the Ribbon.

4. Tap Ctrl + End to place the cursor at the bottom of the document.

5. If necessary, tap Enter a couple of times to provide some blank space at the bottom of the document.

6. Choose Home→Clipboard→Paste 🔳 from the Ribbon to place a copy of the date at the bottom of the document.
   Notice the Paste Options smart tag that popped up at the bottom of the pasted text.

7. Click the smart tag to view its menu, and then click in the document background to close the menu.

8. Tap the Esc key to dismiss the button.

TIP! *If you don't tap Esc, the button will disappear on its own as you work.*

9. Click the Undo 🔳 button to undo the paste.

Move the Inside Address

10. Position the mouse pointer in the margin to the left of the first line of the inside address, and then press and hold down the mouse button and drag to select all three lines.

11. Choose Home→Clipboard→Cut 🔳 from the Ribbon.

12. Tap Ctrl + End to move the cursor to the bottom of the document.

13. Tap Enter if you need space.

Paste Using the Shortcut Keystrokes

14. Tap Ctrl + V to paste the text.

15. Tap Esc to dismiss the Paste Options smart tag.
    Scroll up and notice that the address no longer appears at the top of the document. That's because this was a move, which removes text from one location and pastes it in another.

16. Click the Undo 🔳 twice to undo the move.

17. Click the Save 🔳 button to save your changes.

Editing with Drag and Drop

Drag and drop produces the same result as cut, copy, and paste. It is efficient for moving or copying text a short distance within the same page. You select the text you wish to move and then drag it to the desired destination. If you press and hold Ctrl while dragging, the text is copied to the destination.

 Hands-On 4.9 Use Drag and Drop

In this exercise, you will use drag and drop to move and copy text.

1. Make sure there are a couple of blank lines at the bottom of your document.

2. If necessary, scroll so that you can see both the bottom of the document and the *Terrel Richardson* line in the signature block.

Drag and Drop Move

3. Select the *Terrel Richardson* line, and then release the mouse button.

4. Place the mouse pointer in the highlighted text.
   The pointer now looks like a white arrow.

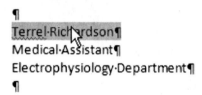

5. Press and hold the mouse button, and follow these steps to move the text:

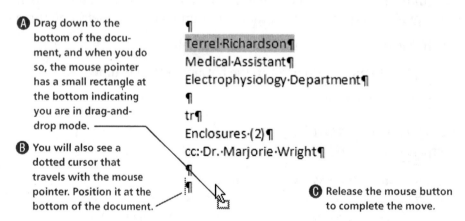

Ⓐ Drag down to the bottom of the document, and when you do so, the mouse pointer has a small rectangle at the bottom indicating you are in drag-and-drop mode.

Ⓑ You will also see a dotted cursor that travels with the mouse pointer. Position it at the bottom of the document.

Ⓒ Release the mouse button to complete the move.

Now you will undo the move and repeat the process, but this time you'll copy the text.

6. Click the Undo button to undo the move.

Drag and Drop Copy

7. Make sure the *Terrel Richardson* line is still selected.

8. Place the mouse pointer inside the selected text, press and hold the Ctrl key and drag the text to the bottom of the document, release the mouse button, and then release the Ctrl key.
   Holding the Ctrl key while dragging is what causes the action to be a copy instead of a move. For this reason, you must release the mouse button before the Ctrl key; otherwise, the action will become a move.

9. Click Undo 🔄 to undo the copy.

10. Leave the document open for the next exercise.
    Soon you will learn to switch between documents so you can copy information from one document to another.

The Clipboard

The Clipboard lets you collect multiple items and paste them into a document. It must be visible on the screen to assemble multiple items; otherwise, only one item at a time is saved for pasting. The Clipboard can hold up to 24 items. When you cut or copy any items exceeding 24, the Clipboard automatically deletes the oldest items.

You click the Dialog Box Launcher 🔲 to display the Clipboard task pane.

The following illustration points out the features of the Clipboard.

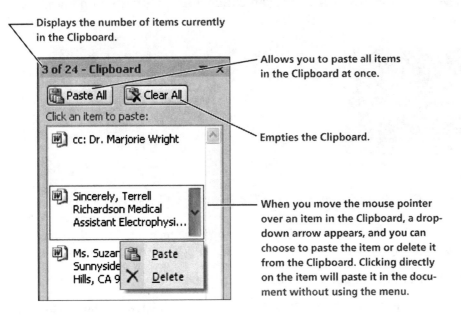

Displays the number of items currently in the Clipboard.

Allows you to paste all items in the Clipboard at once.

Empties the Clipboard.

When you move the mouse pointer over an item in the Clipboard, a drop-down arrow appears, and you can choose to paste the item or delete it from the Clipboard. Clicking directly on the item will paste it in the document without using the menu.

The Clipboard Options button at the bottom of the task pane offers useful options. Click an item in the menu to turn it on or off.

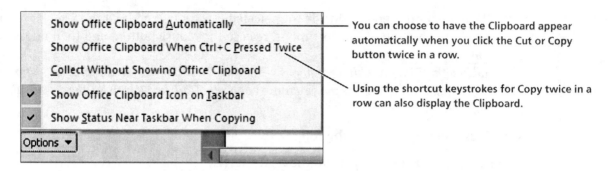

You can choose to have the Clipboard appear automatically when you click the Cut or Copy button twice in a row.

Using the shortcut keystrokes for Copy twice in a row can also display the Clipboard.

Switching Between Documents

There are several techniques for switching between documents. In the next exercise, you will use the taskbar at the bottom of the screen for switching documents. When you have multiple documents open, they will appear as icons on the taskbar. Clicking an icon displays that document in the foreground. In the following illustration, Frost Letter is the active document. The active document icon is darker than the others.

If you have several documents open at the same time, they may gather under one icon. You access them by clicking the icon on the taskbar, then choosing a document from the list.

 Hands-On 4.10   Switch and Copy Between Documents

In this exercise, you will collect several items in the Clipboard, and then you'll switch to another document and paste the text into that document.

1. Open the Medical Release document in the Lesson 04 folder.

2. Go to the taskbar and click the Frost Letter icon to switch back to that document.

3. Click the Dialog Box Launcher in the Home→Clipboard command group, as shown at the right, to open the Clipboard task pane.

4. If there are any items in the Clipboard, click the Clear All button at the top of the task pane.

Copy to the Clipboard

5. Select the three-line inside address, and tap ⌈Ctrl⌉+⌈C⌉ to copy the text to the Clipboard.

6. Select Suzanne Frost, and choose Home→Clipboard→Copy 🗐 to copy the text to the Clipboard.

7. At the beginning of the first paragraph, click and drag to select *Dr. Vijay Singh,* and then use either the shortcut keystrokes or the Copy command on the Ribbon to copy the text.

8. Select and copy the word *arrhythmia* toward the end of the first paragraph.

9. Select *Dr. Marjorie Wright* (but not the paragraph symbol that follows it) and copy the text to the Clipboard.

Switch to the Other Document

10. Go to the taskbar and switch to Medical Release.

11. Click the Dialog Box Launcher 🗔 on the Clipboard group of the Home tab to open the Clipboard task pane.

12. Select the first three lines in Medical Release, as shown here.

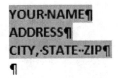

13. Click the inside address in the Clipboard to paste it over the selected text.

14. Select DOCTOR NAME in the salutation, and paste *Dr. Vijay Singh* in its place.

15. The appropriate form for the salutation is title and last name, so select *Vijay* and tap ⌈Delete⌉.

16. In the body paragraph, select DOCTOR NAME and paste *Dr. Marjorie Wright* in its place.

17. In the second line of that paragraph, select MEDICAL CONDITION and paste *arrhythmia* in its place.

18. Select YOUR NAME at the bottom of the document and paste *Suzanne Frost* in its place.

Save the Document

19. Click the Save 🖫 button on the Quick Access toolbar.

20. Click the Close ☒ button at the top of the Clipboard.

21. Choose Office 🗐→Close to close Medical Release.

22. When your original letter appears, close the Clipboard.

23. Leave this document open for the next exercise.

Working with Print Preview

The Print Preview window shows how a document will look when it prints. It is especially useful when printing long documents and those containing intricate graphics and formatting. It is always wise to preview a long or complex document before sending it to the printer.

Displaying Print Preview

You display the Print Preview window by choosing Office→Print menu ▶ button, then clicking the Print Preview command.

Preview Window Features

When you display the Print Preview window, you see a Print Preview Ribbon that replaces the regular Ribbon. The following illustration describes the commands on the Ribbon.

This command opens the Word Options window, where you can change printing defaults.

These checkboxes let you turn the ruler and magnifier on and off.

These commands allow you to move back and forth in your document.

This command closes the Print Preview window.

Clicking this command opens the Print dialog box.

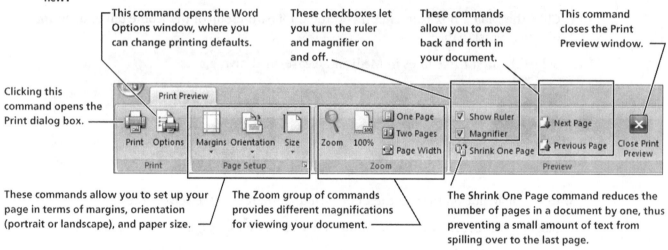

These commands allow you to set up your page in terms of margins, orientation (portrait or landscape), and paper size.

The Zoom group of commands provides different magnifications for viewing your document.

The Shrink One Page command reduces the number of pages in a document by one, thus preventing a small amount of text from spilling over to the last page.

Hands-On 4.11 Use Print Preview

In this exercise, you will practice using Print Preview with the magnifier and the zoom controls.

1. Follow these steps to access the Print Preview window:

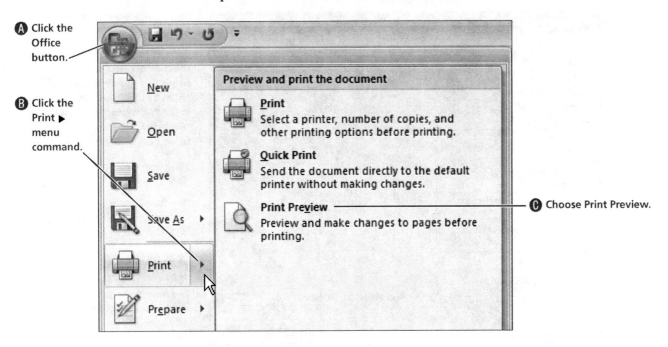

Ⓐ Click the Office button.

Ⓑ Click the Print ▸ menu command.

Ⓒ Choose Print Preview.

!NOTE! *In the future, the preceding command will be written: Choose Office→Print ▸ menu→Print Preview.*

2. Position the mouse pointer over the letter, and notice that it looks like a magnifying glass.

3. Click the mouse button to magnify your letter, and then click again to zoom out.

4. Click the Zoom 🔍 button to view the Zoom dialog box.

5. Choose 200%, and then click OK.

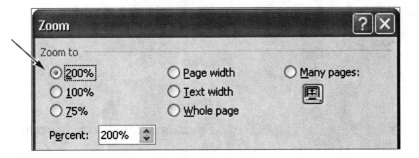

6. Click the mouse button to zoom back out.

7. Click the Page Width 🖳 button on the Ribbon, which causes the page to fill the width of the screen, and then click the mouse button to zoom back out.

8. Click the Close Print Preview ⊠ button to return to the main Word screen.

The Print Dialog Box

FROM THE KEYBOARD

Ctrl + P to open the Print dialog box

The Print dialog box allows you to control how your document prints. The following illustration explains some of the important aspects of the dialog box.

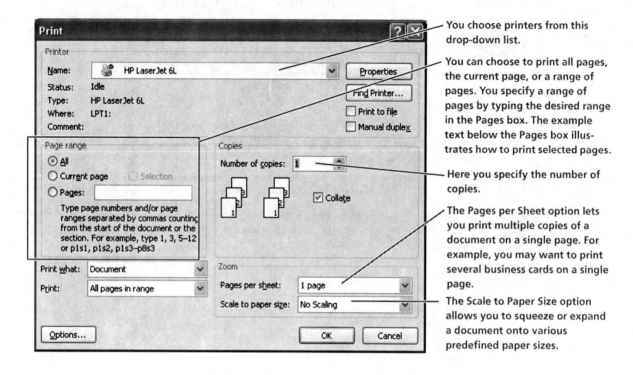

You choose printers from this drop-down list.

You can choose to print all pages, the current page, or a range of pages. You specify a range of pages by typing the desired range in the Pages box. The example text below the Pages box illustrates how to print selected pages.

Here you specify the number of copies.

The Pages per Sheet option lets you print multiple copies of a document on a single page. For example, you may want to print several business cards on a single page.

The Scale to Paper Size option allows you to squeeze or expand a document onto various predefined paper sizes.

 ## Hands-On 4.12   Print the Document

In this exercise, you will send your letter to the printer using the Print dialog box.

1. Tap Ctrl + P to open the Print dialog box.

2. In the Copies area, use the spinner control to specify two copies.

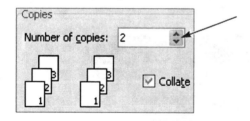

3. Click OK to print two copies of your letter. If your computer is not attached to a local printer, click Cancel to close the Print dialog box.

4. Save 🖫 and close the document.

Concepts Review

True/False Questions

1. The Show/Hide button is used to display nonprinting characters, such as paragraph symbols.   TRUE   FALSE

2. You can select a single word by clicking once on the word.   TRUE   FALSE

3. The Modified Block Style—Indented Paragraphs letter format is the same as the Modified Block Style—Standard format, except the first lines of the body paragraphs are indented a half inch.   TRUE   FALSE

4. Word 2007's new line spacing default is 1.5 lines instead of the standard single (1.0) spacing.   TRUE   FALSE

5. Someone using an older version of Word can read your Word 2007 documents by downloading a compatibility pack from the Microsoft website.   TRUE   FALSE

6. The [Backspace] key deletes the character to the right of the cursor.   TRUE   FALSE

7. You use the [Shift] key to select nonadjacent parts of a document.   TRUE   FALSE

8. Holding the [Shift] key while clicking in a sentence selects the entire sentence.   TRUE   FALSE

9. The Clipboard holds up to 24 entries.   TRUE   FALSE

10. The AutoCorrect feature lets you speed up your work by automatically inserting customized text.   TRUE   FALSE

Multiple Choice Questions

1. Which of the following methods can you use to select a paragraph?

   a. Double-click in the paragraph.

   b. Triple-click in the paragraph.

   c. Triple-click anywhere in the left margin.

   d. None of the above

2. Which key should you press if you want to copy while using drag and drop?

   a. Shift

   b. Ctrl

   c. Alt

   d. Home

3. Which of the following statements is accurate regarding AutoCorrect?

   a. If AutoCorrect corrects something you do not want corrected, your only option is to delete the corrected term and retype it.

   b. If you do not want to use AutoCorrect, you should just ignore it. You cannot turn the feature off.

   c. You cannot delete AutoCorrect entries that come with the Word software.

   d. If Word automatically corrects something that you don't want corrected, an AutoCorrect smart tag option allows you to undo the change.

4. Which of the following statements is correct relative to saving a document?

   a. Word 2007 documents are saved in a docQ format.

   b. The Save button is located on the Mini toolbar.

   c. If you are saving a document for the first time, Word displays the Save As dialog box.

   d. You cannot save a Word 2007 document on a USB flash drive.

Skill Builders

Skill Builder 4.1   Create a Block-Style Letter

In this exercise, you will practice using traditional spacing for a business letter and letting Word Wrap and AutoComplete take effect. You should control the AutoCorrect feature as needed.

1. If necessary, tap Ctrl + N to start a new blank document.

2. Use the Show/Hide ¶ button to display formatting marks.

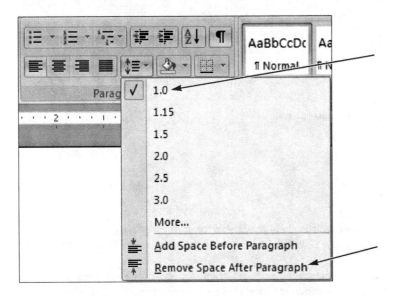

3. Select the paragraph symbol, change the line spacing to 1.0, and then remove the space after paragraphs. (You will need to open the menu twice to do this.)

4. Type the following letter, tapping [Enter] wherever you see a paragraph symbol. Notice the five paragraph symbols at the top of the document. They position the date at approximately 2 inches from the top of the page.

```
¶
¶
¶
¶
¶
September·26,·2007¶
¶
¶
¶
Ms.·Melissa·Thompson¶
Customer·Service·Representative¶
Urbana·Software·Services¶
810·Ivanhoe·Way¶
Urbana,·IL·61801¶
¶
Dear·Ms.·Thompson:¶
¶
I·would·like·to·take·this·opportunity·to·thank·you·for·your·excellent·customer·service.·You·were·patient,·
courteous,·and·very·helpful.·The·installation·assistance·you·provided·was·invaluable.·¶
¶
I·have·already·put·your·program·to·good·use.·As·you·know,·application·programs·can·boost·personal·
productivity.·Your·program·allows·me·to·manage·my·business·much·more·effectively.·I·am·enclosing·the·
$45·fee·you·requested.·¶
¶
Please·send·me·a·receipt·and·a·catalog.¶
¶
Sincerely,¶
¶
¶
¶
Li·Song¶
Administrative·Assistant¶
¶
xx¶
Enclosure¶
¶
```

5. Position the cursor just in front of the sentence starting *I am enclosing the $45* in the second paragraph, and tap [Enter] twice to create a new paragraph.

6. Position the cursor at the end of the new paragraph, just in front of the paragraph symbol.

7. Tap [Delete] twice to remove the two paragraph symbols separating the new paragraph from the following paragraph.

8. If necessary, tap the ⌷Spacebar⌷ to insert a space between the combined sentences.

9. Position the cursor at the end of the first paragraph before the paragraph mark, and tap the ⌷Spacebar⌷ if there is no space at the end of the sentence.

10. Type the sentence **I also appreciate the overnight delivery.**

11. Save the letter in the Lesson 04 folder, and name it **sb-Thompson Letter.**

Skill Builder 4.2   Use the Clipboard and Drag and Drop

In this exercise, you will open a document from your file storage location and use the Clipboard to rearrange paragraphs. You will use drag and drop to move blocks of text.

1. Open the sb-Professional Contacts document in the Lesson 04 folder.
   Notice that the document contains a list of professional contacts. In the next few steps, you will use the Clipboard to reorganize the contacts by profession: all the attorneys will be grouped together, followed by the designers, and then the bookkeepers.

2. Choose Home→Clipboard→Dialog Box Launcher ⬚ from the Ribbon to display the Clipboard.

3. If necessary, click the Clear All button to clear the Clipboard.

4. Select the first attorney contact, *David Roberts, Attorney,* by clicking in front of the contact in the left margin.
   This will select the entire paragraph, including the paragraph mark.

5. Choose Home→Clipboard→Cut ✂ from the Ribbon.
   The item appears on the Clipboard.

6. Select the next attorney, *Lisa Wilson,* and Cut ✂ it to the Clipboard.

7. Cut the remaining attorney contacts to the Clipboard. Use Undo ↺ if you make a mistake. However, be careful because even if you use Undo, the item you cut will remain on the Clipboard.

8. Now Cut ✂ the designer contacts to the Clipboard.
   The bookkeeper contacts should now be grouped together in the document.

9. Tap ⌷Enter⌷ to position the cursor on a new line below the bookkeeper contacts.

10. Click the Paste All button on the Clipboard to paste the attorney and designer contacts.
    Notice that the contacts are pasted in the order they were cut, thus grouping the attorneys together and the designers together.

[Handwritten notes:]

Cut   Control +x
Copy   ✓   + C
Paste   ✓   + V
Highlight   ✓   + A

Create Headings

11. Click the cursor in front of the first bookkeeper contact, and tap [Enter] twice to create blank lines.

12. Click on the blank line above the first bookkeeper and type **Bookkeepers.**

13. Use this technique to create headings for attorneys and designers.

Use Drag and Drop

14. Select the Attorneys heading, the four attorneys, and the blank line below by dragging in the left margin and then releasing the mouse button.

15. Position the mouse pointer on the selection, and drag up until the dotted cursor is just in front of the Bookkeepers heading.

16. Release the mouse button to move the attorneys block above the bookkeepers.

17. Now move the designers above the bookkeepers.

18. Close the Clipboard, and then save and close the file.

Skill Builder 4.3   Edit a Document

In this exercise, you will edit a document that is marked up for changes.

1. Choose Office [icon] →Open.

2. Open the sb-Maine document in the Lesson 04 folder.
   You will edit this document during this exercise. Notice that this document contains formatting that you have not yet learned about. For example, the title is centered and bold, and the paragraphs are formatted with double line spacing. This document is formatted like this because it is a report. You will learn about these formatting techniques in Lesson 5, Creating a Memorandum and a Simple Report. Use these guidelines to make the changes shown in the following illustration:

   - If only one or two characters require deletion, then position the cursor in front of the character(s) and use [Delete] to remove them.
   - If one or more words require deletion, then select the text and use [Delete] to remove the selected text.
   - If a word or phrase needs to be replaced with another word or phrase, then select the desired text and type the replacement text.
   - Use Undo [icon] if you make mistakes.

3. When you have finished, save the changes and close the document.

MAINE – THE PINE TREE STATE

Maine is recognized as one of the most ~~healthy~~ *healthful* states in the nation with temperatures

averaging 70°F and winter temperatures averaging 20°F. It has 3,~~7~~00 miles of coastline, is about *summer*

320 miles long and 210 miles wide, with a total area of 33,215 square miles or about as big as all

of the other five New England States combined. It comprises 16 counties with 22 cities, 424

towns, 51 plantations, and 416 unorganized townships. Aroostook county is so large (6,453

square miles) that it covers an area greater than the combined size of Connecticut. *and Rhode Island*

Maine abounds in natural assets—542,629 acres of state and national parks, including the

92-mile Allagash Wilderness Waterway, Acadia National Park (second most visited national

park in the United States), and Baxter State Park (location of Mt. Katahdin and the northern end

of the Appalachian Trail). Maine has one mountain ~~which~~ *that* is approximately one mile high—Mt.

Katahdin (5,268 ft. above sea level) and also claims America's first chartered city: York, 1641.

Maine's blueberry crop is the largest ~~blueberry crop~~ in the nation—98% of the low-bush

blueberries. Potatoes rank third in acreage and third in production nationally. Maine is nationally

famed for its shellfish; over 46 million pounds of ~~shellfish~~ *lobster* were harvested in 1997. The total of *in the United States*

all shellfish and fin fish harvested was approximately 237 million pounds with a total value of

$273 million ~~during the 1997 fishing season.~~ *in 1997*

LESSON 5

Creating a Memorandum and a Simple Report

In this lesson, you will create a memo and a simple report. You will apply character and paragraph formatting, and you will use Spelling & Grammar check. You will set up custom line spacing and insert page numbers. You will also create bulleted and numbered lists.

LESSON OBJECTIVES

After studying this lesson, you will be able to:

- Insert dates and symbols
- Insert and delete page breaks
- Work with proofreading tools
- Use character and paragraph formatting
- Use bullets and numbering
- Insert page numbers

Case Study: Preparing a Memorandum

Lashanda Robertson is the public affairs representative for Flexico, Inc., a fabric manufacturer specializing in materials for active wear. She regularly issues press releases to clothing manufacturers and other potential customers, trumpeting forthcoming fabrics and materials. Lashanda creates a memorandum to which she attaches her latest press release announcing the new FlexMax line of fabrics for active wear. Memorandums are used for internal communication within a company or organization, whereas business letters are used for external communication.

Lashanda is also interested in report writing. Her son, Bill, is enrolled in an information systems course and he is preparing a report on the importance of computer technology in the twenty-first century. Lashanda knows that reports are used in both business and educational settings. She draws upon her business experience to guide her son in formatting his school report.

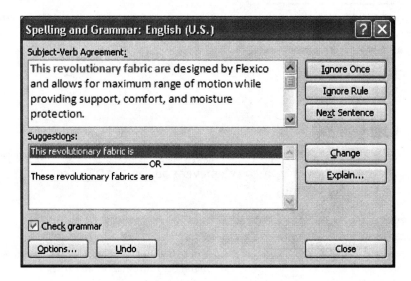

The Spelling and Grammar tool is a powerful proofreading aid.

Search Engines
Knowing how to access information on the Internet typically means that you need to be familiar with search engines. Some of the best known search engines include:

- Google
- AllTheWeb
- Yanoo
- Dogpile
- Ask
- Vivisimo

World Wide Web Consortium Goals
The World Wide Web Consortium (W3C) is an organization that sets standards for the developing common protocols that promote the evolution of the Internet and insure cross-platform communications. Below is a listing of their goals and principles.

1. Universal Access
2. Semantic Web
3. Trust
4. Interoperability
5. Evolvability
6. Decentralization
7. Cooler Multimedia!

(Bullet point titles taken from http://www.w3.org/Consortium/Points)

Bullets and numbering make Bill's report easy to read.

Typing a Memorandum

There are a variety of acceptable memorandum styles in use today. All memorandum styles contain the same elements but with varied formatting. The style shown in the following figure is a traditional memorandum style with minimal formatting.

The introduction includes leads such as MEMO TO: and FROM:. Use a double space between paragraphs, or use the new Microsoft spacing, which automatically adds space after a paragraph. This means you only need to tap Enter once between paragraphs.

The body of the memo comes next.

Extras such as attachment notations go here.

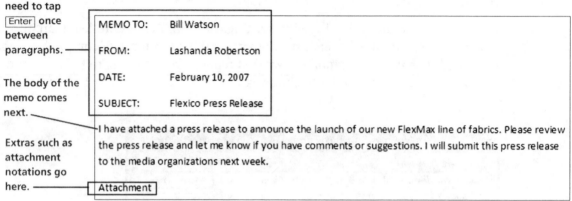

MEMO TO: Bill Watson

FROM: Lashanda Robertson

DATE: February 10, 2007

SUBJECT: Flexico Press Release

I have attached a press release to announce the launch of our new FlexMax line of fabrics. Please review the press release and let me know if you have comments or suggestions. I will submit this press release to the media organizations next week.

Attachment

Introducing Tabs

The Tab key moves the cursor to the nearest tab stop. In Word, the default tab stops are set every $1/2$ inch, thus the cursor moves $1/2$ inch whenever you tap the Tab key. In this lesson, you will use Word's default tab settings.

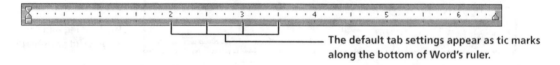

The default tab settings appear as tic marks along the bottom of Word's ruler.

!TIP! *A quick way to turn the ruler on and off is to click the View Ruler button at the top of the scroll bar.*

Inserting and Formatting the Date

You use the Insert→Text→Insert Date and Time 🖫 command on the Ribbon to display the Date and Time dialog box. Word lets you insert the current date in a variety of formats. For example, the date could be inserted as 2/10/07, February 10, 2007, or 10 February 2007.

FROM THE KEYBOARD
Alt + Shift + D
to insert a date

The Update Automatically Option

You can insert the date and time as text or as a field. Inserting the date as text has the same effect as typing the date into a document. Fields, however, are updated whenever a document is opened or printed. For example, imagine you create a document on February 10, 2007, and you insert the date as a field. If you open the document the next day, the date will automatically change to February 11, 2007. The date and time are inserted as fields whenever the Update Automatically box is checked, as shown here.

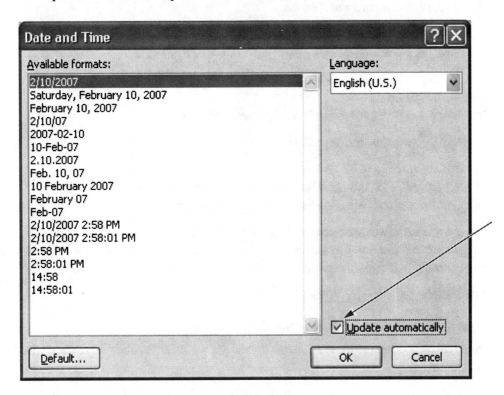

Hands-On 5.1   Set Up a Memo and Insert the Date

In this exercise, you will create a memo and insert the date automatically. You will also try out Word's new 1.15 line spacing and the extra space following paragraphs.

Set Up a Memo

1. Start a new blank document. Make sure the Word window is maximized ▭.

2. If necessary, click the View Ruler 🔲 button at the top of the vertical scroll bar to turn on the ruler.

3. Tap [Enter] twice to space down to approximately 2 inches from the top of the page (1-inch mark on the vertical ruler).
    Using Word's default spacing, you don't have to tap [Enter] as many times as you did in the previous lesson to position the cursor at 2 inches.

4. Type **MEMO TO:** and tap the [Tab] key.
    Notice that the cursor moves to the next $^1/_2$-inch mark on the ruler.

5. If necessary, choose Home→Paragraph→Show/Hide [¶] from the Ribbon to display formatting marks.
    Notice the arrow formatting mark that represents the tab.

6. Type **Bill Watson** and tap [Enter] once.

7. Type **FROM:** and tap [Tab] twice.
    It is necessary to [Tab] twice to align the names. The first tab aligns the cursor at the $^1/_2$-inch mark on the ruler; the second aligns the cursor at the 1-inch position.

8. Type **Lashanda Robertson** and tap [Enter] once.
    You'll notice that Lashanda has a red wavy underline, indicating it is not in Word's dictionary. You will learn more about automatic spell checking later in this lesson.

9. Type **DATE:** and tap [Tab] twice.

Choose a Date Format and Insert the Date

10. Choose Insert→Text→Insert Date & Time 🔲 from the Ribbon to display the Date and Time dialog box.

11. Make sure the Update Automatically box is not checked at the bottom of the dialog box.
    Checking this option instructs Word to insert the date as a field, which would cause you to lose the original date if you open the document at a later date. In this instance, you do not want the date to change.

12. Choose the third date format on the list, and click OK.

13. Complete the remainder of the memorandum, as shown in the following illustration, using the ⌞Tab⌝ to align the text in the Subject line. Bear in mind that you only need to tap ⌞Enter⌝ once between paragraphs.

MEMO TO:	Bill Watson
FROM:	Lashanda Robertson
DATE:	February 10, 2007
SUBJECT:	Flexico Press Release

I have attached a press release to announce the launch of our new FlexMax line of fabrics. Please review the press release and let me know if you have comments or suggestions. I will submit this press release to the media organizations next week.

Attachment

14. Click the View Ruler 🔲 button at the top of the scroll bar to turn off the ruler.

15. Choose Home→Paragraph→Show/Hide ¶ from the Ribbon to turn off the formatting marks.

16. Click the Save 🔲 button, and save the document in Lesson 05 folder as **Robertson Memo.**

17. Leave the memorandum open, as you will modify it throughout this lesson.

Inserting Symbols

Word lets you insert a variety of symbols, typographic characters, and international characters not found on the keyboard. You insert symbols via the Symbol dialog box. The following illustration shows how you access the Symbol dialog box.

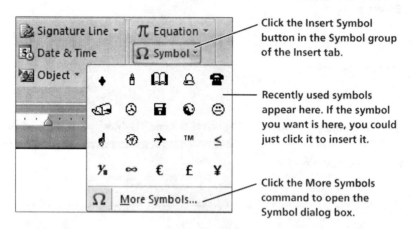

Click the Insert Symbol button in the Symbol group of the Insert tab.

Recently used symbols appear here. If the symbol you want is here, you could just click it to insert it.

Click the More Symbols command to open the Symbol dialog box.

The Special Characters tab displays commonly used special characters, such as the registered trademark ® symbol and various punctuation symbols.

You can choose from several fonts, each displaying a different set of characters in the dialog box. Some fonts, such as Wingdings, contain interesting and fun symbols.

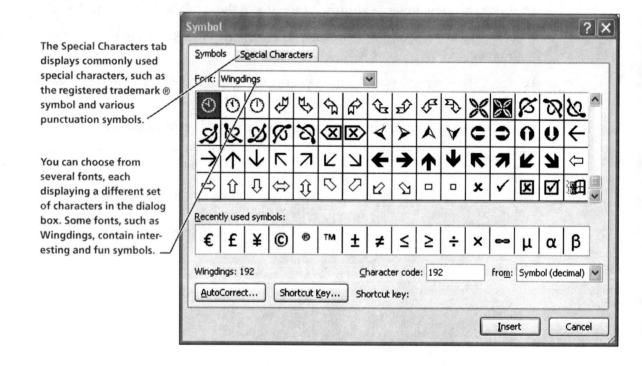

 **Hands-On 5.2   Insert Symbols**

In this exercise, you will add a trademark symbol and a registered trademark symbol to your document.

1. Position the cursor to the right of the word *Flexico* on the *SUBJECT:* line.

2. Click Insert→Symbols→Insert Symbol Ω from the Ribbon, and choose the More Symbols command at the bottom of the menu.

3. When the Symbol dialog box appears, click the Special Characters tab.

4. Choose the registered trademark symbol (an R inside a circle), and then click the Insert button.
   The ® symbol is inserted in the document, and the Symbol dialog box remains open. Word leaves the dialog box open in case you wish to insert additional symbols.

5. Position the cursor to the right of *FlexMax* in the main paragraph. (You may need to drag the dialog box out of the way in order to see the word. To do that, position the mouse pointer on the blue title bar at the top of the dialog box, press and hold the mouse button, drag the dialog box out of the way, and then release the mouse button.)

6. Insert the trademark (™) symbol.
   The trademark (™) symbol indicates that a company claims a phrase or icon as its trademark but has not received the federal protection accompanying the registered trademark (®) symbol.

7. Click the Symbols tab in the Symbol dialog box, and choose different fonts from the Font list to see other sets of symbols.

8. When you finish experimenting, click the Close button to close the dialog box.

9. Click the Save button to save the changes.

Working with Page Breaks

If you are typing text and the cursor reaches the bottom of a page, Word automatically breaks the page and begins a new page. This is known as an automatic page break. The location of automatic page breaks may change as text is added to or deleted from a document. Automatic page breaks are convenient when working with long documents that have continuously flowing text. For example, imagine you were writing a novel and you decided to insert a new paragraph in the middle of a chapter. With automatic page breaks, you could insert the paragraph and Word would automatically repaginate the entire chapter.

You force a page break by choosing Insert→Pages→Page Break from the Ribbon. A manual page break remains in place unless you remove it. You insert manual page breaks whenever you want to control the starting point of a new page.

FROM THE KEYBOARD

Ctrl+Enter to insert a page break

Removing Manual Page Breaks

In Draft view, a manual page break appears as a horizontal line, including the phrase Page Break. You can also see the page break line in Print Layout view if you turn on the Show/Hide feature. You can remove a manual page break by positioning the cursor on the page break line and tapping ⌈Delete⌉, as shown in the following illustration.

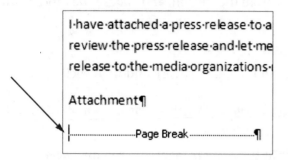

 Hands-On 5.3   Work with Page Breaks

In this exercise, you will practice using manual page breaks. You will insert a page break, thereby creating a new page so you can copy and paste the press release information from another document into your new page.

Insert a Page Break

1. Make sure you are in Print Layout view. If you are not sure, click the View tab and choose Print Layout from the Document Views group at the left edge of the Ribbon. (If the button is highlighted, you are already in Print Layout view.)

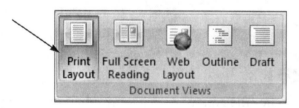

2. Position the cursor at the bottom of the document and, if necessary, tap ⌈Enter⌉ to generate a blank line below the *Attachment* line.

3. Choose Insert→Pages→Page Break ⊟ from the Ribbon.

4. If necessary, scroll down to see the bottom portion of page 1 and the top of page 2.

5. Look at the Status bar at the bottom-left corner of the screen; it shows the page you are on and the total number of pages. (The first number varies, depending on where your cursor is located.) It also displays the number of words in the document.

Page: 1 of 2   Words: 61

Remove the Page Break

6. Scroll up until the *Attachment* line is visible.

7. If necessary, click Home→Paragraph→Show/Hide ¶ to display formatting marks and see the page break.

8. Click to the left of the page break line, and tap Delete.

9. Try scrolling down to the second page and you will see that it is gone.

Reinsert the Page Break

10. Check to see that the cursor is just below the *Attachment* line, and tap Ctrl+Enter to reinsert the page break.
    This shortcut keystroke is useful because you will use page breaks frequently.

11. Click Home→Paragraph→Show/Hide ¶ to hide the formatting marks.
    The cursor should be positioned at the top of the second page.

Copy and Paste from Another Document

12. Click Office→Open and, if necessary, navigate to your file storage location and open Press Release from the Lesson 05 folder.
    Notice that a number of phrases are flagged by the spelling checker (red wavy underlines) and grammar checker (green wavy underlines) in the document. You will take care of those in the next exercise.

13. In the Press Release document, tap Ctrl+A to select the entire document.

14. Tap Ctrl+C to copy the document.
    Now you will switch to your memo.

15. On the taskbar, click the Robertson Memo icon to switch back to that document.

16. Make sure your cursor is at the top of page 2.

17. Choose Home→Clipboard→Paste from the Ribbon.
    The press release is pasted on page 2 of your document. Now you will switch back to the press release and close it.

18. Use the taskbar icon to switch to Press Release.

19. Choose Office→Close to close the file.
    The Robertson Memo should now be in the foreground.

20. Save the file and leave it open for the next exercise.

Working with Proofreading Tools

Word's powerful Spelling and Grammar tool helps you avoid embarrassing spelling and grammar errors. Whether you choose to use the default on-the-fly checking, where Word marks possible errors as you type, or whether you choose to save proofing tasks until you've completed your document content, these tools can help polish your writing. However, these tools are proofreading aids, not the final word. You still need to involve human judgment in a final round of proofing.

■ Spelling checker

■ Grammar checker

Using the Spelling Checker

Word checks a document for spelling errors by comparing each word to the contents of a dictionary. Word also looks for double words such as *the the,* and a variety of capitalization errors.

Word can automatically check your spelling as you type. It flags spelling errors by underlining them with wavy red lines. You can correct a flagged error by right-clicking the error and choosing a suggested replacement word or other option from the menu that pops up.

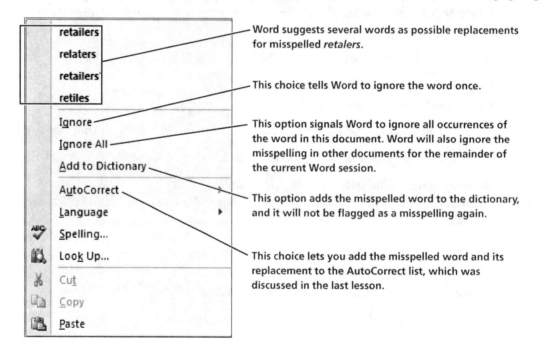

Word suggests several words as possible replacements for misspelled *retalers.*

This choice tells Word to ignore the word once.

This option signals Word to ignore all occurrences of the word in this document. Word will also ignore the misspelling in other documents for the remainder of the current Word session.

This option adds the misspelled word to the dictionary, and it will not be flagged as a misspelling again.

This choice lets you add the misspelled word and its replacement to the AutoCorrect list, which was discussed in the last lesson.

In this exercise, you will use the Ignore All option on the spelling checker pop-up menu to remove the red underlines from all occurrences of the words Flexico *and* FlexMax. *You will also delete a repeated word.*

Spellcheck Using Ignore All

1. Notice that the word *Flexico* in the first line of page 2 has a wavy red underline. This word appears a number of times in the document.
   Flexico *is spelled correctly; it's just that it does not appear in Word's dictionary. As a result, Word flags it as a possible spelling error.*

2. Follow these steps to have the spelling checker ignore all occurrences of *Flexico* and thereby remove the wavy red underline wherever the term appears:

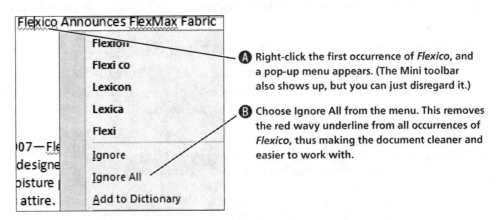

Ⓐ Right-click the first occurrence of *Flexico*, and a pop-up menu appears. (The Mini toolbar also shows up, but you can just disregard it.)

Ⓑ Choose Ignore All from the menu. This removes the red wavy underline from all occurrences of *Flexico*, thus making the document cleaner and easier to work with.

Notice that the word FlexMax *is flagged as a possible misspelling.*

3. Right-click *FlexMax* and choose Ignore All from the pop-up menu.

Work with Double Word Errors

Word flagged a double word error in the first paragraph of the press release.

4. Right-click the word *for* with the wavy red line, and choose the Delete Repeated Word command from the menu.

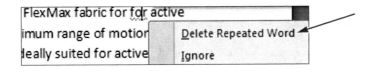

5. Save your file and leave it open for the next exercise.

Using the Grammar Checker

Word has a sophisticated grammar checker that can help you with your writing skills. Like the spelling checker, the grammar checker can check grammar as you type. The grammar checker flags errors by underlining them with wavy green lines. You can correct a flagged error by right-clicking the error and choosing a replacement phrase or other option from the pop-up menu. Be careful when using the grammar checker. It isn't perfect. There is no substitute for careful proofreading.

Grammar checking is active by default. Grammar checking options are available by clicking the Office button, then clicking the Word Options button to display the Word Options window. You can enable or disable the feature by checking or unchecking the boxes in the figure to the right.

When correcting spelling and grammar in Word
☑ Check spelling as you type
☐ Use contextual spelling
☑ Mark grammar errors as you type
☑ Check grammar with spelling

The Spelling and Grammar Dialog Box

FROM THE KEYBOARD

F7 to start the Spelling & Grammar check

Choose Review→Proofing→Spelling and Grammar from the Ribbon to display the Spelling and Grammar dialog box. You may prefer to focus on your document's content and postpone proofing until you're done. You can use the Spelling and Grammar dialog box for that purpose.

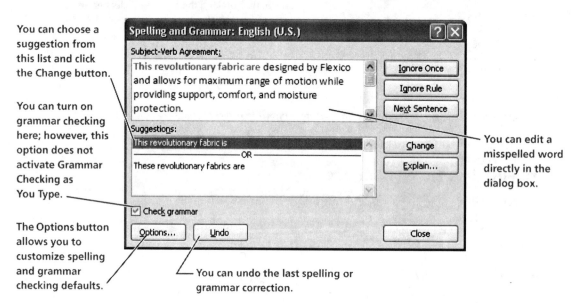

You can choose a suggestion from this list and click the Change button.

You can turn on grammar checking here; however, this option does not activate Grammar Checking as You Type.

The Options button allows you to customize spelling and grammar checking defaults.

You can edit a misspelled word directly in the dialog box.

You can undo the last spelling or grammar correction.

In this exercise, you will make corrections to the Robertson Memo using the Spelling and Grammar dialog box. If you do not see any text underlined in green, the grammar checking options are turned off on your computer. If you see the green grammar check lines in your document, follow the steps to turn the feature on anyway, so you will know where to locate the feature in the future.

1. Click the Office button, and then click the Word Options button to display the Word Options window.

2. Choose Proofing from the menu on the left.

3. Follow these steps to turn on grammar checking:

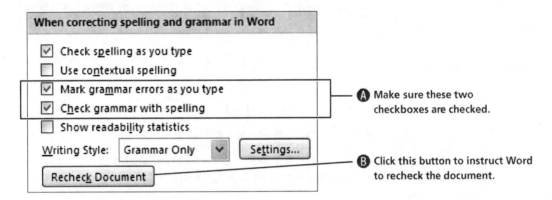

4. When the message box appears, choose Yes to dismiss the message, then click OK to close the window.
   Since you clicked Recheck Document, notice that Flexico *and* FlexMax *have wavy red lines again.*

5. Position the cursor at the beginning of the first line on page 2.

6. Choose Review→Proofing→Spelling & Grammar [ABC] from the Ribbon.
   The Spelling and Grammar dialog box appears, and Flexico *is noted as a possible spelling error.*

7. Click the Ignore All button.

8. Click Ignore All again when *FlexMax* appears as a possible spelling error.
   Now Word points out a possible grammar error.

Use the Grammar Checker

9. Follow these steps to correct the grammatical error:

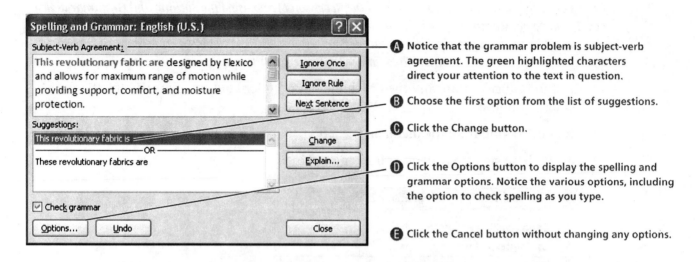

A Notice that the grammar problem is subject-verb agreement. The green highlighted characters direct your attention to the text in question.

B Choose the first option from the list of suggestions.

C Click the Change button.

D Click the Options button to display the spelling and grammar options. Notice the various options, including the option to check spelling as you type.

E Click the Cancel button without changing any options.

The grammar checker locates the next error.

10. The highlighted option *fabric is* in the Suggestions list is the one you want, so click the Change button.

11. The next error is a spelling error, and the suggestion *Delivery* is correct, so click the Change button.

12. Finish checking the rest of the press release using your own good judgment regarding what changes to make. When *Lashanda* is flagged, click the Ignore Once button.

13. When the message appears indicating that the spelling and grammar check is complete, click OK.

14. Save 🖫 the file and leave it open for the next exercise.

Formatting Text

You can format text by changing the font, font size, and color. You can also apply various font formats, including bold, italics, and underline. If you are typing new text and no text is selected, the format settings take effect from the cursor forward or until you change them again. If you wish to format existing text, you must select the text and then apply the desired formats. You can format text using options in the Font dialog box. Display the Font dialog box by clicking the Dialog Box Launcher in the Font group of the Home tab.

FROM THE KEYBOARD
Ctrl + B for bold
Ctrl + U for underline
Ctrl + I for italics

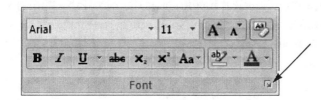

The following illustration describes the Font dialog box.

Scroll here to choose a different font.

Click this drop-down arrow to choose a different font color.

If you change any of the options on the Font tab and then click the Default button, all new documents will be based on the changes you made. In other words, you will have changed the default.

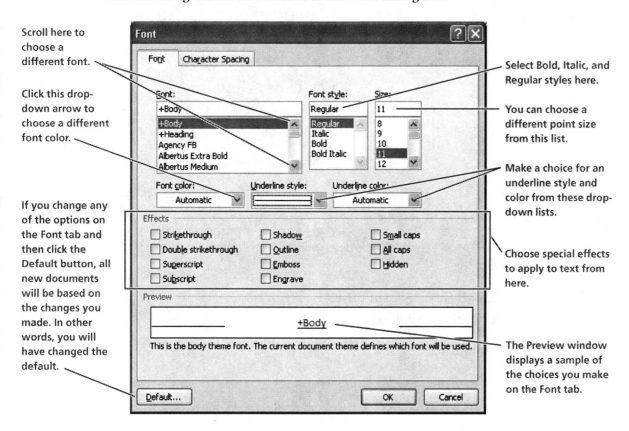

Select Bold, Italic, and Regular styles here.

You can choose a different point size from this list.

Make a choice for an underline style and color from these drop-down lists.

Choose special effects to apply to text from here.

The Preview window displays a sample of the choices you make on the Font tab.

Working with Fonts and Themes

All Word 2007 documents are based on a document theme, which is a set of formatting selections including colors, graphic elements, and fonts, all designed to blend well together. There are various themes you can apply to your documents, and the fonts vary depending on the theme.

The theme-related font choices include two fonts, one for body text and one for headings. That's what the first two entries in the Font list of the Font dialog box represent. This dialog box displays the current theme fonts using the generic +Body and +Heading names. You'll also find the theme fonts for the body and headings at the top of the Font drop-down menu in the Font group of the Home tab. Here they display the actual names of the fonts for the current theme. You'll learn more about themes in *Microsoft Word 2007: Comprehensive*.

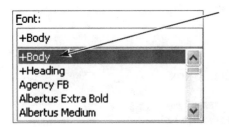

Font list in the Font dialog box

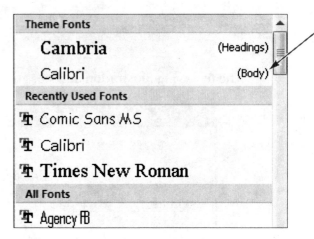

Font list in the Font group on the Home tab

 ## Hands-On 5.6   Format Text

In this exercise, you will use elements from the Font group on the Ribbon, the Font dialog box, and the Mini toolbar to format your text.

Format the Press Release Title Lines

1. Scroll to the top of the second page.

2. Position the mouse pointer in the left margin, and drag down to select the first three heading lines.

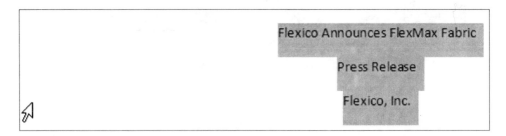

3. Switch to the Home tab on the Ribbon, and then follow these steps to format the lines:

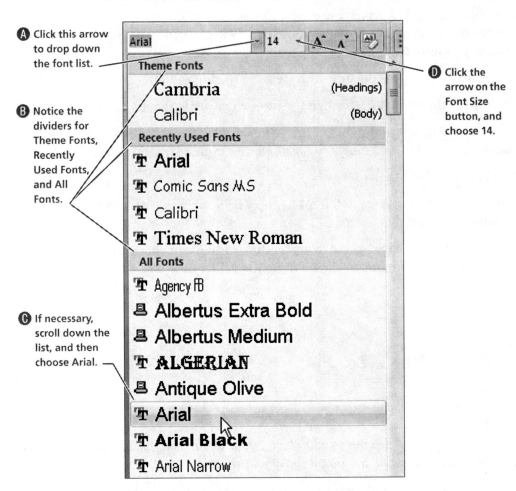

Ⓐ Click this arrow to drop down the font list.

Ⓑ Notice the dividers for Theme Fonts, Recently Used Fonts, and All Fonts.

Ⓒ If necessary, scroll down the list, and then choose Arial.

Ⓓ Click the arrow on the Font Size button, and choose 14.

Format with the Mini Toolbar

At this point you could add bold to the text by using the Bold button in the Font group on the Home tab. However, it might be interesting to try out the Mini toolbar.

4. Make sure the heading lines are still selected. Move the mouse pointer over the selected text. Right-click the selected text to see the toolbar.
   You will also see a pop-up menu if you had to right-click to display the Mini toolbar. Right-clicking in a document typically generates a shortcut menu. You can ignore it for now.

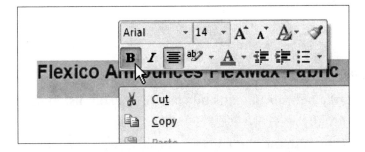

5. Click the Bold **B** button to apply the bold format.

6. Click the Italic **I** button, to apply the format, and then click it again to turn off the italic formatting.

Use Keystrokes to Select and Format

The following steps show you how to select text using the keyboard. In some situations, keyboard selecting can give you greater precision and control. Refer to the Selection Techniques section of Lesson 4 for more information on selecting text with the keyboard.

7. Scroll up to the first page of the document to view the memorandum.

8. Click just in front of the word *MEMO* when the mouse pointer is shaped like an I-beam ⊺.

9. Press and hold the ⎡Shift⎤ key, and then tap the ⎡→⎤ key until *MEMO TO:* is selected. *Since your hands are on the keyboard, this is an opportune time to use a keyboard shortcut.*

10. Press ⎡Ctrl⎤+⎡B⎤ to apply bold to the text.

11. Use the techniques in the previous two steps to apply bold to the *FROM:* heading. Remember, select first, and then format.

12. Now apply bold to the other two headings, using the technique of your choice. You may want to try out the Bold command in the Font group of the Home tab.

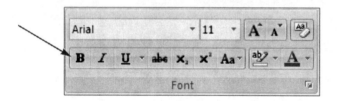

Change the Default Font

In this section of the exercise, you will experiment with changing the default font. You can change the default so that all new documents open in the default font of your choice.

13. Make sure no text is selected, and then click the Dialog Box Launcher ▣ in the bottom-right corner of the Font group.

14. Choose Bodoni MT from the Font list, and then click the Default button in the bottom-left corner of the dialog box.

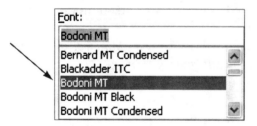

15. When the message box appears asking if you want to change the default font, click Yes.

16. Press ⎡Ctrl⎤+⎡N⎤ to start a new document, and observe the Font list in the Font group. *All new documents now open with that font as the default.*

17. Choose Office→Close to close the blank document.

Reset the Default Font

18. Click the Dialog Box Launcher in the bottom-right corner of the Font group to open the Font dialog box.

19. Make sure the Font tab is in the foreground, and then choose +Body from the top of the list.

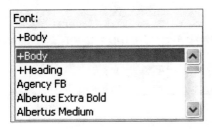

Remember that all documents are based on a document theme, and font choices are a part of the theme. The default body font for the default theme is Calibri, which is represented in this list as +Body. The Font list on the Ribbon displays the actual names of the theme fonts for the theme in effect at the time.

20. Click the Default button, and when the message appears asking if you want to change the default font, click Yes.

21. Save ⊟ your file and leave it open for the next exercise.

The Format Painter

The Format Painter 🖌 lets you copy text formats from one location to another. This is convenient if you want the same format(s) applied to text in different locations. The Format Painter copies all text formats, including the font, font size, and color. This saves time and helps create consistent formatting throughout a document. The Format Painter is located in the Clipboard group on the Home tab, and it also appears on the Mini toolbar.

QR⟩ **QUICK REFERENCE: COPYING TEXT FORMATS WITH THE FORMAT PAINTER**

Task	Procedure
Copy text formats with the Format Painter	▪ Select the text with the format(s) you wish to copy. ▪ Click the Format Painter once if you want to copy formats to one other location, and double-click if you want to copy to multiple locations. ▪ Select the text at the new locations(s) that you want to format. If you double-clicked in the previous step, the Format Painter will remain active, allowing you to select text at multiple locations. You can even scroll through the document to reach the desired location(s). ▪ If you double-clicked, then click the Format Painter button to turn it off.

In this exercise, you will learn to use the Format Painter to copy formats from one text block to another.

Format Text

1. Scroll to page 2, and select the heading *Announcement* just above the first large paragraph of text.

2. When the Mini toolbar appears, follow these steps to apply color to the heading line.

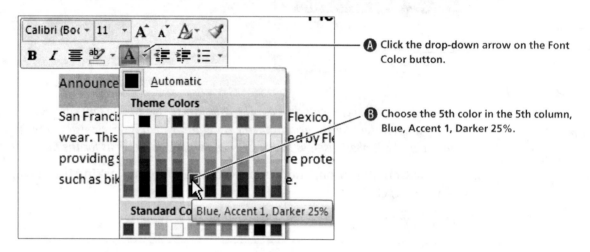

Ⓐ Click the drop-down arrow on the Font Color button.

Ⓑ Choose the 5th color in the 5th column, Blue, Accent 1, Darker 25%.

Notice that the color you selected is in the Theme Colors category. Various themes use different sets of theme colors. These are the theme colors for Word's default theme.

3. Keep the text selected and the Mini toolbar active, and follow these steps to apply additional formats to the text:

Ⓐ Click the Bold button to bold the text.

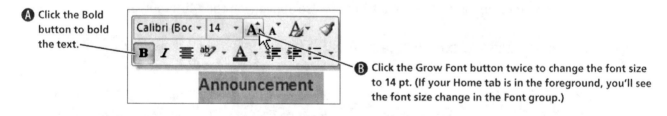

Ⓑ Click the Grow Font button twice to change the font size to 14 pt. (If your Home tab is in the foreground, you'll see the font size change in the Font group.)

Copy Formats to One Location

4. Make sure the heading *Announcement* is selected.

5. Click the Format Painter 🖌 button on the Mini toolbar.
   A paintbrush icon is added to the I-beam mouse pointer once it is positioned over the document.

6. Drag the mouse pointer across the *Delivery and Availability* heading, and then release the mouse button.
   The 14pt bold blue formats should be copied to the heading. The animated paintbrush icon also vanishes because you clicked the Format Painter button just once in the previous step. If you want to copy formats to multiple locations, you must double-click the Format Painter.

Copy Formats to More Than One Location

7. Scroll down so you can see the last two headings on the page.
Make sure the Home tab is in the foreground. This time you'll use the Format Painter in the Clipboard group on the Home Tab.

8. Make sure the *Delivery and Availability* heading is still selected.

9. Double-click the Format Painter.

10. Select the heading *FlexMax Styles* by either dragging the mouse over it or by clicking in front of it in the margin when the mouse pointer is a white arrow.
The formats are applied to the heading.

11. Select the heading *About Flexico* to copy the format to that heading.

12. Choose Home→Clipboard→Format Painter 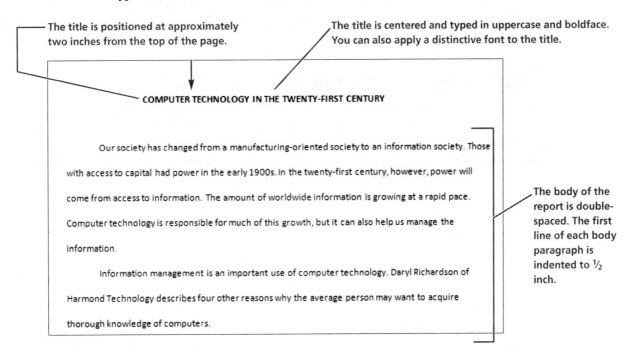 to turn it off.

13. Save 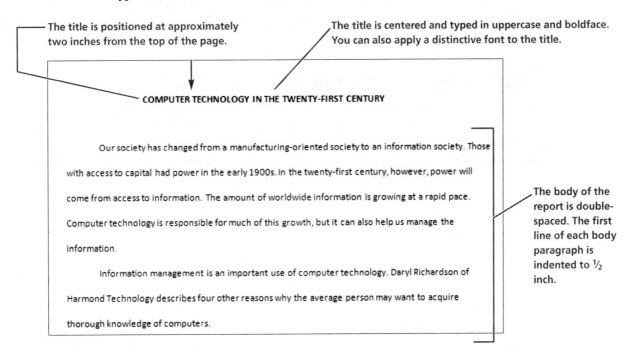 your file and close it.

Formatting Reports

There are a variety of acceptable report formats. The following example shows a traditional business report in unbound format. Different report formats can be used for research papers and other types of documents.

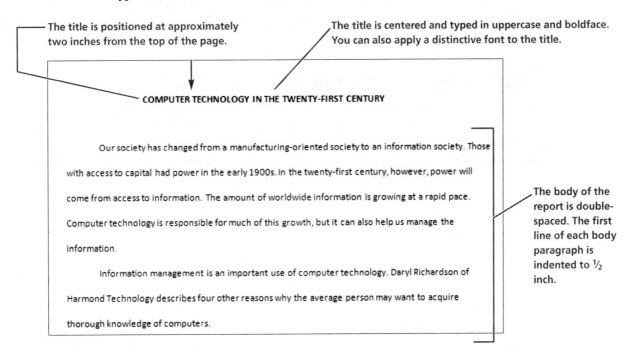

The title is positioned at approximately two inches from the top of the page.

The title is centered and typed in uppercase and boldface. You can also apply a distinctive font to the title.

COMPUTER TECHNOLOGY IN THE TWENTY-FIRST CENTURY

Our society has changed from a manufacturing-oriented society to an information society. Those with access to capital had power in the early 1900s. In the twenty-first century, however, power will come from access to information. The amount of worldwide information is growing at a rapid pace. Computer technology is responsible for much of this growth, but it can also help us manage the information.

Information management is an important use of computer technology. Daryl Richardson of Harmond Technology describes four other reasons why the average person may want to acquire thorough knowledge of computers.

The body of the report is double-spaced. The first line of each body paragraph is indented to ½ inch.

Using Paragraph Formatting

Paragraph formatting includes paragraph alignment, line spacing, paragraph space settings, and bullets and numbering, to mention a few options.

Selecting paragraphs for formatting purposes is a little different from selecting characters. With character formatting, you select the entire block of text you want to format. In the majority of situations this is necessary. With paragraph formatting, you need only click in the paragraph to *select* it. You can highlight the entire paragraph if you wish, but that is not necessary. On the other hand, if you want to apply formatting to more than one paragraph, you must select at least part of each paragraph.

Paragraph Defined

In Word, a paragraph is created anytime you tap the [Enter] key. In other words, a paragraph could consist of several lines that end with an [Enter] or just one line, such as a heading, that ends with an [Enter]. Tapping [Enter] to generate a blank line creates a paragraph, even though there is no text in it. What's more, Word stores formats in the paragraph mark.

Paragraph Formatting Compared to Character Formatting

You use character formatting when you wish to format individual words or a selected block of text. Paragraph formatting affects the entire paragraph.

Character formats are available in the Font group of the Home tab on the Ribbon, while paragraph formats appear in the Paragraph group of the Home tab. Paragraph formats include paragraph alignment, line spacing, borders and shading, bullets and numbering, and indents and tabs.

Using Paragraph Alignment

Paragraph alignment determines how text aligns between the margins. Left alignment gives the paragraph a straight left margin and a ragged right margin. Center alignment is usually applied to headings. Right alignment generates a straight right and a ragged left margin. Justify provides straight left and right margins. You can use several tools to align paragraphs, including the alignment commands in the Paragraph group on the Home tab, the Paragraph dialog box, and the Mini toolbar.

Setting Alignments

The following illustration displays the paragraph alignment commands in the Paragraph group of the Home tab. The Center command is also conveniently located on the Mini toolbar.

Align Text Left
Center
Align Text Right
Justify

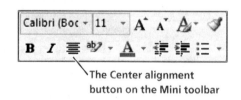

The Center alignment button on the Mini toolbar

Examples

The following illustration shows how the different paragraph alignment settings look in Word.

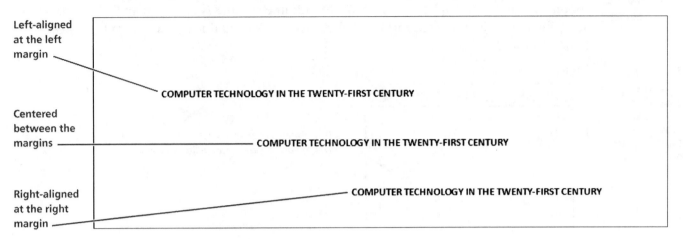

Left-aligned at the left margin

COMPUTER TECHNOLOGY IN THE TWENTY-FIRST CENTURY

Centered between the margins

COMPUTER TECHNOLOGY IN THE TWENTY-FIRST CENTURY

Right-aligned at the right margin

COMPUTER TECHNOLOGY IN THE TWENTY-FIRST CENTURY

Hands-On 5.8   Align Text with the Ribbon and Mini Toolbar

In this exercise, you will practice using the alignment buttons in the Paragraph group of the Home tab and the Center button on the Mini toolbar to align your report heading.

1. Start a blank document, and make sure the Word window is maximized ⬜.

2. If necessary, choose View→Document Views→Print Layout ⬜ to switch to Print Layout view.

3. If the ruler does not appear on the screen, click the View Ruler ⬜ button at the top of the scroll bar.

4. Tap [Enter] enough times to position the cursor approximately 2 inches from the top of the page. (That's 1 inch on the vertical ruler.)

Type the Heading

5. Turn on [Caps Lock] and choose Home→Font→Bold **B** from the Ribbon.

6. Type the report title, **COMPUTER TECHNOLOGY IN THE TWENTY-FIRST CENTURY.**

7. Turn off Bold and [Caps Lock], and then tap [Enter] twice.

8. Position the cursor in the report heading.

Align the Heading

9. Choose Home→Paragraph→Center ⬜ from the Ribbon.

10. Choose Home→Paragraph→Align Text Right ⬜ from the Ribbon.

11. Choose Home→Paragraph→Align Text Left ⬜ from the Ribbon.

12. Right-click on the heading to display the Mini toolbar.

13. Click the Center ⬜ button on the toolbar to center the heading.

14. Save the file in the Lesson 05 folder as **Computer Report,** leave the file open, and continue with the next topic.

Setting Line Spacing

The Line Spacing 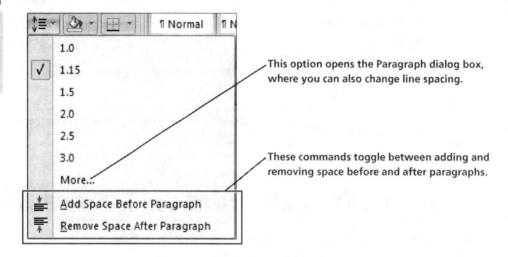 button in the Paragraph group of the Home tab lets you set line spacing for one or more paragraphs. Word 2007's default line spacing is 1.15. You apply line spacing by selecting the desired paragraph(s) and choosing the desired line spacing from the Line Spacing drop-down list.

FROM THE KEYBOARD

[Ctrl]+[1] for single spacing
[Ctrl]+[1.5] for 1.5 spacing
[Ctrl]+[2] for double spacing

This option opens the Paragraph dialog box, where you can also change line spacing.

These commands toggle between adding and removing space before and after paragraphs.

Hands-On 5.9   Set Line Spacing

In this exercise, you will begin by changing to double-spacing. Then you will return to single-spacing for several paragraphs in the document.

1. If necessary, choose Home→Paragraph→Show/Hide [¶] to display formatting characters.

2. Position the cursor on the second paragraph symbol below the title.

3. Choose Home→Paragraph→Line Spacing [≣] from the Ribbon, and click 2.0 for double-spacing.

4. Tap the [Tab] key once to create a $\frac{1}{2}$-inch indent at the start of the paragraph.

5. Now type the following paragraph, but only tap [Enter] once after the last line in the paragraph, since double-spacing is in effect.
   The lines will be double-spaced as you type them.

> Our society has changed from a manufacturing-oriented society to an information society. Those with access to capital had power in the early 1900s. In the twenty-first century, however, power will come from access to information. The amount of worldwide information is growing at a rapid pace. Computer technology is responsible for much of this growth, but it can also help us manage the information.

6. Make sure you tap Enter after the last line. Tap Tab once, and type the following paragraph.
Notice that double-spacing is carried to the new paragraph.

> Information management is an important use of computer technology. Daryl Richardson of
>
> Harmond Technology describes four other reasons why the average person may want to acquire
>
> thorough knowledge of computers.

7. Tap Enter to complete the paragraph, and then press Ctrl+1 (use the 1 in the number row, not the number pad) to set single-spacing.
The shortcut keystrokes can be quite convenient for setting line spacing.

8. Now type the following paragraphs, tapping Enter between paragraphs. You don't need to tap Enter twice because of the default additional spacing after paragraphs. Do not tab at the beginning of these paragraphs.

> Computer skills are becoming more important in the business world. Many companies need employees with excellent computer skills.
>
> The Internet and other information resources provide access to a global database of information.
>
> Computer skills can often simplify one's personal life. Computers can be used to entertain, to manage finances, and to provide stimulating learning exercises for children.
>
> Using computers can provide a sense of accomplishment. Many people suffer from "computerphobia." Learning to use computers often creates a feeling of connection with the information age.

9. Save your document, and continue with the next topic.

Using Bulleted and Numbered Lists

The Bullets and Numbering commands in the Paragraph group on the Home tab provide a quick and easy way to create bulleted and numbered lists. You can apply bullets and numbers to existing lists by selecting the list and clicking the desired command. For a new list, you can turn on bullets or numbers when you begin typing the list. Lists are automatically renumbered if items are inserted or deleted.

Turning Off Bullets and Numbering

When you type a list, you should complete the list by tapping Enter after the last paragraph in the list. You can then turn off bullets or numbering for the first line following the list by clicking the Bullets or the Numbering button. Tapping Enter twice also turns off bullets or numbering.

 Hands-On 5.10   Work with Bullets and Numbering

In this exercise, you will create a bulleted list and a numbered list.

Create a Bulleted List

1. Make sure the cursor is at the end of the document then tap Ctrl + Enter to insert a page break.

2. Choose Home→Paragraph→Line Spacing from the Ribbon, and then choose Remove Space After Paragraph from the menu.

3. Type the following heading and introductory paragraph:

   > Search Engines
   > Knowing how to access information on the Internet typically means that you need to be familiar with search engines. Some of the best known search engines include:

4. Tap Enter twice at the end of the paragraph.

5. Choose Home→Paragraph→Bullets on the Ribbon.
   Word will most likely insert a round bullet, although another bullet style may appear. Don't be concerned if your bullet is not round. You will learn to modify bullets later in this lesson.

6. Type **Google** as the first search engine, and then tap Enter to generate the next bullet.

7. Finish typing the list as shown to the right, tapping Enter after each item to generate the next bullet.

   - Google
   - AllTheWeb
   - Yahoo
   - Dogpile
   - Ask
   - Vivisimo

8. Tap Enter three times following the last item in the list to turn off bullets.

NOTE! *Word only advances one line when you tap Enter twice at the end of the list. The first Enter generates the next bullet or number; the second Enter turns off bullets or numbering and stays on the same line.*

Create a Numbered List

In this section of the exercise, you will type a heading and introductory paragraph. Then you will type a numbered list.

9. Type the following heading and introductory paragraph:

World Wide Web Consortium Goals

The World Wide Web Consortium (W3C) is an organization that sets standards for developing common protocols that promote the evolution of the Internet and insure cross-platform communications. Below is a listing of their goals and principles.

---

10. Tap [Enter] twice at the end of the paragraph.

11. Choose Home→Paragraph→Numbering ▤ from the Ribbon.

12. Type **Universal Access,** and then tap [Enter] to generate the next number.

13. Complete the list as shown:

1. Universal Access
2. Semantic Web
3. Trust
4. Interoperability
5. Evolvability
6. Decentralization
7. Cooler Multimedia!

14. Tap [Enter] twice following the last item to stop the numbering and generate a blank line.

15. Type **(Bullet point titles taken from http://www.w3.org/Consortium/ Points)** to give credit to the W3C website for the list.
    If you tap [Enter] or [Spacebar] after typing the text, Word may format the website address as a hyperlink. It is a Word default to format website addresses as hyperlinks. This setting appears in the Word Options dialog box.

16. Save your file, and continue with the next topic.

Using the Bullets and Numbering Libraries

The arrows ⬝ on the Bullets and Numbering buttons provide access to bullets and numbering libraries, where you can choose a style for your bulleted or numbered list or define new formats.

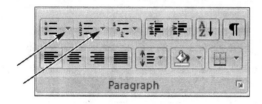

The bullets and numbering libraries shown in the following illustrations display the available built-in styles.

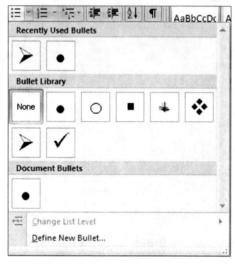

Bullet Library

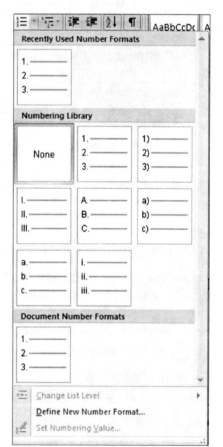

Numbering Library

Hands-On 5.11   Change the Bullet Style

In this exercise, you will choose a different bullet style from the bullets gallery.

1. Select the bulleted list, as shown here.

2. Click the drop-down arrow on the Bullets 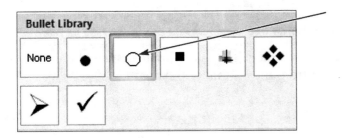 button and choose the circle bullet.
   The position of the circle bullet in the library may vary.

3. Save your file, and leave it open for the next exercise.

Customizing Bullet and Number Styles

You can customize the built-in bullet and number styles. You can define a new bullet or number format by clicking the drop-down arrow on the Bullet or Numbering button and choosing Define New Bullet or Define New Numbering Style.

You can choose from a variety of symbols, pictures, and fonts.

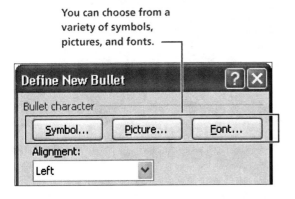

You can select a number style from this list.

You can choose from a variety of fonts to customize your numbering style.

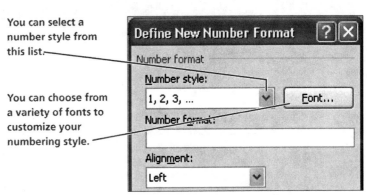

Restart or Continue Numbering

Many documents have more than one numbered list. Sometimes you may want the numbering to continue sequentially from one list to the next. For example, if one list ends with the number 4 you may want the next list to begin with the number 5. When you begin the next list in your document, Word assumes you want to restart numbering at 1. If you want to continue numbering from the previous list, Word provides an AutoCorrect smart tag when you start additional numbered lists in a document. You can click the AutoCorrect Options smart tag and choose Continue Numbering.

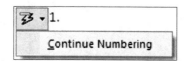

 ## Hands-On 5.12   Experiment with Custom Bullets

In this exercise, you will work with the Define New Bullet dialog box.

1. Click anywhere in your bulleted list.

2. Choose Home→Paragraph→ Bullets 📋 menu ▾ to display the Bullets library, and then choose Define New Bullet from the bottom of the menu.

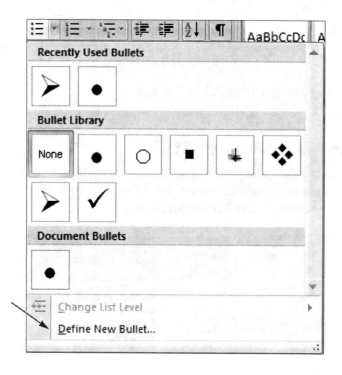

3. When the Define New Bullet dialog box appears, click the Picture button to display the Picture Bullet dialog box.

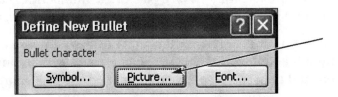

4. Click the bullet of your choice, and then click OK twice to apply the customized bullet.

5. Choose Home→Paragraph→Bullets ☰ ▾ menu ▾ to display the Bullet library. Notice that your new bullet now appears in the library.
The position of the bullet in the library may vary.

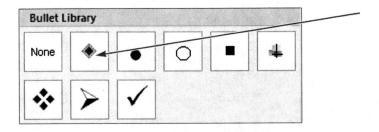

6. Click in the document to close the library.

⚠ TIP! *If you wish to remove a bullet from the library, right-click it and choose Remove from the pop-up menu.*

7. Click Undo ↺ to return the bulleted list to the circle-style bullet.

8. Format the headings on page 2 with bold 12 pt.

9. Save your changes.

Setting Page Numbering

You can insert page numbers at various positions on a page. Page numbering is associated with headers and footers, which you'll learn more about in *Microsoft Word 2007: Comprehensive*.

A page numbering gallery offers a variety of page numbering designs. Choose Insert→Header & Footer→Page Number from the Ribbon to display a menu of varying positions for your page numbers. Choose a position, and then click the desired style to insert page numbers in your document.

 Hands-On 5.13 **Insert Page Numbers**

In this exercise, you will insert page numbers in your report.

1. Choose Insert→Header & Footer→Page Number 🗐 from the Ribbon.

2. Follow these steps to insert page numbering:

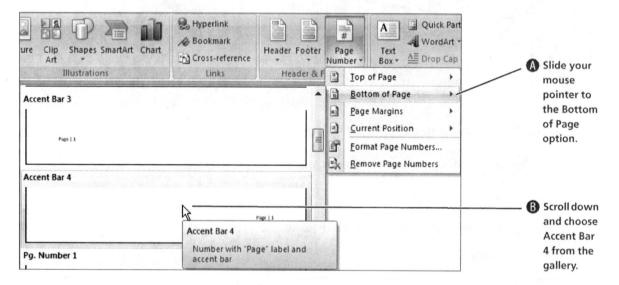

Ⓐ Slide your mouse pointer to the Bottom of Page option.

Ⓑ Scroll down and choose Accent Bar 4 from the gallery.

3. Double-click the body of the document to close the footer area.

4. Scroll through the document and observe the page numbering.
   The numbering appears grayed out, but it will print like normal text. Header and Footer text is grayed out to let you know that it is not part of the body of the document. You'll learn more about Headers and Footers in Microsoft Word 2007: Comprehensive.

5. Save your report and close it.

Concepts Review

True/False Questions

1. When you use paragraph formatting features, you only need to click in the paragraph to select it.   TRUE   FALSE

2. You can use the Format Painter to copy and past formatted text.   TRUE   FALSE

3. Manual page breaks remain in place until you remove them.   TRUE   FALSE

4. Default tab setting appear as small triangles at the bottom of the ruler.   TRUE   FALSE

5. You cannot continue numbering from one list to another within a document.   TRUE   FALSE

6. Word marks a possible grammatical error with a wavy green line.   TRUE   FALSE

7. Word 2007's default line spacing is 1.25.   TRUE   FALSE

8. You can customize the built-in bullets and number styles.   TRUE   FALSE

9. You can use the Mini toolbar to right-align headings in a report.   TRUE   FALSE

10. You can remove a manual page break by clicking it and tapping Delete.   TRUE   FALSE

Multiple Choice Questions

1. When you choose Ignore All from the pop-up menu during a spelling check, it means that _____.
   a. Word will ignore all spelling errors for the rest of the document
   b. grammar checking will be ignored until you manually start it again
   c. Word will ignore all occurrences of the word on which you right-clicked
   d. Word will ignore all repeated words

2. Which of the following items falls into the category of paragraph formatting?
   a. Change line spacing
   b. Change point size
   c. Apply the bold feature
   d. Change to the Cambria (Heading) font

3. To copy text formats to several locations in a document, you select the text containing the formats you want to copy then _____.
   a. click the Format Painter button and select the desired blocks of text
   b. double-click the Format Painter button and select the desired blocks of text
   c. use the Copy button
   d. double-click the Copy button

4. Which shortcut keystrokes do you use to create a manual page break?
   a. Ctrl + Enter
   b. Ctrl + Spacebar
   c. Ctrl + Shift + Enter
   d. Alt + Enter

Skill Builders

Practice Formatting

In this exercise, you will practice working with character formats. Use the Font group on the Home Ribbon for steps 3–6 and use the Mini toolbar for steps 7, 8, and 10.

1. Open sb-Yard Sale from the Lesson 05 folder.

2. Tap [Enter] several times to better align the document on the page.

3. Select the three heading lines, and change the font to Arial, bold, and red.

4. Deselect the text, and then select the first heading line and change it to 18 points.

5. Select the second heading line, and make it 14 points.

6. Make the third heading line 18 points.

7. Apply bold to the date and time in the body.

8. Select the body, and change the font to Comic Sans MS or the font of your choice.

9. Place the cursor in front of *Stop* in the body, and tap [Enter] to provide additional space between the heading lines and the body.

10. Change the heading lines to a different color of your choice.

11. Save 🖫 the file and close it.

Skill Builder 5.2   Create a Memorandum

In this exercise, you will create a memorandum. You will also apply character formatting.

1. Follow these guidelines to create the memorandum shown at the end of this exercise:
   - Position the line *MEMO TO:* approximately 2 inches down from the top of the page.
   - Apply bold to the lead words *MEMO TO:*, *FROM:*, *DATE:*, and *SUBJECT:*.
   - Apply bold formatting to the time and date in the body paragraph.
   - Type your initials at the bottom of the memo.

2. Save the memo in the Lesson 05 folder as **sb-Alexander Memo**, and then close it.

MEMO TO: Jason Alexander

FROM: Tamika Jackson

DATE: Today's Date

SUBJECT: Monthly Sales Meeting

Our monthly sales meeting will be held in the conference room at **10:00 a.m.** on **Thursday, July 24.** Please bring your sales forecast for August and be prepared to discuss any important accounts that you wish to. I will give you a presentation on our new products that are scheduled for release in September. I look forward to seeing you then.

xx

Skill Builder 5.3   Create a Policies and Procedures Document

In this exercise, you will use multiple lists to create a policies and procedures page. You will also use Word's default line spacing and after-paragraph spacing.

Set Up the New Page

1. Start a new blank document.

2. Choose Home→Paragraph→Center ≡ from the Ribbon.

3. Type **OUTDOOR ADVENTURES** and tap [Enter].

4. Type **Policies and Procedures** and tap [Enter] twice.

5. Choose Home→Paragraph→Align Text Left ≡ from the Ribbon.

6. Type **Medical and Injury** and tap [Enter].

7. Choose Home→Paragraph→Numbering ≣ from the Ribbon.
   The new paragraph will be preceded by the number 1.

8. Type **All guests must have medical insurance** and tap [Enter].

⚠**NOTE!** *The after-paragraph spacing for bullets and numbering is less than the normal default.*

9. Complete items 2 and 3 as shown below, tapping [Enter] twice after item 3 to turn off numbering.

Medical and Injury
1. All guests must have medical insurance 2. All guests must sign an injury waiver 3. All guests agree to pay out-of-pocket medical expenses

10. Finish typing the document as shown at the end of the exercise.

11. Select the body of the document.

12. Choose Home→Paragraph→Increase Indent ≣ fives time to reposition the body.

13. Finally, format the title with 18 point bold and the subtitle with 16 point bold.

14. Save the file in the Lesson 05 folder as **sb-Outdoor Adventures,** and then close the document.

OUTDOOR ADVENTURES

Policies and Procedures

Medical and Injury

1. All guests must have medical insurance
2. All guests must sign an injury waiver
3. All guests agree to pay out-of-pocket medical expenses

Cancellations and Refunds

1. A full refund will be given for cancellations with 60 days notice
2. A 50% refund will be given for cancellations with 30 days notice
3. No refund for cancellations with less than 30 days notice

Outdoor Adventures May Cancel Your Trip for the Following Reasons

1. Inclement weather
2. Poor water flow
3. Insufficient number of guests
4. Unavailability of a guide

LESSON 6

Working with Tables

A table is one of Word's most useful tools for organizing and formatting text and numbers. Tables provide a powerful means of communicating information, yet they are flexible and easy to use. Word provides a variety of features that let you set up, modify, and format tables. In this lesson, you will insert tables and quickly apply table styles.

LESSON OBJECTIVES

After studying this lesson, you will be able to:

- Insert a table in a document
- Navigate in a table
- Insert columns and rows in an existing table
- Align table data
- Apply built-in table styles

Case Study: Creating a Diamond-Studded Table

Jonathan Ziady is an administrative assistant for Diamond Financial Services. Blake Daniels, a Diamond customer, asked Jonathan to prepare a statement for his accounts. Normally, Jonathan would prepare a standard statement using Diamond's financial software; however, Blake requested a customized format for this particular statement.

Jonathan uses Word 2007's powerful table features to prepare the custom report that Blake requested. Using the Table button makes it a snap for Jonathan to rapidly generate a new table and get right to work.

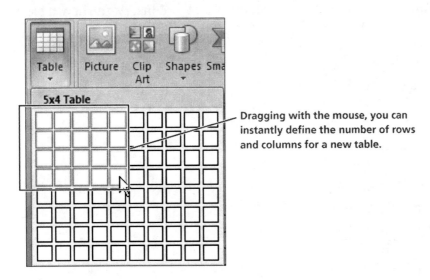

Dragging with the mouse, you can instantly define the number of rows and columns for a new table.

The Table Styles gallery provides a quick and easy way to apply professional-looking formats to tables.

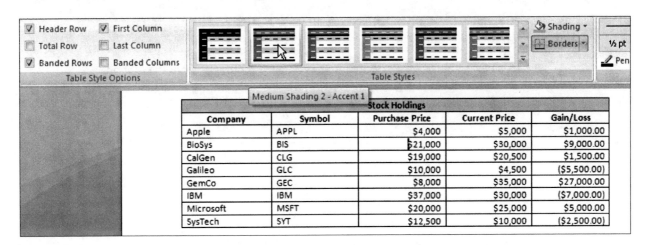

Stock Holdings				
Company	Symbol	Purchase Price	Current Price	Gain/Loss
Apple	APPL	$4,000	$5,000	$1,000.00
BioSys	BIS	$21,000	$30,000	$9,000.00
CalGen	CLG	$19,000	$20,500	$1,500.00
Galileo	GLC	$10,000	$4,500	($5,500.00)
GemCo	GEC	$8,000	$35,000	$27,000.00
IBM	IBM	$37,000	$30,000	($7,000.00)
Microsoft	MSFT	$20,000	$25,000	$5,000.00
SysTech	SYT	$12,500	$10,000	($2,500.00)

Inserting Tables

Tables are composed of cells (rectangles) organized in columns and rows. Word lets you insert, edit, and format text within cells, just as you would in any document. You can also use virtually any text formats within cells.

Using the Table Button Grid

On the Insert tab of the Ribbon, you can use the Table 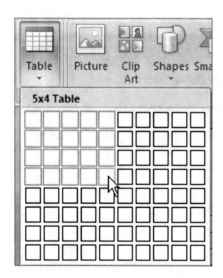 button in the Tables command group to insert a new table. The Table button displays a grid where you specify the number of rows and columns for a table by dragging in the grid. Word inserts the new table at the cursor location.

QR ❯ **QUICK REFERENCE: INSERTING A NEW TABLE**

Task	Procedure
Insert a new table	■ Choose Insert→Tables→Table from the Ribbon.
	■ Drag in the grid to select the desired number of columns and rows.

Hands-On 6.1   Insert a Table

In this exercise, you will use the Table button to insert a table with four columns and eight rows. The table will contain a list of Blake Daniels' stock holdings.

Type the Document Heading

1. Make sure the Word window is maximized ▣ and then start a new document.

2. If necessary, click the View Ruler ▣ button at the top of the scroll bar to display the horizontal and vertical rulers.

3. Use Enter to space down to approximately 2 inches from the top of the page. (That's 1 inch on the vertical ruler.)

4. Choose Home→Paragraph→Center ▤ from the Ribbon, and type the heading **Account Information**.

5. Tap Enter, type **Blake Daniels (1/15/2007)**, and then tap Enter.

6. Choose Home→Paragraph→Align Text Left ▤ from the Ribbon.

Insert the Table

7. Choose Insert→Tables→Table ▦ from the Ribbon.

8. When the grid appears, follow these steps to create a table:

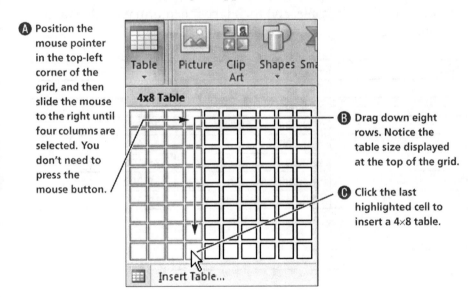

Ⓐ Position the mouse pointer in the top-left corner of the grid, and then slide the mouse to the right until four columns are selected. You don't need to press the mouse button.

Ⓑ Drag down eight rows. Notice the table size displayed at the top of the grid.

Ⓒ Click the last highlighted cell to insert a 4×8 table.

9. Format the Account Information heading with 14pt and bold.

10. Save ▤ the document as **Account Information** in the Lesson 06 folder, and leave the file open for the next exercise.

Navigating in a Table

You can position the cursor in a cell by clicking in the desired cell. However, it is often more efficient to use the keyboard to move between cells. You use the ⌜Tab⌟ key to move forward one cell, while ⌜Shift⌟+⌜Tab⌟ moves you back one cell. If the cursor is in the last cell of the table, tapping ⌜Tab⌟ adds a new row to the bottom of the table.

 Hands-On 6.2   Navigate and Enter Data

In this exercise, you will practice navigating in a table, and then you will enter data in it.

1. Position the cursor in the first cell of the table.

2. Tap ⌜Tab⌟ three times to move to the end of the first row.

3. Tap ⌜Tab⌟ again to move to the beginning of the second row.

4. Tap ⌜Shift⌟+⌜Tab⌟ a few times to move back, one cell at a time.

5. Position the cursor in the last cell of the table, and then tap ⌜Tab⌟.
   Word inserts a new row at the end of the table.

6. Click Undo 🔄 to undo the new row.

Enter Data

7. Position the cursor in the first cell of the table, and then type the information shown in the following table. Remember to use ⌜Tab⌟ to move from cell to cell.

Company	Symbol	Purchase price	Current Price
Apple	APPL	$4,000	$5,000
BioSys	BIS	$21,000	$30,000
CalGen	CLG	$19,000	$20,500
Galileo	GLC	$10,000	$4,500
GemCo	GEC	$8,000	$35,000
IBM	IBM	$37,000	$30,000
SysTech	SYT	$12,500	$10,000

8. Save 💾 the file, and leave it open for the next topic.

Using Table Tools

Table Tools consist of tabs on the Ribbon that are *contextual*, meaning they appear in context with the task you are performing. They are comprised of the the Design tab and the Layout tab. In order to display the tabs, the cursor must be inside a table.

Inserting Rows and Columns

You can insert new rows and columns after a table has been created. Word 2007's Rows & Columns group on the Layout tab contains commands that let you insert rows above or below existing rows and new columns to the right or left of existing columns. If you wish to insert more than one row or column, you must first select the same number of rows or columns that you wish to insert. The following Quick Reference table describes techniques for modifying rows and columns.

QUICK REFERENCE: INSERTING AND DELETING COLUMNS AND ROWS

Task	Procedure
Insert rows	■ Click in the desired row or select the same number of rows that you wish to insert. ■ Choose Layout→Rows & Columns. ■ Choose either Insert Above or Insert Below.
Insert columns	■ Click in the desired column or select the same number of columns that you wish to insert. ■ Choose Layout→Rows & Columns. ■ Choose either Insert Left or Insert Right.
Delete rows or columns	■ Select the desired rows or columns. ■ Choose Layout→Rows & Columns→Delete. ■ From the Delete drop-down menu, choose Delete Cells, Delete Columns, Delete Rows, or Delete Table.

Hands-On 6.3   Insert a Row and a Column

In this exercise, you will practice inserting a new row and a new column in the table.

1. Click anywhere in the last row of the table.

2. Choose Layout→Rows & Columns→Insert Above to insert a new row above the SysTech row.

3. Add the following data to the new blank row.

Microsoft	MSFT	$20,000	$25,000

Now you'll insert a column at the right end of the table.

4. Click anywhere in the last column of the table.

5. Choose Layout→Rows & Columns→Insert Right ⊞ from the Ribbon.
   Word inserts a blank column at the right end of the table.

6. Click the Undo ↺ button to remove the column you added.

7. Save ▣ the file, and leave it open for the next topic.

Selecting Table Data

The mouse pointer changes shape, depending on whether you're selecting a cell, row, column, or the entire table. The following illustrations display the various pointer shapes when selecting in a table.

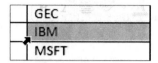

Click to select a cell when the mouse pointer is shaped like a right-tilting black arrow at the left side of a cell.

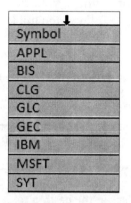

Click to select a column when the mouse pointer is shaped like a down-pointing black arrow at the top of the column.

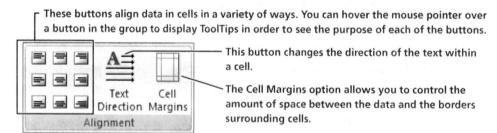

Click to select a row when the mouse pointer is a white arrow in the margin.

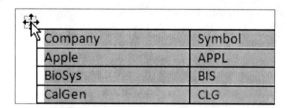

Click the square move handle in the upper-left corner of the table to select the entire table. The mouse pointer must be in the table for the handle to appear.

Aligning Table Data

In this topic, you'll learn to control alignment of data both horizontally and vertically within cells. The Alignment group on the Layout tab makes this task easy to accomplish.

These buttons align data in cells in a variety of ways. You can hover the mouse pointer over a button in the group to display ToolTips in order to see the purpose of each of the buttons.

This button changes the direction of the text within a cell.

The Cell Margins option allows you to control the amount of space between the data and the borders surrounding cells.

Hands-On 6.4   Select Table Entries and Align Data

In this exercise, you will center-align the table headings and right-align the numeric data.

1. Position the mouse pointer in the margin to the left of the table's heading row.

2. When the mouse pointer is shaped like a white arrow, click once to select the row.

3. Choose Layout→Alignment from the Ribbon.

4. In the Alignment group, choose Align Center, as shown here, to center the text both horizontally and vertically within the cells.

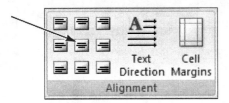

5. Follow these steps to select the numeric data in your table:

Ⓐ Position the mouse pointer at the left edge of the first cell containing numeric data.

Ⓑ Press and hold the mouse button down and drag diagonally to the last number cell to select the entire range of numbers, and then release the mouse button.

Purchase Price	Current Price
$4,000	$5,000
$21,000	$30,000
$19,000	$20,500
$10,000	$4,500
$8,000	$25,000
$37,000	$30,000
$20,000	$25,000
$12,500	$10,000

6. This time choose Align Center Right from the Alignment group to right-align the numbers and center them vertically within the cells.

⚠ **TIP!** *If necessary, place the mouse pointer over the alignment icons and watch for ToolTips to determine which icon applies Align Center Right.*

The numbers are now right-aligned within the cells.

7. Save your file, and leave it open for the next exercise.

Using Table Styles to Format a Table

The Table Styles group located on the Design tab lets you choose from a variety of predefined table formats. These formats automatically apply borders, shading, font colors, font sizes, and other formats to tables. You may be pleasantly surprised to see the professional-looking formatting that results when you apply Table Styles.

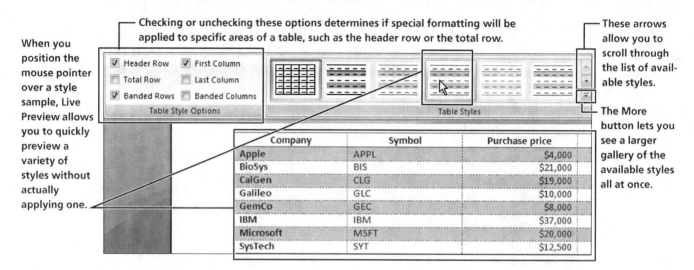

Checking or unchecking these options determines if special formatting will be applied to specific areas of a table, such as the header row or the total row.

These arrows allow you to scroll through the list of available styles.

When you position the mouse pointer over a style sample, Live Preview allows you to quickly preview a variety of styles without actually applying one.

The More button lets you see a larger gallery of the available styles all at once.

☑ Header Row   ☑ First Column
☐ Total Row   ☐ Last Column
☑ Banded Rows ☐ Banded Columns

Table Style Options   Table Styles

Company	Symbol	Purchase price
Apple	APPL	$4,000
BioSys	BIS	$21,000
CalGen	CLG	$19,000
Galileo	GLC	$10,000
GemCo	GEC	$8,000
IBM	IBM	$37,000
Microsoft	MSFT	$20,000
SysTech	SYT	$12,500

 ## Hands-On 6.5   Apply Table Styles

In this exercise, you will add polish to your table by applying one of Word's built-in table styles.

1. Make sure the cursor is in the table.

2. Choose Design→Table Styles from the Ribbon.

Observe the Table Style Gallery

3. Position the mouse pointer in the Table Styles group, and move from one style to another. Notice that Live Preview displays how the style would look if applied to your table.

4. Use the middle scroll arrow, as shown at right, to scroll down and view other built-in table styles.

5. Again, use Live Preview to examine additional styles.

6. Click the More ⬚ button to display a larger sampling of styles, and then scroll through the gallery.

7. Click in the body of the document to close the gallery, and then click the table.

8. Use the scroll buttons to scroll to the second row of table styles.

Apply a Table Style

9. If necessary, place a checkmark in the Header Row and First Column checkboxes in the Table Style Options group, as shown at right, to apply special formatting to those areas of your table. Check or uncheck the remaining boxes, as shown in the illustration.

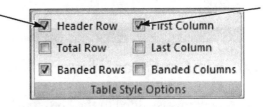

10. Choose the Light List – Accent 1 style (fourth style sample in the second row) to apply that style to your table.

NOTE! *The location may vary based on your screen size and resolution. You can use ToolTips to locate the style, or feel free to choose another style.*

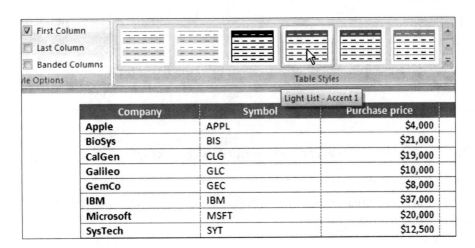

Company	Symbol	Purchase price
Apple	APPL	$4,000
BioSys	BIS	$21,000
CalGen	CLG	$19,000
Galileo	GLC	$10,000
GemCo	GEC	$8,000
IBM	IBM	$37,000
Microsoft	MSFT	$20,000
SysTech	SYT	$12,500

Notice the special formatting on the header row, and notice that bold was applied to the first column. That's the result of options you chose in the Table Style Options group.

11. Save the document, and close it.

Concepts Review

True/False Questions

1. A new row is added to the bottom of a table whenever you tap the [Tab] key. TRUE FALSE

2. You can insert new rows above and below the row containing the cursor. TRUE FALSE

3. You can select an entire column when the mouse pointer appears as a four-headed arrow at the top of the column. TRUE FALSE

4. Controlling cell margins determines the amount of space between the data and the borders surrounding cells. TRUE FALSE

5. You can select a table row when the mouse pointer appears as a black arrow in the margin next to the table. TRUE FALSE

6. When you insert a new column in a table, the new column always appears to the left of the column containing the cursor. TRUE FALSE

7. The mouse pointer must be in a table in order for the move handle to appear in the upper-left corner. TRUE FALSE

8. Word's Table Tools tabs on the Ribbon can be described as contextual. TRUE FALSE

9. Live Preview allows you to view the effect of a table style before you apply it. TRUE FALSE

10. The More button in the Table Styles group allows you to download additional table styles from the Microsoft website. TRUE FALSE

Multiple Choice Questions

1. Word's Table Tools tabs on the Ribbon include which of the following tabs?
   a. Layout
   b. Format
   c. Home
   d. Insert

2. How many rows should you select if you want to insert two rows?
   a. 1
   b. 2
   c. 3
   d. 0

3. Which of the following is not a choice in the Table Style Options group?
   a. Banded Rows
   b. First Column
   c. Header Text
   d. Header Row

4. Which of the following is not included in a table style format?
   a. Font Color
   b. Font Size
   c. Shading
   d. Bullets

Skill Builders

Skill Builder 6.1   Use Table Styles and Merge Cells

In this exercise, you will create a memorandum using Table Styles.

1. Use these guidelines to create the following memorandum:
   - Use proper spacing and formatting for a business memorandum.
   - Create a four-column, six-row table.
   - Enter the data as shown in the following illustration.
   - Use the scroll down ⌄ button in the Table Styles group to scroll down seven rows and apply the sixth format in that row, Medium List 2 – Accent 4. The style location may vary. If necessary, use ToolTips to locate the style, or choose a different style.

2. Save the completed document to the Lesson 06 folder as **sb-Contractors,** and then close it.

Memo To: Linda Fong

From: Reginald Wills

Date: Today's Date

Subject: FastTrack Contractors

Per your request, I am providing you with a list of independent contractors who are qualified to work on the FastTrack project. I have included their names, hourly rates, availability, and telephone numbers.

Independent Contractors for Fast Track

Name	Rate	Availability	Phone
Vanesha Denny	$35/hour	April 15	236-0090
Tanya Simms	$40/hour	Immediate	235-9988
Mukesh Patel	$30/hour	April 21	450-9090
Isaac Stone	$55/hour	Immediate	234-8980
Pat Thomas	$40/hour	May 1	223-4565

Skill Builder 6.2   Insert and Delete Columns and Rows in a Table

In this exercise, you will open a document containing a table. You will add and delete columns and rows.

1. Open sb-Flight Information from your Lesson 06 folder.

2. Position the cursor in the last cell of the table and tap `Tab` to insert a new row at the bottom of the table.

3. Enter the following data in the new row:

Sat	29Sept	AA 983	OK	Q	LV Atlanta AR San Francisco	230P 422P

4. Make sure the cursor is in the last column of the table.

5. Choose Layout→Rows & Columns→Insert Right [icon] from the Ribbon.

6. Type the following information in the new column:

Seat
13B Coach
30B Coach
32E Coach
24A Coach

Delete a Row

7. Select the second row of the table.

8. Choose Layout→Rows & Columns→Delete [icon] from the Ribbon.

9. Choose Delete Rows from the menu.

10. Click the Undo [icon] button to undo the deletion.

Delete a Column

11. Select the Class column.

12. Choose Layout→Rows & Columns→Delete [icon] from the Ribbon.

13. Choose Delete Columns from the menu.

14. Save and close the file.

Skill Builder 6.3   Insert and Format a Table

In this exercise, you will create a table to display your research for your paleontology class. Then you will format the table.

1. Choose Insert→Tables→Table ▦ from the Ribbon.

2. Drag the mouse pointer in the table grid to select four columns and five rows.

3. Click the last highlighted cell to insert the table.

4. Type the table as shown in the following illustration.

Name	Anatomy	Period	Location
Brachiosaurus	Weighed about 80 tons, long neck, front legs longer than hind ones.	Jurassic	Tanzania
Peteinosaurus	Flying reptile.	Triassic	Italy
Polacanthus	Armored all over.	Cretaceous	England
Utahraptor	Large eyes, long clutching hands, and sturdy clawed feet.	Cretaceous	Europe, Asia, and North America

Insert a Column

5. Position the cursor in the Anatomy column.

6. Choose Layout→Rows & Columns→Insert Right ▦ from the Ribbon.

7. Enter the following data in the new column:

Diet
Plants
Insects
Plants
Carnivorous

Add a Row

8. Position the cursor in the Utahraptor row.

9. Choose Layout→Rows & Columns→Insert Above ![icon] from the Ribbon.

10. Enter the following data in the new row:

Protoceratops	Walked on four legs, large head, bulky body, parrot-like beak, knobs of bone on its head.	Plants	Cretaceous	Mongolia

11. Apply a Table Style design of your choice.

Increase Cell Margins

The text in the Anatomy column is a bit too close. You will increase the cell margins to add more white space in the cells.

12. Make sure the cursor is in the table.

13. Choose Layout→Alignment→Cell Margins ![icon] from the Ribbon.

14. Enter **.05** in the Top and Bottom boxes, as shown in the following illustration.

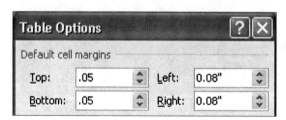

15. Click OK.

16. Save the file as **sb-Dinos** in your Lesson 06 folder.

Unit 2 Assessments

Assessment 2.1   Create a Table and Align Data

In this exercise, you will insert a table, add a column, and apply a table style. You will then adjust the alignment of the data in the table.

1. Insert a two-column, six-row table.

2. Enter the data as shown in the following illustration.

Company	Contact
BPI	David Katz
Exxon	Maria Velasquez
City of Oakland	Michael Gunn
Centron	Ralph Watson
Constructo	Ben Johnson

3. Insert a new column between the Company and Contact columns.

4. Enter the following data:

Word Version
Word 2007
Word 2003
Word 2003
Word 2007
Word 2002

5. Apply the Medium Shading 2 - Accent 1 table style. (The medium shading formats are located in the fifth row of the Table Styles gallery. The position may vary based on your screen size and resolution. If needed, use ToolTips to locate the style.)

6. Center-align the data in all three columns

7. Save the file as **as-Word Versions** in your Unit 2 Assessments folder then close it.

Assessment 2.2   Create a Table and Align Data

In this exercise, you will create a table and align data.

1. Follow these guidelines to create a table for tracking orders:
   - Type **Order Tracking Sheet** as the heading for your document.
   - Format the heading as you deem appropriate.
   - Create a five-column, six-row table.
   - Type the data shown in the following illustration.
   - Align the data and adjust the column widths as shown in the example.
   - Select the table and use the Center alignment button in the Paragraph group of the Home tab to center the table between the margins.

Customer ID	Order Status	Item #	In Stock?	Order Total
233	I	S230	Y	$23.45
234	S	A321	Y	$45.87
341	S	A423	Y	$100.91
567	I	S345	N	$43.23
879	H	D567	N	$78.92

2. Save the document as **as-Order Tracking** in your Unit 2 Assessments folder then close it.

Assessment 2.3   Create a Modified Block-Style Letter

In this exercise, you will practice the skills needed to create a modified block-style letter. You'll turn on the ruler to ensure the correct spacing for the date, the complimentary close, and the signature block.

1. Start a new blank document.
   You will create an AutoCorrect entry for Back Bay Users Group to use in your letter.

2. Click the Office ⬛ button, and then click the Word Options button in the bottom-right corner of the window.

3. In the Word Options window, choose Proofing from the menu on the left.

4. Click the AutoCorrect Options button.

5. When the AutoCorrect dialog box appears, type **bbug** in the Replace box.

6. Type **Back Bay Users Group** in the With box.

7. Click the Add button, and then click OK twice.

8. If necessary, click the View Ruler ⬛ button at the top of the vertical scroll bar to display the ruler.

9. Create the modified block-style business letter shown in the following illustration.

10. Follow these guidelines as you type your letter.
    - Change to single-spacing and remove the after-paragraph spacing.
    - Use Tab to align the date, closing, and signature block at 3 inches on the ruler. (You'll need to tap Tab six times to indent the lines at 3 inches.)
    - Space down the proper distance from the top of the page.
    - Use correct spacing between paragraphs.
    - Use your AutoCorrect shortcut in the first paragraph, rather than typing Back Bay Users Group.

Today's Date

Mrs. Suzanne Lee
8445 South Princeton Street
Chicago, IL 60628

Dear Mrs. Lee:

Thank you for your interest in the Back Bay Users Group. We will be holding an orientation for new members on the first Thursday in April at our headquarters.

Please let us know if you can attend by calling the phone number on this letterhead. Or, if you prefer, you may respond in writing or via email.

Sincerely,

Jack Bell
Membership Chair

11. Save ⊞ the letter to the Unit 2 Assessments folder on your file storage location as **as-Lee Letter.**

12. Switch to the View tab, and remove the checkmark from the Ruler command in the Show/Hide group to turn off the ruler. Then switch back to the Home tab.

13. Delete the AutoCorrect entry you created in this exercise.

14. Print the letter, and then close the document.

Assessment 2.4   Use the Clipboard and Drag and Drop

In this exercise, you will use the Clipboard and the drag-and-drop technique to rearrange items in a list.

1. Open as-Animals in the Unit 2 Assessments folder in your file storage location.

2. Open the Clipboard, and use the Clear All button, if necessary, to empty it.

3. Use the Home→Clipboard→Cut ✂ button to place all the animals on the Clipboard, and then cut all the vegetables to the Clipboard.

4. Position the cursor below the list of minerals, and then use the Paste All button to paste the animals and vegetables back in the document.

5. Use the ⎡Enter⎤ key to put two blank lines between groups and an extra blank line above the minerals, and then type an appropriate title at the top of each group.

6. Use drag and drop to arrange the groups in this order: Animals, Vegetables, Minerals. Remember, when selecting the text, include the blank line below the group.

7. Save 💾 the file and close it.

Assessment 2.5   Edit a Document

In this exercise, you will use your editing skills to make specified changes to a letter.

1. Open the as-Wilson Letter document in the Unit 2 Assessments folder in your file storage location.

2. Edit the document, as shown in the illustration at the end of this exercise.

3. Use Enter to push the entire document down, so that the date is positioned at approximately the 2-inch position.

4. Use Tab to move the date, complimentary close, and signature block to the 3-inch position on the ruler. This will convert the letter from block style to modified block style.

5. When you finish, save the changes, print the letter, and close the document.

Today's Date

~~Ms. Cynthia Wilson~~   Mr. Roosevelt Jackson
~~118 Upper Terrace~~   8 Spring Street
~~Freehold, NJ 08845~~   Martinville, NJ 08836

Dear ~~Ms. Wilson~~:
   Mr. Jackson
                                                        back
Thank you for your recent letter concerning back injuries in your office. Yes, injuries are a
common problem for office workers today. It was estimated by the U. S. Bureau of Labor
Statistics that in one year over ~~490~~,000 employees took time from work due to back injuries.
                  580

Encourage your office employees to make certain their work surface is at a ~~suitable~~ height. They
should also be encouraged to take frequent breaks from their desks.   comfortable

Please
~~Feel free to~~ contact my office if you would like more information.

Sincerely,

Elaine Boudreau
Ergonomics Specialist

Assessment 2.6   Format Characters and Insert Special Characters

In this exercise, you will try out various character formats and insert special characters. Then you will insert and delete a page break.

1. Open as-Formatting from the Unit 2 Assessments folder.

2. Follow the instructions in the exercise document to format lines and insert special characters.

3. Save 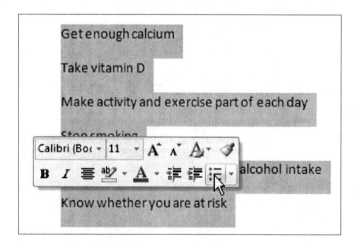 the document and close it.

Assessment 2.7   Use Character Formatting and Lists in a Flyer

In this exercise, you will create a flyer that Lakeville Community Hospital will distribute through their Health Education Department. You will use paragraph alignment, and create bulleted lists. When you complete the exercise, your document should look like the figure at the end of this exercise.

1. Open the file as-Osteoporosis from the Unit 2 Assessments folder.

2. Select the first two lines of the *document,* and format them with bold, center alignment, and 16 point font.

3. Format the heading line, *What is Osteoporosis?,* with bold and 12 point font.

4. Use the Format Painter to copy the formatting from the heading line to the other two heading lines (*What Can You Do to Prevent Osteoporosis?* and *What Can You Do to Help Prevent Falls?*).

Add Bullets to Lists

5. Select *Get enough calcium* through *Know whether you are at risk.*

6. Use the Mini toolbar to apply bullets to the list.

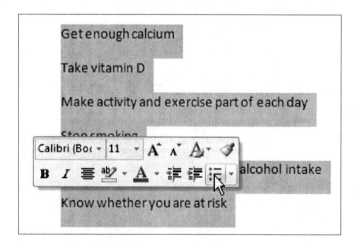

7. Apply bullets to the seven lines at the end of the document.

8. Save the file and close it.

Lakeville Community Hospital
Partners in Prevention

What is Osteoporosis?

Osteoporosis is a disorder that causes your bones to become increasingly porous, brittle, and subject to fracture. Women are four times more likely to suffer from osteoporosis than men. However, there are steps you can take to reduce the risk of bone loss and fracture.

What Can You Do to Prevent Osteoporosis?

- Get enough calcium
- Take vitamin D
- Make activity and exercise part of each day
- Stop smoking
- Cut down on caffeine, salt, and alcohol intake
- Know whether you are at risk

What Can You Do to Help Prevent Falls?

- Have your vision checked
- Stay active to help maintain balance, strength, and coordination
- Wear low-heeled shoes with non-slip soles
- Tie your shoe laces
- Replace slippers that are stretched out of shape and are too loose
- Eliminate all tripping hazards in your home
- Install grab bars and handrails

Assessment 2.8   Use Line Spacing, Numbering, and Indenting

In this exercise, you will create a document with variable line spacing and a numbered list.

1. Follow these guidelines to create the document shown at the end of this exercise:
   - Tap [Enter] enough times to place the cursor at approximately the 2-inch mark in the vertical ruler.
   - Add bold and a 16 point font for the title.
   - Center the title, tap [Enter] after the title, and switch to Align Text Left.
   - Turn off bold, and change to 11 point font.
   - Use single-spacing and double-spacing as necessary to format the document as shown.

2. Save the document in the Unit 2 Assessments folder as **as-Success,** and then close it.

SUCCESS

The quest for success is a driving force in the lives of many Americans. This force drives the business

world and often results in huge personal fortunes. However, success can come in many forms, some of

which are listed below.

1. Many people in America view success monetarily.
2. Our society also views public figures, such as movie stars, athletes, and other celebrities as being successful.
3. Educational achievements, such as earning an advanced degree, are often perceived as successful.

It is easy to see that success means many things to many people. The poet Ralph Waldo Emerson

provides this elegant definition of success:

To laugh often and much' to win the respect of intelligent people and the affection of children; to earn the appreciation of honest critics and endure the betrayal of false friends; to appreciate beauty, to find the best in others; to leave the world a bit better, whether by a healthy child, a garden patch or a redeemed social condition; to know even one life has breathed easier because you have lived. This is to have succeeded.

Unit 3

Excel 2007

In this unit, you will work with essential Excel 2007 features. You will begin by reviewing the new Ribbon interface in Excel. Next, you will move on to creating worksheets. You will also edit worksheets with Cut, Copy, and Paste, drag and drop, and automated features such as AutoFill and AutoComplete. When working with formulas and functions, you will use relative and absolute cells, point mode, and mixed references. In the last lesson of this unit, you will format your worksheets and uncover the "magic" of Excel charting. This unit ends with a series of Assessment exercises.

LESSON 7

Exploring Excel 2007

In this lesson, you will develop fundamental Excel 2007 skills. This lesson will provide you with a solid understanding of Excel so you are prepared to master the advanced features introduced in later lessons. You will learn how to navigate around a worksheet, enter various types of data, and select cells.

LESSON OBJECTIVES

After studying this lesson, you will be able to:

- Explain ways Excel can help your productivity
- Launch the Excel program
- Navigate around the Excel window
- Utilize the tabs and Ribbon to issue commands
- Enter text and numbers into cells
- Distinguish between a text and a number entry in a cell
- Save and "save as" your workbooks
- Close a workbook and exit from Excel

Case Study: Building a Basic Spreadsheet

Charlie Arnold is a volunteer coordinator at South Coast Hospital. Mendy Laubach, the human resources manager for the hospital, has asked Charlie to maintain a list of hours worked by his volunteers from Wednesday to Sunday (Charlie's workweek). Mendy asks Charlie to report the data on a daily basis. After analyzing Mendy's request, Charlie decides that Excel 2007 is the right tool for the job and proceeds to organize the data in a worksheet. Charlie's worksheet is shown in the following illustration.

	A	B	C	D	E	F	G
1	Hospital Volunteers-Hours Worked						
2							
3			Wednesd:	Thursday	Friday	Saturday	Sunday
4	Gift Shop						
5		Evelyn	3	2	4	0	6
6		Gene	4	2	1	7	3
7		Karel	6	1	2	3	3
8		Bill	3	5	2	2	3
9		Total					
10	Candy Stripers						
11		Ginny	7	0	2	1	4
12		Karel	2	4	1	3	2
13		Ann	4	1	5	2	0
14		Total					
15	Bookmobile						
16		Mohamed	3	6	0	3	2
17		Leticia	1	7	2	2	3
18		Maria	5	2	4	2	0
19		Total					

Notice that Excel makes it easy for you to organize your data in columns and rows. The total rows have been included in the example, although you will not learn how to create formulas until Lesson 9.

Presenting Excel 2007

Microsoft Office Excel 2007 is an electronic spreadsheet program. It allows you to work with numbers and data much more efficiently than the pen-and-paper method. Excel is used in virtually all industries and many households for a variety of tasks such as:

- Creating and maintaining detailed budgets

- Keeping track of extensive customer lists

- Performing "what-if" scenarios and break-even analyses

- Determining the profitability of a business or sector

- Creating tables to organize information

- Tracking employee information

- Producing detailed charts to graphically display information

- Creating invoices or purchase orders

- Determining the future value of an investment, the present value of an annuity, or the payment for a loan

- Working with reports exported from small business accounting software programs such as Intuit's QuickBooks®

As you can see from this list, Excel is not just used to crunch numbers. It is a very powerful program that is used not only to work with numbers but also to maintain databases. If you have started a database in Excel, you can even import it into Microsoft Access (the program in the Microsoft Office Suite that is specialized for working with databases). Many people may use Excel to track their databases rather than Access because of its ease of use and because Access is not included in all of the Microsoft Office editions. If you are tracking multiple databases that you wish to include in reports and data queries, you will want to consider utilizing Access, though, as it really is designed to work with multiple tables of data.

NOTE! *Throughout this book, we will look at different personal and business scenarios and how Excel is used to streamline the workflow.*

Starting Excel

The method you use to start Excel depends in large part on whether you intend to create a new workbook or open an existing workbook. A workbook is a file containing one or more worksheets. To create a new workbook, use one of the following methods. Once the Excel program has started, you can begin working in the new workbook that appears.

- Click the button and choose Microsoft Office Excel 2007 from the All Programs menu. (Depending on your installation of Microsoft Office, you may need to choose Microsoft Office from the All Programs menu and then choose Microsoft Office Excel 2007.)

- Click the Microsoft Office Excel 2007 ⊠ button on the Quick Launch toolbar located to the right of the Start button. (This button may not appear on all computers.)

Use one of the following methods if you intend to open an existing Excel workbook. Once the Excel program has started, the desired workbook will open in an Excel window.

■ Navigate to the desired document using Windows Explorer or My Computer and double-click the workbook.

■ Click the button and point to My Recent Documents. You can choose the desired workbooks from the documents list, which displays the most-recently used documents.

Hands-On 7.1   Start Excel

In this exercise, you will help Charlie start the Excel program.

1. Start your computer, and the Windows Desktop will appear.

2. Click the **start** button and choose (All) Programs.

3. Choose the Microsoft Office folder, and then choose Microsoft Office Excel 2007.
   After a pause, the Excel program loads and the Excel window appears.

Exploring the Excel Program Window

When you launch Excel, you will see a blank workbook displayed. The window is filled with many objects and a space for you to create your spreadsheet. Using the figures that follow, you will have an opportunity to learn the names of some of the objects that you can see on your screen.

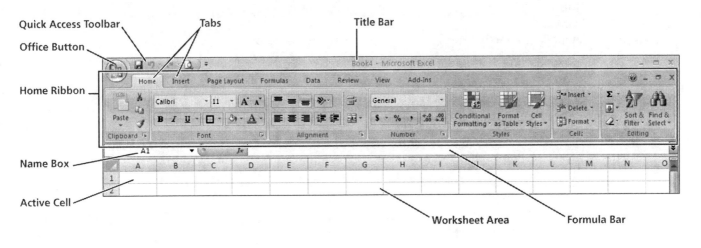

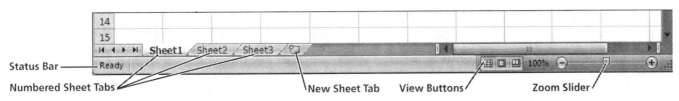

Using Worksheets and Workbooks

Excel displays a blank workbook the moment you start the program. A workbook is composed of worksheets. This is similar to a paper notebook with many sheets of paper. You enter text, numbers, formulas, charts, and other objects in worksheets. By default, Excel displays three worksheets in a new workbook, each accessible by a separate tab at the bottom of the screen. The maximum number of worksheets you can insert is limited only by the amount of memory available on your computer.

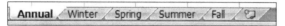

In this example, the sheet tabs are named so that you can organize data for each season as well as track annual information.

A worksheet has a grid structure with horizontal rows and vertical columns. A new worksheet has 16,384 columns and 1,048,576 rows! However, at any given time only a small number of the rows and columns are visible in the worksheet window. The intersection of each row and column is a cell. Each cell is identified by a reference. The reference is the column letter followed by the row number. For example, A1 is the reference of the cell in the top-left corner of the worksheet. So, we refer to this as cell A1.

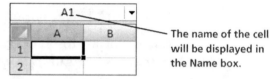

The name of the cell will be displayed in the Name box.

Mousing Around in Excel

The shape of the mouse pointer will change as you move it around the Excel window. The shape of the pointer will let you know what will happen if you click over that spot.

Mouse Pointer Shape	Function
✚	Click to select a cell. Click and drag to select multiple cells.
✛	The fill handle pointer; you will learn what this tool can do for you in Lesson 8, Editing, Viewing, and Printing Worksheets.
↖	Allows you to perform a variety of tasks when clicked, such as issue a command from the Ribbon or select a new tab.
⊹	The move pointer; if you drag with this, it will move cell contents from one location to another.
↔	The resize pointer; dragging this pointer will allow you to change the size of objects such as rows, pictures, and charts.
→ ↓	Select a row or column.
I	Click with the I-beam pointer to enter text, such as in the Formula Bar.

Scrolling Along in a Worksheet

There are two scroll bars visible in the Excel window, both vertical and horizontal. They allow you to see other areas of the worksheet without changing which cell is active. There are three ways to use the scroll bars to view other areas of your spreadsheet.

Click and drag the scroll box to control the scroll more precisely.

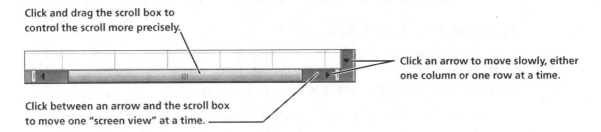

Click an arrow to move slowly, either one column or one row at a time.

Click between an arrow and the scroll box to move one "screen view" at a time.

Navigating in a Worksheet

When you have a cell selected, it is surrounded by a thick line, which indicates that it is the active cell. You can change the active cell by clicking in another cell or by using the keyboard. This is important because data is entered into the active cell. The vertical and horizontal scroll bars let you navigate through a worksheet; however, scrolling does not change which cell is active. After scrolling you will have to select which cell is to be active, either by clicking or using one of the keystrokes listed below.

Keystroke(s)	How the Highlight Moves
→ ← ↑ ↓	One cell right, left, up, or down
Home	Beginning of current row
Ctrl + →	End of current row
Ctrl + Home	Home cell, usually cell A1
Ctrl + End	Last cell in active part of worksheet
Page Down	Down one visible screen
Page Up	Up one visible screen
Alt + Page Down	One visible screen right
Alt + Page Up	One visible screen left
Ctrl + G	Displays Go To dialog box—enter cell reference and click OK

In this exercise, you will practice selecting the active cell in a worksheet so that you can become comfortable enough with the program to help Charlie begin to create his spreadsheet.

Navigate with the Mouse

1. Slide the mouse over the screen and notice the thick cross shape ✛ when it is in the worksheet area.
   If you click with this pointer shape, you will select a cell.

2. Click the cross-shaped pointer on any cell and notice that the cell becomes active.

3. Move the selection five times by clicking in various cells.

Navigate with the Keyboard

Now that you have practiced using the mouse, it is time to learn how to use the keyboard in order to move about a worksheet. You should use the keys on your keyboard that are between the main part and the numeric keypad on the far right.

4. Use the →, ←, ↑, and ↓ keys to position the highlight in cell F10.

5. Tap the Home key and see that the highlight moves to cell A10.
   The Home key always makes the cell in column A of the current row active.

6. Press Ctrl + Home to make A1 the active cell.

7. Tap the Page Down key two or three times.
   Notice that Excel displays the next 30 or so rows (one "visible" screen's worth) each time you tap Page Down.

8. Press and hold down the ↑ key until A1 is the active cell.

Use the Scroll Bars

The scroll bars allow you to see other areas of the Excel worksheet area without changing which cell is active.

9. Click the Scroll Right ▶ button on the horizontal scroll bar until columns AA and AB are visible.
   Excel labels the first 26 columns A–Z and the next 26 columns AA–AZ. A similar labeling scheme is used for the remaining columns out to the final column, XFD.

10. Click the Scroll Down ▼ button on the vertical scroll bar until row 100 is visible.
    Notice that the highlight has not moved. To move the highlight, you must click in a cell or use the keyboard.

11. Take a few minutes to practice scrolling and moving the selection.

Use the Go To Command

As you learned in the preceding Quick Reference table, you can use Ctrl + G *to display the Go To box, where you can go to a specific cell by entering the desired cell reference in the Reference box and clicking OK. You can use* Ctrl + Home *to select cell A1.*

12. Press Ctrl + G to display the Go To dialog box.

13. Type **g250** in the Reference box and click OK.
    Notice that cell references are not case sensitive.

14. Use the Go To command to move to two or three different cells.

15. Press Ctrl + Home to return to cell A1.

Explore the Excel Window

Now that you have learned how to select cells and move around in the window, it is time to explore the Excel window a bit further.

16. Follow these steps to explore the Excel window:

A Notice the Name box.

B Click the Sheet2 tab and notice that a blank worksheet appears. The number of worksheets you can have is limited only by the amount of available memory in the computer.

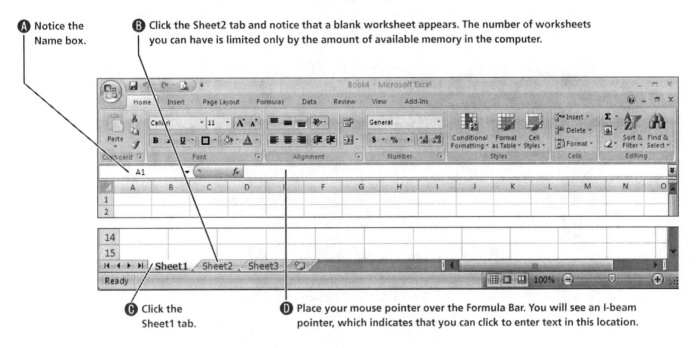

C Click the Sheet1 tab.

D Place your mouse pointer over the Formula Bar. You will see an I-beam pointer, which indicates that you can click to enter text in this location.

17. Press Ctrl + Home to move the highlight to cell A1.

Working with Tabs and Ribbons

In Microsoft Office 2007, Excel does not have the traditional menu and toolbars with which computer users are familiar. You are able to access the commands that will allow you to effectively utilize Excel through the tabs, ribbons, and Office button located at the top of window.

The Office Button

 The Office button, when clicked, accesses a menu that allows you to issue file management commands. File management simply means working with Excel on the level of the "file"—such as creating new files, opening existing files, saving the file you are working on, and printing your file.

The Quick Access Toolbar

Excel 2007 has one remaining toolbar (compared with previous versions), which is located at the top of the window. It is similar to the Quick Launch toolbar in Windows in that it contains commands that you use frequently. It is also customizable, unlike the Ribbon, which is set. The Quick Access toolbar, with the default buttons, is displayed in the following illustration.

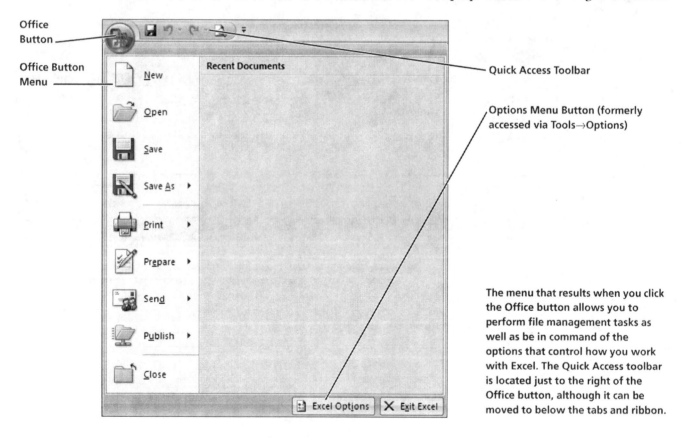

Office Button

Office Button Menu

Quick Access Toolbar

Options Menu Button (formerly accessed via Tools→Options)

The menu that results when you click the Office button allows you to perform file management tasks as well as be in command of the options that control how you work with Excel. The Quick Access toolbar is located just to the right of the Office button, although it can be moved to below the tabs and ribbon.

Customizing the Quick Access Toolbar

The Quick Access toolbar can be customized to include commands that you frequently use. If you regularly use the Open command, you may wish to add it to the Quick Access toolbar, as shown.

Displaying Tabs and Working with Ribbons

2007 new!

The tabs at the top of the Excel window organize the commands into eight categories. The commands appear on ribbons displayed across the screen. In order to view a new tab, you simply need to single-click it. The commands on the Ribbon can be chosen by a single-click as well.

Excel's Home Ribbon

The standard tabs along with the Ribbon are displayed in the preceding illustration. Additional contextual tabs will become visible as necessary. For instance, if you are working with a picture, a picture tab will appear.

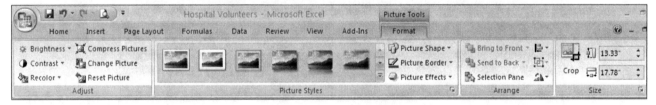

The Ribbon with a contextual tab displayed. When a picture is selected, a special Picture Tools Format tab appears. All of the commands on this ribbon deal with the formatting of the picture.

ScreenTips

A ScreenTip is a little window that appears to describe the function of the object at which you are pointing. ScreenTips appear when you rest your mouse pointer over an option on a ribbon, the Quick Access toolbar, or the Office button. In Excel 2007, there are also Enhanced ScreenTips that appear for some of the commands. An Enhanced ScreenTip is a larger window that is more descriptive than a ScreenTip and also provides a link to an Excel help topic.

When you place your mouse pointer over an object on the Ribbon, a ScreenTip appears.

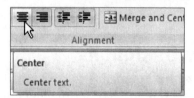

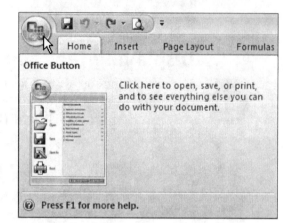

Sometimes you will see an Enhanced ScreenTip when you place your mouse pointer over an object. In this case, you receive an Enhanced ScreenTip explaining the function of the Office button with a link to a help topic.

Dialog Box Launchers

Many of the groups on the Ribbon have Dialog Box Launchers . Clicking on the dialog box launcher will open a window that allows you to issue additional commands.

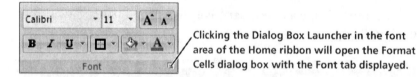

Clicking the Dialog Box Launcher in the font area of the Home ribbon will open the Format Cells dialog box with the Font tab displayed.

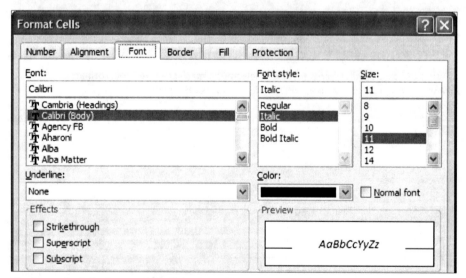

The Font tab of the Format Cells dialog box allows you to make changes to how the font appears in the selected cell(s).

Hiding the Ribbon

There may be times when you do not want the Ribbon displayed at the top of the window. In order to hide it, simply double-click on the tab that is currently displayed. To display the Ribbon once again, click on the tab you wish to view.

QUICK REFERENCE: USING TABS AND RIBBONS AND CUSTOMIZING THE QUICK ACCESS TOOLBAR	
Task	**Procedure**
Hide the Ribbon	■ Double-click the tab of the Ribbon that is displayed.
Unhide the Ribbon	■ Double-click any of the tabs at the top of the window, or click the hidden tab.
Customize the Quick Access toolbar with a Ribbon command	■ Right-click the Ribbon command you wish to add. ■ Choose Add to Quick Access Toolbar.
Customize the Quick Access toolbar with a command not available on the Ribbon	■ Click the Office button. ■ Click the Excel Options button. ■ Click the Customize option in the list to the left. ■ Choose from where you wish the command to come. ■ Click the command you wish to add. ■ Click Add.
Remove a button from the Quick Access toolbar	■ Right-click the button you wish to remove. ■ Choose Remove from Quick Access Toolbar.

 Hands-On 7.3 ## Explore the Tabs, Ribbons, and Quick Access Toolbar

In this exercise, you will have the opportunity to explore the tabs and Ribbon at the top of the Excel window. In addition, you will add a button to the Quick Access toolbar that you feel is important to always have readily available.

Display the Page Layout Ribbon

In this exercise, you will display the Page Layout tab of the Ribbon and open the Page Setup dialog box.

1. Click the Page Layout tab at the top of the window.

The Page Layout tab is displayed.

2. Click the Dialog Box Launcher at the bottom-right corner of the Page Setup section of the Ribbon.

The Page Setup dialog box appears.

3. Click the Cancel button at the bottom of the dialog box to close it.

4. Move your mouse pointer over various commands on the Page Layout tab of the Ribbon display their ScreenTips and explore what will occur if you choose to click them.

Add a Button to the Quick Access Toolbar

In this section, you will add a button to the Quick Access toolbar that will allow you to easily open another workbook.

5. Follow these steps to add Open to the Quick Access toolbar:

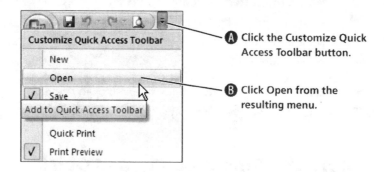

A Click the Customize Quick Access Toolbar button.

B Click Open from the resulting menu.

Notice the ScreenTip that displays below the mouse pointer when you point at a menu option, explaining what will occur if you choose that option. The Open button will appear on the Quick Access toolbar.

The new button appears on the Quick Access toolbar.

Remove a Button from the Quick Access Toolbar

In order to remove the Open button from the Quick Access toolbar, you will repeat the steps you took to add it.

6. Click the Customize Quick Access Toolbar button.

7. Choose Open from the resulting menu.
Excel will essentially "remove the checkmark" from the Open option and remove the button from the toolbar. Leave the Excel window open, as you will continue to work with it in the next exercise.

Entering Data in Excel

You can begin entering data the moment Excel is started. Data is entered into the active cell (the cell with the thick line around it). Text and numbers are used for different purposes in a worksheet. For instance, text entries cannot be used in calculations, whereas number entries can. Text is used for descriptive headings and entries that require alphabetic characters or a combination of alphabetic and numeric characters and spaces. Numbers can be entered directly or can be calculated using formulas. Excel recognizes the data you enter and decides whether the entry is text, a number, or a formula. You will learn about entering formulas in Lesson 9, Working with Formulas and Functions.

Data Types

Entries are defined as one of two main classifications: constant values or formulas. Constant values can be text, numeric, or a combination of both. The one thing that makes an entry constant is that the value does not change when other information changes. Conversely, formula entries display the results of calculations, and a result can change when a value in another cell changes.

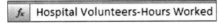

This entry is a constant value; it will not change as other cells are updated.

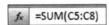

When a formula entry is used, it will refer to one or more cells and will change as the indicated cells are updated.

Completing Cell Entries

Text and numbers are entered by positioning the highlight in the desired cell, typing the desired text or number, and completing the entry. You can use Enter, Tab, or any of the arrow keys (→, ←, ↑, ↓) to complete an entry. The position of the active cell following a cell entry depends on the method by which you complete the entry.

Entry Completion Method	Where the Active Cell Will Appear
Enter	It will move down to the next cell.
Tab	It will move to the next cell to the right.
→ ↑ ↓ ←	It will move to the next cell in the direction of the arrow key.
Esc	The entry will be deleted and the current cell will remain active.

The Enter and Cancel Buttons

The Enter ✔ and Cancel ✖ buttons appear on the Formula Bar whenever you enter or edit an entry. The Enter button completes the entry and keeps the highlight in the current cell. The Cancel button cancels the entry, as does the Esc key.

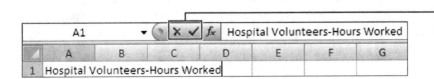

The Cancel and Enter buttons appear when an entry is being entered or edited.

Deleting and Replacing Entries

You can delete an entire entry after it has been completed by clicking in the cell and tapping [Delete]. Likewise, you can replace an entry by clicking in the cell and typing a new entry. The new entry will replace the original entry. You will learn all about editing entries in Lesson 8, Editing, Viewing, and Printing Worksheets.

Long Text Entries

Text entries often do not fit in a cell. These entries are known as long entries. Excel uses the following rules when deciding how to display long entries:

- If the cell to the right of the long entry is empty, then the long entry displays over the adjacent cell.

- If the cell to the right of the long entry contains an entry, then Excel shortens, or truncates, the display of the long entry.

Keep in mind that Excel does not actually change the long entry; it simply truncates the display of the entry. You can always widen a column to accommodate a long entry.

 The entry, Hospital Volunteers-Hours Worked, is a long entry. The entire phrase is entered in cell A1 although it displays over cells A1-D1.

 Hands-On 7.4   Enter Text

In this exercise, you will enter text into your worksheet.

Type a Long Entry

First, you will have the opportunity to see how text can flow into empty cells to the right of its "home" cell.

1. Make cell A1 active by clicking the mouse pointer ✛ in it.

2. Type **Hospital Volunteers-Hours Worked** and tap [Enter].
   The text is entered in the cell and the highlight moves down to cell A2. Excel moves the highlight down when you tap [Enter] because most people enter data column by column. Notice that the entry displays over cells B1, C1, and D1. The long entry would not display over these cells if they contained data.

3. Click cell A1 and note the appearance of the Formula Bar.

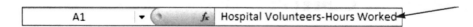

Notice that the Formula Bar displays the name of the active cell (A1) as well as its content. In this example, the cell's content is the title, Hospital Volunteers-Hours Worked. The title is a long entry because it is wider than cell A1. Cells B1-D1 are empty so the long entry is displayed over them. Keep in mind, however, that the entire entry belongs to cell A1. This concept will be demonstrated in the next few steps.

Verify that the Entry Belongs to Cell A1

4. Tap the → key to make cell B1 active.

5. Look at the Formula Bar and notice that cell B1 is empty.
   The long entry belongs to cell A1 even though it is displayed over cells A1–D1.

Type Additional Text Entries

6. Click in cell C3.

7. Type **Wednesday** and tap → once.
   Notice that the entry is completed and the highlight moves to cell D3. You can always use the arrow keys to complete an entry and move the highlight in the desired direction.

8. Type **Thursday** in cell D3 and tap →.
   Notice that the display of Wednesday *is shortened, or truncated. However, the Wednesday entry is still contained in its entirety in cell C3. A long entry is always truncated when the cell to the right contains text or a number.*

9. Enter the remaining text entries shown in the following illustration:

	A	B	C	D	E	F	G
1	Hospital Volunteers-Hours Worked						
2							
3			Wednesd:	Thursday	Friday	Saturday	Sunday
4	Gift Shop						
5		Evelyn					
6		Gene					
7		Karel					
8		Bill					
9		Total					
10	Candy Stripers						
11		Ginny					
12		Karel					
13		Ann					
14		Total					
15	Bookmobile						
16		Mohamed					
17		Leticia					
18		Maria					
19		Total					

If Excel proposes any entries for you as you type, simply continue typing. You will learn more about the AutoFill feature in Lesson 8, Editing, Viewing, and Printing Worksheets.

Working with Numbers

Number entries can contain only the digits 0–9 and a few other characters. Excel initially right-aligns numbers in cells, although you can change this alignment. The following table lists characters that Excel accepts as part of a number entry.

 TIP! *Entering numbers using the numeric keypad is very quick. The keypad is designed like a calculator. It includes its own decimal point and an Enter key.*

Valid Characters in Number Entries

The digits 0–9

The following characters: + – ( ) , / $ % . *

Number Formats

It isn't necessary to type commas, dollar signs, and other number formats when entering numbers. It's easier to simply enter the numbers and use Excel's formatting commands to add the desired number format(s). You will learn how to format numbers soon.

Decimals and Negative Numbers

You should always type a decimal point if the number you are entering requires one. Likewise, you should precede a negative number entry with a minus (–) sign or enclose it in parentheses ( ).

 ## Hands-On 7.5   Enter Numbers

In this exercise, you will practice entering numbers and canceling entries before completion.

Use the Enter Button

1. Position the highlight in cell C5.

2. Type **3** but don't complete the entry.

3. Look at the Formula Bar and notice the Cancel ☒ and Enter ☑ buttons.
   These buttons appear whenever you begin entering or editing data in a cell.

4. Click the Enter ☑ button to complete the entry.
   Notice that the highlight remains in cell C5. You can use the Enter button to complete entries, though it is more efficient to use the keyboard when building a worksheet. This is because the highlight automatically moves to the next cell. The Enter button is most useful when editing entries.

Use the Cancel and the ⌷Esc⌷ Key

5. Position the highlight in cell C6 and type **4**, but don't complete the entry.

6. Click the Cancel ☒ button on the Formula Bar to cancel the entry.

7. Type **4** again, but this time tap ⌷Esc⌷ on the keyboard.
   The ⌷Esc⌷ key has the same effect as the Cancel button.

8. Type **4** once again, and this time tap ⬇ .
   Notice that Excel right-aligns the number in the cell.

9. Enter the remaining numbers shown in the following illustration.

 TIP! *To use the numeric keypad to enter numbers, the* [Num Lock] *light must be on. If it's not, press the* [Num Lock] *key on the keypad.*

	A	B	C	D	E	F	G
1	Hospital Volunteers-Hours Worked						
2							
3			Wednesd:	Thursday	Friday	Saturday	Sunday
4	Gift Shop						
5		Evelyn	3	2	4	0	6
6		Gene	4	2	1	7	3
7		Karel	6	1	2	3	3
8		Bill	3	5	2	2	3
9		Total					
10	Candy Stripers						
11		Ginny	7	0	2	1	4
12		Karel	2	4	1	3	2
13		Ann	4	1	5	2	0
14		Total					
15	Bookmobile						
16		Mohamed	3	6	0	3	2
17		Leticia	1	7	2	2	3
18		Maria	5	2	4	2	0
19		Total					

10. Take a minute to verify that you have correctly entered all the numbers.
    It is so important for you to be accurate when you are entering data into Excel. Learning how to use complex formulas and functions will not do you any good if your original data is inaccurate!

Understanding Save Concepts

One important lesson to learn is to save your workbooks early and often! Power outages and careless accidents can result in lost data. The best protection is to save your workbooks every 10 or 15 minutes or after making significant changes. Workbooks are saved to storage locations such as a USB drive, the My Documents folder, a shared network drive, and websites on the Internet.

The Save Command

The Save button on the Quick Access toolbar and →Save initiate the Save command. If a document has been saved previously, Excel replaces the original version with the new, edited version. If a document has never been saved, Excel displays the Save As dialog box. The Save As dialog box lets you specify the name and storage location of the document. You can also use the Save As dialog box to make a copy of a document by saving it under a new name or to a different location. Your filenames can have up to 255 characters, including spaces, giving you the flexibility to create descriptive names for your workbooks.

Save As Options

2007 new!

In Excel 2007, you are given multiple options as to how to save your workbook. How you save it depends on how it will be used and who will be using it. If you are collaborating with someone who has a previous version of Excel installed on his computer, you will need to save the file in the Excel 97-2003 Format. If you wish to publish your workbook and do not wish for others to make changes to it, you may wish to save it as a PDF file if you have Adobe Acrobat's program. The default format is the Excel 2007 format, which is great to use if everyone who will be utilizing the file has Excel 2007 installed on his computer.

If you click the Save As button, the Save As dialog box will be displayed.

If you place your mouse pointer over this menu button, you will see the menu displayed here that gives you additional options for saving your workbook.

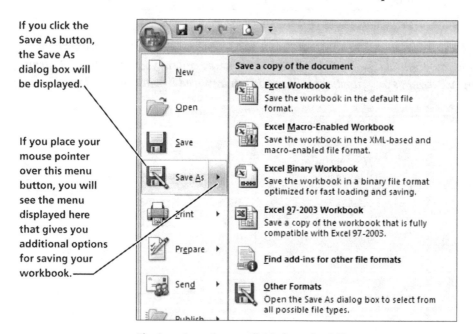

The Save As options available from the Office menu.

Locating Workbooks

Both the Save As and Open dialog boxes (discussed in Lesson 8, Editing, Viewing, and Printing Worksheets) let you locate workbooks on your local drives, in network locations, and on the web. The Places Bar appears on the left side of the Save As and Open dialog boxes. You can use the Places Bar or the Save In list to locate workbooks, as described in the following illustration.

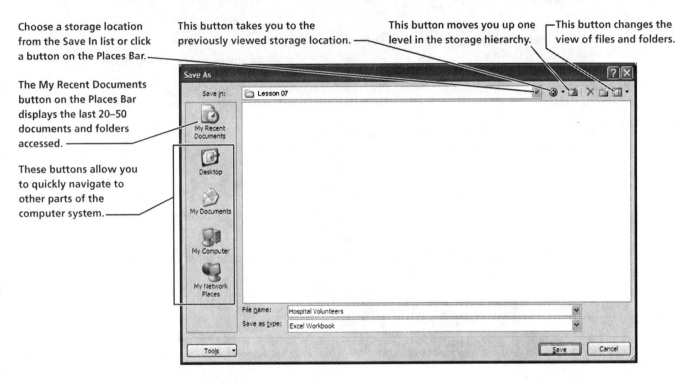

Choose a storage location from the Save In list or click a button on the Places Bar.

This button takes you to the previously viewed storage location.

This button moves you up one level in the storage hierarchy.

This button changes the view of files and folders.

The My Recent Documents button on the Places Bar displays the last 20–50 documents and folders accessed.

These buttons allow you to quickly navigate to other parts of the computer system.

Issuing Commands from the Keyboard

There are many times when it is more convenient to issue a command from the keyboard than to chase it down with your mouse. These commands are termed keyboard shortcuts and can help you to be more efficient as you can enter them "on the fly" without removing your fingers from the keyboard. In this book, you will see keyboard shortcuts displayed in a special feature called From the Keyboard. Whenever you issue a keyboard command, you will first hold down the shortcut key ([Ctrl], [Alt], or [Shift]) and then tap the additional key to issue the command. This is similar to holding down the [Shift] key and then tapping a letter to make it capital. Throughout this book you will be asked to use [Ctrl]+[S] to save your worksheet.

FROM THE KEYBOARD

[Ctrl]+[S] to save

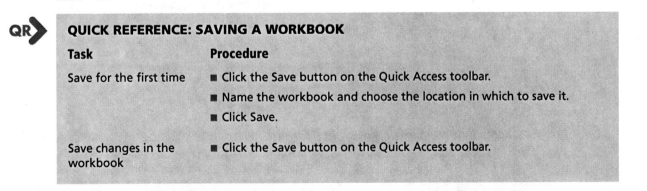

QR **QUICK REFERENCE: SAVING A WORKBOOK**

Task	Procedure
Save for the first time	■ Click the Save button on the Quick Access toolbar.
	■ Name the workbook and choose the location in which to save it.
	■ Click Save.
Save changes in the workbook	■ Click the Save button on the Quick Access toolbar.

QUICK REFERENCE: SAVING A WORKBOOK (CONTINUED)

Task	Procedure
Save in a new location or with a new name	■ Click the Office button and choose Save As.
	■ Change the name of the workbook, the storage location, or both.
	■ Click Save.
Save the workbook in the Excel 97-2003 Format	■ Click the Office button.
	■ Place your mouse pointer over the arrow to the right of Save As.
	■ Click Excel 97-2003 Format in the resulting menu displayed to the right.

 Hands-On 7.6   Save the Workbook

In this exercise, you will save the workbook created in the previous exercises to your file storage location.

1. Click the Save 📄 button on the Quick Access toolbar.
   The Save As dialog box appears because this is the first time you are saving the workbook.

2. Follow these steps to save the workbook:
   Keep in mind that your My Documents folder or other storage location may contain different folders and files than those displayed here.

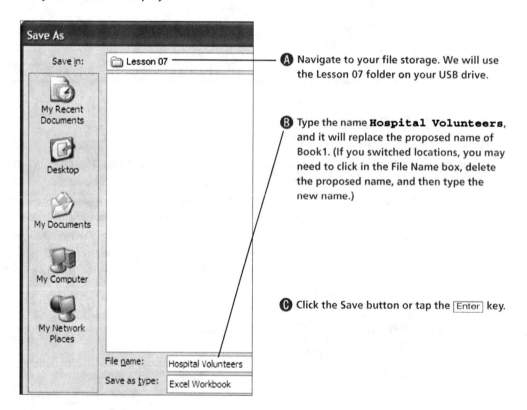

Ⓐ Navigate to your file storage. We will use the Lesson 07 folder on your USB drive.

Ⓑ Type the name **Hospital Volunteers**, and it will replace the proposed name of Book1. (If you switched locations, you may need to click in the File Name box, delete the proposed name, and then type the new name.)

Ⓒ Click the Save button or tap the Enter key.

Notice that the workbook is saved (the name will appear in the Title Bar of the window) and remains on the screen. Leave it open as we will continue to use it for the remaining exercises.

Closing Workbooks

The →Close command is used to close an open workbook. When you close a workbook that has not been saved, Excel prompts you to save the changes. If you choose Yes at the prompt and the workbook has previously been saved, Excel simply saves the changes. If the workbook is new, Excel displays the Save As dialog box, allowing you to assign a name and storage location to the workbook.

 Hands-On 7.7   **Close the Workbook**

In this exercise, you will close the workbook that you have been working on throughout this lesson.

1. Choose →Close.

2. Click the Yes button if Excel asks you if you want to save the changes.
   Notice that no workbook appears in the Excel window. The Excel window always has this appearance when all workbooks have been closed.

Exiting from Excel

You should close Excel and other programs if you are certain you won't be using them for some time. This will free up memory for other programs. When you close Excel, you will be prompted to save any workbooks that have unsaved edits.

- Click the Office button , and then click ✕ Exit Excel to exit the program.
- Clicking the Close button ✕ will close only your current Excel 2007 workbook; any other Excel workbooks that are being used will remain open until you close them.

 Hands-On 7.8   **Exit from Excel**

In this exercise, you will exit from the Excel program.

1. Click the Office button , and then click the ✕ Exit Excel button.
   Excel will close without prompting you to save the workbook because you have not changed it since it was opened last.

Concepts Review

True/False Questions

1. Each workbook can have a maximum of one worksheet.   TRUE   FALSE

2. A worksheet is composed of horizontal rows and vertical columns.   TRUE   FALSE

3. You cannot customize the commands on the Ribbon.   TRUE   FALSE

4. Text entries can contain spaces.   TRUE   FALSE

5. Number entries can contain only the digits 0–9. No other characters are permitted.   TRUE   FALSE

6. A filename can contain spaces.   TRUE   FALSE

7. Text entries can be used in calculations.   TRUE   FALSE

8. The Save As command allows you to save your workbook with a different name.   TRUE   FALSE

9. You should wait to save your workbook until you are done entering all of your data.   TRUE   FALSE

10. When you click the Close button of the workbook you are working on, it will close all open Excel workbooks.   TRUE   FALSE

Multiple Choice Questions

1. Which of the following keystrokes moves the highlight to cell A1?
   a. `End`
   b. `Ctrl` + `Tab`
   c. `Ctrl` + `Home`
   d. `Ctrl` + `Insert`

2. What happens when you insert an entry in the cell to the right of a long text entry?
   a. The display of the long entry is truncated.
   b. The long entry is replaced by the entry in the cell to the right.
   c. It has no effect on the long entry.
   d. None of the above

3. How do you hide the Ribbon?
   a. Choose Home→Hide from the Ribbon
   b. Choose Office button→Hide Ribbon
   c. Double-click the tab that is displayed
   d. Double-click one of the sheet tabs of the workbook

4. What occurs when you tap `Esc` while entering data into a cell?
   a. The workbook will close.
   b. The entry will be entered and the cell to the right will become active.
   c. Nothing, you can continue entering the data into the cell.
   d. The cell entry will be canceled.

Skill Builders

Skill Builder 7.1   Create a Workbook

In this exercise, you will create a workbook. You will start Excel and then enter text and numbers that contain two decimal places.

Start Excel and Enter Text

1. Start Excel by selecting (All) Programs→Microsoft Office→Microsoft Office Excel 2007 from the Start menu.
   Notice that a blank workbook with three worksheets is displayed when you open Excel.

2. Enter text in rows 1 and 3 as shown in the following illustration.
   Try using the Tab *key to enter the data in row 3.*

	A	B	C	D	E	F	G	H
1	Order Tracking Sheet							
2								
3	Order #	Cust ID	Ord Stat	Item #	In Stock?	Ord Tot	Shipping Address	

3. In cells A4:E8 and G4:G8, enter the data shown in the following illustration.
   Make sure to type the entire shipping address in column G.

	A	B	C	D	E	F	G	H	I	J	K
1	Order Tracking Sheet										
2											
3	Order #	Cust ID	Ord Stat	Item #	In Stock?	Ord Tot	Shipping Address				
4	1	341	S	A423	Y		1603 Catalina Avenue, Redondo Beach, CA 90277				
5	2	234	S	A321	Y		Will Pick Up				
6	3	567	I	S345	N		450 Terrace Drive, Santa Clara, CA 95050				
7	4	879	H	D567	N		No address at this point				
8	5	233	I	B444	Y		23 Maple Lane, Crawfordsville, IN 47933				

Enter Numbers with Decimals

4. Click cell F4.

5. Type **100.91** and tap ⎵Enter⎵.
   You should always type a decimal point if the number requires one.

6. Type **45.87** and tap ⎵Enter⎵.

7. Enter the numbers shown in the following illustration into cells F6, F7, and F8.

	A	B	C	D	E	F	G	H	I	J	K
1	Order Tracking Sheet										
2											
3	Order #	Cust ID	Ord Stat	Item #	In Stock?	Ord Tot	Shipping Address				
4	1	341	S	A423	Y	100.91	1603 Catalina Avenue, Redondo Beach, CA 90277				
5	2	234	S	A321	Y	45.87	Will Pick Up				
6		567	I	S345	N	43.23	450 Terrace Drive, Santa Clara, CA 95050				
7		879	H	D567	N	78.92	No address at this point				
8		233	I	B444	Y	23.45	23 Maple Lane, Crawfordsville, IN 47933				

Leave the workbook open, as you will use it in the next exercise.

Skill Builder 7.2   Explore the Excel Window and Save and Close Your Workbook

In this exercise, you will take a look at the features of the Excel window before saving and closing your new workbook.

1. Click to display the data tab of the Ribbon.
   Look at the types of commands available. Many of them will be covered in later lessons of this book.

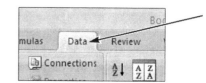

2. Click to display the View tab of the Ribbon.

3. Double-click the View tab to hide the Ribbon.

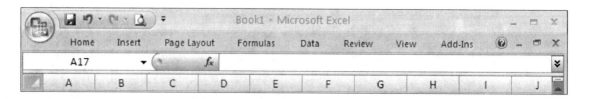

4. Double-click the Home tab to display the Ribbon once again.
   Notice that the Home tab will be displayed because you chose it to redisplay the Ribbon.

5. Click cell H4, and then look at the Formula Bar.

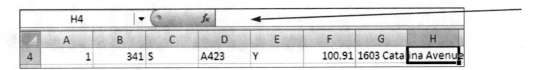

There is nothing displayed because the entire entry is contained in cell G4 and is simply spilling over into cell H4 because it is empty.

6. Type your name, and then click the Enter ☑ button.

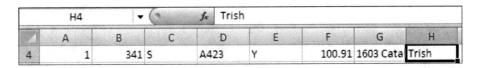

Your name will now appear in cell H4, and the address in cell G4 will be truncated.

7. Tap ⌈Delete⌉.
   Your name will be deleted, and the address from G4 will once again spill over into the cells to the right.

8. Click Save 🖫 on the Quick Access toolbar.

9. Choose to save the workbook in your file storage location (in this example, Lesson 07).

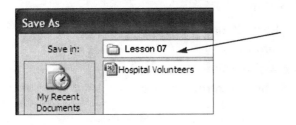

10. Type **sb-Order Tracking**, and tap ⌈Enter⌉.
    The workbook will be saved in the location that you specified.

11. Click the Close ⌈×⌉ button at the top right of the Excel window.
    Your workbook will close. If you have any other workbooks open, they will remain so until you choose to exit from Excel or close them individually.

LESSON 8

Editing, Viewing, and Printing Worksheets

In this lesson, you will expand on the basic skills you learned in Lesson 7. You will learn various methods of editing worksheets: replacing and deleting entries, using Undo and Redo, working with AutoCorrect, and more. You will also learn about printing Excel worksheets and working with different views. When you have finished this lesson, you will have developed the skills necessary to produce carefully edited and proofed worksheets.

LESSON OBJECTIVES

After studying this lesson, you will be able to:

- Open and edit a workbook file
- Use a variety of techniques to select cells and ranges
- Move and copy cell entries
- Undo and redo commands
- Clear cell contents, including formatting
- Use AutoFill and AutoComplete
- Work with various Excel views and the zoom feature
- Preview your worksheet before printing
- Print your worksheet, including printing specific sections of your worksheet

Case Study: Creating a Basic List in Excel

Ken Hazell is the owner of Carmel Automotive Repair. He realizes that Excel would be the best tool to keep track of his employees' personal data. Excel can be used as a simple database to keep track of lists of employees, inventory, or other items. You will learn more about Excel's database features in *Microsoft Excel 2007: Comprehensive*. Microsoft Excel is an important tool for any entrepreneur in today's highly competitive business world.

	A	B	C	D	E
1	Carmel Automotive Repair				
2	Employee Roster				
3					
4	Name	Phone	Position	Employment Date	Lock-up Day
5	Ken Hazell	619-555-3224	Owner		
6	Christina Chu	858-555-3098	Front Office	5/25/2004	Monday
7	Isabella Soprano-Birdsell	619-555-3309	Front Office	3/28/2003	Tuesday
8	Derek Navarro	951-555-0826	Front Office	8/3/2005	Wednesday
9	Jason Rogers	858-555-4987	Front Office	1/5/1999	Thursday
10	Matt Bernardo	858-555-0211	Front Office	4/13/2001	Friday
11	Meredith Baxter	858-555-1002	Mechanic	5/10/2003	
12	George Springhurst	858-555-0021	Mechanic	10/30/2002	
13	Preston Washington	760-555-3876	Mechanic	12/24/2003	
14	Steve Porter	619-555-4016	Mechanic	4/23/2002	
15	David Scott	760-555-0728	Mechanic	7/29/2000	
16	Charlie Simpson	858-555-3718	Mechanic	5/15/2007	
17	Leisa Malimali	619-555-4017	Manager	5/15/2007	

Ken will use this spreadsheet to organize his employees' phone numbers, dates of employment, and the day that each front office worker is responsible for locking up the shop.

Opening Workbooks

FROM THE KEYBOARD
Ctrl + O to open

The Office button →Open command displays the Open dialog box. The Open dialog box lets you navigate to any storage location and open previously saved workbooks. Once a workbook is open, you can browse it, print it, and make editing changes. The organization and layout of the Open dialog box are similar to those of the Save As dialog box.

Hands-On 8.1 Open the Workbook

In this exercise, you will open a workbook that lists the employees of Carmel Automotive Repair.

1. Start Excel.

2. Click the Office [■] button, and then choose the Open command.
   The Open dialog box is displayed.

!NOTE! *In future lessons this command will be written, Choose Office→Open.*

3. Follow these steps to open the CAR Employee Roster workbook:
   Keep in mind that your storage location (such as a USB drive) may contain different folders and files than those displayed here.

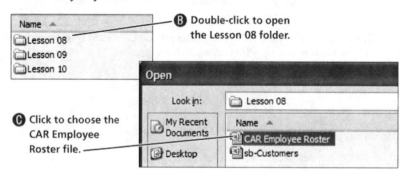

Ⓐ Navigate to your file storage location. This will likely be your USB flash drive.

Ⓑ Double-click to open the Lesson 08 folder.

Ⓒ Click to choose the CAR Employee Roster file.

Ⓓ Click the Open button.

!TIP! *You can also double-click a document in the Open dialog box to open it.*

Editing Entries

You can edit the active cell by clicking in the Formula Bar and making the desired changes. You can also double-click a cell and edit the contents directly there. This technique is known as in-cell editing.

Replacing Entries

Editing an entry is efficient if the entry is so long that retyping it would be time-consuming. Editing can also be helpful when working with complex formulas and other functions that are difficult to re-create. If the entry requires little typing, however, it is usually easier to simply retype it. If you retype an entry, the new entry will be replace whatever is contained in the cell.

Deleting Characters

Use the ⌈Delete⌉ and ⌈Backspace⌉ keys to edit entries in the Formula Bar and within a cell. The ⌈Delete⌉ key removes the character to the right of the insertion point, while the ⌈Backspace⌉ key removes the character to the left of the insertion point.

A ←┊→ B

Tapping ⌈Backspace⌉ will remove the "A".

This is the "flashing" insertion

Tapping ⌈Delete⌉ will remove the "B".

 Hands-On 8.2   Edit Entries

In this exercise, you will use the Formula Bar to revise the contents of cell A2. You will also edit cells B3 and B15 directly in the cells.

Edit in the Formula Bar

1. Click cell A2 to select it.

2. Follow these steps to edit cell A2 using the Formula Bar:

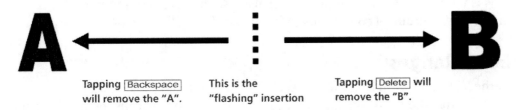

Ⓐ Click in the Formula Bar just to the right of the word *List*.

Ⓑ Tap ⌈Backspace⌉ four times to remove the word *List*, and then type **Roster**.

Ⓒ Click the Enter button.

Replace an Entry

3. Click cell D4.

4. Type **Employment Date** and tap ⌈Enter⌉.
   The entry Employment Date *replaces the entry* Starting Date. *Notice that the cell formatting (underlining the word) applied to the new entry as well. Also note that the new entry is cut off or truncated (as you learned about in the previous lesson) since the cell to the right contains an entry.*

Use In-Cell Editing

5. Double-click cell A7 (the cell with the name Isabella Soprano).

6. Use the mouse or the ➡ key to position the flashing insertion point to the right of the last name, Soprano.

7. Type **–Birdsell**, and then tap ⌈Enter⌋ to complete the change.
   The entry should now read Isabella Soprano-Birdsell.

8. Click the Save 🖫 button to update the changes.
   Clicking the Save button automatically saves changes to a workbook that has previously been saved.

Selecting Cells and Ranges

FROM THE KEYBOARD
⌈Ctrl⌋+⌈A⌋ to select all
⌈Ctrl⌋+⌈Spacebar⌋ to select a column
⌈Shift⌋+⌈Spacebar⌋ to select a row

When you want to change something in a worksheet—for instance, move, copy, delete, format, or print specific data—you must first select the cell(s). The most efficient way to select cells is with the mouse, though you can also use the keyboard method. You can select one or many cells. A group of contiguous (adjacent) cells is called a range.

Excel Ranges

In the last lesson, you learned that each cell has a reference. For example, A1 refers to the first cell in a worksheet. Likewise, a range reference specifies the cells included within a range. The range reference includes the first and last cells in the range separated by a colon (:). For example, the range A4:E4 includes all cells between A4 and E4 inclusive. The following illustration highlights several ranges and their corresponding range references.

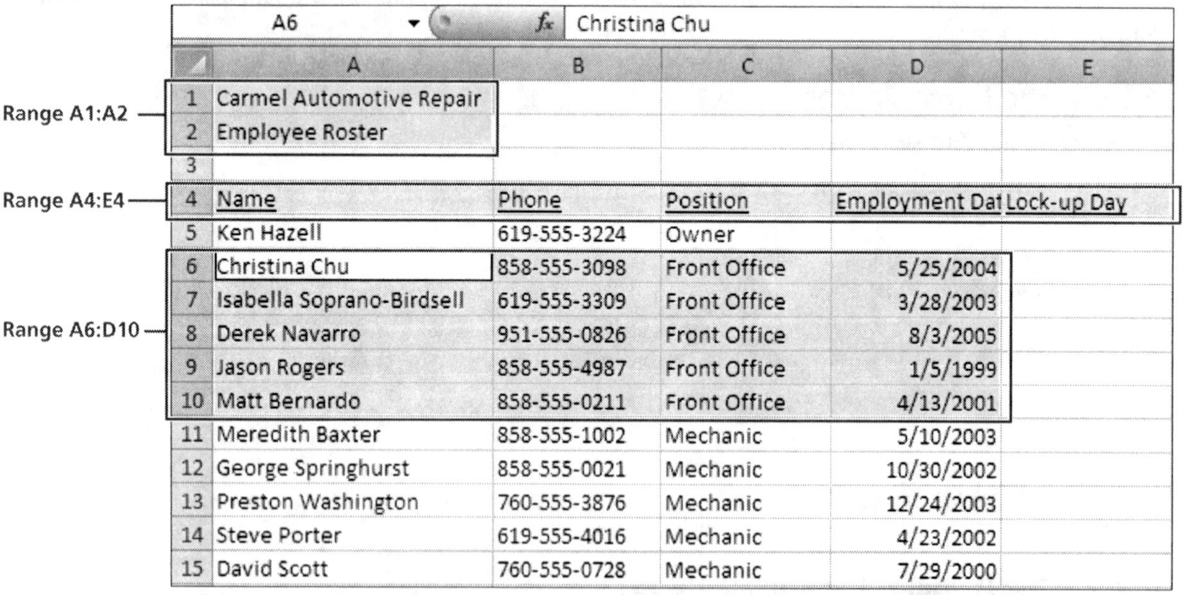

	A6	▼	*fx*	Christina Chu	

	A	B	C	D	E
1	Carmel Automotive Repair				
2	Employee Roster				
3					
4	Name	Phone	Position	Employment Dat	Lock-up Day
5	Ken Hazell	619-555-3224	Owner		
6	Christina Chu	858-555-3098	Front Office	5/25/2004	
7	Isabella Soprano-Birdsell	619-555-3309	Front Office	3/28/2003	
8	Derek Navarro	951-555-0826	Front Office	8/3/2005	
9	Jason Rogers	858-555-4987	Front Office	1/5/1999	
10	Matt Bernardo	858-555-0211	Front Office	4/13/2001	
11	Meredith Baxter	858-555-1002	Mechanic	5/10/2003	
12	George Springhurst	858-555-0021	Mechanic	10/30/2002	
13	Preston Washington	760-555-3876	Mechanic	12/24/2003	
14	Steve Porter	619-555-4016	Mechanic	4/23/2002	
15	David Scott	760-555-0728	Mechanic	7/29/2000	

Range A1:A2 — (rows 1–2, column A)
Range A4:E4 — (row 4)
Range A6:D10 — (rows 6–10, columns A–D)

The selected ranges in the worksheet are shaded, as displayed above. In addition, the first cell in the last range selected, A6, shows no shading and has an outline around it. This indicates that it is the active cell, which is displayed in the Name box and Formula Bar.

The following Quick Reference table describes selection techniques in Excel.

 Hands-On 8.3   Practice Making Selections

In this exercise, you will practice selecting multiple ranges and entire rows and columns using the mouse. You will also use the [Shift] and [Ctrl] keys to practice selecting cell ranges.

Click and Drag to Select a Range

1. Position the mouse pointer ✛ over cell A4.

2. Press and hold down the left mouse button while dragging the mouse to the right until the range A4:E4 is selected, and then release the mouse button.
   Notice that for each range that is selected, the corresponding row and column headers are displayed in orange.

3. Click once anywhere in the worksheet to deselect the cells.

Select Multiple Ranges

4. Follow these steps to select two ranges:

A Select the range A4:E4 as you did in steps 1 and 2 above.

B Press and hold down the [Ctrl] key while dragging to select the range A6:D10.

C Release the [Ctrl] key after the second range is selected.

Both the A4:E4 and A6:D10 ranges are selected now. The [Ctrl] key lets you select more than one range at the same time.

5. Press and hold down the [Ctrl] key while you select another range, and then release the [Ctrl] key.
   You should now have three ranges selected.

6. Make sure you have released the [Ctrl] key, and then click once anywhere on the worksheet to deselect the ranges.
   The highlighting of the previous selections disappears.

Select Entire Rows and Columns

7. Follow these steps to select various rows and columns:

A Click the column A heading to select the entire column.

B Position the mouse pointer on the column C heading and drag to the right until columns C, D, and E are selected.

	A	B	C	D	E
1	Carmel Automotive Repair				
2	Employee Roster				
3					
4	Name	Phone	Position	Employment Dat	Lock-up Day
5	Ken Hazell	619-555-3224	Owner		
6	Christina Chu	858-555-3098	Front Office	5/25/2004	
7	Isabella Soprano-Birdsell	619-555-3309	Front Office	3/28/2003	
8	Derek Navarro	951-555-0826	Front Office	8/3/2005	

Column A will be deselected since you were not holding down the Ctrl *key.*

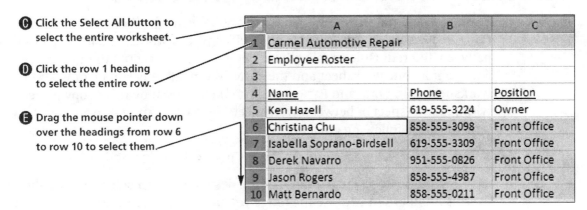

● Click the Select All button to select the entire worksheet.

● Click the row 1 heading to select the entire row.

● Drag the mouse pointer down over the headings from row 6 to row 10 to select them.

	A	B	C
1	Carmel Automotive Repair		
2	Employee Roster		
3			
4	Name	Phone	Position
5	Ken Hazell	619-555-3224	Owner
6	Christina Chu	858-555-3098	Front Office
7	Isabella Soprano-Birdsell	619-555-3309	Front Office
8	Derek Navarro	951-555-0826	Front Office
9	Jason Rogers	858-555-4987	Front Office
10	Matt Bernardo	858-555-0211	Front Office

Use Keyboard Techniques

8. Follow these steps to use keyboard techniques to select cells:

● Click cell A4.

	A	B	C	D	E
4	Name	Phone	Position	Employment Dat	Lock-up Day
5	Ken Hazell	619-555-3224	Owner		
6	Christina Chu	858-555-3098	Front Office	5/25/2004	
7	Isabella Soprano-Birdsell	619-555-3309	Front Office	3/28/2003	
8	Derek Navarro	951-555-0826	Front Office	8/3/2005	
9	Jason Rogers	858-555-4987	Front Office	1/5/1999	
10	Matt Bernardo	858-555-0211	Front Office	4/13/2001	
11	Meredith Baxter	858-555-1002	Mechanic	5/10/2003	
12	George Springhurst	858-555-0021	Mechanic	10/30/2002	
13	Preston Washington	760-555-3876	Mechanic	12/24/2003	
14	Steve Porter	619-555-4016	Mechanic	4/23/2002	
15	David Scott	760-555-0728	Mechanic	7/29/2000	

● Press and hold down the Shift key and click cell E15 to select the range A4:E15.

● Click cell A11.

	A	B	C	D
11	Meredith Baxter	858-555-1002	Mechanic	5/10/2003
12	George Springhurst	858-555-0021	Mechanic	10/30/2002
13	Preston Washington	760-555-3876	Mechanic	12/24/2003
14	Steve Porter	619-555-4016	Mechanic	4/23/2002
15	David Scott	760-555-0728	Mechanic	7/29/2000

● Press and hold down the Shift key, and then tap → three times and ↓ four times.

The range A11:D15 is selected. Notice that the Shift *key techniques give you precise control when selecting. You should use the* Shift *key techniques if you find selecting with the mouse difficult or if you have a large range to select that is not entirely visible on your screen.*

9. Take a few moments to practice selection techniques. See if you can select any portion of a worksheet you wish.

Working with Cut, Copy, and Paste

FROM THE KEYBOARD
Ctrl + C to copy
Ctrl + X to cut
Ctrl + V to paste

The Cut, Copy, and Paste commands are available in all Office 2007 applications. With Cut, Copy, and Paste, you can move or copy cells within a worksheet, between worksheets, or between different Office applications. For example, you could use the Copy command to copy a range from one worksheet and the Paste command to paste the range into another worksheet. Cut, Copy, and Paste are most efficient for moving or copying cells a long distance within a worksheet or between worksheets. Cut, Copy, and Paste are easy to use if you remember the following guidelines:

- You must select cells before issuing a Cut or Copy command.

- You must position the highlight at the desired location before issuing the Paste command. This is important because the range you paste will overwrite any cells in the paste area.

You can also right-click on a cell or range of cells in order to get a shortcut menu specific to the selection. The Cut, Copy, and Paste commands are available on this menu as well. There are many ways to issue commands; your job is to simply figure out which method works best for you!

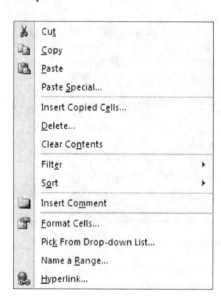

When you right-click a cell or range of cells, a shortcut menu appears that provides options specific to the selection. Notice that you can choose to Cut, Copy, and Paste from this menu.

The Office Clipboard

The Office Clipboard lets you collect items from any Office worksheet or program and paste them into any other Office document. For example, you can collect a paragraph from a Word document, data from an Excel worksheet, and a graphic from a PowerPoint slide and then paste them all into a new Word document. The Office Clipboard can also be used within a single application like Excel to collect several items and then paste them as desired. The Office Clipboard can hold up to 24 items.

How It Works

You can place items on the Office Clipboard using the standard Cut and Copy commands; however, the Office Clipboard task pane must first be displayed. It is displayed by clicking the Launcher button in the Clipboard area of the Home Ribbon.

Moving Cells via Drag and Drop

Drag and Drop produces the same results as Cut, Copy, and Paste. However, Drag and Drop is usually more efficient if you are moving or copying entries a short distance within the same worksheet. If the original location and new destination are both visible in the current window, then it is usually easier to use Drag and Drop. With Drag and Drop, you select the cells you wish to move or copy, and then you point to the edge of the selected range and drag the range to the desired destination. If you press the Ctrl key while dragging the selected area, the cells are copied to the destination. Drag and Drop does not place items on the Office Clipboard, however, so you will want to use either the Cut or the Copy command if you wish to work with the Clipboard.

Editing Cells via Right-Dragging

Right-dragging is a variation of the Drag and Drop technique. Many beginners find Drag and Drop difficult to use because they have difficulty controlling the mouse. This difficulty is compounded if they are trying to copy entries using Drag and Drop. This is because copying requires the Ctrl key to be held while the selected range is dragged. With the right-drag method, the right mouse button is used when dragging. When the right mouse button is released at the destination, a pop-up menu appears. The pop-up menu gives you several options including Move, Copy, and Cancel. This provides more control because there is no need to use the Ctrl key when copying, and you have the option of canceling the move or copy.

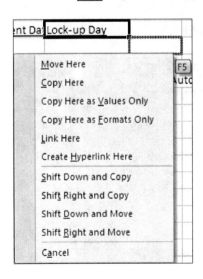

When you right-drag and drop, you will receive a pop-up menu at the destination so that you can choose whether to move or copy the data. Many of the rest of the options displayed will be covered in subsequent lessons.

QUICK REFERENCE: CUTTING, COPYING, AND PASTING

Command	Discussion	Procedure
Cut	The Cut command removes entries from selected cells and places them on the Office Clipboard.	■ Select what you wish to move or copy. ■ Click the Cut ✂ button, or press Ctrl + X.
Copy	The Copy command also places entries on the Office Clipboard, but it leaves a copy of the entries in the original cells.	■ Select what you wish to move or copy. ■ Click the Copy 📋 button, or press Ctrl + C.
Paste	The Paste command pastes entries from the Office Clipboard to worksheet cells beginning at the highlight location.	■ Click once where you wish the clipboard contents to be pasted. ■ Click the Paste 📋 button, or press Ctrl + V.

 ## Hands-On 8.4   Move and Copy Selections

In this exercise, you will have the opportunity to use the Cut, Copy, and Paste commands as well as drag and drop to move and copy selections.

Copy and Paste

1. Click cell A1 to select it.

2. Make sure the Home tab is displayed, locate the Clipboard command group, and then click the Copy 📋 button on the Ribbon.
   A "marquee" will dance around the selection that you have copied and placed on the clipboard.

3. Click cell C2.

4. Choose Home→Clipboard→Paste 📋 from the Ribbon to paste the selection in cell C2.

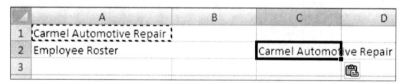

The contents of cell A1 will remain there as well as appear in cell C2 when you choose to copy the selection. Notice the dashed lines around the cell that is being copied and the Paste Options button that appears to the bottom right of the cell in which the selection was pasted.

Cut and Paste

5. Right-click cell C2.
   When you right-click a cell, a shortcut menu appears with options specific to the cell, as well as the Mini Toolbar.

6. Choose Cut from the shortcut menu.

7. Right-click cell E2 and choose Paste from the shortcut menu.

C	D	E	F
		Carmel Automotive Repair	

Cell C2 will now be empty since the contents were moved to cell E2.

Drag and Drop

8. Follow these steps to move the contents of cell E2 via drag and drop:

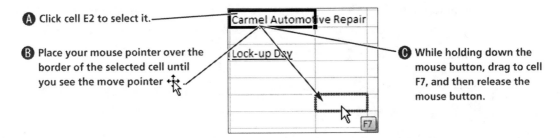

Ⓐ Click cell E2 to select it.

Ⓑ Place your mouse pointer over the border of the selected cell until you see the move pointer ✛

Ⓒ While holding down the mouse button, drag to cell F7, and then release the mouse button.

When you drag a cell with this method, Excel shows what cell the selection will be dropped into by displaying it on a ScreenTip as well as placing a highlight around the cell.

Right-Drag a Selection

9. Select cell E4, and then place your mouse pointer over the border of the selected cell until you see the move pointer as shown at right. ✛

10. Start dragging with the right (not the left) mouse button. Keep the right mouse button held down until told to release it in the next step.

11. Drag down to cell F5, and then release the right mouse button.
    A pop-up menu appears, listing your choices for the right-drag.

12. Choose Copy Here from the pop-up menu.
    The contents of cell E4 remain in the cell and are copied to the destination cell, F5.

Using Undo and Redo

Excel's Undo button lets you reverse actions that have occurred in Excel. You can reverse simple actions such as accidentally deleting a cell's content or more complex actions such as deleting an entire row. Most actions can be undone, but those that cannot include printing and saving workbooks. The Undo command can become your best friend when you have to undo an action that you are not sure how you issued. Don't you wish life had an undo button at times!

The Redo button reverses an Undo command. Use Redo when you undo an action but then decide to go through with that action after all. The Redo button will be visible on the Quick Access toolbar only after you have undone an action.

Undoing Multiple Actions

FROM THE KEYBOARD
Ctrl+Z to undo
Ctrl+Y to redo

Clicking the arrow ▾ on the Undo button displays a list of actions that can be undone. You can undo multiple actions by dragging the mouse over the desired actions. However, you must undo actions in the order in which they appear on the drop-down list.

When you click the arrow on the Undo button, you will see a list of previous commands.

Limitations to "Undoing"

In Excel, there are some times when the Undo command will not work. If you click the Office button and choose any command, it cannot be undone (such as saving a workbook). When an action cannot be undone, Excel will change the Undo ScreenTip to "Can't Undo."

QR▶

QUICK REFERENCE: UNDOING AND REDOING ACTIONS	
Task	**Procedure**
Undo the last command	▪ Click the Undo 🔄 button on the Quick Access toolbar or tap Ctrl+Z.
Undo a series of commands	▪ Click the drop-down arrow 🔄 ▾ on the Undo button to display a list of previous commands.
	▪ Choose the last command that you wish to have undone.
Redo an undone command	▪ Click the Redo 🔄 button on the Quick Access toolbar.

In this exercise, you will delete the contents of a cell and then use Undo to reverse the deletion. When you do, the original data will display in the cell again. You will also use Redo to reverse an Undo command.

Delete the Entry and Use Undo and Redo

1. Click the column A heading to select the entire column.

2. Tap [Delete].
   All of the contents in column A have been deleted! There are many times that you will use Undo in order to reverse an action you did not wish to make.

3. Click Undo 🔄 to restore the entry.

4. Follow these steps to undo the last four commands from the previous section:

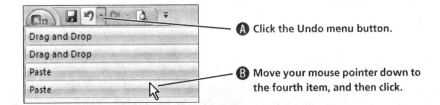

   A Click the Undo menu button.

   B Move your mouse pointer down to the fourth item, and then click.

   Excel undoes your last four commands.

5. Click the Redo 🔄 button four times to restore the four actions that you "undid."

6. Use [Ctrl]+[S] to save the changes, but don't close the workbook.
   Remember, as you learned in the last lesson, you must hold down the [Ctrl] key first and then tap the [S] to issue the Save command.

Clearing Cell Contents and Formats

FROM THE KEYBOARD
[Delete] to clear cell contents

In Excel, you can format cell content by changing the font style, size, and color. You can also add enhancements such as bold, italics, and underline. Cells with numeric data can be formatted as currency, dates, times, percents, and more. In Lesson 10, Formatting Worksheets and Charting Basics you will learn how to format cells.

Clicking the Clear 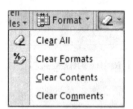 button displays a menu that lets you clear content, formats, and comments from cells. The submenu also contains an All option that clears all of these items from the selected cell(s).

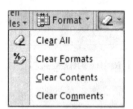

Clicking the Clear button in the Editing section of the Home Ribbon will display a menu that shows all of the options for clearing cell contents.

Excel's Options for Clearing Cells

Contents	Clearing the content has the same effect as tapping the [Delete] key. The cell contents are deleted, but any format applied to the cell remains and will be in effect when new data is entered in the cell.
Formats	The Formats option removes all text and number formats, leaving unformatted entries in the cell(s).
Comments	You can insert comments in cells to document your worksheet. The Comments option also removes comments from the selected cells.
All	This command will clear everything listed above.

One of the most useful functions of Excel's Clear command is removing numeric value formats. This is because once a cell is formatted as a particular numeric format, such as a date or currency, Excel remembers that formatting even if the cell contents are deleted.

QUICK REFERENCE: CLEARING CELL CONTENTS AND FORMATTING

Task	Procedure
Clear the contents of a cell	■ Select the cell or range that you wish to clear. ■ Choose Home→Editing→Clear on the Ribbon. ■ Choose Clear Contents from the resulting menu.
Clear the formatting from a cell	■ Select the cell or range that you wish to clear. ■ Choose Home→Editing→Clear on the Ribbon. ■ Choose Clear Formats from the resulting menu.
Clear contents and formatting from a cell	■ Select the cell or range that you wish to clear. ■ Choose Home→Editing→Clear on the Ribbon. ■ Choose Clear All from the resulting menu.

Hands-On 8.6   Clear Cell Contents and Formatting

In this exercise, you will enter a number formatted as a date and a number formatted as currency. You will also use the Clear command to delete cell contents and cell formats.

1. Click cell F5.

2. Choose Home→Editing→Clear ⟨2·⟩ from the Ribbon, choose Clear Formats, and then tap Enter twice.
   The contents of the cell were underlined, a type of formatting. When you choose to clear only the formats, the contents will remain and only the formatting is removed. Notice that the contents are no longer underlined.

3. Click the Undo ⟨↺⟩ button on the Quick Access toolbar.

4. Ensure that cell F5 is selected, and then click the Clear ⟨2·⟩ button and choose Clear All.

5. Type your name and tap Enter.
   Notice that the contents are no longer underlined in cell F5 since you cleared "all" (formatting and contents) from it.

6. Use Ctrl+Z to undo the typing of your name.

7. Click cell F7 and tap Delete.
   The Delete key functions the same as if you had clicked the Clear button and chosen Clear Contents. Any formatting will remain in the cell.

8. Click the Save ⟨💾⟩ button.

Using Auto Features

Excel offers many "auto" features that help you to work more efficiently. AutoFill allows you to quickly fill a range of cells. AutoComplete makes it easy to enter long entries by typing an acronym or series of characters, which are "converted" to the desired entry. AutoCorrect can also assist in correcting commonly misspelled words.

Working with AutoFill

AutoFill allows you to quickly extend a series, copy data, or copy a formula into adjacent cells by selecting cells and dragging the fill handle. You will learn about using AutoFill to copy formulas in Lesson 9, Working with Formulas and Functions If the selected cell does not contain data that AutoFill recognizes as a series, the data will simply be copied into the adjacent cells. The fill handle is a small black square at the bottom-right corner of the active cell. A black cross appears when you position the mouse pointer on the fill handle. You can drag the fill handle to fill adjacent cells as described below.

■ Copy an entry—If the entry in the active cell is a number, a formula, or a text entry, the fill handle copies the entry to adjacent cells.

- Expand a repeating series of numbers—If you select two or more cells containing numbers, Excel assumes you want to expand a repeating series. For example, if you select two cells containing the numbers 5 and 10 and drag the fill handle, Excel will fill the adjacent cells with the numbers 15, 20, 25, etc.

- AutoFill of date entries—If the active cell contains any type of date entry, Excel will determine the increment of the date value and fill in the adjacent cells. For example, if the current cell contains the entry Q1 and you drag the fill handle, AutoFill will insert the entries Q2, Q3, and Q4 in the adjacent cells.

The following table and illustrations provide examples of series that AutoFill can extend.

Selected Cells	Extended Series
Mon	Tue, Wed, Thu
Monday	Tuesday, Wednesday, Thursday
Jan	Feb, Mar, Apr
January	February, March, April
Jan, Apr	Jul, Oct, Jan
1, 2	3, 4, 5, 6
100, 125	150, 175, 200
1/10/07	1/11/07, 1/12/07, 1/13/07
1/15/07, 2/15/07	3/15/07, 4/15/07, 5/15/07
1st Qtr	2nd Qtr, 3rd Qtr, 4th Qtr

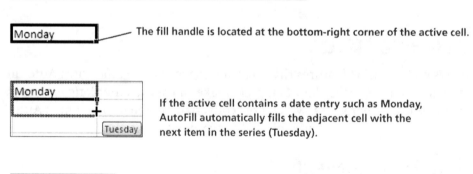

The fill handle is located at the bottom-right corner of the active cell.

If the active cell contains a date entry such as Monday, AutoFill automatically fills the adjacent cell with the next item in the series (Tuesday).

The completed series with the AutoFill Options button displayed

AutoFill Options

The AutoFill Options 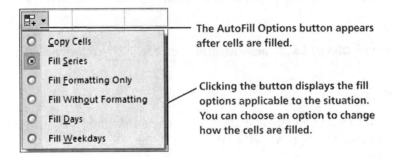 button appears below your filled selection after you fill cells in a worksheet. A menu of fill options appears when you click the button.

The AutoFill Options button appears after cells are filled.

Clicking the button displays the fill options applicable to the situation. You can choose an option to change how the cells are filled.

If you choose to Fill without Formatting, you can fill cells without copying the formatting from the original cell.

AutoComplete vs. AutoFill

The AutoComplete feature is useful when you want the same entry repeated more than once in a column. AutoFill allows you to select a cell and fill in entries either by completing a series or copying the source cell, whereas AutoComplete works within a cell as you type. If the first few characters you type match another entry in the column, then AutoComplete will offer to complete the entry for you. You accept the offer by tapping Enter or reject the offer by typing the remainder of the entry yourself.

| 15 | David Scott | 760-555-0728 | Mechanic |
| 16 | Charlie Simpson | 858-555-3718 | mechanic |

In this situation, an "m" was typed and the AutoComplete feature kicked into gear, suggesting that you may be interested in completing the entry as *Mechanic* since you have already typed that entry earlier in the column. In order to accept *Mechanic* as the entry, you would simply tap Enter.

!TIP! *AutoComplete will complete the entry "case sensitive."*

In this exercise, you will enter two new employees in the worksheet and use AutoComplete to aid in your entries. In addition, you will look at how to use AutoFill to complete a series of the days of the week.

Use AutoComplete

1. Click cell A16 and type **Charlie Simpson**, and then tap Tab to move to the next cell to the right.

2. Type **858-555-3718** and tap Tab .

3. Type **m** and notice that Excel will suggest *Mechanic* as the entry. Tap Tab to accept the suggestion and move to the next cell to the right.
   Notice that the entry will be capitalized just as it is in the cells above.

4. Type today's date, and then type Enter .
   Notice that when you tap Enter , it will take you to cell A17 where you can begin typing the next entry of the list.

5. Type **Leisa Malimali** and tap Tab .

6. Type **619-555-4017** and tap Tab .

7. Type **M** in cell C17.
   Excel will suggest Mechanic *as it did in the previous row. In this case, Leisa is a manager, so you will need to continue typing your entry. Make sure that you have typed in a capital M as it will not pull from the previous entries.*

8. Continue typing **anager** and tap Tab .
   Excel will replace the AutoCorrect suggestion with the entry that you type, Manager.

9. Type today's date and tap Enter .

Use AutoFill to Expand a Series

In this section of the exercise, you will help Ken to fill in the column showing the front office employee responsible for locking up each day.

10. Click cell E6.

11. Type **Monday**, and then click the Enter ✔ button.
    Now that cell E6 contains Monday, Excel will recognize it as the beginning of the series including Tuesday, Wednesday, Thursday, and so forth. E6 will remain the active cell.

12. Follow these steps to fill the adjacent cells:

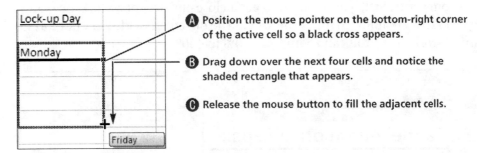

A Position the mouse pointer on the bottom-right corner of the active cell so a black cross appears.

B Drag down over the next four cells and notice the shaded rectangle that appears.

C Release the mouse button to fill the adjacent cells.

Excel recognizes days of the week (Monday), quarters (1st Qtr, Quarter 1, First Quarter), months (January), and other date values as the beginning of a series. You can expand any of these series with the fill handle.

13. Click the AutoFill Options button and note the various fill options.
    If desired, you can choose an option to change how the cells are filled.

14. For now, just tap Esc to dismiss the menu.

Exploring the Many Views of Excel

When you change the view in Excel, it does not change how the worksheet will print. For instance, if you change the zoom to 300%, the worksheet will appear much larger on the screen but will still print normally. There are other views in Excel that will aid you in working with your file and assist you in making changes to the final printed worksheet. There is an additional view option that will be covered in *Microsoft Excel 2007: Comprehensive*, Page Break Preview, that allows you to set where pages will break when printed.

The View tab on the Ribbon provides options for how to view your workbook, which screen elements to show or hide, control of the zoom, and other window display options such as Freeze Panes and Split Window. This lesson will cover Page Layout view and Zoom. Remember that your Ribbon may appear differently, depending on the size of your Excel window.

Working in Page Layout View

Page Layout view allows you to see how your spreadsheet will appear when you print it, page by page. You can even add headers and footers and edit your worksheet in this view.

Zooming the View

The Zoom control lets you zoom in to get a close-up view of a worksheet and zoom out to see the full view. Zooming changes the size of the onscreen worksheet but has no effect on the printed worksheet. You can zoom from 10% to 400%.

You can move the slider to change the zoom.

You can also click the Zoom Out and Zoom In ⊕ buttons to change the zoom.

Clicking the Zoom button will open the Zoom dialog box so that you can set the zoom more precisely.

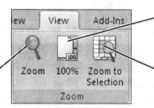

The 100% button allows you to quickly return the zoom to 100%.

The Zoom to Selection button on the Ribbon will customize the zoom to display the selected range of cells.

QR▶

QUICK REFERENCE: WORKING WITH EXCEL'S VIEWS	
Task	**Procedure**
Change the zoom of a worksheet	■ Click and drag the zoom slider at the bottom right of the worksheet window.
Zoom in to a selection	■ Select the range you wish to zoom in on. ■ Display the View Ribbon. ■ Click the Zoom to Selection button in the Zoom area.
View a worksheet in Page Layout view	■ Display the View Ribbon. ■ Click the Page Layout View button in the Workbook Views group of the Ribbon.

Hands-On 8.8   Change Views and Use the Zoom Control

In this exercise, you will practice using commands to change the zoom and switch between Page Layout and Normal views.

Change the Zoom

1. Follow these steps to adjust the zoom percentage:

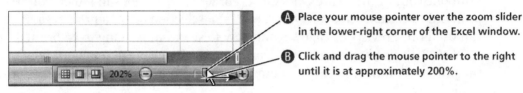

A Place your mouse pointer over the zoom slider in the lower-right corner of the Excel window.

B Click and drag the mouse pointer to the right until it is at approximately 200%.

C Release the mouse button.

2. Click the Zoom Out ⊖ button several times until the zoom displays 100%.

3. Drag to select the range A1:E17.

4. Click the View tab to display the View Ribbon.

5. Click the Zoom to Selection button in the Zoom area of the Ribbon.

6. Choose View→Zoom→100% from the Ribbon.

Switch Between Page Layout and Normal Views

7. Choose View→Workbook Views→Page Layout View from the Ribbon.
   Notice that this view will allow you to see how the worksheet will print and allows you to simply click to add headers and footers.

8. Choose View→Workbook Views→Normal from the Ribbon.
   The worksheet will return to Normal view, and you are ready to proceed to the next section.

Printing Worksheets

Excel gives you many ways to print your work. The method you choose depends on what you want to print. The basic print command, for instance, offers you print options such as printing specified pages, a selected range, or the entire workbook. Additional choices include printing multiple copies and collating options.

The Quick Print 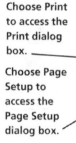 button can be added to the Quick Access toolbar. When clicked, it will print one copy of the entire worksheet. For large workbooks in which you frequently want to print only a certain selection, you can print a selection or set a print area. Before printing, you can use Print Preview or Page Layout view to see what is going to be printed. In *Microsoft Excel 2007: Comprehensive*, you will learn how to change page setup options such as changing the print orientation, printing column headings on every page, setting the print area, and many others.

Print Preview

The Print Preview command displays the Print Preview window. Print Preview lets you see exactly how a worksheet will look when printed. Print Preview can save time, paper, and wear and tear on your printer. It is especially useful when printing large worksheets and those with charts and intricate formatting. It is always wise to preview a large or complex worksheet before sending it to the printer. When you display the Print Preview window, the normal Ribbons are replaced by a Print Preview Ribbon. Print Preview is a very valuable tool in looking at how your worksheet will look when printed, but you are not able to edit your worksheet when you are in print preview mode (you will want to use Page Layout view for this purpose).

Choose Print to access the Print dialog box.

Choose Page Setup to access the Page Setup dialog box.

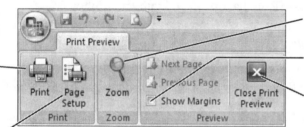

You can zoom in and out to check your worksheet to be printed more closely.

You can show margins and adjust them in the Print Preview window.

Use the Close Print Preview command to close the preview window and return to your worksheet.

The Print Preview Ribbon, which is displayed after you click the Print Preview button on the Quick Access toolbar.

Print the Worksheet

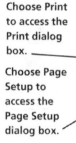 You can customize your Quick Access toolbar to include the Quick Print button, which sends the entire worksheet to the current printer. You must display the Print dialog box if you want to change printers, adjust the number of copies to be printed, or set other printing options such as printing only selected cells. The Print dialog box is displayed by clicking the Office button and choosing the Print command. The following illustration explains the most important options available in the Print dialog box.

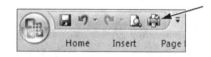

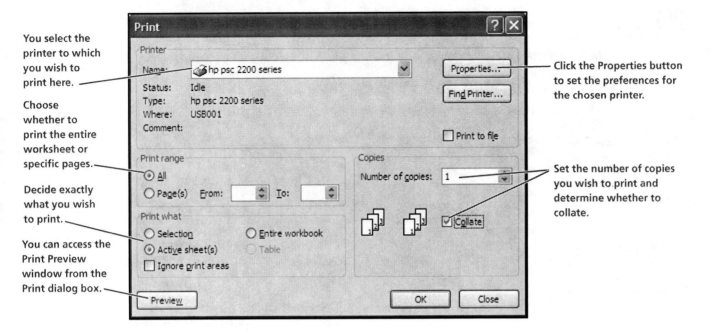

You select the printer to which you wish to print here.

Choose whether to print the entire worksheet or specific pages.

Decide exactly what you wish to print.

You can access the Print Preview window from the Print dialog box.

Click the Properties button to set the preferences for the chosen printer.

Set the number of copies you wish to print and determine whether to collate.

Printing Selections

Many times you will want to print only a range of cells. You can do this by selecting the desired cells, displaying the Print dialog box, choosing to print the selection, and clicking OK. You also use this technique to print nonadjacent selections within a worksheet or workbook. For example, use this technique to print two non-adjacent sections of a worksheet or two or more sections on different worksheets. Non-adjacent selections print on separate pages.

FROM THE KEYBOARD
Ctrl + P to print

 TIP! *To print a selection, you must select the cell range before displaying the Print dialog box.*

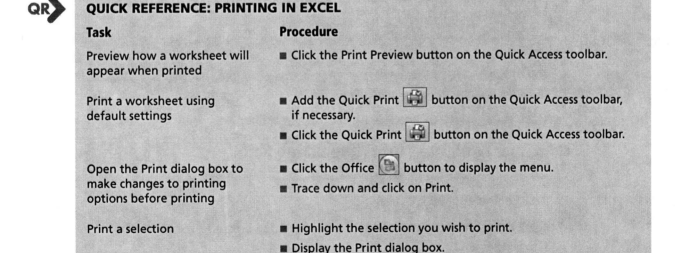

QUICK REFERENCE: PRINTING IN EXCEL

Task	Procedure
Preview how a worksheet will appear when printed	■ Click the Print Preview button on the Quick Access toolbar.
Print a worksheet using default settings	■ Add the Quick Print button on the Quick Access toolbar, if necessary. ■ Click the Quick Print button on the Quick Access toolbar.
Open the Print dialog box to make changes to printing options before printing	■ Click the Office button to display the menu. ■ Trace down and click on Print.
Print a selection	■ Highlight the selection you wish to print. ■ Display the Print dialog box. ■ Click in the circle to the left of Selection. ■ Click OK.

Hands-On 8.9   Preview and Print a Worksheet

In this exercise, you will preview the worksheet you have been working on and send it to the printer.

Preview How Your Worksheet Will Print

1. Follow these steps to preview the worksheet before printing:

Ⓐ Click the Office button.

Ⓑ Trace your mouse down to the arrow to the right of Print.

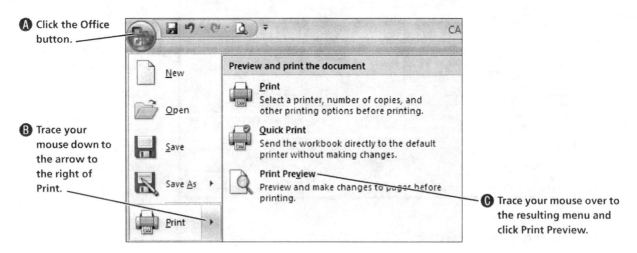

Ⓒ Trace your mouse over to the resulting menu and click Print Preview.

⚠ **NOTE!** *In future lessons, this command will be written Choose Office →Print menu ▼ →Print Preview. The ▼ notation indicates that you will click the arrow on the button to access a menu of options.*

2. Click the Zoom button to zoom in on your worksheet and then again to zoom out.

3. Click in the box to the left of Show Margins.

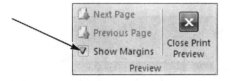

Notice that Excel will display the page margins as dotted lines, which you can adjust by clicking and dragging in the Print Preview window.

4. Click the Close Print Preview button on the Ribbon.

Print Your Worksheet Using the Dialog Box

5. Click the Office button to display the menu.

6. Trace down and click Print.

7. Look at the options available in the Print Dialog box, and then click OK to print the worksheet.

8. Tap ⌷Ctrl⌷+⌷s⌷ to save your worksheet.

9. Click the Office button and choose Close.

Concepts Review

True/False Questions

1. Excel allows you to undo all commands issued. TRUE   FALSE

2. Double-clicking in a cell lets you revise the contents of the cell without replacing the entire contents. TRUE   FALSE

3. When you delete the contents of a cell using the Delete key on the keyboard, the formatting remains. TRUE   FALSE

4. If you drag and drop using the left mouse button, you will be able to choose the command to issue when the mouse button is released. TRUE   FALSE

5. You cannot delete the formats in a cell without deleting the contents as well. TRUE   FALSE

6. You select an entire row by clicking the row header. TRUE   FALSE

7. Page Layout view allows you to add headings and footers to your worksheet. TRUE   FALSE

8. You can print a group of cells without printing the entire worksheet. TRUE   FALSE

9. Changing the zoom in a worksheet will change the way it prints. TRUE   FALSE

10. AutoFill allows you to easily enter contents into cells that have been entered into another cell in the column. TRUE   FALSE

Multiple Choice Questions

1. What happens when you enter text in a cell that already contains an entry?
   a. The text replaces the original entry.
   b. Excel rejects the new entry, keeping the original entry intact.
   c. The cell contains both the original entry and the new entry.
   d. None of the above

2. Which command can be issued when you click the Clear button on the Ribbon?
   a. Clear the entire worksheet.
   b. Clear the formatting from a cell.
   c. Clear the formula from a cell.
   d. None of the above

3. What must you do before issuing a Cut or Copy command?
   a. Choose Home→Clipboard→Cut, or Home→ Clipboard→ Copy from the Ribbon.
   b. Double-click the cell from which you wish to cut or copy.
   c. Click the column header of the cell from which you wish to cut or copy.
   d. Select the cell(s) you wish to cut or copy.

4. What does the Print Preview view allow you to do?
   a. Add headers and footers to your worksheet.
   b. Observe how your spreadsheet will look when printed.
   c. Edit your worksheet.
   d. Both a and b

# Skill Builders

Skill Builder 8.1   Edit a Worksheet

In this exercise, you will edit a worksheet. This exercise demonstrates that sometimes it is easier to replace entries while at other times it is easier to edit them.

Replace Several Entries

1. Start Excel and choose Office→Open.

2. Navigate to the Lesson 08 folder in your file storage location and open sb-Customers.

3. Click cell B4.

4. Type **Ralph** and tap ⎡Enter⎤.
   Notice that it is easy to replace the entry because the name Ralph is easy to type.

5. Replace the name *Calvin* in cell B6 with the name **Stephen**.

Edit Using the Formula Bar

6. Click cell D4.

7. Click in the Formula Bar just in front of the telephone prefix *333*.

8. Tap ⎡Delete⎤ three times to remove the prefix.

9. Type **222** and complete ✔ the entry.

10. Change the area code in cell D8 from *814* to **914**.
    In these entries, it was easier to edit than to retype entire phone numbers.

Use In-Cell and "Your Choice" Editing

11. Double-click cell E4.

12. Use ⎡→⎤ or ⎡←⎤ to position the insertion point in front of the word Lane.

13. Tap ⎡Delete⎤ four times to remove the word *Lane*.

14. Type **Reservoir** and complete the entry.

15. Edit the next five addresses using either the Formula Bar or in-cell editing. The required changes appear bold in the following table.

Cell	Make These Changes
E5	2900 **Carleton** Drive, San Mateo, CA 94401
E6	**2300** Palm Drive, Miami, FL 33147
E7	888 Wilson Street, **Concord**, CA 94565
E8	320 Main Street, **Pittsburgh**, PA 17951
E9	5120 132nd Street, Los Angeles, CA **90045**

Leave the workbook open as you will use it for Skill Builder 8.2

Skill Builder 8.2 Use AutoComplete and AutoFill

In this exercise, you will add data to the worksheet you created in Skill Builder 8.1 by using AutoComplete and AutoFill.

Use AutoComplete

1. Click cell B10, and type **ja**.
   Notice that AutoComplete does not suggest an entry when you only type a "j" as there are two "j" entries in the column.

2. Tap [Enter] to accept the suggested entry of Jack.

3. Using the following figure, complete the customer's information, using AutoComplete in column F.

	A	B	C	D	E	F
9	Judy	Alioto	(213) 222-3344	5120 132nd Street, Los Angeles, CA 95544	West
10	Jack	LaRue	(360) 444-0489	359 Peninsula Avenue, Port Angeles, WA 98363	West

Use AutoFill

4. Click cell A4.
   Before using AutoFill, you must first select the cell that you will be using as the basis for the fill information.

5. Place your mouse pointer over the fill handle at the bottom-right corner of the selected cell, drag down through cell A10, and then release the mouse button when the ScreenTip shows C-07.

	A	B
3	Customer #	Firstna
4	C-01	Ralph
5		Willie
6		Steph
7		Susan
8		Jack
9		Judy
10		Jack
11		C-07

	A
3	Customer #
4	C-01
5	C-02
6	C-03
7	C-04
8	C-05
9	C-06
10	C-07

Notice that Excel recognizes C-01 as the beginning of a series (C-02, C-03, C-04, ...).

Enter Additional Customers

6. Enter the following three customers, in rows 11–13, into the list, using AutoFill and AutoComplete when possible.

	A	B	C	D	E	F
10	C-07	Jack	LaRue	(360) 444-0489	359 Peninsula Avenue, Port Angeles, WA 98363	West
11	C-08	Edgar	Martinez	(206) 111-1111	11 Mariners Way, Seattle, WA 98101	West
12	C-09	Trevor	Hoffman	(619) 555-1111	51 Camino de Padres, San Diego, CA 92101	West
13	C-10	Derek	Jeter	(212) 222-5555	2 Yankee Avenue, New York, NY 10002	East

7. Use ⌈Ctrl⌉+⌈S⌉ to save your workbook, then leave it open for the next exercise.

Skill Builder 8.3   Move and Copy Cell Contents

In this exercise, you will use the workbook from Skill Builder 8.2 and move and copy the contents of cells.

1. Click to select cell E1.

2. Choose Home→Clipboard→Cut from the Ribbon.

3. Click cell A1, and choose Home→Clipboard→Paste.

4. Select A11:F11, and copy the range using the keyboard command ⌈Ctrl⌉+⌈C⌉.

5. Click cell A14, and paste the range using ⌈Ctrl⌉+⌈V⌉.
   This can come in handy if you have a new entry that is very similar to an existing one!

6. Use ⌈Ctrl⌉+⌈Z⌉ to undo the Paste command.

7. Close ⌈X⌉ Excel, choosing to save your workbook.

Working with Formulas and Functions

The magic of the Excel spreadsheet lies in its ability to crunch numbers and make sense of data. The heart of this magic lies in the formulas and functions that are used for this number crunching. In this lesson, you will be introduced to creating and modifying basic formulas and functions in Excel. You will learn how to reference cells in formulas as well as how to use another automated feature of Excel, AutoSum. Sit back and relax as you begin to discover the true power of Excel.

LESSON OBJECTIVES

After studying this lesson, you will be able to:

■ Create formulas to calculate values, utilizing the proper syntax and order of operations

■ Use a variety of methods to create statistical functions to determine the sum, average, maximum, and minimum of a range of numbers

■ Use relative and absolute cell references in formulas and functions

■ Modify and copy formulas and functions

■ Display the formulas contained within cells rather than the resulting value

Case Study: Creating a Spreadsheet with Formulas

The Big Bear Mountain Inn is a 200-room hotel located next to a ski resort. The manager of the hotel, Glen Livingston, has asked the accountant, Tammy McJagger, to prepare commission and monthly projected profit reports for the first quarter. Commissions are not paid for in-house bookings but are paid to outside agencies who book rooms for the inn.

Tammy has set up a workbook with two worksheets, one to track commissions and the other to help Glen view how the projected profit changes based on occupancy. Your job will be to help Tammy create the necessary formulas and functions for the workbook.

	A	B	C	D	E
1	**Big Bear Mountain Inn**				
2	*First Quarter Commissions*				
3					
4			Nights Booked		
5	Booking Agent	January	February	March	1st Qtr Total
6	Betty's Better Travel	250	486	274	1010
7	Mountain Travel Agency	342	276	299	917
8	Rent Online 4 Less	74	149	101	324
9	Sea to Mountain Travel	113	109	88	310
10	Skiingtrips.com	337	265	124	726
11	Total	1116	1285	886	3287
12	Average	223.2	257	177.2	657.4
13	Maximum	342	486	299	1010
14	Minimum	74	109	88	310

The Commissions worksheet will show the number of nights booked by each agency that is due a commission.

	A	B	C	D	E	F
1	**Big Bear Mountain Inn**					
2	*Monthly Projected Profits*					
3						
4	Projected Nights Booked	3,000	3,750	4,500	5,250	5,700
5	Occupancy Rate	50%	63%	75%	88%	95%
6	Revenue	$ 267,000	$ 333,750	$ 400,500	$ 467,250	$507,300
7	Operating Cost	260,000	275,000	290,000	305,000	314,000
8	Advertising	3,500	3,500	3,500	3,500	3,500
9	Commissions	14,632	14,632	14,632	14,632	14,632
10	Office Expenses	5,000	5,000	5,000	5,000	5,000
11						
12	Total Costs	283,132	298,132	313,132	328,132	337,132
13	Gross Profit	(16,132)	35,618	87,368	139,118	170,168
14	Net Profit	$ (12,099)	$ 26,714	$ 65,526	$ 104,339	$127,626
15	Gross Profit vs. Revenue	-6%	11%	22%	30%	34%
16						
17	Average Room Rate	$ 89		Commission Rate		15%
18	Monthly Fixed Operating Cost	$ 200,000		Tax Rate		25%
19	Nights Per Month	6,000		Variable Cost per Night	$ 20.00	

The Monthly Projected Profits worksheet will help Glen to understand how his bottom line changes in relation to occupancy rate.

Working with Formulas and Functions

A formula is simply a math problem done in Excel. You can add, subtract, multiply, divide, and group numbers and cell contents in order to make your data work for you. A function is a prewritten formula that helps to simplify complex procedures, both for numbers and for text. For instance, a formula can be used to sum a group of numbers, to determine the payment amount on a loan, and to search for text.

Using AutoSum

FROM THE KEYBOARD

 for Autosum

The power of Excel becomes apparent when you begin using formulas and functions. The most common type of calculation is summing a column or row of numbers. In fact, this type of calculation is so common that Excel provides the AutoSum feature specifically for this purpose.

The **Σ AutoSum ▾** button on the Home tab automatically sums a column or row of numbers. When you click AutoSum, Excel proposes a range of cells. Excel will first look "up" for a range to sum, and if a range is not found there, it will next look left. You can accept the proposed range or drag in the worksheet to select a different range. When you complete the entry, Excel places a SUM function in the worksheet, which adds the numbers in the range.

You can include empty cells in the range that you wish to AutoSum, although if you are averaging a range of cells you will want to include only those cells with a value that should be included in the average.

⚠ **TIP!** *If your Excel window is smaller, the button may be displayed like this:* **Σ ▾**.

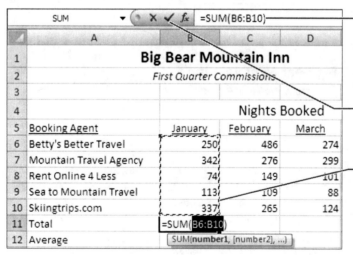

Excel will look "up" and propose to sum the range B6:B10 in cell B11 and display it in the Formula Bar. All formulas begin with an equals (=) sign. SUM is a built-in function that adds the numbers in a range (B6:B10 in this

When you click the Enter ✔ button on the Formula Bar to complete the entry, the total should be 1116.

A flashing marquee (marching ants) surrounds the range B6:B10. AutoSum assumes you want to add together all cells above B11 until the first empty cell (or cell not containing a number) is reached. The marquee identifies this range of cells.

Other Functions Available Through the AutoSum Button

The AutoSum button does not stop at simply summing a group of numbers. The following statistical functions are also available as automated features: average, count numbers, maximum, and minimum.

Auto Function	Description
Sum	Adds the cells indicated in the formula
Average	Averages the values in the cells indicated in the formula
Count	Counts the number of values in the cells indicated in the formula
Maximum	Returns the maximum value in the cells indicated in the formula
Minimum	Returns the minimum value in the cells indicated in the formula

!TIP! *Once you have entered a function in a cell, you can use AutoFill to copy it to adjacent cells.*

Status Bar Functions and Customization

The status bar, which is displayed at the bottom of the Excel window, allows you to view information about a range of numbers without actually inserting a function in the worksheet. You can customize the status bar to display the following functions: Average, Count, Numerical Count, Minimum, Maximum, and Sum. To customize the status bar, right-click anywhere on it and click to add or remove features. Other than functions, you can also customize additional features of the status bar such as zoom, signatures, overtype mode, and macros.

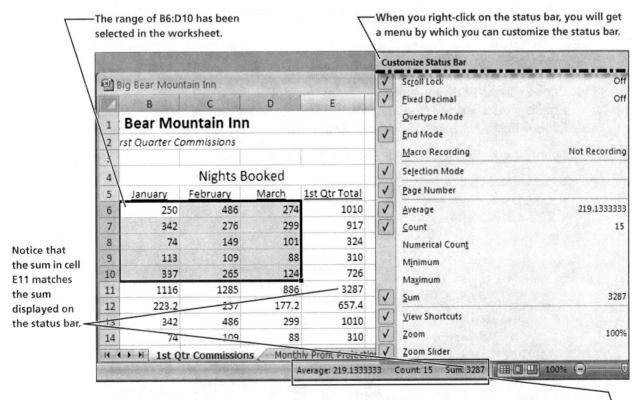

The range of B6:D10 has been selected in the worksheet.

When you right-click on the status bar, you will get a menu by which you can customize the status bar.

Notice that the sum in cell E11 matches the sum displayed on the status bar.

By default, Excel displays the sum, average, and count values of the selected range on the status bar.

Hands-On 9.1   Use AutoSum and Status Bar Functions

In this exercise, you will use AutoSum to calculate the number of rooms booked by each agency to whom you pay a commission, as well as the quarterly totals. You will also explore the functions on the status bar.

Open an Excel File

1. Start Excel.

2. Open the Big Bear Mountain Inn workbook from the Lesson 09 folder in your file storage location.
   Take a look at the workbook. There are two tabs at the bottom of the window: 1st Qtr Commissions and Monthly Profit Projection. On the Monthly Profit Projection worksheet, there are bookings entered; it will be up to you to calculate the total, average, maximum, and minimum values.

Use AutoSum

3. Click cell B11.

4. Choose Home→Editing→Sum **Σ** from the Ribbon.
   Excel displays a marquee (marching ants) around the part of the spreadsheet where it thinks the formula should be applied. You can change this selection as necessary.

5. Follow these steps to complete the AutoSum formula.

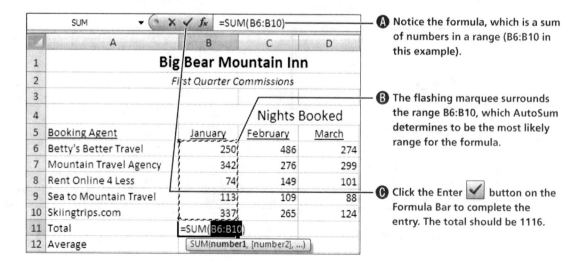

Ⓐ Notice the formula, which is a sum of numbers in a range (B6:B10 in this example).

Ⓑ The flashing marquee surrounds the range B6:B10, which AutoSum determines to be the most likely range for the formula.

Ⓒ Click the Enter ✓ button on the Formula Bar to complete the entry. The total should be 1116.

6. Click in cell C11.

7. Choose Home→Editing→Sum $\boxed{\Sigma}$ from the Ribbon and complete $\boxed{\checkmark}$ the entry.

8. Use the preceding technique to calculate the column total in cell D11.

Calculate the Quarterly Totals

9. Click in cell E6.

10. Choose Home→Editing→Sum $\boxed{\Sigma}$ from the Ribbon.
   Notice that since there are no values above cell E6, Excel will look to the left to find a range to sum, B6:D6.

11. Tap $\boxed{\text{Enter}}$ to complete the entry.

12. Use the preceding technique to calculate the row total in cell E7.

Override the Range AutoSum Proposes

13. Click in cell E8, and then choose Home→Editing→Sum $\boxed{\Sigma}$ from the Ribbon.
   Excel will assume you want to sum the cells E6 and E7, above E8. This assumption is incorrect. Excel made this assumption because there were two cells above E8, which is enough to make a range.

14. Follow these steps to override the proposed range:

A Position the mouse pointer over cell B8, and then click and drag to the right until the range B8:D8 is selected.

| 8 | Rent Online 4 Less | 74 | 149 | 101 | =SUM(B8:D8) |
| 9 | Sea to Mountain Travel | 113 | 109 | 88 | SUM(number1, [number2], ...) |

B Notice that the new range, B8:D8, appears in the formula.

C Tap $\boxed{\text{Enter}}$ to complete the formula.

Use AutoFill to Extend a Formula

You can use AutoFill, which was introduced in the previous lesson, to extend a formula just as you used it to extend a series of days of the week.

15. Follow these steps to AutoFill the formula in cell E8 to the three cells below it:

A Click cell E8.

B Position your mouse pointer over the fill handle at the bottom-right corner of the cell until you see the thin cross, and then press the left mouse button and drag down through cell E11.

	A	B	C	D	E
5	Booking Agent	January	February	March	1st Qtr Total
6	Betty's Better Travel	250	486	274	1010
7	Mountain Travel Agency	342	276	299	917
8	Rent Online 4 Less	74	149	101	324
9	Sea to Mountain Travel	113	109	88	
10	Skiingtrips.com	337	265	124	
11	Total	1116	1285	886	
12	Average				

C Release the mouse button to fill the formula into the cells.

Use AutoCalculate

16. Drag to select the range B6:D10.

17. Look at the Status bar to see the sum value displayed by AutoCalculate.

18. Click the save  button, but leave the spreadsheet open for the next exercise.

Creating Formulas

You have already learned how to compute totals with AutoSum. AutoSum provides a convenient method for summing a range of numbers. However, you will need to use many other types of formulas in Excel. In fact, many worksheets, such as financial models, require hundreds or even thousands of complex formulas.

Beginning Character in Formulas

As you saw in the AutoSum discussion in the previous section, functions begin with an equals (=) sign. If you are typing a formula in a cell, it is recommended that you also begin it with an equals (=) sign, even though you can begin it with a plus (+) or a minus (−) sign. It is best to adopt one method in order to create consistency.

Cell and Range References

Formulas derive their power from the use of cell and range references. For example, in the previous exercise, you used AutoSum to insert the formula =SUM(B6:B10) in cell B11. Because the range reference (B6:B11) was used in the formula, you were able to copy the formula across the row using the fill handle. There are two important benefits to using references in formulas.

- When references are used, formulas can be copied to other cells.

- Since a reference refers to a cell or a range of cells, the formula results are automatically recalculated when the data is changed in the referenced cell(s).

The Language of Excel Formulas

Formulas can include the standard arithmetic operators shown in the following table. You can also use spaces within formulas to improve their appearance and readability. Notice that each formula in the table begins with an equals (=) sign. Also, keep in mind that each formula is entered into the same cell that displays the resulting calculation.

QUICK REFERENCE: USING ARITHMETIC OPERATORS IN FORMULAS

Operator	Example	Comments
+ (addition)	=B7+B11	Adds the values in B7 and B11
– (subtraction)	=B7–B11	Subtracts the value in B11 from the value in B7
* (multiplication)	=B7*B11	Multiplies the values in B7 and B11
/ (division)	=B7/B11	Divides the value in B7 by the value in B11
^ (exponentiation)	=B7^3	Raises the value in B7 to the third power (B7*B7*B7)
% (percent)	=B7*10%	Multiplies the value in B7 by 10% (0.10)
( ) (grouping)	=B7/(C4–C2)	Subtracts the value in C2 from the value in C4 and then divides the result by the value in B7

 TIP! *When typing a cell reference in a formula, you can simply type the column letter in lowercase and Excel will capitalize it for you.*

Please Excuse My Dear Aunt Sally

Excel formulas follow the algebraic hierarchy you learned about way back in middle or high school. This means that the formula completes operations in a specific order. You may have learned to memorize this hierarchy with the mnemonic "Please Excuse My Dear Aunt Sally":

Please-	Parentheses (grouping symbols)
Excuse-	Exponents
My-	Multiplication
Dear-	Division
Aunt-	Addition
Sally-	Subtraction

In order to control the order of operations, you can use parentheses to cause Excel to add before multiplying or subtract before dividing. Take a look at the following examples to see how the order of operations works with and without parentheses and how the resulting value will be different.

=53+7*5=53+35=88   Multiplication then addition

=(53+7)*5=(60)*5=300   Parentheses then multiplication

Hands-On 9.2   **Use the Keyboard to Create a Basic Formula**

In this exercise, you will use the keyboard to enter formulas into the spreadsheet.

1. Click the Monthly Profit Projection sheet tab at the bottom of the Excel window.

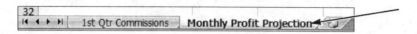

2. Click cell B6.

3. Type **=B4*B17** in the cell, and then tap ⌷Enter⌷ to complete the formula.
   In order to calculate the revenue, you will need to multiply the number of nights booked (B4) by the average room rate (B17).

4. Click cell B5.

5. Type **=b4/b19** in the cell, and then tap ⌷Enter⌷ to complete the formula.
   Formulas are not case sensitive. Notice that regardless of whether you type the cell references as upper- or lowercase, the formula will work properly. In this example, the cell has been formatted to display a percentage for you. You will learn how to apply different number formats in Lesson 10, Formatting Worksheets and Charting Basics.

Using Cell References in Formulas

A cell reference identifies which cell or range of cells contains the values to use in a formula. Cell references are one of three types: relative, absolute, or mixed. All formulas use the relative cell reference unless you specifically instruct Excel to use another type. You used relative cell references in the formulas you created in the last exercise. As this lesson continues, you will learn about the other two types of cell references.

Relative Cell References

A relative cell reference means the cell is *relative* to the cell that contains the formula. For example, when you create a formula in cell C3 to subtract A3 minus B3 (=A3–B3), Excel finds that the first value is two cells to the left of the formula. The second value is one cell to the left of the formula.

When you copy a formula, the cell references update automatically and refer to new cells relative to the new formula cell. For example, if you copied the formula mentioned in the previous paragraph down to cell C4, the new formula would be A4 minus B4 (=A4–B4). The first and second values are still relative to the same number of cells to the left of the formula cell.

◢	A	B	C	D	E	F
12	Total Costs	=SUM(B7:B10)	=SUM(C7:C10)	=SUM(D7:D10)	=SUM(E7:E10)	=SUM(F7:F10)
13	Gross Profit	=B6-B12	=C6-C12	=D6-D12	=E6-E12	=F6-F12

Notice that when a formula utilizing relative cell references in column B is copied through to column F, the cells referenced in the copied formulas will refer to cells relative to where they are pasted.

Point Mode

One potential danger that can occur when typing formulas is accidentally typing the incorrect cell reference. This is easy to do, especially if the worksheet is complex. Point mode can help you avoid this problem. With point mode, you can insert a cell reference in a formula by clicking the desired cell as you are typing the formula. Likewise, you can insert a range reference in a formula by dragging over the desired cells. You will use point mode in the next exercise.

Absolute Cell References

You have been using relative references thus far in this course. Relative references are convenient because they update automatically when formulas are moved or copied. In some situations, you may not want references updated when a formula is moved or copied. You must use absolute or mixed references in these situations. Absolute references always refer to the same cell, regardless of which cell the formula is moved or copied to. You can refer to cells on other worksheets or in other workbooks as well. In *Microsoft Excel 2007: Comprehensive*, you will learn about referring to cells in other locations.

Creating Absolute References

You create absolute references by placing dollar signs in front of the column and row components of the reference: for example, $C$1. You can type the dollar signs as you enter a formula or add them later by editing the formula. The following illustration shows an example of how absolute references are used in formulas.

	A	B	C	D	E	F
12	Total Costs	=SUM(B7:B10)	=SUM(C7:C10)	=SUM(D7:D10)	=SUM(E7:E10)	=SUM(F7:F10)
13	Gross Profit	=B6-B12	=C6-C12	=D6-D12	=E6-E12	=F6-F12
14	Net Profit	=B13*(1-$F$18)	=C13*(1-$F$18)	=D13*(1-$F$18)	=E13*(1-$F$18)	=F13*(1-$F$18)
15	Gross Profit vs. Revenue	=B13/B6	=C13/C6	=D13/D6	=E13/E6	=F13/F6

Cell B14 displays a formula that has both a relative cell reference (B13) and an absolute cell reference ($F$18).

When copied to cell C14, the relative cell reference will refer to the cell relative to where it is pasted (C13), but the absolute cell reference will remain the same.

Mixed References

You can mix relative and absolute references within a reference. For example, the reference $C1 is a combination of an absolute reference to column C and a relative reference to row 1. Mixed references are useful when copying many types of formulas.

Using the F4 Function Key

You make a reference absolute or mixed by typing dollar signs while entering the reference. You can also click in front of a reference in the Formula Bar and use the F4 function key to insert the dollar signs. The first time you tap F4, dollar signs are placed in front of both the column and row components of the reference. If you tap F4 again, the dollar sign is removed from the column component, thus creating a mixed reference. If you tap F4 a third time, a dollar sign is placed in front of just the column component and removed from the row component. One more tap of F4 will return you to a relative cell reference.

What-If Analysis

Another great advantage to using cell references in formulas is that it allows you to perform what-if analyses. A what-if analysis is as simple as changing the value in a cell that is referenced in a formula and observing the overall change in the data. You can perform these simple analyses at any time by replacing the value(s) in referenced cells. The Undo command can come in very handy when performing a what-if analysis as it provides a quick way to return the worksheet to the original values. If you wish to perform an extensive what-if analysis and not worry about losing your original data, you may wish to save your workbook under a different name as a "practice" file.

 ## Hands-On 9.3   Create Formulas Using Cell References

In this exercise, you will use absolute cell references to create formulas that can be copied to other cells.

Enter a Formula Using Point Mode

1. Click cell B7, and type **=** to begin a formula.

2. Click cell B18, and then tap the F4 function key.

 NOTE! *If you have a keyboard that uses the function keys for other purposes, you may have to tap the F Lock key to be able to utilize F4 for absolute or mixed references in Excel.*

> *Tapping F4 will make the B18 cell reference an absolute by adding the $ symbol to both the column and row references. Take a look at the Formula Bar and you will see $B$18.*

3. Type **+(** to continue the formula.

4. Click cell F19, and then tap F4.

5. Type *, and then click cell B4.

6. Type **)**, and then click the Enter ☑ button to complete the formula.
   *You have created a formula using point mode consisting of both absolute and relative cell references. Notice how the formula appears in the Formula Bar: =$B$18+($F$19*B4). This means that no matter where you copy this formula to, it will always reference cells B18 and F19.*

Enter Fixed Values and Calculate the Commissions

7. Click cell B8, type **3500**, and then tap Enter to complete the entry.

8. Click cell B10, type **5000**, and then tap Enter.

9. Click the 1st Qtr Commissions tab.

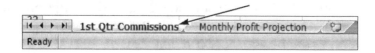

10. Select the range B11:D11, and then look at the Status bar to determine the average number of commissionable nights booked per month.

Average: 1095.666667   Count: 3   Sum: 3287

Notice that the average number of nights you will be paying a commission on in the first quarter is 1,096 (rounded up). We will use this figure to calculate the commissions for the monthly profit projection sheet.

11. Click the Monthly Profit Projection tab to return to that worksheet.

12. Click cell B9, and enter the formula **=1096*$B$17*$F$17** to calculate the commissions. Tap [Enter] to complete the entry.

Now that you have learned how to use point mode as well as type formulas, you can choose which method to use for the rest of this exercise. Remember, though, that point mode is much more accurate, especially with large and complex worksheets.

Calculate the Total Costs and Profits

13. Click cell B12, and choose Home→Editing→Sum **Σ** from the Ribbon.

14. Click and drag to select B7:B10 as the range, and then tap [Enter].

15. Enter **=B6-B12** in cell B13, tapping [Enter] to complete the entry.
Now that you have calculated the gross profit, you can calculate the net profit since you know the tax rate.

16. Enter **=B13*(1-$F$18)** in cell B14, tapping [Enter] to complete the entry.

17. Enter **=B13/B6** in cell B15, tapping [Enter] to complete the entry.
You have now entered all of the formulas for column B. In the next exercise, you will learn how to edit the contents of cells B5 and B6 to reflect absolute cell references where necessary.

18. Take a look at the formulas displayed in the figure below to see how using absolute cell references differs from using relative cell references.

	A	B	C	D	E	F
4	Projected Nights Booked	=100*30	=125*30	=150*30	=175*30	=190*30
5	Occupancy Rate	=B4/$B$19	=C4/$B$19	=D4/$B$19	=E4/$B$19	=F4/$B$19
6	Revenue	=B4*$B$17	=C4*$B$17	=D4*$B$17	=E4*$B$17	=F4*$B$17
7	Operating Cost	=$B$18+($F$19*B4)	=$B$18+($F$19*C4)	=$B$18+($F$19*D4)	=$B$18+($F$19*E4)	=$B$18+($F$19*F4)
8	Advertising	3500	3500	3500	3500	3500
9	Commissions	=1096*$B$17*$F$17	=1096*$B$17*$F$17	=1096*$B$17*$F$17	=1096*$B$17*$F$17	=1096*$B$17*$F$17
10	Office Expenses	5000	5000	5000	5000	5000
11						
12	Total Costs	=SUM(B7:B10)	=SUM(C7:C10)	=SUM(D7:D10)	=SUM(E7:E10)	=SUM(F7:F10)
13	Gross Profit	=B6-B12	=C6-C12	=D6-D12	=E6-E12	=F6-F12
14	Net Profit	=B13*(1-$F$18)	=C13*(1-$F$18)	=D13*(1-$F$18)	=E13*(1-$F$18)	=F13*(1-$F$18)
15	Gross Profit vs. Revenue	=B13/B6	=C13/C6	=D13/D6	=E13/E6	=F13/F6
16						
17	Average Room Rate	89		Commission Rate		0.15
18	Monthly Fixed Operating Cost	200000		Tax Rate		0.25
19	Nights Per Month	=200*30		Variable Cost per Night		20

Modifying and Copying Formulas

You can modify and copy formulas in much the same way that you learned to edit and copy cells in the last lesson. We will use the tools learned previously and apply them to formulas in the next exercise.

Modifying Formulas

You can modify formulas in either the Formula Bar or the cell. If you select a cell and enter a new formula, it replaces the previous contents of the cell.

When you select a formula in order to edit it, you will see colored lines around all of the cells that are referenced by the formula. This can help you to visually determine if the formula is correct.

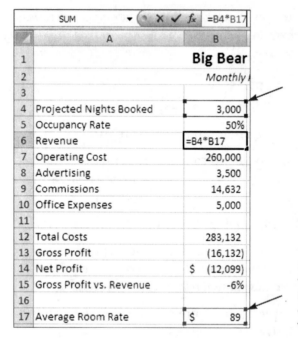

Notice that when the formula in B6 is selected for editing (as indicated by the insertion point in the Formula Bar), Excel will graphically display the cells that are being referenced by the formula, in this case cells B4 and B17.

Copying Formulas

You can use either the Copy and Paste commands with formulas or AutoFill in order to copy them to new cells. You can copy formulas to one cell at a time or to a range of cells using either method.

If you use AutoFill, the AutoFill Options button will appear once you have released the mouse button. Clicking this button will allow you to customize your fill.

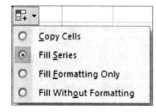

You can change what was copied in the cells through AutoFill by clicking the AutoFill Options button and choosing a different option.

Hands-On 9.4   Modify and Copy Formulas

In this exercise, you will use previously learned techniques to modify and copy formulas in order to complete your profit projection.

1. Click cell B5, and enter **=B4/$B$19** to replace the current formula.
   Make sure you tap Enter *to complete the entry of the formula or it will continue to build when you click the next cell!*

2. Click cell B6, and then follow these steps to edit the formula in the cell.

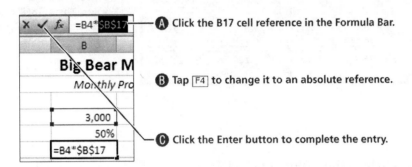

Ⓐ Click the B17 cell reference in the Formula Bar.

Ⓑ Tap F4 to change it to an absolute reference.

Ⓒ Click the Enter button to complete the entry.

Use Copy and Paste Commands to Copy a Formula

3. Click cell B5, and then use Ctrl+C to copy the formula.

4. Click cell C5, and then use Ctrl+V to paste the formula in the new cell.
   This method works great if you need to copy a formula to just one cell. You can use these commands to copy a formula to a range of cells as well.

5. Select the range D5:F5, and then use Ctrl+V.
   The formula that you copied in step 3 is now pasted to the range of cells selected.

6. Click in cell D5, and look at the formula in the Formula Bar.

D5	▾	f_x	=D4/$B$19	
	A	B	C	D
4	Projected Nights Booked	3,000	3,750	4,500
5	Occupancy Rate	50%	63%	75%

Notice that the relative cell reference now indicates cell D4, whereas the absolute cell reference is still looking to cell B19.

Use AutoFill to Copy Formulas

7. Follow these steps to copy the formula from cell B6 to the range C6:F6.

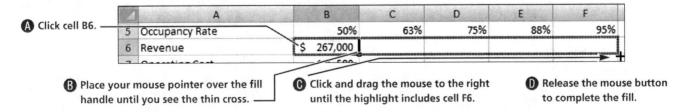

Ⓐ Click cell B6.

	A	B	C	D	E	F
5	Occupancy Rate	50%	63%	75%	88%	95%
6	Revenue	$ 267,000				

Ⓑ Place your mouse pointer over the fill handle until you see the thin cross.

Ⓒ Click and drag the mouse to the right until the highlight includes cell F6.

Ⓓ Release the mouse button to complete the fill.

Next, you will use AutoFill to copy formulas from B7:B15 all the way through F7:F15.

8. Select the range B7:B15.

9. Place your mouse pointer over the fill handle at the bottom right of the selected range.

10. When you see the thin cross **+**, drag to the right until the highlight includes the cells in column F.

260,000	275,000	290,000	305,000	314,000
3,500	3,501	3,502	3,503	3,504
14,632	14,632	14,632	14,632	14,632
5,000	5,001	5,002	5,003	5,004
283,132	298,134	313,136	328,138	337,140
(16,132)	35,616	87,364	139,112	170,160
$ (12,099)	$ 26,712	$ 65,523	$ 104,334	$ 127,620
-6%	11%	22%	30%	34%

Once you have AutoFilled the cells, the AutoFill Options button appears. Notice that the Advertising and Office Expenses rows have filled across as a series rather than copying the initial value. The AutoFill Options button will help you to solve this problem.

11. Click the AutoFill Options ▦ button.

12. Click in the circle to the left of Copy Cells.
Excel revises the AutoFilled formula that filled in as a series (3,500; 3,501; 3,502; 3,503; and 3,504) rather than copying 3,500 all the way across.

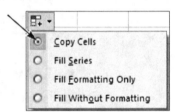

- ◉ Copy Cells
- ○ Fill Series
- ○ Fill Formatting Only
- ○ Fill Without Formatting

Displaying Formulas

FROM THE KEYBOARD
Ctrl + □ to show formulas

Excel normally displays the results of formulas in worksheet cells. However, you may need to display the actual formulas from time to time. Displaying the formulas can be helpful, especially in complex financial worksheets. Displaying formulas can help you understand how a worksheet functions. It can also be used to "debug" the worksheet and locate potential problems.

To display formulas, you will use the Show Formulas button on the Formulas tab of the Ribbon. You can edit a formula in this view, but you will need to show values again to see the result. In order to view the values once again, click the Show Formulas button again.

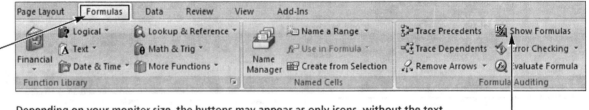

Depending on your monitor size, the buttons may appear as only icons, without the text descriptors, or as large buttons.

C	D	E
Big Bear Mountain Inn		
Monthly Projected Profits		
=125*30	=150*30	=175*30
=C4/$B$19	=D4/$B$19	=E4/$B$19
=C4*$B$17	=D4*$B$17	=E4*$B$17
=$B$18+($F$19*C4)	=$B$18+($F$19*D4)	=$B$18+($F$19*E4)
3500	3500	3500
=1096*$B$17*$F$17	=1096*$B$17*$F$17	=1096*$B$17*$F$17
5000	5000	5000
=SUM(C7:C10)	=SUM(D7:D10)	=SUM(E7:E10)
=C6-C12	=D6-D12	=E6-E12
=C13*(1-$F$18)	=D13*(1-$F$18)	=E13*(1-$F$18)
=C13/C6	=D13/D6	=E13/E6

When you choose to show formulas, you will see the formulas in the cells rather than the values as before. If a cell does not contain a formula, the contents will be visible in this view.

QUICK REFERENCE: VIEWING FORMULAS

Task	Procedure
Display or hide the formulas in a workbook	Choose Formulas→Formula Auditing→Show Formulas from the Ribbon.

 Hands-On 9.5   **Display Formulas in a Worksheet**

In this exercise, you will display the formulas in the profit projection worksheet to see how it is constructed and to be able to troubleshoot any potentially inaccurate formulas.

1. Choose Formulas→Formula Auditing→Show Formulas from the Ribbon.
   Take a look at the worksheet. You can use this feature to easily examine your formulas more closely.

2. Choose Formulas→Formula Auditing→Show Formulas from the Ribbon.
   The values will be displayed once again.

Using Formula AutoComplete

 2007 new! Excel 2007 includes a feature that serves to assist you in creating and editing formulas. Formula AutoComplete will jump into action once you have typed an equals (=) sign and the beginning letters of a function in a cell. It works by displaying a list of functions beginning with the typed letters below the active cell.

Functions Defined

A function is a predefined formula that performs calculations or returns a desired result. Excel has more than 400 built-in functions. You construct functions using a set of basic rules known as syntax. Fortunately, most functions use the same or similar syntax. This syntax also applies to the MIN, MAX, AVERAGE, and COUNT functions.

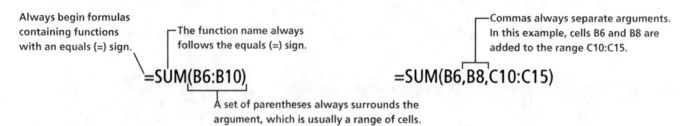

Always begin formulas containing functions with an equals (=) sign.

The function name always follows the equals (=) sign.

Commas always separate arguments. In this example, cells B6 and B8 are added to the range C10:C15.

=SUM(B6:B10)   =SUM(B6,B8,C10:C15)

A set of parentheses always surrounds the argument, which is usually a range of cells.

 QUICK REFERENCE: USING FORMULA AUTOCOMPLETE TO ENTER A FORMULA INTO A CELL

Task	Procedure
Use Formula AutoComplete	■ Type an equals (=) sign and begin typing the desired formula.
	■ Double-click the formula once you see it in the list.
	■ Select the range to which you wish to apply it.
	■ Type a closed parenthesis,), to finish the formula.
	■ Complete the entry.

 Hands-On 9.6   Use Formula AutoComplete

In this exercise, you will have an opportunity to use the Formula AutoComplete feature to create a formula.

1. Display the 1st Qtr Commissions worksheet by clicking the sheet tab.

2. Click cell B12.

3. Type **=ave** and observe the list that results.

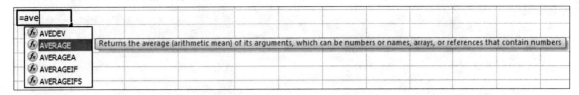

When you use Formula AutoComplete, Excel will show you a list of functions that begin with the letters you type in. If you click on a function in the list, a ScreenTip will display the results you will obtain if you select it.

4. Double-click AVERAGE in the list.
Excel will fill in the formula name for you. It will be up to you to select the range next.

5. Drag to select cells B6:B10 as the range for the formula.

NOTE! *You do not include total rows or columns when completing most functions.*

6. Type **)** to complete the function, and then tap Enter.

7. Click on cell B12, and use the fill handle to copy the function to the range of C12:E12.

11	Total	1116	1285	886	3287
12	Average	223.2	257	177.2	657.4
13	Maximum				

You now have the average number of bookings for each month and the entire quarter.

Using the Function Wizard

The Function Wizard *fx* button displays the Insert Function dialog box. This dialog box provides access to all of Excel's built-in functions. It allows you to locate a function by typing a description or searching by category. When you locate the desired function and click OK, Excel displays the Function Arguments box. The Function Arguments box helps you enter arguments in functions. The Insert Function box and the Function Arguments box are shown in the following illustrations.

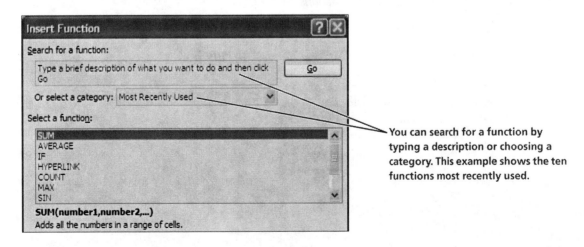

You can search for a function by typing a description or choosing a category. This example shows the ten functions most recently used.

The Function Arguments box appears when you choose a function and click OK. ——

You can type the argument (typically a range) in this box or select the desired range in the worksheet. ——

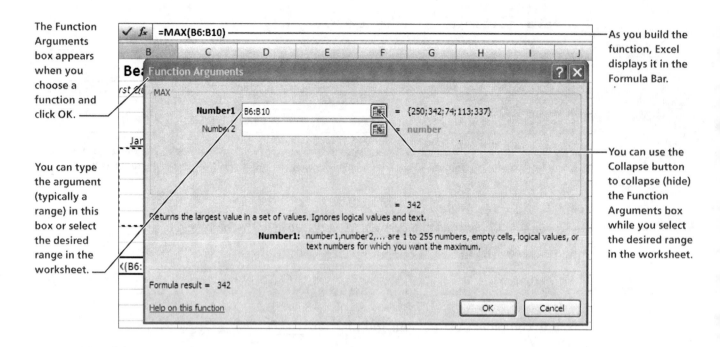

=MAX(B6:B10)

As you build the function, Excel displays it in the Formula Bar.

You can use the Collapse button to collapse (hide) the Function Arguments box while you select the desired range in the worksheet.

Function Arguments

MAX

Number1 B6:B10   = {250;342;74;113;337}
Number2   = number

= 342

Returns the largest value in a set of values. Ignores logical values and text.

Number1: number1,number2,... are 1 to 255 numbers, empty cells, logical values, or text numbers for which you want the maximum.

Formula result = 342

Help on this function   OK   Cancel

NOTE! *The ScreenTip for the Function Wizard* f_x *is displayed as Insert Function.*

QR▶ **QUICK REFERENCE: USING THE FUNCTION WIZARD TO ENTER A FUNCTION IN A CELL**

Task	Procedure
Create a function using the Function Wizard	▪ Select the cell(s) in which you wish to enter a function.
	▪ Click the Function Wizard button.
	▪ Choose the desired function and click OK.
	▪ Select the range to which you wish to apply the function.
	▪ Click OK.

Hands-On 9.7   Use the Function Wizard

In this exercise, you will complete the commissions worksheet by using the Function Wizard to create both the maximum and minimum functions.

1. Click in cell B13.

2. Follow these steps to create the Maximum function.

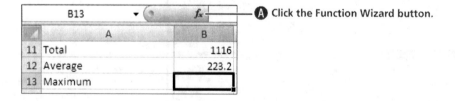

Ⓐ Click the Function Wizard button.

	A	B
11	Total	1116
12	Average	223.2
13	Maximum	

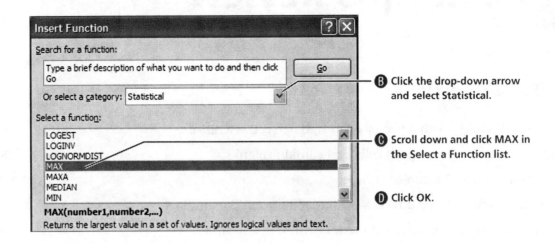

Ⓑ Click the drop-down arrow and select Statistical.

Ⓒ Scroll down and click MAX in the Select a Function list.

Ⓓ Click OK.

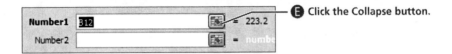

Ⓔ Click the Collapse button.

Ⓕ Click and drag to select the range B6:B10.

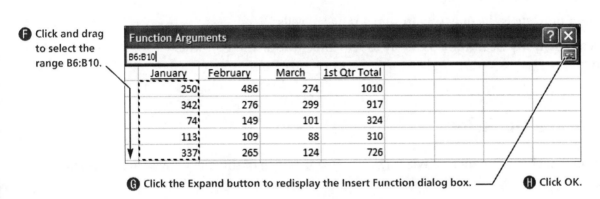

Ⓖ Click the Expand button to redisplay the Insert Function dialog box.

Ⓗ Click OK.

3. Use the fill handle to copy the formula to the range of C13:E13.

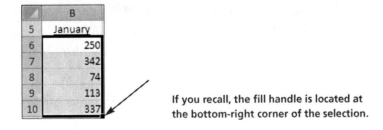

If you recall, the fill handle is located at the bottom-right corner of the selection.

4. Using the steps outlined in step 2, create the Minimum function in cell B14.

5. Copy the function in cell B14 to the range of C14:E14.

6. Save your workbook and close Excel.

Concepts Review

True/False Questions

1. All formulas begin with an equals (=) sign or a cell reference.　　TRUE　FALSE

2. AutoSum can total a range of cells that contains blanks.　　TRUE　FALSE

3. MIN and MAX are examples of functions.　　TRUE　FALSE

4. Function arguments are always surrounded by quotation marks (" ").　　TRUE　FALSE

5. You can use more than one arithmetic operator in a formula.　　TRUE　FALSE

6. When you type a cell reference in a formula, you must type the column letter in uppercase.　　TRUE　FALSE

7. You use F4 to make a cell reference absolute.　　TRUE　FALSE

8. You can use AutoFill to copy a formula.　　TRUE　FALSE

9. Formula AutoComplete is the only way to sum a range of cells.　　TRUE　FALSE

10. "Please Excuse Sally My Dear Aunt" is a way to remember the arithmetic order of operations.　　TRUE　FALSE

Multiple Choice Questions

1. Which button launches the Function Wizard?
   a. AutoSum
   b. Insert Function
   c. Create Function
   d. AutoFunction

2. Which function calculates the highest value in a selection?
   a. COUNT
   b. MIN
   c. MAX
   d. AVERAGE

3. Which of the following statements about using AutoSum is true?
   a. AutoSum automatically sums a non-adjacent column or row of numbers.
   b. AutoSum automatically sums an adjacent column or row of numbers.
   c. AutoSum can sum only a list of values in the column above.
   d. None of the above

4. Which cell reference contains dollar signs?
   a. Absolute
   b. Relative
   c. Mixed
   d. Both a and c

Skill Builders

Skill Builder 9.1   Use the AutoSum Function

In this exercise, you will use AutoSum to compute totals.

1. Open the sb-Benefit Plan workbook from the Lesson 09 folder in your file storage location.

2. Click cell C10, and then choose Home→Editing→Sum 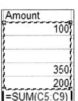 from the Ribbon.
   Notice that Excel proposes the formula =SUM(C8:C9). Excel proposes this incorrect formula because there are empty cells in the range you are to sum.

3. Drag the mouse pointer over the range C5:C9.
   The flashing marquee will surround the range C5:C9.

4. Complete the entry.
   The total should equal 650.

5. Use the techniques described in the preceding steps to compute the totals in cells E10, G10, and I10.

6. Save the changes to your workbook and close it.

Skill Builder 9.2   Create Simple Formulas

In this exercise, you will create formulas using the keyboard as well as the point-and-click method.

1. Open the sb-Orders and Returns workbook from the Lesson 09 folder in your file storage location.

2. Click cell B18.

3. Type **=**.

4. Click in cell B4, and type **+**.

5. Click in cell B9, and type **+**.

6. Click in cell B14, and tap Enter.

7. Use AutoFill to copy the formula to cells C18 and D18.

8. Using the techniques described in the preceding steps, create a formula in cell B19 that totals the exchanges from all three stores.

9. Create another formula in cell B20 that totals the returns from all three stores.

10. Use AutoFill to copy the formulas into the appropriate cells.

11. Take a few minutes to examine the formulas in the Formula Bar.

12. When finished, save and close the workbook.

Skill Builder 9.3   Use Formula AutoComplete and AutoFill

In this exercise, you will calculate averages by using the Formula AutoComplete feature.

1. Open the sb-Greeting Cards workbook from the Lesson 09 folder in your file storage location.

2. Click cell B8.

3. Begin typing the formula **=aver**, and then tap Tab to choose AVERAGE as the function.

4. Drag to select B3:B6, and then tap Enter.
   The result should equal 33.

5. Use the fill handle to copy the formula across row 8.

6. Click cell B17.

7. Use Formula AutoComplete to average the range B12:B15.
   The result should equal 23.5. Once again, you can type the function name and arguments in lowercase and Excel will convert them to uppercase.

8. Use the fill handle to copy the formula across row 17.

9. Click cell B20.

10. Use point mode to enter the formula =B7-B16, and complete the entry.
    The result should be 38.

11. Use the fill handle to copy the formula across row 20.

12. Save and close the workbook.

Skill Builder 9.4   Use Absolute References and Perform a What-If Analysis

In this exercise, you will create a worksheet that calculates commissions as total sales multiplied by the commission rate. You will change the commission rate to see the impact this change has on the total sales. You will use an absolute reference when referencing the commission rate.

1. Start a new workbook, and set up the following worksheet. Type all numbers as shown.

	A	B	C	
1	January Commission Report			
2				
3	Commission Rate		10%	
4				
5		Sales	Commission	
6	Ahmed	42000		
7	James	38000		
8	Sierra	65000		
9	Malik	18000		
10	Joseph	29000		

2. Click cell C6, and enter the formula **=B6*$C$3** in the cell.
   The result should be 4200. Cell C3 needs an absolute reference because you will copy the formula down the column and because the new formulas must also reference C3.

3. Use the fill handle to copy the formula down the column to cells C7 through C10.

4. Click cell C3, and change the percentage to **15%**.
   By this time, you should see the benefit of setting up values first (such as the commission rate) and referencing them in formulas. It allows you to perform what-if analyses. In most cases, you will need absolute references when referencing variables in this manner. Absolute references are necessary whenever you copy a formula that references a variable in a fixed location.

5. Change the commission percentage back to **10%**.

6. Save the workbook as **sb-January Commissions** in the Lesson 09 folder and close it.

LESSON 10

Formatting Worksheets and Charting Basics

In this lesson, you will learn how to use several of Excel's formatting features to enhance your worksheets. You will also learn how to manipulate the structure of worksheets. By the end of this lesson, you will be able to create basic Excel charts that will impress your boss, co-workers, and family members.

LESSON OBJECTIVES

After studying this lesson, you will be able to:

- Format worksheets using a variety of methods: Ribbon, mini toolbar, Format Cells dialog box
- Horizontally align and indent cell entries
- Merge and center the contents of cells
- Format cell borders and fill colors
- Modify column width and row height
- Insert and delete columns, rows, and cells
- Create a variety of different chart types
- Move and size embedded charts
- Preview and print charts

Case Study: Formatting and Charting with Excel

Mendy Dobranski runs a computer and QuickBooks consulting business. She is working on her 3rd Quarter Income Statement for 2008. So far she has entered all of the data, but the report looks very drab and boring. She is now ready to spruce it up by using many of Excel's formatting features.

Mendy's Computer Services				
Income Statement				
3rd Quarter 2008				
	July	August	September	Quarter Total
INCOME				
Computer Tutoring	$ 1,750	$ 1,900	$ 1,550	$ 5,200
Contract Teaching	1,300	1,250	1,650	4,200
QuickBooks Consulting	4,350	4,125	3,900	12,375
Total Income	$ 7,400	$ 7,275	$ 7,100	$ 21,775

Mr. Fitzpatrick is creating a test blueprint in order to ensure that the test he is about to create for Lesson 9, Working with Formulas and Functions, is aligned to the learning objectives in the lesson. You will be working with the structure of the worksheet in order to make it look just right.

	A	B	C	D	E	F	G	H
1		Mr. Fitzpatrick's Class						
2		Test Blueprint						
3			Categories					
4		Content Outline	Knowledge	Comprehension	Application	Analysis	Total	Percentage
5			(Number of Items)					
6	1.	Create formulas to calculate values, utilizng the proper syntax and order of operations						
7	a.	The student can create a formula using the proper mathematical operators.			2		2	6%

Christie Giamo is the founder and CEO of Autosoft, a rapidly growing software development company. Christie has asked her sales manager, Andy Broderick, to prepare charts depicting revenue for the 2007 fiscal year. Andy uses Excel's charting tools to produce impressive charts to meet Christie's high standards.

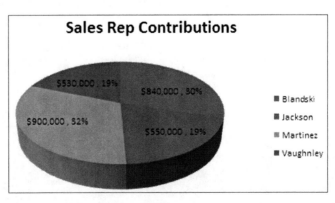

A pie chart produced by Andy.

Formatting Worksheets

Formatting deals with changing how the data in your worksheet looks, not with changing the data itself. In Excel and other Office programs, you can format text by changing the font, font size, and font color. You can also apply various font enhancements, including bold, italic, and underline. To format cells, select the desired cell(s) and apply formats using buttons on the Home tab of the Ribbon, by using the Format Cells dialog box, or by using the mini toolbar that appears when you right-click a cell or select text.

Formatting Entries with the Ribbon

The Font group on the Home tab of the Ribbon provides you with many popular formatting commands.

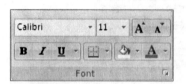

The Font group on the Home tab of the Ribbon makes finding formatting options easy.

Using the Mini Toolbar

The mini toolbar, a new feature in the Office 2007 Suite, will appear when text is selected. It will appear transparent until you move the mouse pointer over it. If you right-click a cell, the mini toolbar will appear non-transparent, ready to use. The mini toolbar will allow you to format the selected text without having to have the Home tab of the Ribbon displayed. This can be extremely convenient when you are primarily working with another tab of the Ribbon.

If you select text, the mini toolbar will appear transparent.

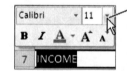
Once the mouse pointer is placed over mini toolbar or you right-click a cell, the mini toolbar will appear "solid."

The mini toolbar will appear when text is selected, such as when "INCOME" is selected above.

Live Preview

In Office 2007, you will have the opportunity to preview how many formatting changes will look before actually issuing the command. Where this feature is available, you will see how the selected area will look when you place your mouse pointer over the formatting option.

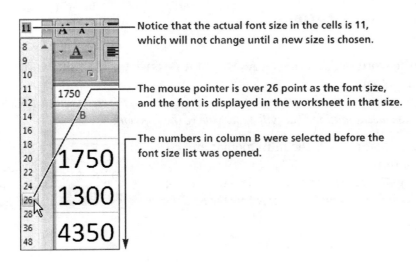

Notice that the actual font size in the cells is 11, which will not change until a new size is chosen.

The mouse pointer is over 26 point as the font size, and the font is displayed in the worksheet in that size.

The numbers in column B were selected before the font size list was opened.

 ## Hands-On 10.1　Format Cells with the Ribbon and Mini Toolbar

In this exercise, you will begin to format the worksheet by using both the Ribbon and the mini toolbar.

Open an Excel File

1. Start Excel.

2. Open the Mendy's Computer Services workbook in the Lesson 10 folder in your file storage location.
   You will see a worksheet displayed that contains all of the data and formulas but that is very much in need of some "beautification"! We will begin by changing the font size of the entire worksheet.

Use the Ribbon to Format

In this section, you will first select the entire worksheet. This means that any formatting that is applied will affect the contents of the whole worksheet.

3. Follow these steps to change the font size for the entire worksheet:

Ⓐ Click the Select All button at the top left of the worksheet.

Ⓑ Ensure that the Home tab is displayed on the Ribbon.

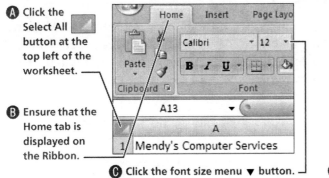

Ⓒ Click the font size menu ▼ button.　Ⓓ Choose 12.

Notice that as you move the mouse pointer over the font size list, Excel will allow you to preview how the worksheet would appear if each font size were selected.

Use the Mini Toolbar to Format

4. Click cell A6.

5. Double-click the word *INCOME* in cell A6 two times—once to select the word, and once to open the mini toolbar.
   The first time you double-click, the cell will be available for editing; the second time, INCOME will be selected and a translucent mini toolbar will appear above the selection.

6. Move the mouse pointer over the mini toolbar and click the Bold **B** button.
   When you move your mouse pointer over the transparent mini toolbar, it will become visible and you can choose the Bold option.

7. Right-click cell A12.
   Right-clicking a cell will also display the mini toolbar.

8. Click the Bold **B** button on the mini toolbar.

9. Use Ctrl + S to save your work before you move to the next topic.

Using Excel's Alignment and Indent Features

Excel allows you to alter how the text is aligned within cells. In addition to the standard left, center, right, and justify horizontal alignments, you can indent the contents within a cell from either edge.

Aligning Entries

The Align Left ⬛, Center ⬛, and Align Right ⬛ buttons on the Home tab of the Ribbon let you align entries within cells. By default, text entries are left aligned and number entries are right aligned. To change alignment, select the cell(s) and click the desired alignment button.

Indenting Cell Entries

The Increase Indent ⬛ button and Decrease Indent ⬛ button in the Alignment group on the Home tab of the Ribbon let you offset entries from the edges of cells. If a cell entry is left aligned, it will indent from the left edge, and if it is right aligned, it will indent from the right edge. Indenting is useful for conveying the hierarchy of entries. The following illustration shows indented cells:

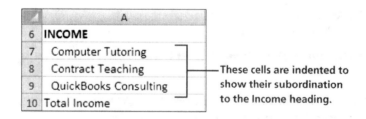

These cells are indented to show their subordination to the Income heading.

Merge and Center Command

The Merge & Center button merges selected cells and changes the alignment of the merged cell to center. This technique is often used to center a heading across columns. You split a merged and centered cell by clicking the Merge & Center button again. The Merge & Center menu button (see the following illustration) displays a menu with additional merge options.

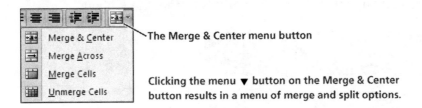

The Merge & Center menu button

Clicking the menu ▼ button on the Merge & Center button results in a menu of merge and split options.

	A	B	C	D	E
1	Mendy's Computer Services				
2	Income Statement				
3	3rd Quarter 2008				

Cells A1:E1 are merged, and the Mendy's Computer Services heading is centered above columns A–E. The entire heading is contained within cell A1.

QUICK REFERENCE: WORKING WITH ALIGNMENTS AND INDENTS

Task	Procedure
Change the alignment in cells	■ Select the cells in which you wish to change the alignment. ■ Click the appropriate button in the Alignment group on the Home tab of the Ribbon.
Indent a cell or range of cells	■ Select the cells that you wish to indent. ■ Click the appropriate button in the Alignment group on the Home tab of the Ribbon.
Merge and center a range of cells	■ Select the cells you wish to merge. ■ Display the Home tab of the Ribbon. ■ Choose Home→Alignment→Merge & Center.

In this exercise, you will set the alignment in cells as well as indent entries.

Change the Alignment in Cells

1. Select the range B5:E5.

2. Choose Home→Alignment→Align Text Right ![icon] from the Ribbon.

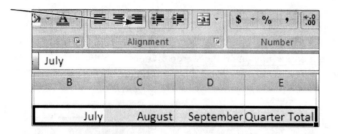

Indent Cell Entries

3. Follow these steps to indent entries in a range of cells:

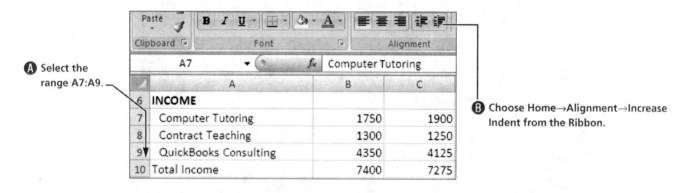

Ⓐ Select the range A7:A9.

Ⓑ Choose Home→Alignment→Increase Indent from the Ribbon.

4. Select the range A13:23.

5. Choose Home→Alignment→Increase Indent ![icon] from the Ribbon.
   Now both the types of income and the expenses have been "set off" from the left edge of the cell.

Merge and Center a Range of Cells

6. Select the range A1:E1.

7. Choose Home→Alignment→Merge & Center from the Ribbon.
   The entry from cell A1 is now centered over columns A through E.

8. Click cell C1.
   Notice that A1 is displayed in the Name box. While cell C1 is merged with A1, B1, D1, and E1, it essentially no longer exists!

9. Select A2:E2.

10. Choose Home→Alignment→Merge & Center from the Ribbon.

11. Repeat steps 9 and 10 for the range A3:E3.

Formatting Numbers

Excel lets you format numbers in a variety of ways. Number formats change the way numbers are displayed, though they do not change the actual numbers. Once a number formatting has been applied to a cell, it remains with the cell—even if the contents are deleted. The following table describes the most common number formats.

Number Format	Description
General	Numbers are formatted with the General Style format by default. It does not apply any special formats to the numbers.
Comma	The Comma Style format inserts a comma after every third digit in the number. It also inserts a decimal point and two decimal places, which can be removed if desired.
Currency	The Currency Style format is the same as the Comma format except that it adds a dollar ($) sign in front of the number.
Percent	A percent (%) sign is inserted to the right of the number in the Percent Style. The percentage is calculated by multiplying the number by 100.

TIP! *If you begin an entry with a dollar sign, the Currency Style format will automatically be applied.*

The following table provides several examples of formatted numbers.

Number Entered	Format	How the Number Is Displayed
5347.82	General	5347.82
5347.82	Comma with 0 decimal places	5,348
5347.82	Comma with 2 decimal places	5,347.82
5347.82	Currency with 0 decimal places	$5,347
5347.82	Currency with 2 decimal places	$5,347.82
.5347	Percentage with 0 decimal places	53%
.5347	Percentage with 2 decimal places	53.47%

Using the Number Command Group

The Number group on the Home tab of the Ribbon allows you to format your numbers in a variety of ways, with the most common styles displayed as buttons. The top area of the group displays the number formatting of the selected cell(s). Clicking the menu button to the right of the current number formatting displays a menu of additional number format options.

If you click the Dialog Box Launcher button in the Number group, the Format Cells dialog box will appear with the Number tab displayed.

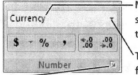

Notice that the number style of the selected cell(s) is displayed at the top of the group (in this example it is Currency).

This menu button displays additional formatting styles.

Clicking the Dialog Box Launcher button will open the Format Cells dialog box with the Number tab selected.

Using Accounting and Currency Styles

There are two number styles that apply currency symbols (such as dollar signs) to numbers. You will notice a difference in where the dollar sign is placed based on the style you select. If you choose the

$5,347.82

$ 5,347.82

In the Currency Style, the dollar sign will be placed next to the number.

In the Accounting Style, the dollar sign will be fixed at the left edge of the cell.

accounting style, currency symbols will appear fixed at the left of the cells. The currency style, on the other hand, will display the currency symbol next to the number in the cell.

Applying the Percent Style

Once you apply formatting to a cell, it will remain until you change or clear it, regardless of whether there is any data contained in the cell. In order to apply the Percent Style, you have two options.

■ Select the cells that you wish to format as Percent Style and apply the formatting. If you format the cells first, you can type 25 and it will be formatted as 25%.

■ Type the value in the cell first, and then apply the Percent Style formatting. If you type in the value first, you will need to type it in as a decimal. For instance, you will need to type in .25 in order for it to format properly as 25%. If you type in 25 and then apply Percent Style formatting, it will appear as 2500%.

Displaying Negative Numbers

Negative number displays can be either preceded by a minus sign or surrounded by parentheses. You can also display negative numbers in red. The Currency option and Number option in the Format Cells dialog box let you choose the format for negative numbers.

The negative number format you choose affects the alignment of numbers in the cells. If the format displays negative numbers in parentheses, a small space equal to the width of a closing parenthesis appears on the right edge of cells containing positive numbers. Excel does this so the decimal points are aligned in columns containing both positive and negative numbers.

16	Internet	45	45
17	Professional Dues	0	500
18	Rent	1500	1500
19	Software	-50	0
20	Subscriptions	25	0

When the numbers are formatted as General Style, the negative numbers will be displayed with a minus sign in front of them.

16	Internet	45.00	45.00
17	Professional Dues	-	500.00
18	Rent	1,500.00	1,500.00
19	Software	(50.00)	-
20	Subscriptions	25.00	-

When you choose the Comma Style format, you can accept the default negative number format with parentheses or change it to display a minus sign in the Format Cells dialog box. If you choose to format negative numbers with parentheses, the positive numbers will be set a bit further from the right edge of the cell in order for the decimal points to be aligned. Notice also that the cells containing the number 0 are displayed with dashes.

 ## Hands-On 10.3   Format Numbers

In this exercise, you will apply various number formatting options to the worksheet.

1. Follow these steps to apply Currency Style format to a range of cells:

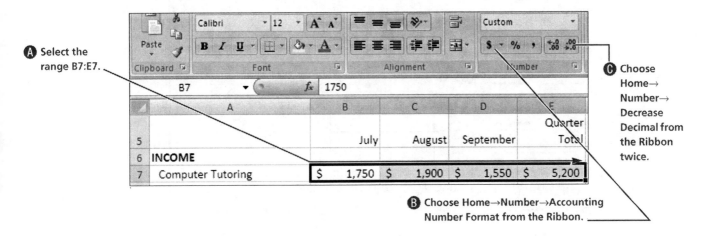

A Select the range B7:E7.

B Choose Home→Number→Accounting Number Format from the Ribbon.

C Choose Home→ Number→ Decrease Decimal from the Ribbon twice.

Notice that the Accounting Number Format will display the dollar sign as fixed at the left edge of the cells. "Custom" will be displayed as the number format since you changed the number of decimal places of the Currency Style.

2. Select the range B8:E9.

3. Choose Home→Number→Comma Style 🔳 from the Ribbon.

4. Choose Home→ Number→Decrease Decimal 🔳 from the Ribbon twice.

5. Select the range B10:E10, hold down ⌐Ctrl⌐, and select the range B24:E25.
Remember that by using ⌐Ctrl⌐, you can select multiple ranges to which you can apply formatting.

6. Choose Home→Accounting Number Format $\boxed{\$}$ from the Ribbon.

7. Choose Home→Decrease Decimal $\boxed{\overset{.00}{\rightarrow .0}}$ from the Ribbon twice.

8. Select the range B13:E23.

9. Apply Comma Style formatting with no decimals to the selection.

10. Select the range A25:E25.

11. Choose Home→Font→Bold $\boxed{\mathbf{B}}$ from the Ribbon.

12. Use $\boxed{\text{Ctrl}}+\boxed{\text{S}}$ to save your work.
    Notice that all of the 0 entries are now displayed as dashes with comma formatting applied.

Using the Format Cells Dialog Box

We have discussed the Number and Alignment tabs of the Format Cells dialog box; now we will examine in more depth how to truly utilize this important dialog box. There are six tabs in the Format Cells dialog box that allow you to format different aspects of your worksheet: Number, Alignment, Font, Border, Fill, and Protection.

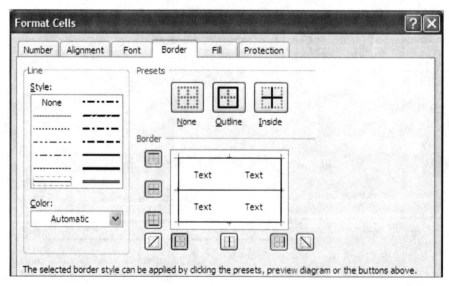

The Border tab of the Format Cells dialog box allows you to set the borders for the selected cells. In this example, a line will appear around the entire selection as well as between each row that is selected.

Borders and Fill Color

The Borders 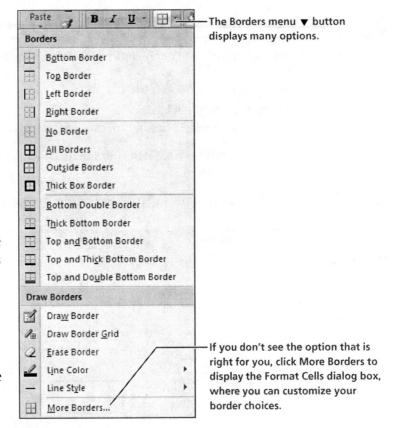 button on the Home tab of the Ribbon lets you add borders to cell edges. When you click the Borders menu ▼ button, a list of options appears. You can apply a border style to all selected cells by choosing it from the list. You can also choose More Borders from the bottom of the list to display the Borders tab of the Format Cells dialog box.

The image displayed on the Borders button on the Ribbon will change based on the last border applied. This feature makes it easy to apply the same border formatting throughout the workbook.

The Borders menu ▼ button displays many options.

If you don't see the option that is right for you, click More Borders to display the Format Cells dialog box, where you can customize your border choices.

Applying Fill Colors and Patterns

The Fill Color 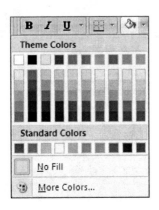 button on the Home tab of the Ribbon lets you fill the background of selected cells with color. When you click the Fill Color menu button, a palette of colors appears. You can apply a color to all selected cells by choosing it from the palette. The fill color is independent of the font color used to format text and numbers. The Format Cells dialog box has a Fill tab that lets you apply fill colors and a variety of patterns and effects.

This palette of colors results when you click the Fill Color menu ▼ button. The color you choose will fill the cell but will not affect the color of the font.

In this exercise, you will apply borders and fill coloring to the worksheet.

Apply Borders to a Selection

1. Select the range A1:E25.
   When you choose A1, you will actually be choosing the entire merged cell that spans across column E.

2. Choose Home→Font→Borders menu ▼→More Borders from the Ribbon.

3. Follow these steps to apply the border formatting:

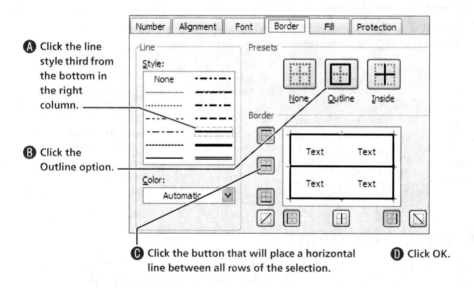

Ⓐ Click the line style third from the bottom in the right column.

Ⓑ Click the Outline option.

Ⓒ Click the button that will place a horizontal line between all rows of the selection.

Ⓓ Click OK.

Notice that the Borders button now displays the icon ▦▾, which represents the More Borders option on the Borders menu. It will always display the last option selected from the Borders menu.

4. Use Ctrl + Z to undo the borders.

5. Select the range B9:E9, hold down the Ctrl key, and select the range B23:E23. Then release the Ctrl key.

6. Click the Borders menu ▼ button.

7. Choose the Bottom Border option to place a border along the bottom of the selected cells.

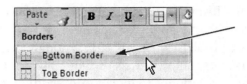

A border will appear along the bottom of both of the selected ranges. The Borders button will now display the Bottom Border icon.

8. Select the range B25:E25.

9. Click the Borders button drop-down arrow, and choose Top and Double Bottom Border.

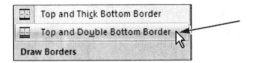

Apply Fill Color to a Range

10. Select the range A6:E6, hold down the Ctrl key, and select A12:E12. Then release the Ctrl key.

11. Follow these steps to apply a fill color to the selected ranges:

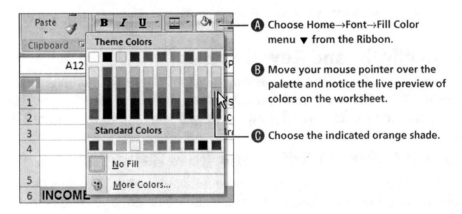

Ⓐ Choose Home→Font→Fill Color menu ▼ from the Ribbon.

Ⓑ Move your mouse pointer over the palette and notice the live preview of colors on the worksheet.

Ⓒ Choose the indicated orange shade.

12. Click away from the selection to view the color in the selected ranges.
Notice that the cells are now orange, but the text has remained black.

13. Use Ctrl + S to save your work.

14. Close the workbook.

Modifying Columns and Rows

As you have seen, many entries do not fit within the default column size. Worksheets can also appear overcrowded with the standard row heights, which may tempt you to insert blank rows to make the worksheet more readable. The problem with this "fix," though, is that it can cause problems down the road when you begin to use some of Excel's more powerful features. In this section, you will use more time-saving techniques to fix column width and row height issues, such as changing multiple columns and rows at the same time and using AutoFit to let Excel figure out the best width or height. Both of these commands simply require you to select multiple columns or rows before issuing the command.

	A	B	C	D	E	F
1	Test Bluepr	Content Outline	Categories			
2			Knowledg	Comprehe	Applicatic	Analysis
3			(Number of Items)			
4	1.	**Create formulas to calculate values, utilizng the proper syntax and order of operations**				

You can see that we have a lot of work to do here in resizing rows and columns!

Column Widths and Row Heights

There are a variety of methods for changing widths of columns and heights of rows. They can be performed on either one or multiple columns or rows. Probably the most efficient way to adjust widths and heights is to simply drag the heading lines of the column(s) or row(s).

Standard Column Widths and Row Heights

Each column in a new worksheet has a standard width of 8.43 characters, where the default character is Calibri 11 point. Each row has a standard height of 15 points, which is approximately one-fifth of an inch.

AutoFit

You can adjust both column widths and row heights with the AutoFit command. AutoFit adjusts column widths to fit the widest entry in a column. Likewise, AutoFit adjusts row heights to accommodate the tallest entry in a row. The following Quick Reference table discusses AutoFit options and other commands for setting column widths and row heights.

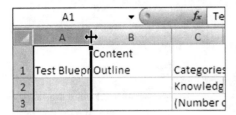

When you point to the border between columns or rows, a double-pointed arrow lets you know you can manually drag to change its size or double-click to issue the AutoFit command.

QUICK REFERENCE: CHANGING COLUMN WIDTHS AND ROW HEIGHTS

Technique	Procedure
Set a precise column width	■ Select the column for which you wish to change the width. ■ Choose Home→Cells→Format→Column Width from the Ribbon. ■ Type in the column width you desire. ■ Click OK.
Set column widths with AutoFit using the Ribbon	■ Select the column(s) for which you wish to change the width. ■ Choose Home→Cells→Format→AutoFit Column Width from the Ribbon.
Set column widths with AutoFit by double-clicking	■ Select a single or multiple columns for which you wish to change the width. ■ Double-click between any two selected headings or to the right of the selected single column heading. Make sure you double-click only when you see the double arrow ⟺ mouse pointer. ■ This will AutoFit all selected columns.
Set a precise row height	■ Select the row for which you wish to change the height. ■ Choose Home→Cells→Format→Row Height from the Ribbon. ■ Type in the row height you desire. ■ Click OK.
Set row heights with AutoFit	■ Select the row for which you wish to change the height. ■ Choose Home→Cells→Format→AutoFit Row Height from the Ribbon. You can also select multiple rows and double-click between any two selected headings. This will AutoFit all selected rows.
Manually adjust column widths and row heights	■ Select the desired columns or rows and drag the column or row heading lines.

In this exercise, you will change the column width and row height to ensure that the cell entries fit properly.

1. Open the Mr. Fitzpatrick's Content Outline file from the Lesson 10 folder in your file storage location.

Adjust Column Widths

2. Follow these steps to resize column A:

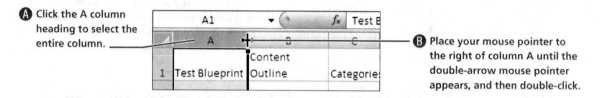

Ⓐ Click the A column heading to select the entire column.

Ⓑ Place your mouse pointer to the right of column A until the double-arrow mouse pointer appears, and then double-click.

Notice that the column is resized to fit the widest entry, which is in row 1. We will be merging and centering the title in row 1, so this column is too wide for our use.

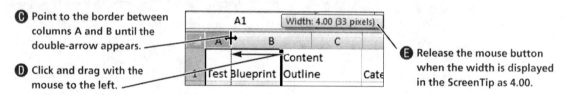

Ⓒ Point to the border between columns A and B until the double-arrow appears.

Ⓓ Click and drag with the mouse to the left.

Ⓔ Release the mouse button when the width is displayed in the ScreenTip as 4.00.

Set a Precise Column Width

3. Click the column B header to select the entire column.

4. Follow these steps to precisely set the column width:

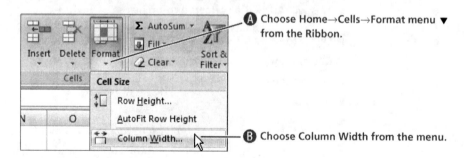

Ⓐ Choose Home→Cells→Format menu ▼ from the Ribbon.

Ⓑ Choose Column Width from the menu.

Ⓒ Type **60**, and then tap ⌶Enter⌶.

The column has been sized much larger to accommodate the larger cell entries, which have "spread out" since the cells are formatted to wrap text.

Use AutoFit to Adjust the Row Height

5. Click the header for row 4, and then drag down through row 23.
   Rows 4 through 23 should now be selected. Any command issued will apply to all selected rows.

6. Choose Home→Cells→Format menu ▼→AutoFit Row Height from the Ribbon as shown.
   All of the selected rows will shrink to fit the tallest entry.

7. Use [Ctrl] + [S] to save your work.

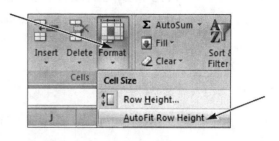

Inserting and Deleting Columns, Rows, and Cells

You can insert and delete columns, rows, and cells as needed in your worksheets. You probably figure that you will have plenty of rows and columns since you start out with more than 1,000,000 and 16,000 of them, respectively. The ability to insert and delete will come in handy when you want to restructure your worksheet after it has been created.

Inserting and Deleting Rows and Columns

Excel lets you insert and delete rows and columns. This gives you the flexibility to restructure your worksheets after they have been set up. The Quick Reference table in this section discusses the various procedures used to insert and delete rows and columns.

Inserting and Deleting Cells

If you want to insert or delete only cells, not entire rows or columns, you need to issue a command to insert or delete cells. This will allow you to add or remove a "chunk" or range of cells from your worksheet. This may cause problems because it alters the structure of your entire worksheet. For this reason, use this feature cautiously.

Shift Cells Option

When you add or remove a range of cells from your worksheet, you will need to tell Excel how to shift the surrounding cells to either make room for the addition or fill the space from the deletion.

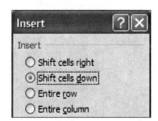

There are four Shift Cells options for you to choose from when you insert cells.

The Appearance of the Cells Group Commands

The buttons in the Cells group of the Home tab of the Ribbon will appear differently depending on the size of your Excel window (which may be determined by the size of your monitor).

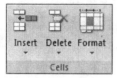

The figure on the left displays how the Cells group buttons will be displayed in a larger window, whereas the figure on the right displays the buttons as displayed in a smaller window. In the exercise steps, you will see the illustrations depicting the larger Ribbon buttons.

QUICK REFERENCE: INSERTING AND DELETING ROWS, COLUMNS, AND CELLS	
Task	**Procedure**
Insert rows	■ Select the number of rows you wish to insert (the same number of new rows will be inserted above the selected rows). ■ Choose Home→Cells→Insert from the Ribbon.
Insert columns	■ Select the number of columns you wish to insert (the same number of new columns will be inserted to the left of the selected columns). ■ Choose Home→Cells→Insert from the Ribbon.
Delete rows	■ Select the rows you wish to delete. ■ Right-click the selection and choose Delete.
Delete columns	■ Select the columns you wish to delete. ■ Right-click the selection and choose Delete.
Insert cells	■ Select the cells in the worksheet where you want the inserted cells to appear. ■ Choose Home→Cells→Insert from the Ribbon. ■ Choose the desired Shift Cells option.
Delete cells	■ Select the cells you wish to delete. ■ Choose Home→Cells→Delete from the Ribbon. ■ Choose the desired Shift Cells option.

In this exercise, you will insert and delete rows, as well as insert cells into the worksheet.

Delete Unnecessary Rows

1. Select rows 15 and 23, using the ⃞Ctrl key to select nonadjacent rows.
    The rows in which there are no objectives listed are now selected.

2. Choose Home→Cells→Delete menu ▾→Delete Sheet Rows from the Ribbon.

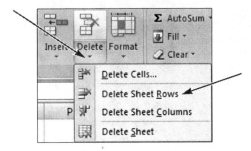

Add Another Row to the Sheet

3. Select row 8.
    When you choose to insert a row, it will be placed above the row you have selected.

4. Point (don't click) over the Insert Home→Cells→Insert ⊞ button on the Ribbon as shown.
    Notice that when you place your mouse pointer over the Insert button, there is a line that divides it into two halves. If you click above or to the left of the line (depending on how large the Ribbon appears on your computer), a new cell, row, or column will be inserted above or to the left of your selection. If you click below or to the right of the line, a menu appears from which you can select a command.

5. Click the Insert ⊞ button (not the menu ▾ button).

6. Enter the text in the following illustration into the appropriate cells.

	A	B	C	D	E
8	d.	The student will demonstrate how to use functions on the status bar in order to determine the minimum and maximum values in a range of cells.			2

7. Follow these steps to copy the necessary formulas:

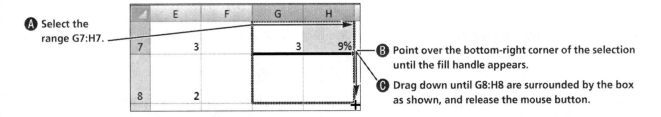

Ⓐ Select the range G7:H7.

Ⓑ Point over the bottom-right corner of the selection until the fill handle appears.

Ⓒ Drag down until G8:H8 are surrounded by the box as shown, and release the mouse button.

All of the formulas and functions have automatically been updated since cell references were used in creating the worksheet.

Insert Cells into the Worksheet

You have discovered that you want to merge and center the contents of cell A1 over the entire worksheet. You will need to "bump" everything in columns B through H down one row.

8. Select the range B1:H1.

9. Follow these steps to insert the cells and shift your existing data down:

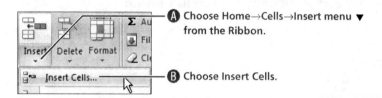

Ⓐ Choose Home→Cells→Insert menu ▼ from the Ribbon.

Ⓑ Choose Insert Cells.

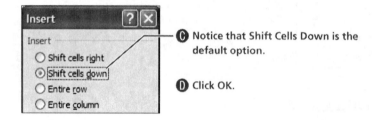

Ⓒ Notice that Shift Cells Down is the default option.

Ⓓ Click OK.

10. Select cell A3.

11. Choose Home→Cells→Insert ⊞ from the Ribbon.
    Everything in column A, below cell A3, will be shifted down one cell.

12. Select row 1.

13. Choose Home→Cells→Insert ⊞ from the Ribbon again.
    Since you selected an entire row first, a new row will be inserted.

Time to Format!

Now that we have shaken up the structure of the worksheet a bit, we will do some formatting to make it more presentable.

14. Follow these steps to enter text and then merge and center a range:

    ■ Select cell A1 and then type **Mr. Fitzpatrick's Class**.

    ■ Tap Enter.

    ■ Select the range A1:H1.

    ■ Choose Home→Alignment→Merge & Center ⊞ from the Ribbon.

    ■ Choose Home→Font→Font Size ▼→24 from the Ribbon.

15. Merge & Center ⊞ A2:H2, and then change the font size to 20.

16. Move (cut and paste) the contents of B3 to A3, and then merge and center ⊞ A3:B3.

17. Select B3:B4, and then click the Merge & Center 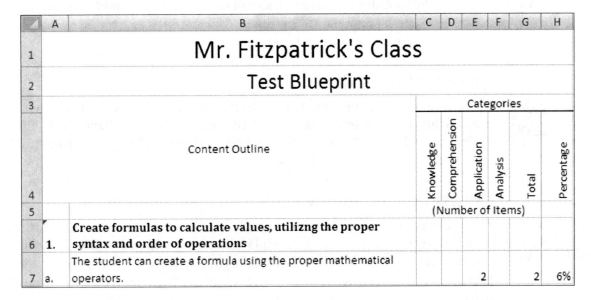 button twice.
    Notice that the Merge & Center command works for both horizontal and vertical ranges.

18. Merge and center ☰ C3:H3, and then place a border along the bottom of the cells.

19. Merge and center ☰ C5:G5.

20. Right-align ☰ B25:B26.

21. Select columns C through H.

22. Choose Home→Cells→Format menu ▾→AutoFit Column Width from the Ribbon.

23. Select row 3.

24. Choose Home→Cells→Format menu ▾→AutoFit Row Height from the Ribbon.
    When you are finished, your worksheet should resemble the following figure.

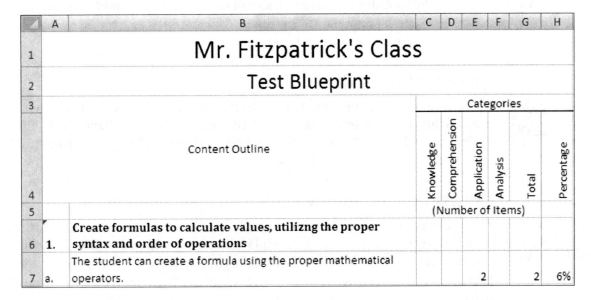

25. Use Ctrl + S to save your work.

Creating Charts in Excel

Numerical data is often easier to interpret when presented in a chart. You can embed a chart in a worksheet so that it appears alongside the worksheet data, or you can place the chart on a separate worksheet. Putting the chart on a separate worksheet prevents the chart from cluttering the data worksheet. Regardless of their placement, charts are always linked to the data from which they are created. Thus, charts are automatically updated when worksheet data changes. Charts are made up of individual objects including the chart title, legend, plot area, value axis, category axis, and data series. You can apply many options and enhancements to each object.

Integrated Chart Engine

New to Office 2007, a chart engine is integrated throughout the suite of programs. It is now easy to create a chart in Microsoft Word or PowerPoint as well as in Excel. Once you have mastered the topics in this lesson, you will be able to understand how to create charts in the other Microsoft Office applications as well! When a chart is created in another application, it is actually saved and stored as an Excel chart.

Introducing OfficeArt

OfficeArt is a new feature in Office 2007 that allows you to draw and format shapes. Charts are drawn with OfficeArt so you can format them with effects available to all OfficeArt shapes, such as realistic 3-D effects, shadow and glow effects, and gradient or texture fill effects. You will learn much more about OfficeArt in *Microsoft Excel 2007: Comprehensive*.

Creating New Charts

FROM THE KEYBOARD
F11 to place a chart on its own sheet

Charts can be created by choosing the chart type from the Insert tab of the Ribbon. If you want to see the entire list of chart types displayed before you make your choice, you can open the Insert Chart dialog box. When you create a chart, you have the option of either embedding it into the current worksheet where the data is or placing it on a separate sheet of its own. To place a chart on its own sheet, simply select it and then tap the F11 key. A new chart will be created on a separate sheet, and the embedded chart will remain as well. When you use the F11 key, the chart on the new sheet will be based on the default chart type, not the type that is embedded in the worksheet. An advantage of creating charts based on data within a workbook is that the chart data will automatically be updated when changes are made to the source data.

Choosing the Proper Source Data

It is important to select the proper data on which to base your chart. In addition to selecting the raw data for the chart, you will also want to ensure that you select any "total" rows that should be included in the chart. You should make sure that you select the proper row and column headings for your column and bar charts. If you notice that any of these important pieces are missing, you will need to reselect your source data.

Chart Types

Excel provides 11 major chart types. Each chart type also has several subtypes from which you can choose. Excel has a chart for every occasion.

Built-In Chart Types

Each chart type represents data in a different manner. You can present the same data in completely different ways by changing the chart type. For this reason, you should always use the chart type that most effectively represents your data. The three most common chart types are column, pie, and line. You will be creating all three types in this lesson.

User-Defined Charts

Excel lets you create and save customized charts to meet your particular needs. For example, you can create a customized chart that contains the name of your company and its color(s) in the background and use it as the basis for all new charts of that type.

The 11 major chart types are displayed along the left side. Click a type to see all of the subtypes displayed.

You can create and manage your own chart templates.

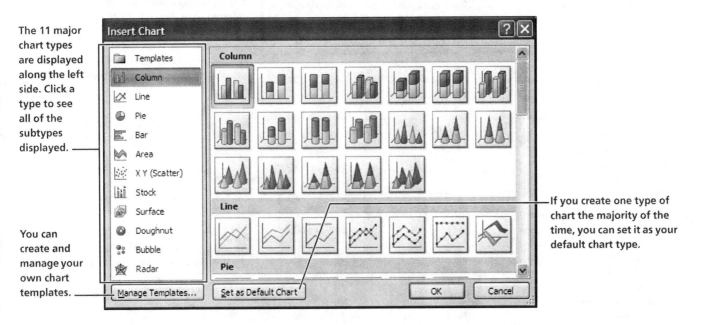

If you create one type of chart the majority of the time, you can set it as your default chart type.

Column Charts and Bar Charts

Column charts compare values (numbers) using vertical bars. Bar charts compare values using horizontal bars. Each column or bar represents a value from the worksheet. Column charts and bar charts are most useful for comparing sets of values (called data series). Column and bar charts can be created in 2-D or 3-D formats.

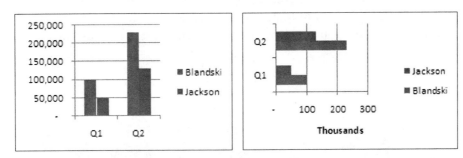

The column chart on the left and the bar chart on the right are displaying the exact same data, but the chart types are different. In this situation, the charts are showing a comparison of the quarterly sales for two employees, Blandski and Jackson.

Category Axis and Value Axis

The horizontal line that forms the base of a column chart is the category axis. The category axis typically measures units of time such as days, months, and quarters, although it can also measure products, people, tests, and other categories. The vertical line on the left side of a column chart is the value axis. The value axis typically measures values such as dollars. Most chart types (including column and bar charts) have a category and a value axis. The following illustrations show the worksheet data and one of the two column charts you will create in the next exercise. The illustrations show the objects included on most column charts and the corresponding data used to create the chart. Take a few minutes to study the following illustrations carefully.

	A	B	C	D	E
1	Autosoft 2007 Quarterly Sales				
2					
3		Q1	Q2	Q3	Q4
4	Blandski	100,000	230,000	280,000	230,000
5	Jackson	50,000	130,000	170,000	200,000
6	Martinez	120,000	120,000	320,000	340,000
7	Vaughnley	90,000	50,000	120,000	270,000
8					
9	Total	$ 360,000	$ 530,000	$ 890,000	$ 1,040,000

The following chart was created using the selected data shown here. Notice that the Total row was not included in the selection. The column chart compares the sales numbers for the individual quarters, but it does not include the total sales from row 9.

This is the vertical value axis. Excel created the numbering scale (0–400,000) after it determined the range of values included in the chart.

This is the horizontal category axis. The category axis labels (Q1, Q2, Q3, and Q4) were taken from row 3 of the selected worksheet cells.

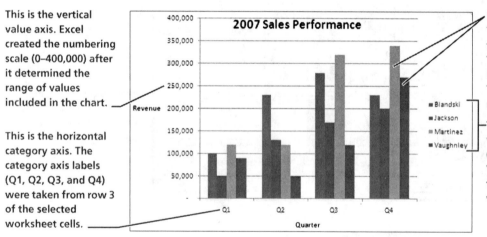

Notice the chart columns. The columns represent values from the various data series. The first data series are the Blandski numbers in row 4. The first column in each quarter represents the Blandski numbers.

This is a legend that identifies the various columns. The legend text (Blandski, Jackson, Martinez, and Vaughnley) was taken from the first column of the selected worksheet cells.

Notice that the chart includes a chart title (2007 Sales Performance), a value axis title (Revenue), and a category axis title (Quarter).

Chart and Axis Titles

Excel allows you to create titles for your charts as well as the value and category axes. If you choose a range of information that includes what appears to Excel to be a title, Excel will include it in the new chart. You can always edit this title if it is not correct.

Pie Charts

Pie charts are useful for comparing parts of a whole. For example, pie charts are often used in budgets to show how funds are allocated. You typically select only two sets of data when creating pie charts: the values to be represented by the pie slices and the labels to identify the slices. The following illustration shows a worksheet and an accompanying 3-D pie chart. Notice that the worksheet has a Total column. You will create a pie chart based on the Total column in the next exercise.

	A	B	C	D	E	F
3		Q1	Q2	Q3	Q4	Totals
4	Blandski	100,000	230,000	280,000	230,000	$840,000
5	Jackson	50,000	130,000	170,000	200,000	$550,000
6	Martinez	120,000	120,000	320,000	340,000	$900,000
7	Vaughnley	90,000	50,000	120,000	270,000	$530,000

The names in column A will become labels in the legend. The numbers in column F will determine the sizes of the slices.

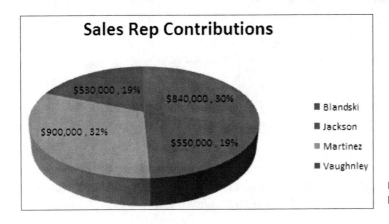

Excel calculates the percentages based on the numbers you select.

The Chart Tools

When a chart is selected, various Chart Tools will be displayed as additional tabs on the Ribbon. These tabs allow you to make changes to the design, layout, and formatting of the chart.

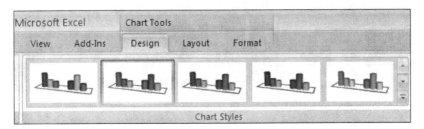

When a chart is selected, the Chart Tools will be displayed, adding the Design, Layout, and Format tabs to the Ribbon.

!TIP! *These additional Ribbon tabs are called contextual tabs.*

QUICK REFERENCE: CREATING A CHART

Task	Procedure
Create a chart	▪ Enter the data you wish to chart into Excel. ▪ Select the data range for the chart. ▪ Display the Insert tab of the Ribbon. ▪ Choose the type of chart from the Charts group.
Add a title to a chart	▪ Select the chart to which you wish to add a title. ▪ Choose Layout→Labels→Chart Title from the Ribbon to display the title options. ▪ Choose how you wish the title to appear. ▪ Select the default title "Chart Title," and type in the title you wish for your chart.
Add axis titles to a chart	▪ Select the chart to which you wish to add an axis title. ▪ Choose Layout→Labels→Axis Titles from the Ribbon to display the axis options. ▪ Choose whether you wish to apply a horizontal or vertical axis title. ▪ Choose how you wish the title to appear. ▪ Select the default title "Axis Title," and type in the title you wish for your axis. ▪ Repeat these steps for the other axis.

Hands-On 10.7   Create Charts

In this exercise, you will create two charts: a column chart and a pie chart. One chart will be embedded in the worksheet and the other will be placed on a separate worksheet.

Create an Embedded 2-D Column Chart

1. Open the workbook named Autosoft Quarterly Sales from the Lesson 10 folder.

2. Select the range A3:E7.

3. Follow these steps to create a clustered column chart:

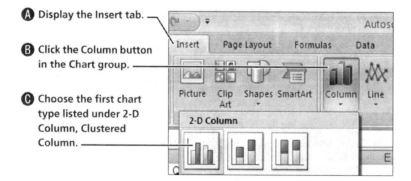

Ⓐ Display the Insert tab.

Ⓑ Click the Column button in the Chart group.

Ⓒ Choose the first chart type listed under 2-D Column, Clustered Column.

The chart will appear embedded in the Sales worksheet with the default properties for the clustered column chart type displayed. The data in the chart is based on the range of cells you preselected.

4. Look at the Ribbon and notice that the Chart Tools are now displayed.
   Notice that the chart is covering part of the data. You will learn how to move charts around a sheet in the next exercise.

Edit the Chart and Axis Titles

5. Choose Chart Tools→Layout→Labels→Chart Title →Centered Overlay Title from the Ribbon.

6. Follow these steps to title the chart:

Ⓐ Select the default title, *Chart Title.*

Ⓑ Type the new title as shown here.

Ⓒ Click anywhere outside of the title text box to accept the new title.

7. Choose Layout→Labels→Axis Titles 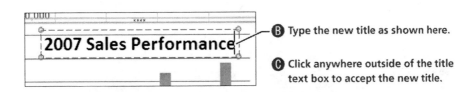→Primary Horizontal Axis Title→Title Below Axis from the Ribbon.

8. Drag to select the default title, *Axis Title.*

9. Type in the new horizontal axis title, **Quarter**, and then click away to accept the new title.

10. Choose Layout→Labels→Axis Titles 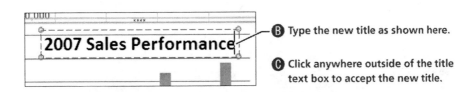→Primary Vertical Axis Title→Horizontal Title from the Ribbon.

11. Select the default title, *Axis Title.*

12. Type in the new vertical axis title, **Revenue**, and then click away to accept the new title.

Create a Pie Chart on a New Sheet

13. Select cell F3 and type the word **Totals**.

14. Select the range F4:F7.

15. Choose Home→Editing→AutoSum **Σ** from the Ribbon to compute the totals for column F.
    Excel calculates the total annual sales for each sales rep. Your totals should match those displayed in the figure for step 17.

16. Format the range of F4:F7 as Currency Style with no decimals.

17. Follow these steps to select the range for the chart:

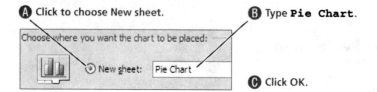

A Drag to select A4:A7.

B While holding `Ctrl`, drag to select F4:F7.

	A	B	C	D	E	F
3		Q1	Q2	Q3	Q4	Totals
4	Blandski	100,000	230,000	280,000	230,000	$840,000
5	Jackson	50,000	130,000	170,000	200,000	$550,000
6	Martinez	120,000	120,000	320,000	340,000	$900,000
7	Vaughnley	90,000	50,000	120,000	270,000	$530,000

18. Choose Insert→Charts→Pie →Pie in 3-D from the Ribbon as shown. *The new chart will appear embedded on the Sales worksheet. We will place it on a separate sheet in the next step.*

19. Choose Design→Location→Move Chart from the Ribbon.

20. Follow these steps to move it to a new sheet named Pie Chart:

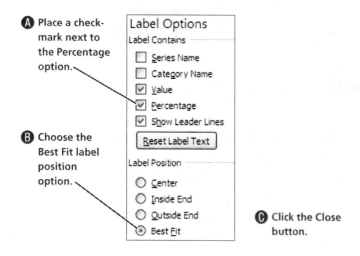

A Click to choose New sheet.

B Type **Pie Chart**.

Choose where you want the chart to be placed:

⦿ New sheet: | Pie Chart |

C Click OK.

Edit the Chart

21. Choose Layout→Labels→Chart Title →Above Chart from the Ribbon.

22. Select the default title and type **Sales Rep Contributions** then click outside of the Title box to accept the new title.

23. Choose Layout→Labels→Data Labels →More Data Label Options from the Ribbon. *The Format Data Labels dialog box appears.*

24. Follow these steps to format the data labels:

A Place a check-mark next to the Percentage option.

B Choose the Best Fit label position option.

Label Options

Label Contains
- ☐ Series Name
- ☐ Category Name
- ☑ Value
- ☑ Percentage
- ☑ Show Leader Lines

[Reset Label Text]

Label Position
- ○ Center
- ○ Inside End
- ○ Outside End
- ⦿ Best Fit

C Click the Close button.

Excel will display both the value and the percentages in each pie slice wherever they "best fit."

25. Save the workbook and leave it open for the next exercise.

Manipulating and Printing Embedded Charts

When a chart is selected, it is surrounded by a light blue border with sizing handles displayed. A selected chart can be both moved and resized when it is selected.

Moving Embedded Charts

Charts that are embedded in a worksheet can be easily moved to a new location. This can be accomplished by a simple drag, but you need to ensure that you click the chart area and not a separate element. Regardless of whether a chart is embedded within a worksheet or moved to a separate tab, the chart data will automatically update when values are changed in the source data.

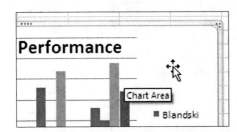

A four-pointed arrow indicates that you can drag to move this selected chart.

Sizing Embedded Charts

In order to size a chart, it must first be selected. You simply need to drag a sizing handle when the double-arrow mouse pointer is displayed. In order to change a chart size proportionately, hold [Shift] while dragging a corner handle.

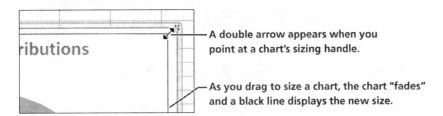

— A double arrow appears when you point at a chart's sizing handle.

— As you drag to size a chart, the chart "fades" and a black line displays the new size.

Deleting Charts

It is a very simple process to delete an embedded chart—just select the chart area and tap [Delete]. You can always use the Undo command if you delete an embedded chart by mistake. You delete a chart that is on its own tab by deleting the worksheet. This action cannot be undone, so Excel warns you with a prompt to confirm the deletion.

Previewing and Printing Charts

You can use the Print Preview and Print commands that you learned about in Lesson 8, Editing, Viewing, and Printing Worksheets to preview and print charts. If a chart is on a separate worksheet, you must first activate it by clicking the sheet tab. If a chart is embedded, you must first select the chart before issuing the Print Preview or Print commands. In Print Preview, the chart will display in black and white or in color, depending on the type of printer to which your computer is connected.

QUICK REFERENCE: MANIPULATING AND PRINTING EMBEDDED CHARTS

Task	Procedure
Move an embedded chart	■ Drag the selected chart to a new location with the move pointer while it is positioned over the chart area.
Change the chart size	■ Drag any sizing handle.
Change the size of a chart while maintaining original proportions	■ Press ⎡Shift⎤ while dragging a corner sizing handle.
Delete a chart	■ Embedded Chart: Select the chart and tap ⎡Delete⎤. ■ Worksheet Chart: Delete the worksheet.
Preview how a chart will look when printed	■ Select the chart by either clicking it if it is embedded or clicking the tab on which it is placed. ■ Choose Office→Print menu ▶ →Print Preview.
Print a chart	■ Ensure that the chart you wish to print is selected. ■ Choose Office→Print.

Hands-On 10.8   Move, Resize, and Print a Chart

In this exercise, you will move, resize and print the column chart that you created in the previous exercise.

Move an Embedded Chart

1. Display the Sales worksheet.

2. Click once on the embedded chart in the Sales sheet to select it.
   Sizing handles appear around the border of the chart.

3. Follow these steps to move the chart:

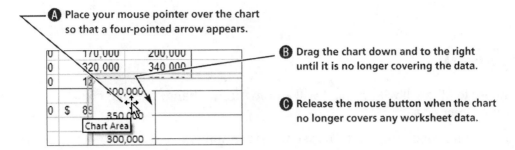

A Place your mouse pointer over the chart so that a four-pointed arrow appears.

B Drag the chart down and to the right until it is no longer covering the data.

C Release the mouse button when the chart no longer covers any worksheet data.

You will see a rectangle "ghost" as you drag, showing you where the chart will land if you release the mouse button at that location.

Size a Chart

4. Follow these steps to resize the chart to be smaller:

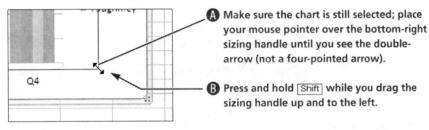

A Make sure the chart is still selected; place your mouse pointer over the bottom-right sizing handle until you see the double-arrow (not a four-pointed arrow).

B Press and hold `Shift` while you drag the sizing handle up and to the left.

C Release the mouse button about one-half inch from the corner to decrease it by one-half inch then release the `Shift` key.

Notice that Excel resized the width and height proportionately. This is because you held down the `Shift` key as you resized the chart.

Preview How an Embedded Chart Will Print

5. Ensure the embedded chart on the Sales worksheet is still selected then choose Office→Print menu ▶ →Print Preview.
The column chart appears in the Print Preview window.

6. Choose Print Preview→Preview→Close Print Preview ⊠ from the Ribbon.

7. Click in a cell away from the chart to deselect it.

8. Choose Office→Print menu ▶ →Print Preview.
Notice that when the chart is not selected, Excel will print the worksheet along with the embedded chart.

9. Choose Print Preview→Preview→Close Print Preview ⊠ from the Ribbon.

Print a Chart

10. Display the Pie Chart worksheet.

11. Choose Office→Print; retrieve the printout.
Excel will print one copy of your chart to the default printer.

12. Save and close the workbook.

Concepts Review

True/False Questions

1. When you choose to fill a cell with color, it will automatically change the font color to one that complements it.   TRUE   FALSE

2. The Merge and Center command can be used only with numbers.   TRUE   FALSE

3. The Comma Style inserts a dollar sign in front of numbers.   TRUE   FALSE

4. You can change a font's style and size but not its color.   TRUE   FALSE

5. Titles can be centered across multiple columns.   TRUE   FALSE

6. Row heights cannot be adjusted using AutoFit.   TRUE   FALSE

7. New columns are inserted to the left of selected columns.   TRUE   FALSE

8. Embedded charts are updated when the worksheet data changes.   TRUE   FALSE

9. Column charts are most useful for comparing the parts of a whole.   TRUE   FALSE

10. You must select an embedded chart before you can move or size it.   TRUE   FALSE

Multiple Choice Questions

1. Which feature allows you to easily apply formatting when the Home tab of the Ribbon is not displayed?
   a. Mini toolbar
   b. Quick Access toolbar
   c. Live Preview
   d. None of the above

2. What must you do before clicking the Merge & Center button?
   a. Click the cell that contains the entry you wish to center.
   b. Select the cells you wish to center the entry across, making sure the entry is included in the selection.
   c. Select the entire row that contains the entry you wish to merge.
   d. None of the above

3. How many rows are inserted if you select three rows and choose the Home→Cells→Insert command from the Ribbon?
   a. One, above the selection
   b. Three, below the selection
   c. Three, above the selection
   d. None; that is not the correct command

4. Which chart type would you use to compare sales figures for a variety of departments over a period of time?
   a. Column
   b. Pie
   c. Doughnut
   d. Bubble

Skill Builders

Skill Builder 10.1 Format a Worksheet with the Ribbon

In this exercise, you will format a worksheet using commands available on the Home tab of the Ribbon.

1. Open the sb-PTA Budget Formatting workbook in the Lesson 10 folder from your file storage location.

2. Change the font for the entire worksheet to Arial Narrow.

3. Select A1, A7, A16, and A31 using the [Ctrl] key.

4. Choose Home→Font→Bold **B** from the Ribbon.

5. Select B8:D8, B14:D14, B17:D17, and B30:D30 using the [Ctrl] key.

6. Choose Home→Number→Accounting Number Format **$** from the Ribbon.

7. Select B9:D13 and B18:D29 using the [Ctrl] key.

8. Choose Home→Number→Comma Style **,** from the Ribbon.

9. Select D5.

10. Ensuring the Home tab is displayed, click the Number Format menu ▼ button and choose Currency from the list.
    If you click the Accounting Number Format **$** *button, the cell will be formatted differently, so make sure to choose Currency from the Number Format list as displayed. Notice that it is formatted with a different number format option and therefore appears different from cells B8, C8, etc.*

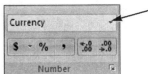

11. Right-align the entry in cell A5.

12. Select the range B31:D31, and then complete these formatting steps:
    - Change the number formatting to Accounting.
    - Apply a border to the range with a Top and Bottom Double Border.

13. Merge and center the ranges A1:D1, A2:D2, and A3:D3

14. Select the range B6:D6 and change the font size to 9.

15. Save and close your workbook.

Skill Builder 10.2 Insert and Delete Rows

In this exercise, you will modify an order entry worksheet by removing and inserting line items.

1. Open the sb-Andrew's Office Supplies file from the Lesson 10 folder in your file storage location.

Create Formulas

2. Click cell D7, and enter a formula that calculates the Extended Price as the Quantity multiplied by the Unit Price.
The result should be 239.7.

3. Copy the Extended Price formula down through rows 8–11.

4. Use AutoSum to compute the subtotal for the extended prices in column D.

5. Calculate the Sales Tax as the Subtotal multiplied by 7.75%.

6. Calculate the Total as the Subtotal plus the Sales Tax.

7. Select all of the numbers in columns C–D and change the decimals to 2.

Delete a Row and Insert New Rows

The customer has decided to cancel the electric pencil sharpeners from his order and add toner cartridges.

8. Select row 8 by clicking the row heading.

9. Choose Home→Cells→Delete ⬛ (taking care not to click the menu ▼ button) from the Ribbon.
The Subtotal, Sales Tax, and Total should be automatically recalculated.

10. Click anywhere in row 10, and choose Home→Cells→Insert ⬛ menu ▼→Insert Sheet Rows from the Ribbon.

11. Add the following item, and be sure to use a formula in cell D10, which can be copied via the fill handle from D9:

	A	B	C	D
10	Toner cartridge	10	119.00	1190.00

12. Select row 12, and choose Home→Cells→Insert ⬛ from the Ribbon.
Notice that if you select the entire row below where you wish to insert a row, you can simply click the Insert button without having to choose the menu button and the Insert Sheet Rows command on the menu.

13. Add the following item to the new row, tapping Tab after typing 145 in cell C12, as Excel will automatically calculate the value in cell D12:

	A	B	C	D
12	Two-line phone	5	145.00	725.00

14. Click in cell D13 and notice that the SUM function has been updated automatically to include the value in cell D12 that was added when you inserted the row.
Excel adjusted the formula reference because the rows inserted were within the range referenced in the formula.

15. Select columns A, C, and D, and use the AutoFit command to adjust the column widths.

16. Manually size column B so that the word *Quantity* in B6 is visible.
You will not want to AutoFit column B as it will fit to Baltimore Petroleum *in B4, which is much too wide.*

17. Save and close the workbook.

Skill Builder 10.3 Create a Column Chart

In this exercise, you will create a column chart to display student enrollment at a university.

Expand a Series

1. Open the workbook named sb-Enrollments from the Lesson 10 folder in your default storage location.
Notice that the enrollment data has been completed in column B but that the years have not been completed in column A. In column A, the first two years (1991 and 1992) form the beginning of the series 1991–2007. The best way to expand this series is with the fill handle.

2. Select cells A4 and A5.

3. Drag the fill handle down to row 20 to expand the series.

4. Choose Home→Alignment→Align Text Left 📇 from the Ribbon.

Create the Chart

5. Select the range A3:B20.
This range includes the enrollment data and the Year *and* Total Enrollment *headings.*

6. Choose Insert→Charts→Column 📊 →Clustered Column from the Ribbon.
Take a moment to study the chart and notice the problem. Excel is interpreting the years 1991–2007 as numbers. The numbers appear as a data series in the chart. The years are the short columns to the left of the tall, thin enrollment data columns. The years should actually be displayed as labels on the horizontal category axis. You will correct this next.

7. Choose Design→Data→Select Data 📊 from the Ribbon.
This will allow you to modify the data series plotted in the chart.

8. Follow these steps to remove the years from the series and to add them as horizontal (category) axis labels:

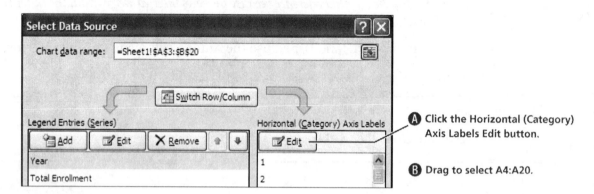

A Click the Horizontal (Category) Axis Labels Edit button.

B Drag to select A4:A20.

Excel will display the axis label range you proposed in the Axis Labels dialog box.

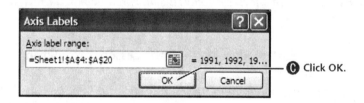

C Click OK.

Take a careful look at the Select Data Source dialog box now. Notice that the chart data range is no longer displayed because it is too complex. In addition, the years from cells A4:A20 will now be displayed as the horizontal (category) axis labels.

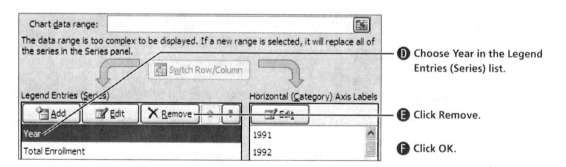

D Choose Year in the Legend Entries (Series) list.

E Click Remove.

F Click OK.

Take a few moments to study your worksheet and chart. Be sure you understand the relationship between the worksheet data and the chart. Notice that with only one data series, Excel automatically uses the column header for that data as the chart title.

Create a Horizontal Axis Title for the Chart

9. Choose Layout→Labels→Axis Titles 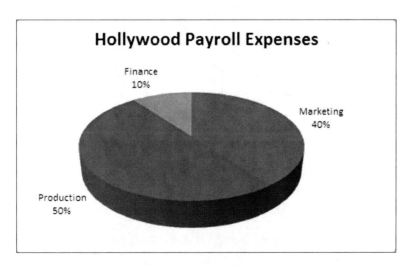→Primary Horizontal Axis Title→Title Below Axis from the Ribbon.

10. Select the default title and replace it with **Year**.

11. Select B4:B20.

12. Apply Comma Style , formatting with no decimals .00→.0 .
    Notice that when you format the source data, it will also translate to the chart data.

13. Save and close your workbook.

Skill Builder 10.4   Create Pie Charts

In this exercise, you will create two pie charts to illustrate employee expenses for Hollywood Productions, a motion picture production company. The pie charts will show how employee costs are divided among departments and how one department's employee costs are allocated. You will create each chart on a separate chart sheet.

Create the Company Chart

1. Open the workbook named sb-Hollywood Productions Expenses from the Lesson 10 folder in your default storage location.

2. Use the ⎡Ctrl⎤ key to select B3:D3 and B7:D7.

3. Choose Insert→Charts→Pie →Pie in 3-D from the Ribbon, and create the pie chart shown on a separate chart sheet named **Hollywood Payroll Expenses**.
   Make sure the chart title and data labels match the chart shown here. Also, notice that the chart does not include a legend.

Hollywood Payroll Expenses

Finance 10%

Marketing 40%

Production 50%

Create a Pie Chart for the Marketing Department

4. Ensure that the Payroll Data worksheet tab is displayed.

5. Select A4:B6.

6. Choose Insert→Charts→Pie →Pie in 3-D from the Ribbon.

7. Title the chart **Marketing Payroll Costs**.

8. Create data labels for the pieces of the pie, showing both the category name and percentage, outside at the end of each slice.

9. Delete the legend.

10. Place the chart on a separate sheet named **Marketing Chart**.

11. Save and close your workbook.

Unit 3 Assessments

Assessment 3.1   Create a New Workbook

In this exercise, you will create a new worksheet and then save and close the workbook.

1. Start Excel by selecting (All) Programs from the Start menu.

2. Choose Office→New, and then tap ⌷Enter⌷.
This allows you to create a new workbook while leaving the current one open.

3. Create the worksheet shown in the following illustration. Make sure the numbers match.

	A	B	C	D	E
1	Big City Diner Q1 Expenses				
2					
3	Item		January	February	March
4	Building	Rent	800	800	800
5		Utilities	340	400	250
6		Phone	250	200	300
7		Insurance	350	0	0
8		Total			
9					
10	Food Cost	Produce	2500	2320	1700
11		Meat	4000	3400	3700
12		Grains	1000	1200	890
13		Total			
14					
15	Salaries	Simmons	800	780	800
16		Swanson	750	650	870
17		Martinez	900	780	680
18		Richardso	1200	1000	990
19		Total			
20					
21	Other	Advertisir	500	300	0
22		Uniforms	0	340	0
23		Janitorial	200	200	200
24		Misc	100	2000	0
25		Total			

4. Save the workbook as **as-Q1 Expenses**, and then close it.

Assessment 3.2   Select, Move, and Copy in a Worksheet

In this exercise, you will practice selecting various ranges and cells in order to move and copy them.

1. Open the workbook named as-Menu from the Unit 3 Assessments folder in your file storage location.

2. Select A7:B27; try using the Shift technique.

3. Place your mouse pointer over the edge of the selection until you see the move pointer, and then click and drag up until the top left of the selection is in row 3.
   The selection will now be contained in the range A3:B23.

4. Copy the contents of cell A4 into cell A12.

5. Select A18:B23 and issue the Cut command.

6. Click cell A20 and issue the Paste command.

7. Save the worksheet and leave it open for the next exercise.

Assessment 3.3   Work with Undo, Clear, and AutoComplete

In this exercise, you will work with the workbook from Assessment 3.2 to clear formatting, undo commands, and use AutoComplete.

1. The as-Menu worksheet from Assessment 3.2 should still be open; if it is not, open it from your default storage location.

2. Select column B by clicking the column header.

3. Choose Home→Editing→Clear→Clear Formats from the Ribbon.
   Notice that the numbers remain in column B, but they are no longer formatted as currency.

4. Click the Undo button on the Quick Access toolbar to bring back the cleared formatting.

5. Click cell A9 and type **s**, observing the AutoComplete option that appears.

6. Tap Enter to accept the AutoComplete suggestion.

7. Click cell A9 and tap Delete to clear the contents of the cell.

8. Choose Office→Print menu ▼→Print Preview.
   Take a look at how the menu will print. Notice the simplified Ribbon that is displayed in this specialized setting.

9. Choose Print Preview→Print from the modified Ribbon.

10. Print the menu for your instructor.

11. Save the changes to the workbook and exit from Excel.

Assessment 3.4   Create a Financial Report

In this exercise, you will create a worksheet by entering data, creating formulas, and using absolute references. You will also save, print a section of, and close the workbook.

1. Open the as-2008 Projected Net Income workbook from the Unit 3 Assessments folder in your file storage location.

2. Use these guidelines to create the following financial report:

   - Type the headings, labels, and numbers as shown in the following illustration. Use AutoFill whenever possible to copy cells or complete a series (for example, with the Q1, Q2, Q3, and Q4 headers).

   - Use formulas to calculate the numbers in rows 6–9. The formulas should multiply the revenue in row 4 by the variables in rows 15–19. For example, the employee costs in cell B6 are calculated as the revenue in cell B4 multiplied by the percentage in cell B15. Use absolute references in these formulas when referring to the variables so you can copy the formulas across the rows. You must use absolute references to get full credit for this assessment!

   - Use AutoSum to calculate the total costs in row 10.

   - Calculate the gross profit in row 12 as Revenue – Total Costs.

   - Calculate the net profit in row 13 as Gross Profit * (1 – Tax Rate). Once again, use absolute references when referring to the tax rate in cell B19.

3. Perform a what-if analysis on your worksheet by changing the percentages in rows 15–19. Make sure the report recalculates correctly when the values are changed.

4. Print the worksheet.

5. Select the range A1:E13, and print just that area.

6. Issue the command to show the formulas in the worksheet.

7. Print the range A1:E13.
   Notice that the column widths are automatically increased to accommodate the width of the formulas. This will cause it to print on two pages.

8. Save the workbook, and then close it.

	A	B	C	D	E
1	2008 Projected Income				
2					
3		Q1	Q2	Q3	Q4
4	Revenue	345000	390000	480000	500000
5					
6	Employee Costs				
7	Capital Expenditures				
8	Manufacturing				
9	Marketing & Sales				
10	Total Costs				
11					
12	Gross Profit				
13	Net Profit				
14					
15	Employee Costs	18%			
16	Capital Expenditures	22%			
17	Manufacturing	17%			
18	Marketing & Sales	16%			
19	Tax Rate	40%			

Assessment 3.5   Format Text and Numbers

In this exercise, you will format and add enhancements to text and numbers.

1. Open the workbook named as-Atlantic Pools Formatting in the Unit 3 Assessments folder on your file storage location.

2. Format B5:F5, B10:F10, and B11:F11 in Currency Style with 0 decimals using the Ribbon.

3. Format rows B6:F9 in Comma Style with 0 decimals.

4. Apply bold formatting to the entries in rows 10 and 11.

5. Format the title with bold, and change the font size to 14.

6. Format the column and row headings with bold.

7. Save your worksheet and leave it open for the next exercise.

Assessment 3.6   Work with Vertical Alignment and Text Rotation

In this exercise, you will create a worksheet, practice creating formulas, and change the vertical alignment and text rotation.

1. Open a new Excel file and enter all text, numbers, and dates as shown in the illustration at the end of this exercise. Follow these guidelines to create the large paragraph shown near the top of the worksheet:

   ■ Use the Merge & Center command to merge cells A2:H2.

   ■ Set the height of row 2 to 75.00 points.

   ■ Turn on the Wrap Text option.

   ■ Type the text in the large merged cell.

   ■ Change the vertical alignment to center and the horizontal alignment to left.

2. Apply the borders as shown. You will want to merge and center the contents of A5, F5, G5, and H5 with the empty row 4 cells above. Merge and center B4:C4 and D4:E4.

3. Use formulas in column F to calculate the number of days between the two tests.

4. Format the entries in column F with the General Style number format.

5. Use formulas in column G to calculate the point increase between the two test scores.

6. Use formulas to calculate the percentage increase in column H. The percentage increase is calculated as the point increase in column G divided by the first test score in column C.

7. Use the AVERAGE function to calculate the averages in cells F12 and H13.

8. Add a border around cells A12–H13.

9. Format all numbers, dates, and text as desired. Adjust row heights and column widths as shown. Format the percentage increases in column H as Percent Style with no decimals.

10. Print the worksheet when you have finished.

11. Save the workbook as **as-Performance Evaluations** and close it.

Grade 10 Performance Evaluations

This worksheet copyter the percentage increase in test scores for students who have been receiving special assistance. The average number of days required to achieve the results is also shown.

	Student	First Test		Second Test		Number of Days Between Tests	Point Increase	Percentage Increase
		Date	Score	Date	Score			
6	Helen Chang	2/3/2008	78	3/30/2008	87			
7	Clara Levy	2/5/2008	77	3/28/2008	82			
8	Miranda Simek	2/5/2008	65	4/5/2008	80			
9	Tariq Aziz	3/10/2008	64	4/1/2008	72			
10	Elizabeth Crawford	3/12/2008	68	4/2/2008	78			
11	Bernice Barton	2/1/2008	72	3/10/2008	88			
12	Average Days							
13	Average Increase							

Assessment 3.7   Create a Worksheet and Pie Chart

In this exercise, you will create a worksheet and a pie chart based on the data in the worksheet. You will also apply a style to the worksheet, insert formulas in the worksheet, and move, resize, and explode a piece of the pie chart.

1. Use the guidelines to create the worksheet and chart shown in the following illustration:

   ■ Type all numbers and text entries as shown, but use formulas to calculate the New Balance in column E and the Totals, Highest, and Lowest values in rows 9–11. The formula for New Balance is New Balance = Beginning Balance + Purchases – Payments. Calculate the Totals in row 9 with AutoSum, and use the MIN and MAX functions for the Highest and Lowest calculations in rows 10 and 11.

   ■ Use the font size of your choice for the title cell A1, merge and center the title across the worksheet, and then format the remainder of the worksheet with the theme of your choice.

   ■ Create the embedded 3-D pie chart shown in the illustration. The pie chart slices represent the new balance percentages of each customer. The pie chart does not represent any of the data in rows 9–11.

   ■ Adjust the position and size of the embedded chart as shown in the illustration.

   ■ Explode the Bishop slice, and adjust the chart rotation and elevation.

   ■ Bold all pie slice labels, and format the chart title with bold and italic by using commands on the Home tab of the Ribbon.

2. Print the worksheet and embedded chart on the same page.

3. Save the workbook as **as-Accounts Receivable Report** in your Unit 3 Assessments folder, and then close it.

	A	B	C	D	E
1	**Mary's Imported Rugs: Accounts Receivable Report**				
2					
3	**Customer**	**Beginning Balance**	**Purchases**	**Payments**	**New Balance**
4	Allison	$ 4,000	$ 2,300	$ 2,000	$ 4,300
5	Washington	3,450	1,000	2,450	2,000
6	Bishop	6,500	2,100	3,000	5,600
7	Worthington	3,400	500	3,400	500
8	Cosby	3,000	3,400	5,000	1,400
9	Totals	$ 20,350	$ 9,300	$ 15,850	$ 13,800
10	Highest	$ 6,500	$ 3,400	$ 5,000	$ 5,600
11	Lowest	$ 3,000	$ 500	$ 2,000	$ 500
12					

Customers with Outstanding Balances

Cosby 10%
Worthington 4%
Bishop 41%
Allison 31%
Washington 14%

Unit 4

PowerPoint 2007 and Access 2007

In this unit, you will work with PowerPoint 2007 and Access 2007. In the first lesson, you will navigate the PowerPoint window, use document themes, and review the new Ribbon interface. Then, you will create your own slide show, complete with bulleted lists, clip art, and transitions. In the Access lessons, you will open, navigate, and close database objects; view forms and reports; and run queries. You will also use tables and add records to a database using a form, as well as sort, delete, edit, and filter records. This unit ends with a series of Assessment exercises.

LESSON 11

Creating and Delivering a Presentation

In this lesson, you will create a PowerPoint presentation for the Pinnacle Pet Care pet clinic. Throughout the lesson, you will be using many PowerPoint features to develop the presentation. You will be working with document themes, text layout styles, and the Master slide. Working with the printing function of PowerPoint 2007, you will examine page setup, print preview, print setup, and output formats. Then you will enhance the Pinnacle Pet Care presentation. You will use clip art to add interest and slide transitions to "bring the presentation to life." By the end of the lesson, your presentation will be ready for delivery. Equipped with the tips and techniques for a successful presentation, you will practice its delivery to the Pet World trade show.

LESSON OBJECTIVES

After studying this lesson, you will be able to:

- Apply a document theme to a new presentation
- Insert new slides
- Add text to a slide
- Manage bulleted items
- View a slide show
- Print a presentation
- Add clip art pictures to a presentation
- Add transition effects to a slide show

Case Study: Creating a Presentation

Al Smith, owner of Pinnacle Pet Care, has been invited to make a presentation representing his firm to the Pet World trade show. Al's goal is to introduce Pinnacle Pet Care to trade show attendees and entice them with a promotional offer. Al decides to use PowerPoint with his new notebook computer and video projection system to develop and deliver his presentation. Al chose PowerPoint because it is easy to learn and seamlessly integrates with his other Microsoft Office applications. Al's dynamic speaking abilities, coupled with PowerPoint's robust presentation features, are sure to win over the trade show attendees.

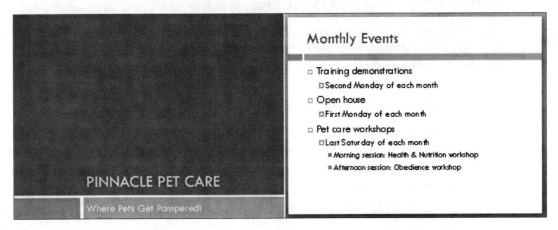

Slides from the Pinnacle Pet Care presentation

Presenting PowerPoint

PowerPoint 2007 is an intuitive, powerful presentation graphics program that enables you to create dynamic, multimedia presentations for a variety of functions. Whether you are developing a one-on-one presentation for your manager or a sophisticated presentation for a large group, PowerPoint provides the tools to make your presentation a success. PowerPoint allows you to project your presentation in a variety of ways. Most presentations are delivered via a computer projection display attached to a notebook computer. There are also other ways to deliver presentations. For example, you can deliver a presentation as an online broadcast over the Internet or convert it to web page format.

PowerPoint provides easy-to-use tools that let you concentrate on the content of your presentation instead of focusing on the design details. Using PowerPoint's built-in document themes, you can rapidly create highly effective professional presentations.

Starting PowerPoint

The method you use to start PowerPoint depends in large part on whether you intend to create a new presentation or open an existing presentation. To create a new presentation, use one of the following methods. After the PowerPoint program has started, you can begin working in the new presentation that appears.

- Click the **start** button, and then choose All Programs→Microsoft Office→Microsoft Office PowerPoint 2007.

- Navigate to the desired document by using Windows Explorer or My Computer and double-click the presentation.

 Hands-On 11.1   Start PowerPoint

In this exercise, you will start PowerPoint.

1. Click the **start** button.

2. Choose All Programs→Microsoft Office→Microsoft Office PowerPoint 2007.
   PowerPoint will open, and the PowerPoint program window will appear.

Navigating the PowerPoint Window

The PowerPoint 2007 program window has changed dramatically from prior versions of the program. The task pane, toolbars, and menu bar have all been replaced by the Ribbon. The following illustration provides an overview of the program window.

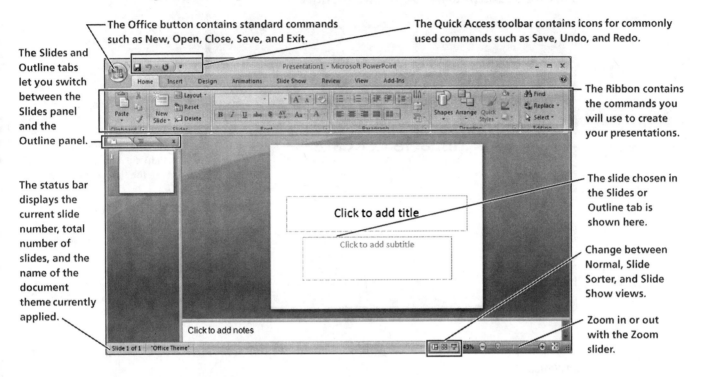

The Office button contains standard commands such as New, Open, Close, Save, and Exit.

The Quick Access toolbar contains icons for commonly used commands such as Save, Undo, and Redo.

The Slides and Outline tabs let you switch between the Slides panel and the Outline panel.

The status bar displays the current slide number, total number of slides, and the name of the document theme currently applied.

The Ribbon contains the commands you will use to create your presentations.

The slide chosen in the Slides or Outline tab is shown here.

Change between Normal, Slide Sorter, and Slide Show views.

Zoom in or out with the Zoom slider.

Inserting Text

PowerPoint slides have placeholders set up for you to type in. For example, the title slide currently visible on the screen has placeholders for a title and subtitle. You click in the desired placeholder to enter text on a slide. For example, to enter the title on a slide, you click in the title placeholder and then type the text. Do not press the Enter key; the placeholders are already formatted with word wrap. The placeholders also are already formatted with font and paragraph settings to make a cohesive presentation. As you will see shortly, it's easy to make changes to the formatting of slides by applying a theme.

In this exercise, you will enter a title and subtitle for the presentation.

1. Follow these steps to add a title and subtitle:

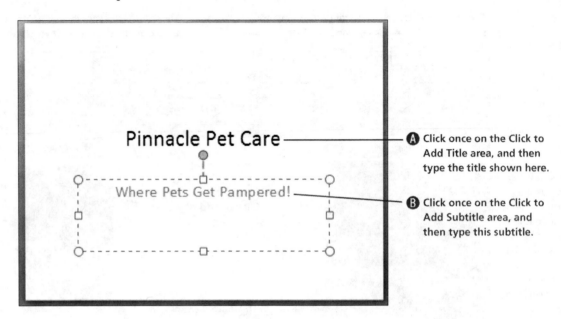

Pinnacle Pet Care ⎯⎯⎯⎯ **(A)** Click once on the Click to Add Title area, and then type the title shown here.

Where Pets Get Pampered! ⎯⎯⎯ **(B)** Click once on the Click to Add Subtitle area, and then type this subtitle.

PowerPoint enters the titles. At this point you have a title slide, but it looks rather plain. This is about to change.

Using Document Themes

You can use PowerPoint's built-in document themes, which provide a ready-made backdrop for your presentations, to easily format all slides in a presentation. When you use a document theme, your presentation automatically includes an attractive color scheme, consistent font style and size, and bulleted lists to synchronize with the design and style of the presentation. Document themes also position placeholders on slides for titles, text, bulleted lists, graphics, and other objects. By using document themes, you can focus on content by simply filling in the blanks as you create the presentation. You access document themes from the Themes group on the Design tab.

Choosing a Theme

There are many document themes included with PowerPoint 2007. Match the theme to the type of presentation you are giving. Keep the design appropriate to the function and the audience.

Finding Additional Themes

New themes are sent to Microsoft daily, so if you just can't find the right one, browse the Microsoft Office Online website for new themes. You can easily browse the site by selecting Design→Themes→More→Search Office Online.

This area displays the themes used in the current presentation.

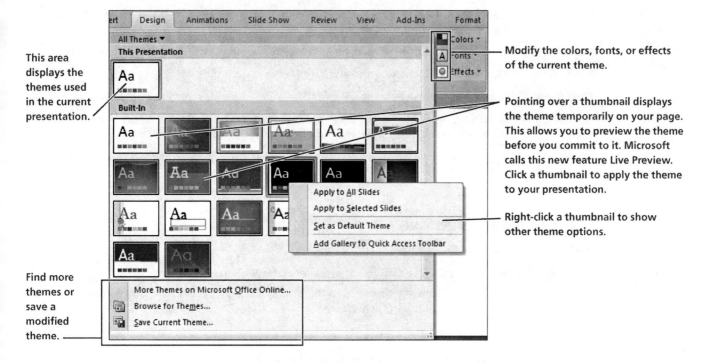

Modify the colors, fonts, or effects of the current theme.

Pointing over a thumbnail displays the theme temporarily on your page. This allows you to preview the theme before you commit to it. Microsoft calls this new feature Live Preview. Click a thumbnail to apply the theme to your presentation.

Right-click a thumbnail to show other theme options.

Find more themes or save a modified theme.

Using the PowerPoint Ribbon

The PowerPoint Ribbon is organized into seven default tabs: Home, Insert, Design, Animations, Slide Show, Review, and View. Like other Office 2007 applications, additional tabs appear when certain elements on a slide are selected. These additional tabs, called contextual tabs, offer commands specific to the selected element; for example, selecting a picture on a slide results in the Picture Tools Format tab being shown. Deselecting the picture returns the Ribbon to its original state with the seven default tabs.

Each tab contains many commands, which are organized in groups. Each group is labeled across the bottom and contains a variety of buttons or button menus.

The Home tab displays several groups of buttons.

The Clipboard group has buttons to copy, paste, and apply the Format Painter.

Each tab on the Ribbon contains several groups of buttons and button menus for performing various tasks.

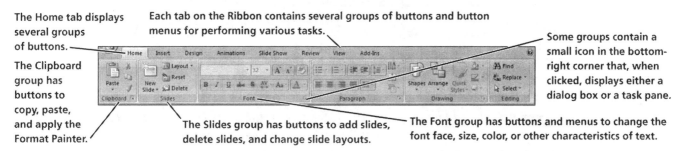

Some groups contain a small icon in the bottom-right corner that, when clicked, displays either a dialog box or a task pane.

The Slides group has buttons to add slides, delete slides, and change slide layouts.

The Font group has buttons and menus to change the font face, size, color, or other characteristics of text.

DEFAULT TABS IN THE POWERPOINT RIBBON

Tab Name	General Tasks
Home	Perform standard tasks, such as copy/paste, add/remove slides, format text, and find/search/replace.
Insert	Insert graphical elements such as shapes, pictures, clip art, charts, tables, WordArt, and media clips.
Design	Format slides with themes, colors, and backgrounds, and align elements on a slide.
Animations	Manage slide transitions and animate elements on a slide.
Slide Show	Create and view slide show presentations of all slides or selected slides.
Review	Proof your text with spellchecker and thesaurus features, translate text to another language, and create comments for reviewers.
View	Change presentation views, show/hide rulers and gridlines, adjust the zoom, change the color mode, or organize multiple document windows.

QUICK REFERENCE: APPLYING A THEME

Task	Procedure
Apply a theme to a presentation	■ Choose Design→Themes from the Ribbon. ■ Choose a theme from the display, or click the More ⯆ button to view additional themes.

Hands-On 11.3 Apply a Document Theme

In this exercise, you will choose a document theme and apply it to the presentation.

1. Follow these steps to choose a theme for the presentation:
   Depending on your monitor resolution, you may see a different number of thumbnails in the Themes group.

Ⓐ Display the Design tab.

Ⓑ Locate the Themes command group.

Ⓒ Point (don't click) over the third theme from the left and notice that the theme's name appears as a ToolTip.

PowerPoint displays a Live Preview of the theme on your title slide. This gives you a good idea of the overall design of the theme. Notice that the fonts and locations have changed for the title and subtitle. A different theme can radically redesign your presentation.

 NOTE! *Throughout this book, this command will be written as follows: Choose Design →Themes →[Theme command] from the Ribbon.*

2. Point (don't click) over several more theme thumbnails.
   You see a Live Preview of each theme on the actual slide. The themes visible on the Ribbon are just a small portion of those available, however.

3. Choose Design→Themes→More ⬇ as shown at right.
   PowerPoint displays all of the currently available themes. It also gives options to look for additional themes online or elsewhere on your computer.

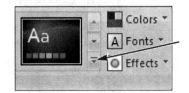

4. Follow these steps to choose a theme:

Ⓐ Point (don't click) to preview the Technic theme. Notice the ToolTip that appears to display the theme name. (The themes are listed in alphabetical order.)

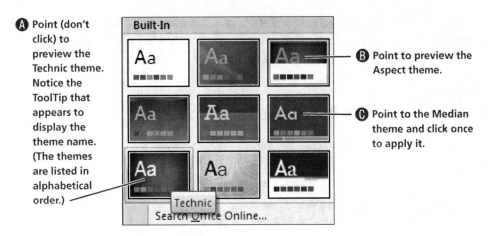

Ⓑ Point to preview the Aspect theme.

Ⓒ Point to the Median theme and click once to apply it.

PowerPoint applies the theme to your presentation.

Creating a Basic Presentation

There is more to creating a presentation than placing one slide after another. Like Al Smith of Pinnacle Pet Care, you are in the process of creating an image. Choosing the appropriate slide layout, just like choosing the appropriate design, will influence how well your audience understands your message. Use the following guidelines when choosing your slide design and layout:

■ **Know your audience:** Will you be speaking to accountants or artists?

■ **Know your purpose:** Are you introducing a product or giving a report?

■ **Know your expectations:** When the last word of this presentation has been given, how do you want your audience to respond to your facts? Are you looking for approval for a project or customers for a product?

Adding Slides

You can use two methods to add slides to a presentation:

- Choose Home→Slides→New Slide 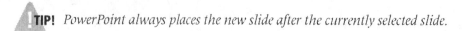 from the Ribbon.

- Right-click a slide on the Slides panel, and then choose New Slide from the pop-up, or context, menu.

TIP! *PowerPoint always places the new slide after the currently selected slide.*

The Slides panel displays thumbnails of your presentation while you work in the Normal view. The Slide Sorter view also displays thumbnails of your slides. This view can be useful when there are more slides than can fit in the Slides panel display.

 Hands-On 11.4   Add a New Slide

In this exercise, you will add a new slide to the presentation and then enter content.

1. Follow these steps to add a new slide:

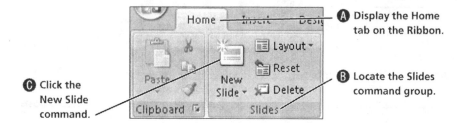

Ⓐ Display the Home tab on the Ribbon.

Ⓑ Locate the Slides command group.

Ⓒ Click the New Slide command.

NOTE! *Throughout this book, a Ribbon command like this will be written as follows: Choose Home→ Slides→New Slide* *from the Ribbon.*

PowerPoint adds a new slide to the presentation immediately after the title slide.

2. Click once in the title placeholder and then type **Our Services** as the title.

3. Click once on the Click to Add Text placeholder and then type the following list. Tap the Enter key after each list item except the last one.

- **Complete medical care** Enter
- **Boarding** Enter
- **Grooming** Enter
- **Training**

PowerPoint adds a bullet in front of each line.

Indenting Bulleted Lists

When using PowerPoint, you can effortlessly create bulleted lists to outline the thrust of your presentation. The bulleted list layout is an outline of five levels. A different bullet character and indentation is used for each level. The following illustration shows the Monthly Events slide you will create in the next exercise.

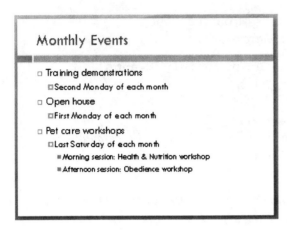

This bulleted list has three levels. An orange square is used for first-level paragraphs, and an indented blue square is used for second-level paragraphs.

Working with Bulleted Lists

When you use a document theme, each paragraph is automatically formatted as a bulleted list. The format includes a bullet style, indentation level, font type, and font size for each bulleted paragraph. This outline for the bulleted list is held within a placeholder or text box. The following Quick Reference table describes the various techniques that can be used with bulleted lists.

Working with List Levels

Indenting a bullet is referred to as *demoting a bullet,* or *increasing the list level.* Typically, a main bullet point has one or more sub-bullets. These sub-bullets, which are smaller than the main bullet, are created by increasing the list level. When a list level is increased, the bullets are indented toward the right. You demote a bullet by choosing the Home→Paragraph→Increase List Level button on the Ribbon. Conversely, decreasing a bullet's indent by moving it more toward the left and increasing the bullet size is referred to as *promoting a bullet,* or *decreasing the list level.* You promote a bullet by choosing the Home→Paragraph→Decrease List Level button on the Ribbon. PowerPoint supports a main bullet and up to eight sub-bullets.

QUICK REFERENCE: WORKING WITH BULLETED LISTS	
Task	**Procedure**
Turn bullets on and off	■ Select the desired paragraph(s).
	■ Choose Home→Paragraph→Bullets ▤ from the Ribbon.
Promote bullets by using the Ribbon	■ Select the desired paragraph(s).
	■ Choose Home→Paragraph→Decrease List Level ▤ from the Ribbon, or use Shift + Tab.
Demote bullets by using the Ribbon	■ Select the desired paragraph(s).
	■ Choose Home→Paragraph→Increase List Level ▤ from the Ribbon, or tap the Tab key.

Hands-On 11.5   Create a Bulleted List

In this exercise, you will create a new slide, and then you will enter information into a multilevel bulleted list. The most efficient way to create multilevel bulleted lists is to first type the entire list.

Create the List

1. Choose Home→Slides→New Slide 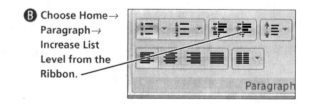 from the Ribbon.
   PowerPoint creates a new slide after the current slide.

2. Click in the title placeholder and then type **Monthly Events**.

3. Click once in the text placeholder.

4. Type **Training Demonstrations** and tap Enter.
   PowerPoint formats the new paragraph with the same large bullet. Paragraph formats are carried to new paragraphs when you tap the Enter key.

5. Tap the Tab key.
   PowerPoint indents the line. It also introduces a new bullet style for the level-2 heading. The small blue square bullet is part of the Median theme you applied previously.

6. Type **Second Monday of each month**.
   PowerPoint formats the line in a smaller font too.

7. Tap the Enter key.
   PowerPoint maintains the same level-2 heading level for the next line.

8. While holding down the Shift key, tap the Tab key once.
   PowerPoint promotes the new line back to level 1, which is the level of the first text line on the slide.

Manipulate Heading Levels

You can also adjust the heading level after you have typed a line.

9. Type the following lines:
   - ■ **Open House**
   - ■ **First Monday of each month**
   - ■ **Pet Care Workshops**

10. Follow these steps to indent the second bullet:

Ⓐ Click once anywhere within the text line to be indented.

Ⓑ Choose Home→ Paragraph→ Increase List Level from the Ribbon.

PowerPoint indents the paragraph and changes the bullet style. Demoting a paragraph makes it subordinate to the preceding paragraph.

11. Click the Increase List Level 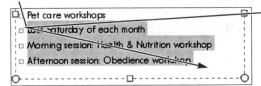 button three more times.

    The bullet style changes and the indent increases each time you choose the command. Also, the font size and font style change with each bullet increase. These formats are determined by the Median theme, on which the presentation is based.

12. Click Home→Paragraph→Decrease List Level ⬚ from the Ribbon three times until the bullet reaches the second indentation, the blue square bullet style.

    With each promotion, the bullet style changes.

Indent Multiple Bullets

13. Click once at the end of the last line and then tap Enter.

14. Type the following new lines:

    ■ **Last Saturday of each month**

    ■ **Morning session: Health & Nutrition workshop**

    ■ **Afternoon session: Obedience workshop**

15. Follow these steps to select the last three lines for your next command:

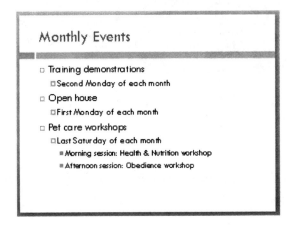

Ⓐ Point at the beginning of the text in the second line, taking care that a four-pointed arrow is not visible.

Ⓑ Drag down and to the right to select (highlight) the end of the last line, and then release the mouse button.

Ⓒ Ignore a context menu that may be visible for a moment. Take care not to click anywhere else on the slide before you perform the next step.

16. Choose Home→Paragraph→Increase List Level ⬚ from the Ribbon.

    PowerPoint indents the three selected lines.

17. Click anywhere outside the border to deselect the text.

18. Using the same method, select the last two lines and increase the list level. Your slide should match the following illustration.

> **Monthly Events**
>
> ☐ Training demonstrations
>   ☐ Second Monday of each month
> ☐ Open house
>   ☐ First Monday of each month
> ☐ Pet care workshops
>   ☐ Last Saturday of each month
>   ■ Morning session: Health & Nutrition workshop
>   ■ Afternoon session: Obedience workshop

Choosing the Slide Layout

There are nine slide layouts in PowerPoint 2007, one for any given situation. Slide layouts are named for the type of data they will contain. For example, the Title layout needs only a title and subtitle. The Title and Content layout will hold other information on the slide, so it has a title and a bulleted list for points. Likewise, the Content with Caption layout is divided into three sections: title, text to one side, and an area for clip art or additional text. The slide layout organizes the information you put into the presentation by giving it a place on the slide. Use the command Home→Slides→Layout ▼ to change the layout of your slides. The new layout is applied to all selected slides. Changing layouts is easy. When you click on the new style, the layout is transferred to the selected slide.

Clicking the Layout button from the Slides group on the Home tab allows you to apply a new layout to the selected slide(s).

 ## Hands-On 11.6 Change the Slide Layout

In this exercise, you will add a new slide and then change its layout.

1. If necessary, select the Monthly Events slide from the Slides panel on the left side of your screen.

2. Choose Home→Slides→New Slide ⬚ from the Ribbon.
PowerPoint adds another slide to the end of the presentation. Like the previous two slides, this one is set up to display a bulleted list.

3. Follow these steps to choose a new layout for the slide:

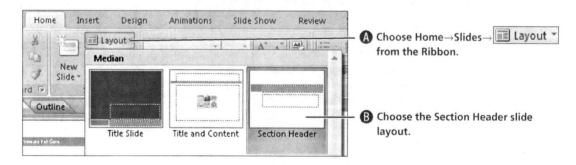

Ⓐ Choose Home→Slides→ ⬚ Layout ▼ from the Ribbon.

Ⓑ Choose the Section Header slide layout.

PowerPoint applies the new layout. Now there are two placeholders for a title and subtext.

4. Enter the following text:

- **Title: `Questions?`**
- **Text: `End of our brief presentation`**

Your slide should resemble the following illustration.

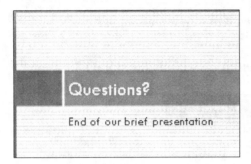

Saving the Presentation

The byword in PowerPoint is to save early and save often. You can use the Save button on the Quick Access toolbar or use the Office→Save command. If it's the first time a presentation has been saved, the Save As dialog box will appear because the file will need a name and location on your computer. You can also use the Save As dialog box to make a copy of a presentation by saving it under a new name or to a different location. If the file has already been saved, PowerPoint replaces the previous version with the new edited version. When saving PowerPoint files, you can use filenames with as many as 255 characters.

FROM THE KEYBOARD

`Ctrl`+`S` to save

Hands-On 11.7   Save the Presentation

In this exercise, you will save the presentation by giving it a name and a location on your computer.

1. Click the Save  button on the Quick Access toolbar, as shown at right.
   PowerPoint displays the Save As dialog box because this presentation has not yet been given a filename.

2. Follow these steps to save the presentation to your file storage location:

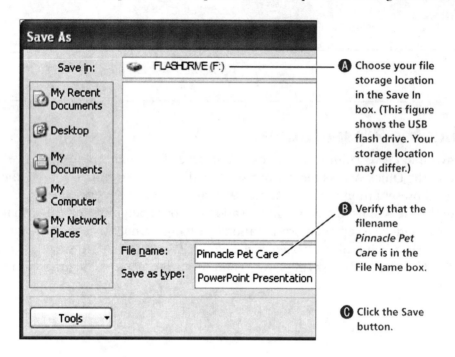

PowerPoint saves the presentation.

Delivering the Slide Show

The slides are created, and the presentation is complete. The first phase of the presentation development is over. The next phase, delivering the presentation, is just beginning. Before you stand before an audience, familiarize yourself with the following tips.

Delivery Tips

It is not only what you say, it is how you say it that makes the difference between an engaging and an unsuccessful presentation. Lead your audience. Help them to focus on the message of your presentation, not on you as the presenter. Use the following *PEER* guidelines to deliver an effective presentation:

- **Pace:** Maintain a moderate pace. Speaking too fast will exhaust your audience, and speaking too slowly may put them to sleep. Carry your audience with you as you talk.

- **Emphasis:** Pause for emphasis. As you present, use a brief pause to emphasize your point. The pause you take will give your audience time to absorb the message.

- **Eye contact:** Address your audience. Always face your audience while speaking. A common mistake is to speak while walking or facing the projection screen. Don't waste all of the work you have done in the presentation by losing the interest of your audience now. If you are speaking from a lectern or desk, resist the temptation to lean on them. Stand tall, make eye contact, and look directly at your audience.

- **Relax:** You are enthusiastic and want to convey that tone to the audience. However, when you speak, avoid fast movement, pacing, and rushed talking. Your audience will be drawn to your movements and miss the point. Remember that the audience is listening to you to learn; this material may be old hat to you, but it's new to them. So speak clearly, maintain a steady pace, and stay calm.

Navigating Through a Slide Show

You can use the mouse and/or simple keyboard commands to move through a slide show. This is often the easiest way to navigate from one slide to the next.

> **FROM THE KEYBOARD**
> Spacebar or → to advance a slide
> Backspace or ← to back up a slide

The Slide Show Toolbar

 The Slide Show toolbar is your navigator during the slide show. Notice that the Slide Show toolbar has options to go to the next and previous slides and to end the slide show. The Slide Show toolbar also lets you use a pen tool to draw on the slide and make other enhancements. However, use of this toolbar is unnecessary when you present a simple slide show like this one.

QR⟩

QUICK REFERENCE: USING BASIC SLIDE SHOW NAVIGATION	
Task	**Procedure**
Advance a slide	■ Click once with the mouse, or ■ Tap the Spacebar, →, Page Down, or Enter key.
Back up a slide	■ Tap the Backspace or ← key.
Display the Slide Show toolbar	■ Move the mouse around on the screen for a moment.

In this exercise, you will navigate through your slide show.

Before You Begin: The Pinnacle Pet Care presentation should be open in PowerPoint.

1. Click once on the first slide in the Slides panel as shown at right.
   The Slides panel along the left side of the PowerPoint window is a handy way to navigate to various slides. You will start your presentation by displaying the Title slide.

2. Choose View→Presentation Views→Slide Show ⬛ from the Ribbon.
   PowerPoint displays your title slide in full-screen view. All toolbars and other screen objects are hidden from view.

3. Move the mouse around the screen for a moment.
   Notice the Slide Show ⬛⬛⬛ *toolbar that appears near the bottom-left corner of the screen when the slides are in full-screen view.*

4. Click the mouse anywhere on the screen to move to the next slide.

5. Tap the [Page Down] key twice and then tap [Page Up] twice by using the keys near the main keyboard (not the keys on the numeric keypad).
   PowerPoint displays the next or previous slide each time you tap these keys.

Manipulate the Slide Show Toolbar

6. Click the Slide Options button on the Slide Show toolbar. Choose Go to Slide→Monthly Events.
   In the Go to Slide menu, your entire presentation is outlined by title. Simply choose the slide you want to see.

7. Click the Slide Options button on the Slide Show toolbar then choose Go to Slide→ Pinnacle Pet Care.
   As you can see, there are many ways to navigate slides in an electronic slide show.

End the Slide Show

8. Continue to click anywhere on the screen until the last slide appears (the Questions slide).

9. Click once on the last slide.
   The screen turns to a black background, with a small note at the top.

10. Click anywhere on the black screen to exit the slide show and return to the main PowerPoint window.

11. Feel free to practice running your slide show again.

12. When you have finished, click the Save ⬛ button to save any changes to your presentation.

Printing Your Presentation

Ninety percent of the time, you will be viewing or projecting the presentations you create from a PC or notebook computer. However, there may be times when a hard copy of the presentation is needed. Here you will simply explore the options of printing a presentation.

Knowing What You Can Print

PowerPoint can create the following types of printouts:

- Slides: Prints each slide of a presentation on a separate page

- Handouts: Prints one or more slides per page, leaving room for attendees to jot notes during the presentation

- Speaker Notes: Prints each slide on a separate page, with any speaker notes you created for the slide below

Using Print Preview

The Print Preview window lets you see how each slide will be printed. You can then refine the appearance before printing. The following illustration describes the options available from the Print Preview window.

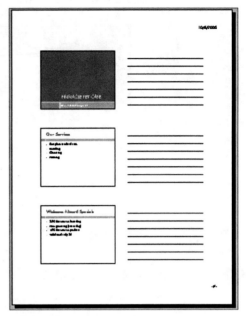

An example of a handout with three slides per page

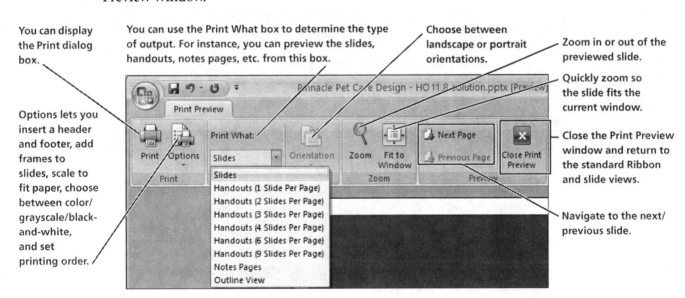

You can display the Print dialog box.

You can use the Print What box to determine the type of output. For instance, you can preview the slides, handouts, notes pages, etc. from this box.

Choose between landscape or portrait orientations.

Zoom in or out of the previewed slide.

Quickly zoom so the slide fits the current window.

Options lets you insert a header and footer, add frames to slides, scale to fit paper, choose between color/grayscale/black-and-white, and set printing order.

Close the Print Preview window and return to the standard Ribbon and slide views.

Navigate to the next/previous slide.

Hands-On 11.9   Use Print Preview

In this exercise, you will work with the Print Preview feature of PowerPoint.

1. Choose Office→Print ►→Print Preview.

2. Follow these steps to open the Print Preview window:

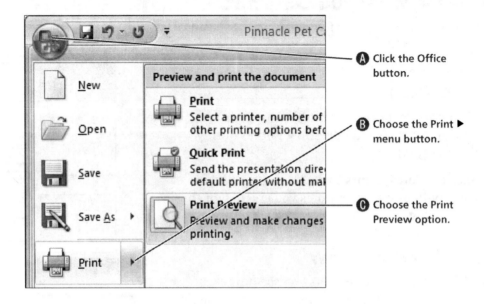

Ⓐ Click the Office button.

Ⓑ Choose the Print ► menu button.

Ⓒ Choose the Print Preview option.

PowerPoint displays the print preview in a new window, with a single Print Preview tab on the Ribbon.

3. Follow these steps to examine the Print Preview options:

Ⓐ Click the Print What menu and select Handouts (4 Slides per Page).

Ⓑ Choose Notes pages in the Print What menu and take note of how it affects the preview of your print job.

Ⓒ Change the zoom control to 100% and then experiment with other zoom settings.

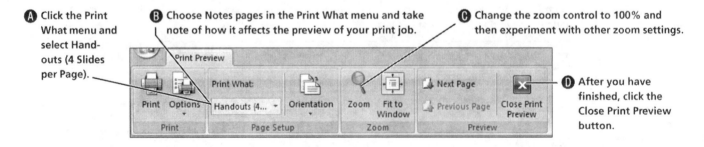

Ⓓ After you have finished, click the Close Print Preview button.

The normal PowerPoint window reappears.

Using Page Setup and Output Formats

If you need to print the presentation itself or transparencies for overhead projection, use the Page Setup dialog box. The Page Setup dialog box can be displayed by choosing Design→Page Setup→Page Setup from the Ribbon. Examine the Page Setup options, along with the different types of output formats you can use by studying the Page Setup dialog box that follows:

PowerPoint sets the size options depending on the output format. However, you can always manually adjust the size.

PowerPoint provides a variety of output formats in the Slides Sized For menu. Available sizes include overhead transparencies, letter paper, banner, and other various sizes.

The orientation options affect the default orientation of the objects in the presentation.

Hands-On 11.10 Explore the Page Setup Box

In this exercise, you will learn about the options provided in the Page Setup dialog box.

1. Choose Design→Page Setup→Page Setup as shown at right to display the Page Setup dialog box.

2. Click the Slides Sized For list and examine the various output formats.

3. Examine the Orientation section of the Page Setup dialog box. *Notice that there are separate settings for printing slides and printing notes and handout pages.*

4. Click the Cancel button when you have finished examining options in the Page Setup box to close the box without applying the settings.

Using the Print Dialog Box

FROM THE KEYBOARD
Ctrl+P to display
the Print box

The Print dialog box allows you to change printers, specify the number of copies to be printed, print a range of slides, and modify the color of the slide for print.

The Print Range section allows you to print all slides, the current slide, or a range of slides. To specify a range of slides, check Slides and type the desired slide numbers in the Slides box.

The Print What section allows you to print slides, meeting handouts, speaker notes, or the outline. This option is also available through Print Preview.

The Name section allows you to choose a printer.

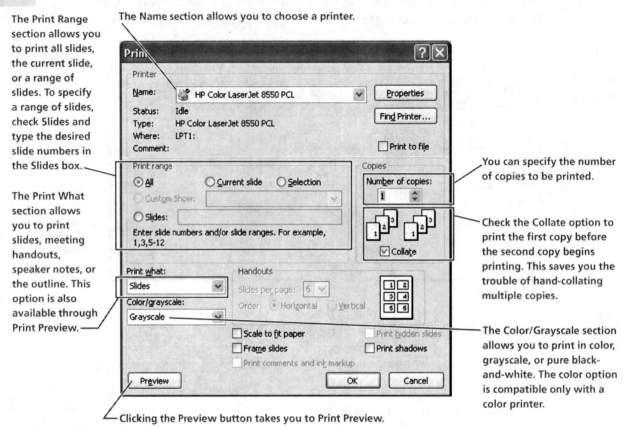

You can specify the number of copies to be printed.

Check the Collate option to print the first copy before the second copy begins printing. This saves you the trouble of hand-collating multiple copies.

The Color/Grayscale section allows you to print in color, grayscale, or pure black-and-white. The color option is compatible only with a color printer.

Clicking the Preview button takes you to Print Preview.

Using the Print Shortcut

If you have customized your Quick Launch toolbar to display the Quick Print icon, you may find it tempting to just click the Quick Print button. However, before this becomes a habit, know that a click of this button sends the entire presentation to the current printer, whether or not you want to make adjustments. If you are working with a document theme that has a colored background, the printing process will not only be painstakingly slow, but may also waste your toner or ink!

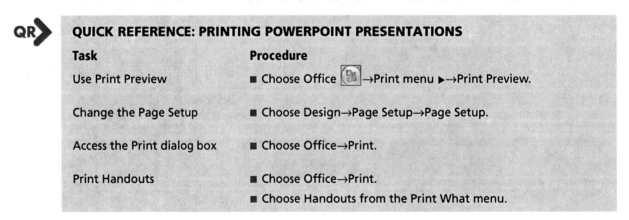

QUICK REFERENCE: PRINTING POWERPOINT PRESENTATIONS

Task	Procedure
Use Print Preview	■ Choose Office ⬛ →Print menu ▶→Print Preview.
Change the Page Setup	■ Choose Design→Page Setup→Page Setup.
Access the Print dialog box	■ Choose Office→Print.
Print Handouts	■ Choose Office→Print.
	■ Choose Handouts from the Print What menu.

Hands-On 11.11 Print Handouts

In this exercise, you will explore the Print dialog box.

1. Save the presentation.

TIP! *It's always a good idea to save a file before you print it. If anything goes wrong, your latest work won't be lost.*

2. Choose Office →Print to display the Print dialog box.

3. Follow these steps to print handouts:

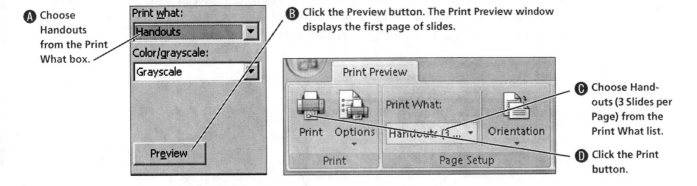

A Choose Handouts from the Print What box.

B Click the Preview button. The Print Preview window displays the first page of slides.

C Choose Handouts (3 Slides per Page) from the Print What list.

D Click the Print button.

The Print dialog box reappears, ready for you to send your print command.

4. Click OK to complete the print command.
   PowerPoint sends the handouts print job to the printer.

5. Click the Print Preview→Preview→Close Print Preview button.
   The normal PowerPoint window appears.

6. Close ☒ the presentation.

Working with Clip Art

Adding clip art to your presentations will help you emphasize key points and add polish to the presentation as a whole. Microsoft Office 2007 has a clip art collection of more than 130,000 pieces of art—and it grows daily. There is clip art available for any occasion. In addition to clip art, you can use other media types with PowerPoint slides, including Drawing Objects (AutoShapes), photographs, movies, and audio (sound) files.

Using Text and Object Layouts

Earlier, you worked with slides that included a title or title and text combination. The slide layouts you used allowed you to easily create slides with a standardized title and bulleted text. Many of PowerPoint's layouts, including the Title and Content layout and the Two Content layout, provide placeholders for titles, text, and various types of content including tables, charts, clip art, pictures, diagrams, organizational charts, and movies.

Some slide layouts include a group of six icons.

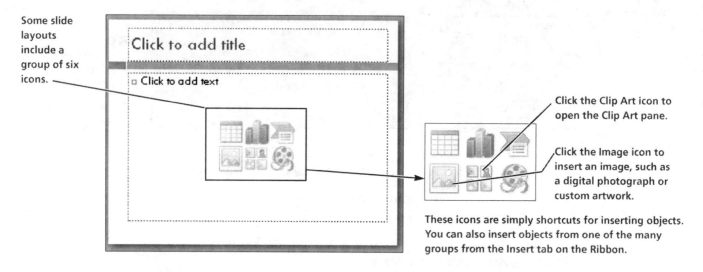

Click the Clip Art icon to open the Clip Art pane.

Click the Image icon to insert an image, such as a digital photograph or custom artwork.

These icons are simply shortcuts for inserting objects. You can also insert objects from one of the many groups from the Insert tab on the Ribbon.

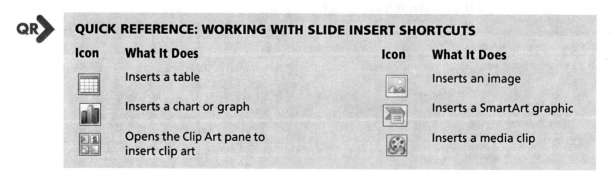

QR **QUICK REFERENCE: WORKING WITH SLIDE INSERT SHORTCUTS**

Icon	What It Does	Icon	What It Does
	Inserts a table		Inserts an image
	Inserts a chart or graph		Inserts a SmartArt graphic
	Opens the Clip Art pane to insert clip art		Inserts a media clip

Hands-On 11.12 Get a Slide Ready for Clip Art

In this exercise, you will get a slide ready to accept clip art. The clip art will be added in the next exercise.

1. Open the Pinnacle Pet Care Animation presentation from the Lesson 11 folder on your file storage location.

2. If necessary, choose View→Presentation Views→Normal to display the presentation in Normal view.
   If it was not visible before, the Slides/Outline panel appears on the left side of the PowerPoint window.

3. If necessary, choose the Slides tab in the Slides/Outline panel.
   It will be easier to monitor your slide layouts if you are using the Slides panel rather than the Outline panel.

4. Select the Our Services slide from the Slides panel.

5. Choose Home→Slides→New Slide .
   A new slide is inserted below Our Services. The new slide uses the same layout as the Our Services slide.

Choose a Layout and Format Text

6. Follow these steps to apply a slide layout suitable for clip art:

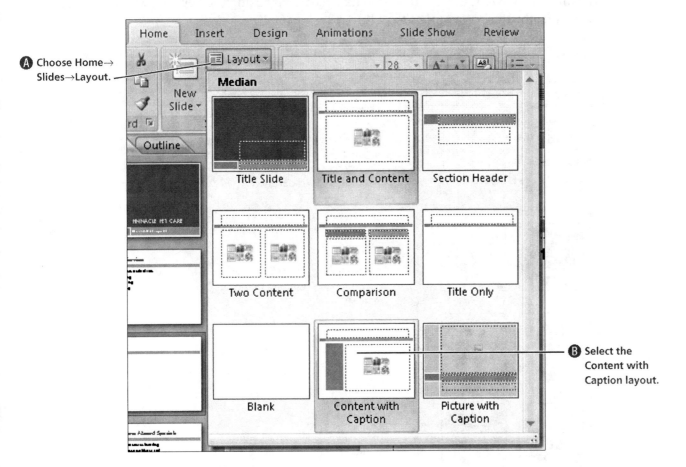

Ⓐ Choose Home→Slides→Layout.

Ⓑ Select the Content with Caption layout.

7. In the Title placeholder, type **Our Recent Success.**

8. In the narrow left text box, type **Best in Show** Enter **Excellence in Customer Service** Enter **National Association of Animal Lovers**.

9. Select the text *Best in Show* and increase the font size to 28 from the Home→Font→Font Size menu ▾ button.

10. Choose Home→Font→Bold to make the text bold.

11. Select the text *National Association of Animal Lovers*.

12. Choose Home→Font→Italic to make the text italic.
    Your slide is ready to have clip art added.

Searching for Clip Art with the Clip Art Task Pane

Finding clip art is easy: Click the Clip Art ▦ icon in the slide placeholder to bring the Clip Art task pane to the right side of your screen. Alternatively, you can select Insert→Illustrations→Clip Art from the Ribbon. You search for clip art by typing a keyword and clicking the Go button. Each piece of clip art is associated with keywords that describe its characteristics. For example, the images shown in the illustration can be located by using the keyword *awards* or *prizes*. The following illustration describes the Clip Art task pane:

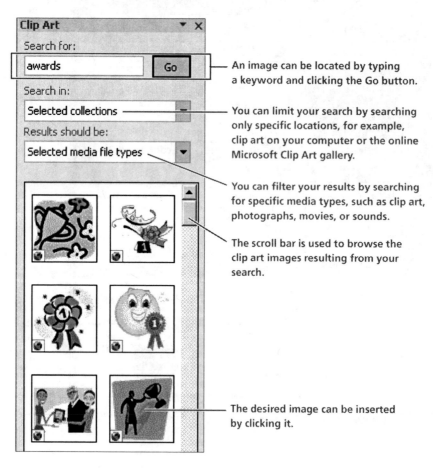

An image can be located by typing a keyword and clicking the Go button.

You can limit your search by searching only specific locations, for example, clip art on your computer or the online Microsoft Clip Art gallery.

You can filter your results by searching for specific media types, such as clip art, photographs, movies, or sounds.

The scroll bar is used to browse the clip art images resulting from your search.

The desired image can be inserted by clicking it.

In this exercise, you will insert clip art.

1. On the Our Recent Success slide, click the Clip Art ⊞ icon as shown to open the Clip Art task pane.

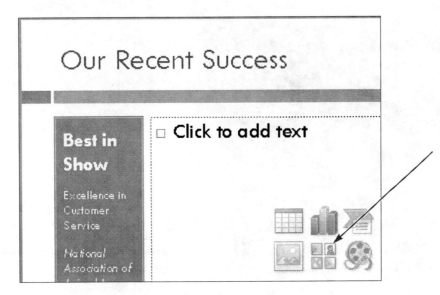

2. Configure the Clip Art task pane as shown:

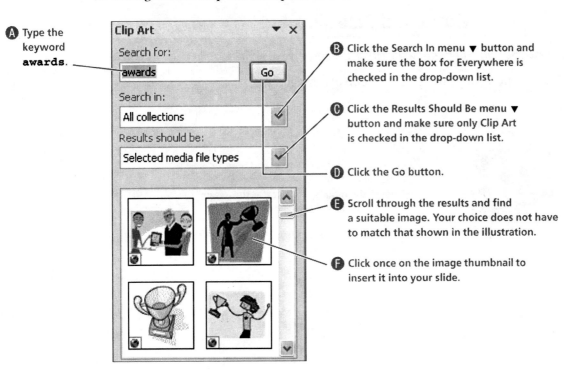

Ⓐ Type the keyword **awards**.

Ⓑ Click the Search In menu ▼ button and make sure the box for Everywhere is checked in the drop-down list.

Ⓒ Click the Results Should Be menu ▼ button and make sure only Clip Art is checked in the drop-down list.

Ⓓ Click the Go button.

Ⓔ Scroll through the results and find a suitable image. Your choice does not have to match that shown in the illustration.

Ⓕ Click once on the image thumbnail to insert it into your slide.

The clip art image is inserted on the slide and replaces the large text box.

Moving, Sizing, and Rotating Objects

When you click an object (such as a clip art image), sizing handles and a rotate handle appear. You can easily move, size, and rotate selected objects as described in the following illustration.

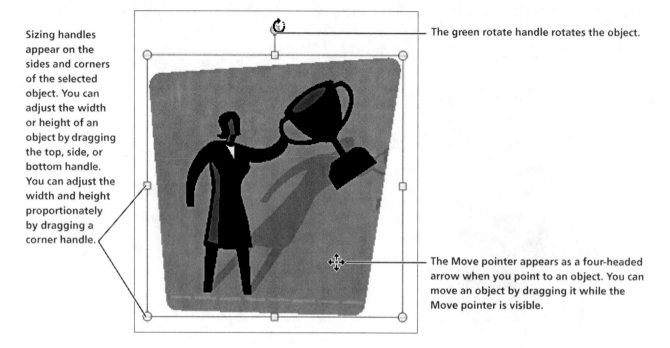

Sizing handles appear on the sides and corners of the selected object. You can adjust the width or height of an object by dragging the top, side, or bottom handle. You can adjust the width and height proportionately by dragging a corner handle.

The green rotate handle rotates the object.

The Move pointer appears as a four-headed arrow when you point to an object. You can move an object by dragging it while the Move pointer is visible.

 ## Hands-On 11.14 **Move and Size Clip Art**

In this exercise, you will manipulate clip art, sizing and moving it to place it on the slide.

1. Follow these steps to rotate the clip art image:

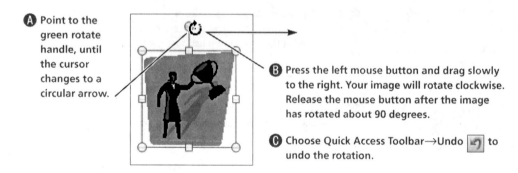

A Point to the green rotate handle, until the cursor changes to a circular arrow.

B Press the left mouse button and drag slowly to the right. Your image will rotate clockwise. Release the mouse button after the image has rotated about 90 degrees.

C Choose Quick Access Toolbar→Undo to undo the rotation.

2. Follow these steps to resize the clip art image:

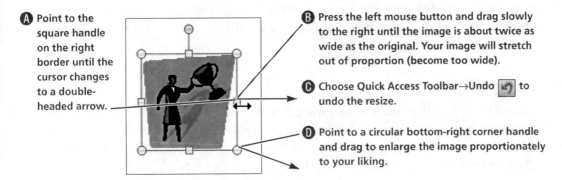

A Point to the square handle on the right border until the cursor changes to a double-headed arrow.

B Press the left mouse button and drag slowly to the right until the image is about twice as wide as the original. Your image will stretch out of proportion (become too wide).

C Choose Quick Access Toolbar→Undo to undo the resize.

D Point to a circular bottom-right corner handle and drag to enlarge the image proportionately to your liking.

3. Point to the image itself (not the border or a resize handle) until the pointer becomes a four-headed arrow. Drag the image so it is centered next to the bar of text. Compare your slide with the following illustration.

4. Save your presentation.

Inserting Clip Art without an Existing Placeholder

If your slide does not have the shortcut icons to insert clip art, you can still insert an image by displaying the Clip Art task pane and choosing Insert→Illustrations→Clip Art from the Ribbon.

Formatting Clip Art

After your image is on the slide, use the various groups on the contextual Format tab to add effects or align your image. You can add borders, drop-shadows, bevels, or rotate your image in 3-D from the Format→Picture Styles group. Other groups on the Format tab allow you to align, flip, crop, or perform basic image editing tasks.

QR▶

QUICK REFERENCE: PERFORMING CLIP ART TASKS

Task	Procedure
Insert a clip art image	■ Click the Clip Art shortcut on the slide to display the Clip Art task pane. ■ Enter a keyword and configure the Search In and Results Should Be options. ■ Click the Go button. ■ Click the desired thumbnail to insert the clip art in your slide.
Resize a clip art image	■ Click the clip art image to display its border. ■ Drag any square handle along the top, bottom, or sides of the clip art's border to resize the image wider or taller. ■ Drag any circular handle in the clip art's corners to resize the image proportionately.
Move a clip art image	■ Point to the image until the mouse pointer becomes a four-headed arrow. ■ Drag the image to the desired location.
Rotate a clip art image	■ Click the clip art image to display its border. ■ Point to the green rotate handle on top of the clip art's border until the mouse pointer becomes a circular arrow. ■ Drag left or right to rotate the image.
Format a clip art image	■ Click the clip art image to display its border. ■ Select a command from the Format→Picture Styles group on the Ribbon.

In this exercise, you will work with the Ribbon to insert and format an image on your slide.

Insert the Image

1. Display the title slide.

2. Choose Insert→Illustrations→Clip Art ⊞ from the Ribbon if the Clip Art task pane is not already visible.
   The Clip Art task pane should be displayed on the right side of your screen.

3. Follow these steps to insert clip art on the title slide:

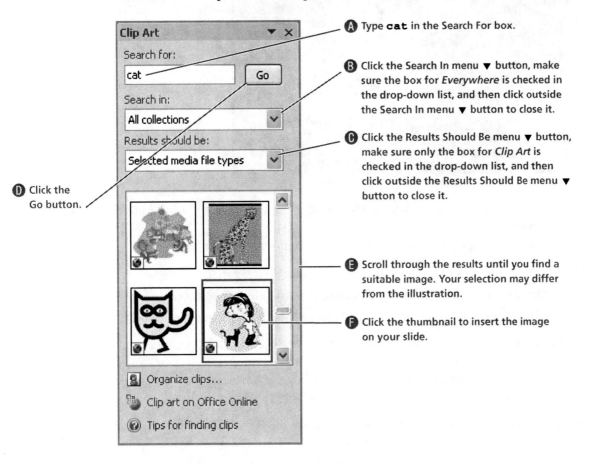

Ⓐ Type **cat** in the Search For box.

Ⓑ Click the Search In menu ▼ button, make sure the box for *Everywhere* is checked in the drop-down list, and then click outside the Search In menu ▼ button to close it.

Ⓒ Click the Results Should Be menu ▼ button, make sure only the box for *Clip Art* is checked in the drop-down list, and then click outside the Results Should Be menu ▼ button to close it.

Ⓓ Click the Go button.

Ⓔ Scroll through the results until you find a suitable image. Your selection may differ from the illustration.

Ⓕ Click the thumbnail to insert the image on your slide.

Size and Position the Image

In the next few steps, you will use the Format contextual tab to experiment with effect options.

4. Drag the top-right circular handle toward the top-right corner of your slide to enlarge the image proportionately. Be careful not to size it too large. The image should still fit on the slide.

5. Choose Format→Arrange→ Align →Align Center from the Ribbon to center the image horizontally.
Selecting an image object forces the display of the contextual Format tab.

6. Follow these steps to format the image:
   - Make sure the image displays handles to indicate it is selected.
   - Choose Format→Picture Styles→Picture Effects ⬜ from the Ribbon.

7. Roll your cursor over several of the items in the Picture Effects gallery to view a Live Preview of each effect.
As you have seen with other commands, Live Preview makes it easy to anticipate the effect of a command without the need to undo it if you don't like the effect.

8. Choose Format→Picture Styles→Picture Effects ⬜→Glow→Accent Color 6, 18 pt. Glow as shown in the following illustration.

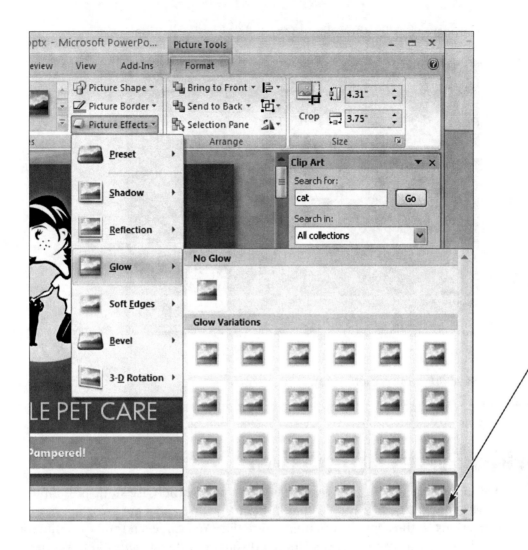

PowerPoint applies a glowing effect to the edge of the image.

9. Close the Clip Art task pane.

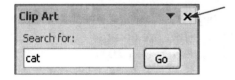

10. Compare your finished slide to the following illustration.

The completed title slide

11. Save 💾 your presentation.

Working with Animation

Animation can add life, energy, and vibrancy to an otherwise static presentation. In PowerPoint 2007, animation comes in many flavors. There are preset animation schemes, transitions, audio clips, and custom animation. You can even time the animation to synchronize with your prepared speech throughout the presentation. Animation, used sparingly, can beautifully accentuate a key point.

Applying Slide Transitions

A transition in PowerPoint is the animation between slides. Transitions put zest and excitement in your presentation and provide distinct breaking points between slides. There are more than 50 transition effects available in PowerPoint 2007.

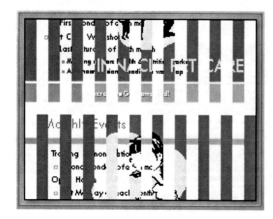

The Comb Vertical transition occurring between two slides

Creating Transitions in Slide Sorter View

Most of the time, you will want to apply the same transition to the entire presentation. Using the Slide Sorter view is a quick and easy way to accomplish this task. You can apply transitions to a single slide, multiple slides, or to all slides in a presentation. When you apply a transition, it animates the entire slide, not individual elements of the slide.

Selecting Slides for Transitions

To easily select all slides in a presentation from Slide Sorter view, click to select the first slide in the presentation. If necessary, scroll to the bottom of the Slide Sorter window pane, press and hold the Shift key, click the last slide in the presentation, and then release the Shift key. All slides will be selected. After the slides are selected, choose Animations→Transitions to This Slide from the Ribbon, and select a transition effect. The transition will be applied to all selected slides. You can also use this same method from the Normal view's Slides panel to select all slides in a presentation.

To apply a transition to a single slide, simply select a single slide in either Normal or Slide Sorter view, and then choose a slide transition from Animations→Transitions to This Slide. The transition will be applied to the selected slide.

The Animations Tab

The Animations tab contains the Transitions to This Slide group, which you use to implement your slide transitions. The Animations tab contains commands to apply transitions, sound, and other animation options to slides.

More than 50 slide transitions are listed here. Simply click on a thumbnail to apply the transition to the selected slide(s).

Use the scroll bar or click the More button to view all the available transitions.

Select an optional sound effect to play during the transition.

Select the speed of the transition.

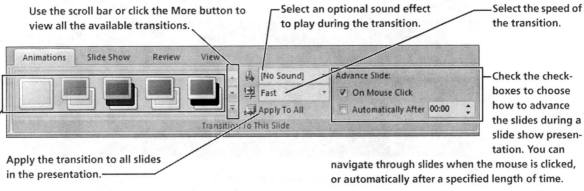

Apply the transition to all slides in the presentation.

Check the checkboxes to choose how to advance the slides during a slide show presentation. You can navigate through slides when the mouse is clicked, or automatically after a specified length of time.

QUICK REFERENCE: ADDING TRANSITIONS TO A PRESENTATION

Task	Procedure
Add transitions to an entire presentation	■ From Slide Sorter view, press Ctrl+A to select all slides in a presentation. ■ Choose Animations→Transition to This Slide and select the desired transition.
Set a transition for individual slides	■ Select the slide(s) to which you wish to apply a special transition. (Remember that transitions are seen when navigating to a slide when a slide loads.) ■ Choose Animations→Transition to This Slide and select the desired transition.

Hands-On 11.16 Apply Transition Effects

In this exercise, you will apply the Dissolve transition to all slides except the title slide.

Choose Transition Effects

1. Choose View→Presentation Views→Slide Sorter ⊞ from the Ribbon.

2. Choose the Animations tab from the Ribbon.

3. Follow these steps to select multiple slides and choose a transition effect:

Ⓐ Click once on the Our Services slide.

Ⓑ Press and hold the Shift key, and click the Contact Us slide. Then you can release the Shift key. (This selects all slides except the opening title slide.)

Ⓓ Choose Dissolve from the Fades and Dissolves category. (A preview of the effect briefly appears on all selected slides.)

Ⓒ Click the More button and locate the Fades and Dissolves category.

Ⓔ Set the transition speed to Medium.

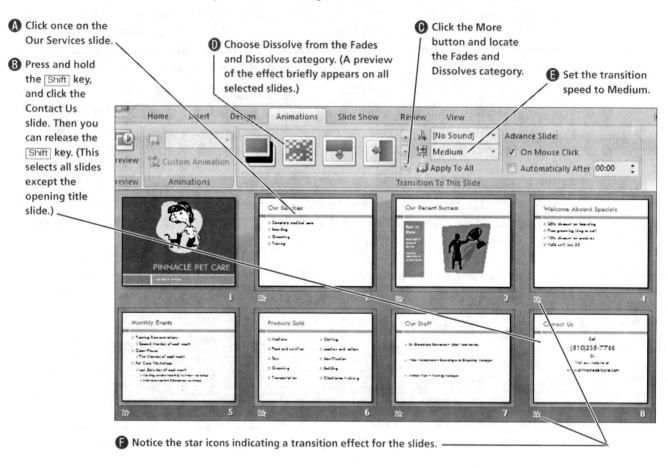

Ⓕ Notice the star icons indicating a transition effect for the slides. ───────

The title slide does not have the star icon because there is no transition applied to it.

Run the Presentation

4. Click the title slide.

At this point, only the title slide should be selected. In the next step, you will run the presentation. Selecting the title slide will force the presentation to begin with that slide.

5. Choose View→Presentation Views→Slide Show from the Ribbon.

The title slide appears without a transition. The title slide would have opened with the Dissolve transition if you had applied the transition to it.

6. Click the mouse button to advance to the next slide.

When you use the transition effect, the title slide dissolves into the Our Services slide.

7. Continue to click the mouse button until you reach the end of the presentation and the Slide Sorter window reappears.

8. Save your presentation.

9. Close the presentation.

10. Exit PowerPoint.

Concepts Review

True/False Questions

1. Document themes give presentations a consistent format and appearance.   TRUE   FALSE

2. There is no difference between the Quick Print button on the customized Quick Access toolbar and the Print command in the Office menu.   TRUE   FALSE

3. A slide's layout cannot be changed after the slide has been created.   TRUE   FALSE

4. The Slide Sorter view is useful in selecting slides when you have more slides than can fit in the Normal view Slides panel.   TRUE   FALSE

5. PowerPoint automatically wraps your text to a second line when your text reaches the edge of the text box.   TRUE   FALSE

6. You can insert clip art from Normal view or Slide Show view.   TRUE   FALSE

7. When searching for clip art in PowerPoint, you can find photographs, movies, and sounds in addition to images.   TRUE   FALSE

8. To apply a transition to multiple slides, you must use Slide Sorter view.   TRUE   FALSE

9. Increasing a bulleted paragraph's list level (indenting) reduces the size of the bullet.   TRUE   FALSE

10. To navigate a presentation in Slide Show view, you must use the Slide Show toolbar.   TRUE   FALSE

Multiple Choice Questions

1. What PowerPoint feature allows you to transform the appearance of an entire presentation by using a single command?
   a. Document themes
   b. Style templates
   c. WordArt styles
   d. Slide Show view

2. Which command allows you to convert a slide from containing placeholders for a title and bullets to placeholders for a title, a clip art image, and a caption?
   a. Layout
   b. Slides
   c. Themes
   d. Background Styles

3. Which of the following actions can be performed on clip art placed on slides?
   a. Rotation
   b. Sizing
   c. Moving
   d. Only b and c
   e. All of the above

4. Which command allows you to convert a slide from a single column of text to two columns of text?
   a. Layout
   b. Slides
   c. Themes
   d. Background Styles

Skill Builders

Skill Builder 11.1   Create a Presentation

In this exercise, you will create a presentation for the Tropical Getaways travel service. The presentation will be used to sell potential customers a tropical getaway to paradise. The managers of Tropical Getaways will be delivering the presentation to an audience of more than 40 people.

1. Start the PowerPoint program.
   A new presentation appears when PowerPoint starts. To gain practice creating a new presentation, you will close that and create a new one.

2. Follow these steps to close the existing presentation:

   A Click the Office button.

   B Choose the Close command.

   The presentation closes.

3. Choose Office [icon] →New.
   The New Presentation window appears.

4. Double-click the Blank Presentation choice.
   A new presentation with a single slide is created.

Apply a Document Theme

5. Choose Design→Themes, and choose the Civic theme.
   PowerPoint applies the theme to your presentation.

6. Click in the Title placeholder and type the title **Tropical Getaways**.

7. Click in the Subtitle placeholder and type the subtitle **Adventures in Paradise**.
   As you type, the text is converted to uppercase because that is a design element of this particular document theme.

8. Save  your presentation as **sb-Tropical Getaways** on your file storage location.

Set Up Another Slide

9. Choose Home→Slides→New Slide from the Ribbon.
   A single-column, bulleted list slide will be added to the presentation. Notice that the Civic document theme is applied to the new slide.

10. Choose Home→Slides→ Layout →Two Content from the Ribbon.
    A new two-column layout is applied to the slide.

11. Click in the Title placeholder and type the title **Most Popular Destinations**.

12. Add the following text to the bulleted list on the left:

    ■ **Tahiti**

    ■ **Maui**

    ■ **Oahu**

    ■ **Cancun**

13. Add the following text to the bulleted list on the right:

    ■ **Caribbean**

    ■ **Fiji**

    ■ **Singapore**

    ■ **Australia**

    After you finish typing, your slide should look similar to the following illustration.

Most Popular Destinations

- Tahiti   - Caribbean
- Maui   - Fiji
- Oahu   - Singapore
- Cancun   - Australia

14. Save your presentation.

Set Up the Remaining Slides

15. Choose Home→Slides→New Slide 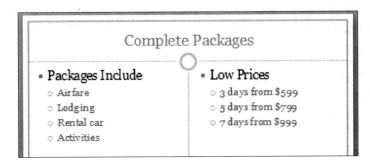 from the Ribbon.
    A third slide is added to the presentation. The new slide has the same Two Content layout as the previous slide.

16. In the Title placeholder, enter the phrase **Complete Packages**.

17. In the first bullet of the left bulleted list, enter the phrase **Packages Include** and tap Enter.

18. Choose Home→Paragraph→Increase List Level from the Ribbon.
    The bullet is indented and a new bullet character is applied by the design template.

19. Add the following text to the bulleted list on the left:
    - **Airfare**
    - **Lodging**
    - **Rental car**
    - **Activities**

20. In the first bullet of the bulleted list on the right, enter the phrase **Low Prices** and tap Enter.

21. Choose Home→Paragraph→Increase List Level from the Ribbon.
    The bullet is indented, and a new bullet character is applied by the design template.

22. Add the following text to the bulleted list on the right:
    - **3 days from $599**
    - **5 days from $799**
    - **7 days from $999**

    After you finish typing, your slide should look similar to the following illustration.

23. Choose Home→Slides→New Slide to add a fourth slide to your presentation.

24. Choose Home→Slides→Layout →Title and Content to change the slide layout to a single column.

25. Enter the title **Travel Now and Save!**

26. Type the following bullet points in the text box:

   - **Package 1**
   - **5 days in Oahu**
   - **$429 per person**
   - **Package 2**
   - **7 days in Tahiti**
   - **$1,299 per person**

27. Select the *5 days in Oahu* and *$429 per person* paragraphs and increase their list level.

28. Select the *7 days in Tahiti* and *$1,299 per person* paragraphs and increase their list level. *After you finish typing, your slide should look similar to the following illustration.*

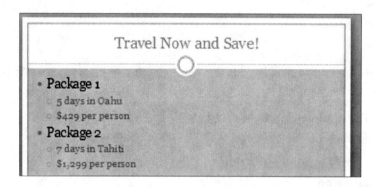

29. Choose Home→Slides→New Slide to add the final slide to the presentation.

30. Type **Tropical Getaways** for the title.

31. Type the following in the text box:

   - **Angelica Escobedo**
   - **(310) 544-8870**

32. Click the dashed border around the text box so it turns solid, and choose Home→ Paragraph→Bullets ▤ to remove the bullets. *The bullets are removed from all paragraphs in the text box.*

33. Select Home→Paragraph→Center ![center icon] from the Ribbon to center the text on the slide.
    After you finish typing, your slide should look similar to the following illustration.

Tropical Getaways

Angelica Escobedo
(310) 544-8870

34. Save ![save icon] the presentation.
    Leave the presentation open if you will continue to the next exercise.

Skill Builder 11.2 Deliver a Slide Show

In this exercise, you will practice delivering the Tropical Getaways presentation.

Before You Begin: The sb-Tropical Getaways presentation created in Skill Builder 11.1 should be open in PowerPoint.

1. Select the first slide from the Slides panel on the left side of your screen.

2. Choose View→Presentation Views→Slide Show ![slide show icon] from the Ribbon.
   The Title slide will occupy your whole screen as the slide show starts.

3. Walk through the presentation by clicking each slide until the presentation is ended.

4. Click once more to return to the PowerPoint program window.

5. Choose View→Presentation Views→Slide Show ![slide show icon] from the Ribbon to start the slide show again.

6. After the slide show begins, position the mouse pointer at the bottom-left corner of the screen to display the Slide Show toolbar.

7. Click the Slide Options button as shown at right on the Slide Show toolbar.

8. Choose Go to Slide→Travel Now and Save!
   Notice that the Go to Slide drop-down menu displays the title of each slide in your presentation.

9. Use the Slide Options button on the Slide Show toolbar to end the slide show by choosing End Show.

10. Save the presentation.
    Leave the presentation open for the next exercise.

Skill Builder 11.3   Print the Presentation

In this exercise, you will print a slide.

Before You Begin: The sb-Tropical Getaways presentation edited in Skill Builder 11.1 should be open in PowerPoint.

1. Select the second slide, Most Popular Destinations, from the Slide panel.

2. Choose Office→Print to display the Print dialog box.

3. In the Print dialog box, choose a printer to use for this print job.
   If a printer is already assigned, examine the dialog box.

4. Under Print Range, choose Current Slide to print only the current slide, not the entire presentation.
   This is only a test to see how a slide will look on paper.

5. In the Print What section, choose Slides.

6. Under Color/Grayscale, choose Grayscale.
   Save your ink color. Using either grayscale or pure black-and-white results in a white background with black text, which is acceptable for a draft copy.

7. Click Preview to verify your settings.

8. Choose Print Preview→Print→Print to return to the Print dialog.

9. Click OK to print your slide.

10. Save and close the presentation.

Skill Builder 11.4 Insert Clip Art

In this exercise, you will add clip art to the Tropical Getaways Animation presentation.

1. Open the sb-Tropical Getaways Animation presentation from your Lesson 11 folder.

2. Choose View→Presentation Views→Normal  from the Ribbon.

3. Choose the Travel Categories slide (the second slide).

4. Choose Home→Slides→Layout→Two Content, as shown at right, to change the layout of the slide.

5. Click the Clip Art ▦ icon on the slide to display the Clip Art task pane.

6. Enter the keyword **safari.**

7. Verify that Search In is set to Everywhere and that Results Should Be is set to only Clip Art, and then click the Go button.

8. Choose a clip art image that appeals to you and click OK.
   If necessary, size and position your clip art image. Your slide may differ from the illustration.

Two Content

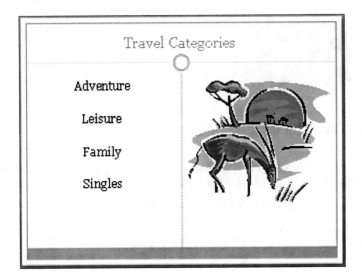

9. Save your presentation and continue with the next exercise.

Skill Builder 11.5 Format Clip Art

In this exercise, you will format clip art to add visual appeal to the presentation.

Before You Begin: The sb-Tropical Getaways Animation presentation from the Lesson 11 folder should be open.

1. Choose the Travel Now and Save! slide (the fifth slide).

2. Choose Home→Slides→Layout→Two Content to change the layout of the slide.

3. Display the Clip Art task pane if necessary, and then enter the keyword **tropics.**

4. Verify that Search In is set to Everywhere and that Results Should Be is set to only Photographs, and then click the Go button.

5. Choose a clip art photograph that appeals to you and click OK.
   If necessary, size and position your clip art photograph. Your slide may differ from the illustration.

6. Verify that the photograph is selected (you see its border with resize handles), and then choose Format→Picture Styles→More ⟱ and select a style from the gallery.
   The illustration shows the Rotated White style applied. Your slide may differ.

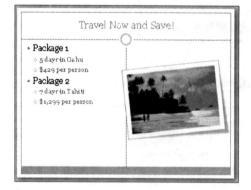

7. Close the Clip Art task pane.

8. Save the changes to your presentation.

Skill Builder 11.6 Apply Slide Transitions

In this exercise, you will apply slide transitions to your presentation.

Before You Begin: The sb-Tropical Getaways Animation presentation from the Lesson 11 folder should be open.

1. Choose View→Presentation Views→Slide Sorter from the Ribbon.

2. Select the first slide, and then $\boxed{\text{Shift}}$+click the last slide.
   This selects all the slides in the presentation.

3. Choose Animations→Transitions to This Slide→More $\boxed{\bar{\ }}$, and then select a transition effect from the gallery.

4. Choose Animations→Preview to preview the effect on each slide.

5. If you are unhappy with your effect, choose Animations→Transitions to This Slide→More $\boxed{\bar{\ }}$ and select a different transition.

6. Save your presentation.

LESSON 12

Exploring Access 2007

Have you ever wondered how service agents who take your order over the telephone know what questions to ask about the products you order...or how sportscasters come up with little-known facts about teams and players in a flash? In most cases, these service agents and sportscasters have access to a powerful database from which they obtain the information.

In this lesson, you will take a tour of the Access 2007 application window and explore a database file to identify the structure of a database and how the elements of a database work together to aid people in all walks of life locate data and information efficiently. Exploring a new program provides valuable insight into the program and its features. Exploring an active database will help you unravel some of the mysteries surrounding data storage and retrieval.

LESSON OBJECTIVES

After studying this lesson, you will be able to:

- Define what a database is
- Identify the types of objects Access databases contain
- Launch Access 2007 and identify elements of the application window
- Open a database and use the Navigation Pane
- Open database objects, navigate within database objects, and close the objects
- Close a database properly and exit Access 2007

Case Study: Exploring Access 2007

Sara Wong has just accepted a position with Labyrinth Exports where she will be managing the data entry department. Her first day on the job, Sara focuses on familiarizing herself with the existing database that the data entry clerks use in an effort to learn what data they enter and how the database is set up. She also wants to review the data entry forms that the data entry clerks use to update and maintain the database.

The employee name shown in the form also appears in the Orders table.

Data about an employee appears in the Employee Details form.

Defining Access Databases

If you have ever used a phone book, a catalog, retrieved a note card from a card file, or pulled a file from a file cabinet, you have used a database. If you have ever used an index or a table of contents in a book, you have used a type of database. Each of these items consists of individual pieces of *data* that, when combined, make up a *database*.

What Is a Database?

A *database* is a collection of related data stored together in one electronic file. Historically, individuals and businesses have used databases to store vast amounts of data in an organized fashion to facilitate quick and easy retrieval of facts, figures, and information. Prior to the computer age, database records were stored on index cards, on columnar tablets, and in file folders stored in file cabinets. While these data storage methods are still around today, computer based databases have reduced the storage requirements of data and have improved the efficiency of data retrieval. As a result, reports from sportscasters, historians, politicians, stock sales, unemployment records, and many other details can be reported with amazing accuracy—and very quickly.

Database Structures

Early electronic databases stored data in flat files—that is, in one gigantic pool of information all stored together like family photos stored in a large box. Flat files contained repetitive data in many entries.

Someone had to type this product name four times.

This long product name was typed twice.

Product	Quantity	Unit Cost	Date Receiv	Posted To In
Labyrinth Exports Almonds	20	$8.00	01/22/2007	☑
Labyrinth Exports Beer	100	$10.00	01/22/2007	☑
Labyrinth Exports Beer	50	$10.00	04/04/2007	☑
Labyrinth Exports Beer	60	$10.00	01/22/2007	☑
Labyrinth Exports Beer	300	$10.00	04/05/2007	☑
Labyrinth Exports Boysenberry Spread	100	$19.00	01/22/2007	☑
Labyrinth Exports Cajun Seasoning	40	$16.00	01/22/2007	☑
Labyrinth Exports Cajun Seasoning	40	$16.00		☐
Labyrinth Exports Chai	40	$14.00		☐
Labyrinth Exports Chai	40	$14.00	01/22/2007	☑
Labyrinth Exports Chocolate	100	$10.00	01/22/2007	☑
Labyrinth Exports Chocolate	100	$10.00	01/22/2007	☑
Labyrinth Exports Chocolate Biscuits Mix	20	$7.00	01/22/2007	☑

Data entry in a flat file database requires lots of repetition.

Modern database programs, such as Access 2007, work more efficiently to store data. Such database programs are often referred to as *object-oriented databases* because they store data in different tables to eliminate the need for repetitive data entry. Such database management systems (DBMS) organize data by placing data into various tables. For example, a business might place basic information about its customers—name, address, city, state, and ZIP—into one table, and data such as order details—date of order, item ordered, item description, number ordered, and unit price—into another table. A business might also place a list of employees and data related to the employees into one table and reference the employee who sold merchandise with order details. As a result, data processing becomes more efficient—data entry personnel can enter only data that is unique rather than retyping data that is stored in a different table.

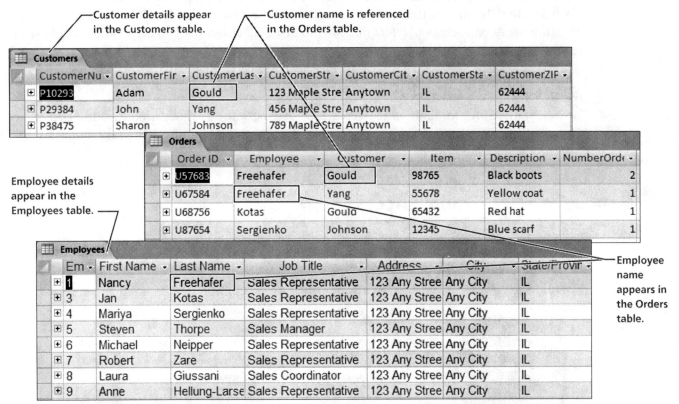

Customer details appear in the Customers table.

Customer name is referenced in the Orders table.

Employee details appear in the Employees table.

Employee name appears in the Orders table.

These three tables from an object-oriented database reduce repetitive data entry because, by storing some data in different tables, it is no longer necessary to retype the data in other tables—a simple reference to one piece of information is sufficient.

Learning to use Access 2007 helps you understand and appreciate data retrieval used by professionals in many walks of life.

Exploring the Access Environment

When you launch Access 2007, one of the first things you will notice is that, unlike other Microsoft Office applications, Access displays a Getting Started welcome screen rather than a new blank file. Because of the number of different objects used to organize data in the database, Access lets you determine how to proceed: either to open an existing database or create a new one.

Launching Access 2007

The basic procedures for launching Access 2007 are the same as those used to launch other Microsoft Office applications. After you launch Access, you are prompted to take action to create or open a database.

 ### Hands-On 12.1   Launch Access 2007

In this exercise, you will launch Access 2007 from the Start menu.

1. Click the Start button on the taskbar.

2. Follow these steps to launch Microsoft Office Access 2007:

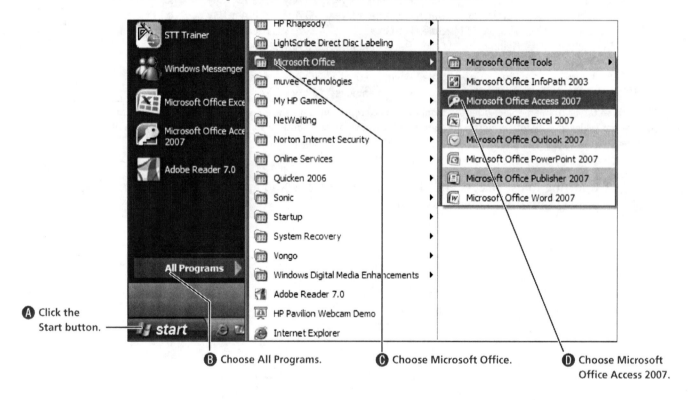

A Click the Start button.

B Choose All Programs.

C Choose Microsoft Office.

D Choose Microsoft Office Access 2007.

The Access 2007 program window appears.

NOTE!   *In future lessons, a Start menu command like this will be written as: Choose All Programs→Microsoft Office→Microsoft Office Access 2007.*

TIP! *After you launch Access for the first time, the program appears on the Start menu. You can launch Access directly from the Start menu rather than displaying the menus from the All Programs list.*

Identifying Elements of the Access Window

 As noted, Access, unlike other Microsoft Office applications, displays a welcome or splash screen each time you launch it. From this screen, you can choose to create a new database, open an existing database, or open a sample database.

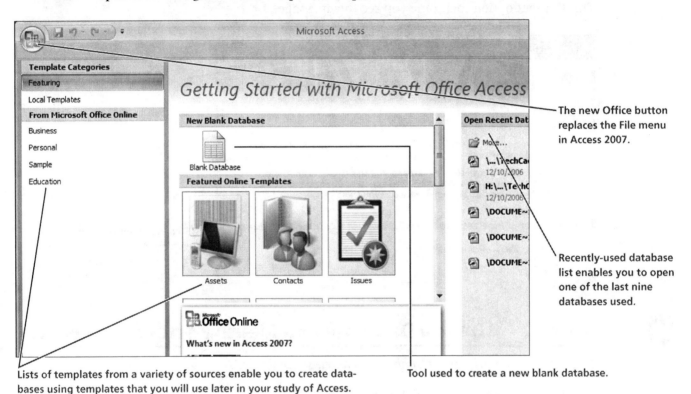

The new Office button replaces the File menu in Access 2007.

Recently-used database list enables you to open one of the last nine databases used.

Lists of templates from a variety of sources enable you to create databases using templates that you will use later in your study of Access.

Tool used to create a new blank database.

Opening a Database and Identifying Features of the Database Window

The procedures for opening an existing file in Access 2007 are basically the same as those found in other Microsoft Office applications. You can choose one of the following procedures:

FROM THE KEYBOARD
Ctrl+O to open

■ Select the file from the Open Recent Database list on the Getting Started with Microsoft Office Access screen.

■ Click the Office button and point to the Open command to display the Recent Documents submenu and select the recently used database to open.

■ Open the file from the Open dialog box.

TIP! *The list of Recent Documents appears when you point to the Open command. As a result, you can select a recently used document from the list to open it.*

Enabling Macros Controlling Database Security

Most database files contain *macros*—programming codes that automate common tasks. Because Access 2007 is highly security conscious, settings that may be active within Access prevent these macros from running without your "permission." The files you use throughout this book have been checked before posting on the website, scanned for viruses, etc., so it's okay to open them and enable database content. If security settings in Access 2007 on your system are set above "low," the message you see onscreen when you open files notifies you of blocked content and provides instructions on how to proceed. You should select the Enable This Content option each time you see this message.

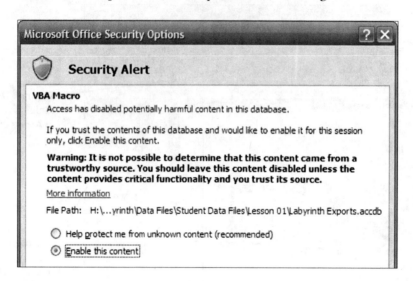

Depending on your security setting, Access may display an alert when you open any database file containing macros.

 Hands-On 12.2   Open a Database and Identify Screen Elements

In this exercise, you will open a database and review screen features.

1. Follow these steps to open a database file:

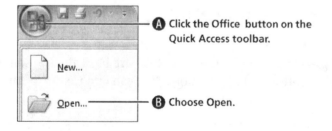

Ⓐ Click the Office button on the Quick Access toolbar.

Ⓑ Choose Open.

!NOTE!   *Later in this book, a command like this will be written Choose Office→Open from the Quick Access toolbar.*

The Open dialog box displays the last folder from which you opened an Access file.

2. Follow these steps to open the file:

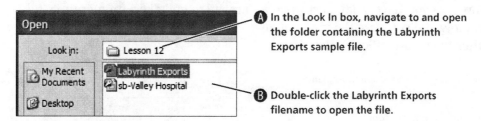

Ⓐ In the Look In box, navigate to and open the folder containing the Labyrinth Exports sample file.

Ⓑ Double-click the Labyrinth Exports filename to open the file.

3. Click the Options button on the following Business Bar as shown, if prompted.

4. Follow these steps to enable the content, if necessary:

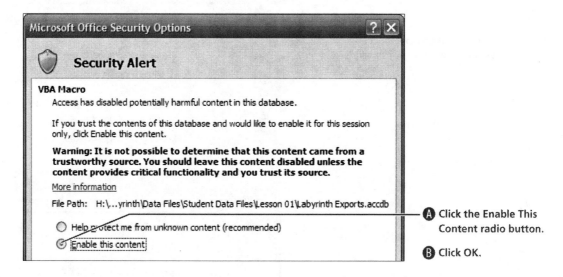

Ⓐ Click the Enable This Content radio button.

Ⓑ Click OK.

The sample database contains a start-up option that enables each person opening the database to log in.

5. Complete your login to the database by following these steps:

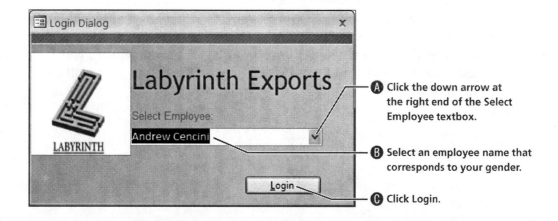

Ⓐ Click the down arrow at the right end of the Select Employee textbox.

Ⓑ Select an employee name that corresponds to your gender.

Ⓒ Click Login.

Identifying Features of the Database Window

Now that you have a database open and ready to go, take a moment to study the layout of the window and compare the visual elements of the window with the features you have seen in other Microsoft Office applications.

The title bar shows the database name and the version of Access you are using.

The Ribbon contains four tabs to display Access tools.

The work area shows a tab with the name of the object that is displayed.

The double-chevron at the top of the Navigation Pane is called the Shutter Bar Open/Close button and enables you to open and close the Navigation Pane.

The Navigation Pane appears down the left side of the window.

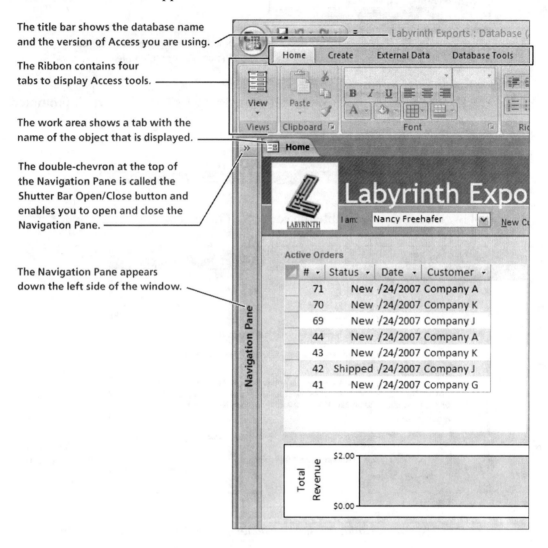

Using the Navigation Pane

If you have used Microsoft Office Excel, you know that navigating within a worksheet or workbook is different from navigating within paragraphs of a document. Navigating within an Access database is also different from navigating in a document. As you begin working with the database, some basic procedures for using the Navigation Pane will enable you to navigate the file more efficiently.

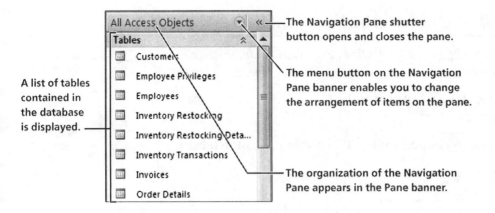

A list of tables contained in the database is displayed.

The Navigation Pane shutter button opens and closes the pane.

The menu button on the Navigation Pane banner enables you to change the arrangement of items on the pane.

The organization of the Navigation Pane appears in the Pane banner.

Object Types

Objects on the Navigation Pane are grouped according to object type. You can expand and collapse each object list to view each object type. You can also select an object from the Navigation Pane banner to display only one object type.

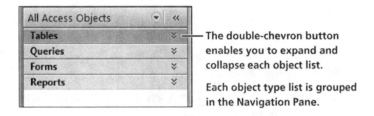

The double-chevron button enables you to expand and collapse each object list.

Each object type list is grouped in the Navigation Pane.

The Navigation Pane Menu

The arrangement of items on the Navigation Pane menu is set when the database is created. Because those who use databases work differently, Access provides a variety of arrangements for displaying database items. These arrangements can vary from database to database to contain arrangements unique to the database; however, options to display database objects by type, date created, and date modified are standard. In addition to selecting the arrangement of objects, the menu contains tools that enable you to display one list of objects at a time.

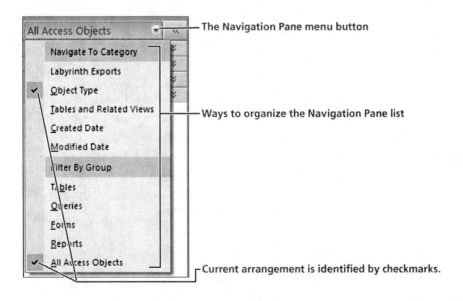

The Navigation Pane menu button

Ways to organize the Navigation Pane list

Current arrangement is identified by checkmarks.

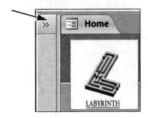

In this exercise, you will use the Navigation Pane to display database objects, expand and collapse object lists, and reorganize database objects.

1. Click the Shutter Bar ⟩⟩ button for the Navigation Pane, as shown at right, to open it.

2. Click the Collapse ⌃ button for the Tables group, as shown below.

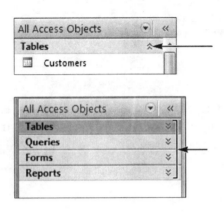

Notice that expand buttons appear for all objects.

Group buttons for the four main object types contained in Access databases are now visible. You'll learn more about each type of database object in the next section.

3. Follow these steps to examine the other object types in this database:

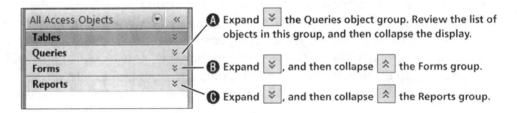

Ⓐ Expand ⌄ the Queries object group. Review the list of objects in this group, and then collapse the display.

Ⓑ Expand ⌄ , and then collapse ⌃ the Forms group.

Ⓒ Expand ⌄ , and then collapse ⌃ the Reports group.

4. Follow these steps to change the display of objects in the Labyrinth Exports database Navigation Pane:

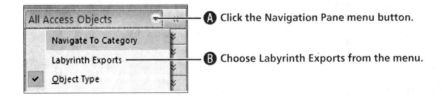

Ⓐ Click the Navigation Pane menu button.

Ⓑ Choose Labyrinth Exports from the menu.

A list specifically for the Labyrinth Exports database appears.

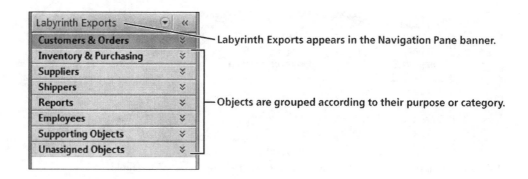

Labyrinth Exports appears in the Navigation Pane banner.

Objects are grouped according to their purpose or category.

5. Click the Navigation Pane menu ⊙ button, and then choose Object Type to return the Navigation Pane display to its original format.

The Navigation Pane returns to its All Access Objects mode.

Opening, Navigating, and Closing Database Objects

As you have already discovered, Access databases contain a variety of different objects to display data and information. As a result, Access is known as an *object-oriented* database program. Each of these objects appears in the Navigation Pane when it is open. Access is also a *relational database management system* (RDMS) because each of the objects contained in the database is related to other objects in the database.

Each type of object in an Access database has a specific purpose. Some are used to input data, others are used to store raw data, and still others are used to select and report specific data. Each object type has a different icon to help you identify what type of object it is. The object icon appears in the object tab or title bar, as well as beside each object in the object list.

QUICK REFERENCE: WORKING WITH OBJECT TYPES IN ACCESS DATABASES

Object Type	Object Icon	Description
Tables	🗔	The basic objects in a database that contain the data used in all other database objects. Tables hold the data and are also used as input objects because you can use the tables to add data to a database.
Forms	🗔	Objects used to display and input data in a layout that is more aesthetically pleasing than table layout.
Reports	🗔	The object in Access databases that processes table data and presents the data as meaningful information. Reports are output objects.
Queries	🗔	Objects used to retrieve data contained in tables on the basis of specific criteria and conditions.

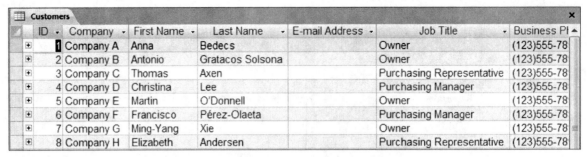

This *table* displays customer data. Notice the column and row layout of the table.

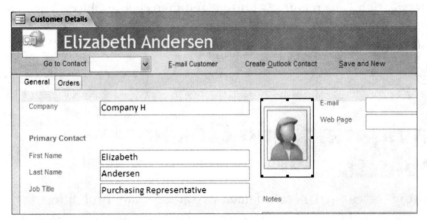

Forms display data about one customer at a time and offer a more appealing layout and design.

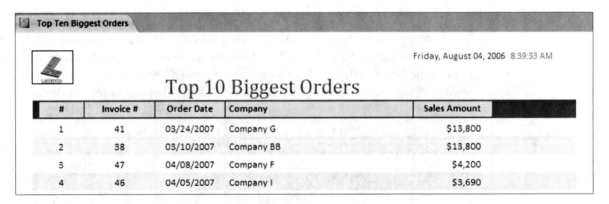

Reports summarize data and display meaningful information.

Inventory Sold	
Product ID	Quantity Sold
Labyrinth Exports Chai	15
Labyrinth Exports Syrup	50
Labyrinth Exports Cajun Seasoning	40
Labyrinth Exports Olive Oil	25
Labyrinth Exports Boysenberry Sprea	100
Labyrinth Exports Dried Pears	40
Labyrinth Exports Curry Sauce	65

Queries display the columns of data that meet the criteria you set—in a column and row layout.

As you complete this section, you will learn more about each object type and its purpose within the database.

Working with Tabbed Objects

The default setting in Access is to display items as tabbed objects within the database. When objects in a database are set to display as tabbed items, Access displays as much of each object as it can fit within the work area of the Access window. As a result, the entire object fills the work area and all objects are layered, one on top of another, with tabs at the top of the work area to identify each object. Each object, therefore, is the same size. You can switch from one object to the next simply by clicking the object tab.

Tabs appear at the top of the work area to identify objects. Notice the object icon beside the object name.

Working with Tables

A database table is the basic object of any database because tables store all of the raw data placed into the database. All other objects in a database are based on data stored in tables. In the Labyrinth Exports database, you will find a number of tables, each of which holds data related in some way to other tables in the database.

Three key terms are used in relation to the data stored in Access databases:

- **Field:** The basic unit of database tables that holds one piece of data, such as first name, last name, street address, ZIP code, date of birth, and so forth.

- **Record:** A collection of all fields related to one item, such as all fields of data for each person or company, all items placed on an order, and personnel information for each employee.

- **File:** A collection of all related records stored together, such as all employee records found in a table, all customers, all suppliers, and so forth.

As you review the following sample table and work with tables, you will see how these elements fit together.

The Customers table is highlighted in the Navigation Pane.

The first cell in the table is outlined by a colored border to indicate that it is active.

The Customers table appears in the work area and the object tab is highlighted to show it is active.

Each column of the table represents a field, and the field name appears as the column heading.

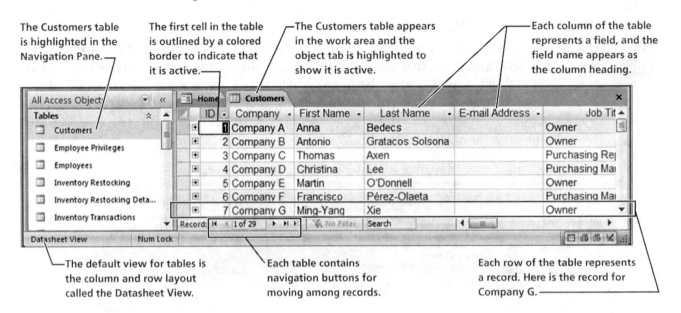

The default view for tables is the column and row layout called the Datasheet View.

Each table contains navigation buttons for moving among records.

Each row of the table represents a record. Here is the record for Company G.

 ## Hands-On 12.4   Browse a Table

In this exercise, you will open a table, review the structure of the table, and navigate within the table.

1. Expand the Tables list in the Navigation Pane and double-click the Customers table name to open the table.

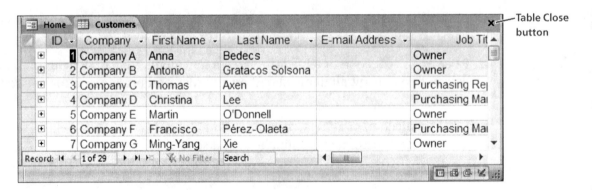

Table Close button

Notice the column and row layout of the table and the active insertion point in the ID column of the first record (row). Each column represents a field *in the database and each row represents a* record.

2. Press Tab to move to the Company column.
You can continue to press Tab to move to the next column (field) until you reach the last column containing data. Pressing Tab from the last column of the first row (record) moves the cursor to the first column (field) in the second row (record).

3. Follow these steps to move among table records using table navigation buttons:

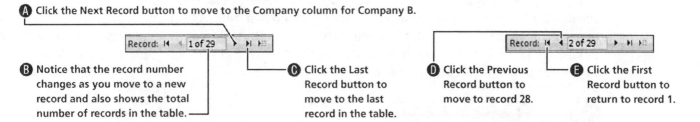

Ⓐ Click the Next Record button to move to the Company column for Company B.

Record: ◄ 1 of 29 ► ►I ►▪

Ⓑ Notice that the record number changes as you move to a new record and also shows the total number of records in the table.

Ⓒ Click the Last Record button to move to the last record in the table.

Record: I◄ ◄ 2 of 29 ► ►I ►▪

Ⓓ Click the Previous Record button to move to record 28.

Ⓔ Click the First Record button to return to record 1.

4. Click the Customer table close button to close the table.

Viewing Forms

Database tables present a continuous list of records in a table-grid layout so that you can view multiple records onscreen at the same time. A database *form* is an object built from fields contained in tables that are positioned in a layout so that each table record (or row) appears in the form window one record at a time. As with other objects, forms can be set to display as tabbed items in the database work area, as the following form shows, or in separate windows onscreen.

This form is formatted to appear as a tabbed object in the database work area.

Fields from the table appear in the form but in a different arrangement.

Navigating Data in Forms

Forms display many of the same navigation tools available in tables. The main difference in the display is that records appear onscreen one record at a time. As a result, when you navigate to a specific record, only the data for one item appears. In tables, one record was active as you navigated the table even though multiple records displayed at the same time because of the column and row layout of the tables.

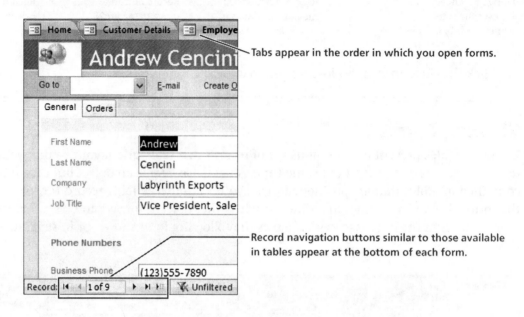

Tabs appear in the order in which you open forms.

Record navigation buttons similar to those available in tables appear at the bottom of each form.

Forms Containing Special Features

Forms vary from the very simple to more sophisticated layouts. Some forms, such as the Home form displayed when you open the Labyrinth Exports database, contain buttons and links to open other database objects or perform tasks such as closing forms and other objects.

Links in the Home form: Those on the left are formatted as hyperlinks to link to products, while those on the right open forms and other database objects for viewing.

Hands-On 12.5   View and Navigate Forms

In this exercise, you will open forms, identify key features of forms, navigate within the form, and close the form.

1. Collapse ⌃ the Tables list in the Navigation Pane and expand ⌄ the Forms list.

2. Follow these steps to open two forms:

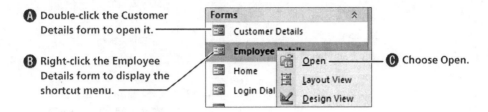

A Double-click the Customer Details form to open it.

B Right-click the Employee Details form to display the shortcut menu.

C Choose Open.

3. Follow these steps to navigate between open forms and records within each form:

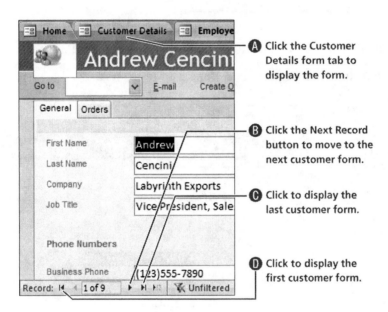

A Click the Customer Details form tab to display the form.

B Click the Next Record button to move to the next customer form.

C Click to display the last customer form.

D Click to display the first customer form.

4. Follow these steps to display employee form eight:

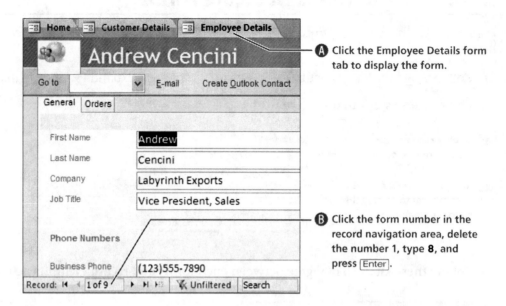

Ⓐ Click the Employee Details form tab to display the form.

Ⓑ Click the form number in the record navigation area, delete the number 1, type **8**, and press Enter.

5. Double-click the Product Details form in the Forms list to open it.

6. Follow these steps to navigate records using this pop-up form:

Ⓐ Click the Go to Product down arrow and select any product in the list.

Ⓑ Click the Order/Purchase History tab in the form window.

Ⓒ Click the Go to Product down arrow again and select a different product.

Ⓓ Click the Close button at the bottom of the form window.

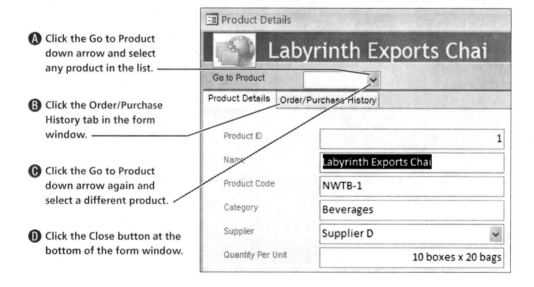

7. Right-click the Employee Details form tab and choose Close All.

Viewing Reports

Tables and forms display data contained in databases as it is entered and stored in the database. They serve as input objects because you can use both tables and forms to add data to the database. *Reports*, on the other hand, process and summarize data and display it as useful and meaningful information on a printed document. Reports can display data in different formats—as columnar information, charts, tables, and so forth—and can also include subtotals and totals.

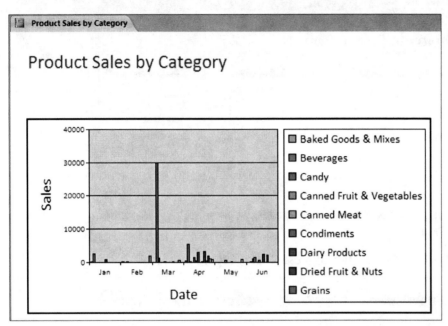

A report can display information as a chart. Notice this object appears as a tabbed object in the database work area.

Top 10 Biggest Orders

#	Invoice #	Order Date	Company	Sales Amount
1	41	03/24/2007	Company G	$13,800
2	38	03/10/2007	Company BB	$13,800
3	47	04/08/2007	Company F	$4,200
4	46	04/05/2007	Company I	$3,690
5	58	04/22/2007	Company D	$3,520
6	79	06/23/2007	Company F	$2,490
7	77	06/05/2007	Company Z	$2,250
8	36	02/23/2007	Company C	$1,930
9	44	03/24/2007	Company A	$1,675
10	78	06/05/2007	Company CC	$1,560

This report displays information in columns and rows. It, too, is formatted as a tabbed object.

In this exercise, you will open reports, review the information contained in the reports, and close the reports.

1. Collapse ⊼ the Forms list and expand ⊻ the Reports list in the Navigation Pane.

2. Double-click the Employee Phone Book report to open it.

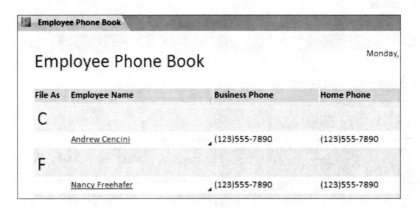

Notice that this report simply displays data in an organized columnar layout for printing and easy reference.

3. Double-click the Top Ten Biggest Orders report to open it.

This report analyzes data contained in the Orders table and identifies the 10 orders that contain the highest sales amount. The format of the table contains a colorful layout and a graphic.

4. Follow these steps to explore report views:

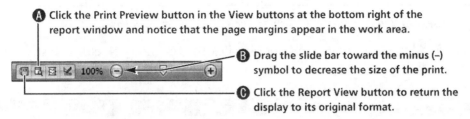

Ⓐ Click the Print Preview button in the View buttons at the bottom right of the report window and notice that the page margins appear in the work area.

Ⓑ Drag the slide bar toward the minus (–) symbol to decrease the size of the print.

Ⓒ Click the Report View button to return the display to its original format.

!NOTE! *View buttons are available for all database objects. They vary according to object type.*

5. Close the Employee Phone Book report (leaving the Top Ten Biggest Orders report open) and collapse the Reports list in the Navigation Pane.

Glimpsing the Power of Queries

You have now explored three different types of database objects and identified how each object fits into the overall scheme of the database. The purpose of all databases is to store data in such a way that you can retrieve required data and information in the quickest, most efficient manner. In Access and many other database programs, *queries* are the tools that enable you to achieve this goal. A *query* is a database object that enables you to select data and records from database tables on the basis of criteria you set. Only records and data that meet the criteria are shown when you run the query; other records are filtered out. Queries can display data from more than one table in the same datasheet. Remember the sportscaster who reports interesting statistics on the spur of the moment? Queries make his work easy.

When you open a query, Access runs the query and displays only the data requested in the query. As a result, the minute you double-click a query, you'll be able to view the data you want to view. Queries can display data from more than one table or from a single table, depending on the data required to obtain the desired query results.

Notice that Access compared the Qty Available value with the Reorder Level value, and when the number in the Qty Available column is less than the Reorder Level value, the item appears in the datasheet.

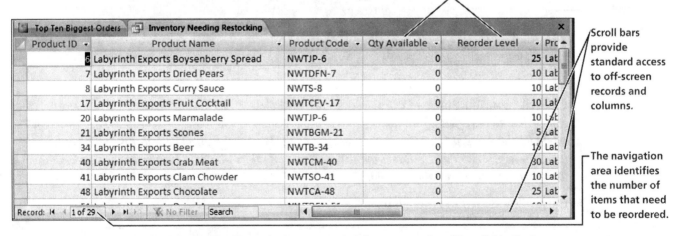

Scroll bars provide standard access to off-screen records and columns.

The navigation area identifies the number of items that need to be reordered.

The Inventory Needing Reordering query displays only those items that show a quantity of 0 available. Notice, again, that the query datasheet resembles the column and row layout of tables, often with fields from more than one table shown together in one datasheet.

Hands-On 12.7   Run Queries

In this exercise, you will run queries to display select data, and close queries.

1. Expand 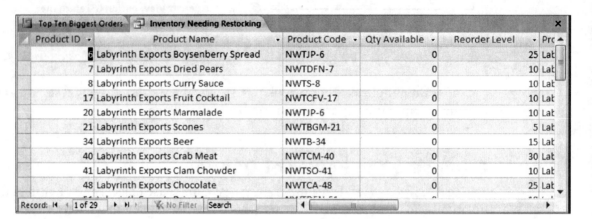 the Queries list and double-click the Inventory Needing Restocking query to run it.

Product ID	Product Name	Product Code	Qty Available	Reorder Level	Prc
6	Labyrinth Exports Boysenberry Spread	NWTJP-6	0	25	Lat
7	Labyrinth Exports Dried Pears	NWTDFN-7	0	10	Lat
8	Labyrinth Exports Curry Sauce	NWTS-8	0	10	Lat
17	Labyrinth Exports Fruit Cocktail	NWTCFV-17	0	10	Lat
20	Labyrinth Exports Marmalade	NWTJP-6	0	10	Lat
21	Labyrinth Exports Scones	NWTBGM-21	0	5	Lat
34	Labyrinth Exports Beer	NWTB-34	0	15	Lat
40	Labyrinth Exports Crab Meat	NWTCM-40	0	30	Lat
41	Labyrinth Exports Clam Chowder	NWTSO-41	0	10	Lat
48	Labyrinth Exports Chocolate	NWTCA-48	0	25	Lat

Record: 1 of 29   No Filter   Search

2. Scroll down the datasheet and review all records listed.

3. Run the Top Ten Orders by Sales Amount query and study the datasheet.

The records display in order on the basis of the amount of sales, from highest to lowest.

Ten records display, those representing the highest order sales amount.

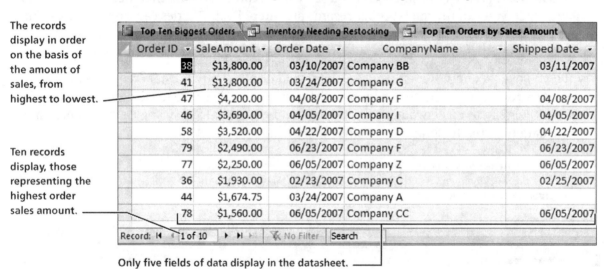

Order ID	SaleAmount	Order Date	CompanyName	Shipped Date
38	$13,800.00	03/10/2007	Company BB	03/11/2007
41	$13,800.00	03/24/2007	Company G	
47	$4,200.00	04/08/2007	Company F	04/08/2007
46	$3,690.00	04/05/2007	Company I	04/05/2007
58	$3,520.00	04/22/2007	Company D	04/22/2007
79	$2,490.00	06/23/2007	Company F	06/23/2007
77	$2,250.00	06/05/2007	Company Z	06/05/2007
36	$1,930.00	02/23/2007	Company C	02/25/2007
44	$1,674.75	03/24/2007	Company A	
78	$1,560.00	06/05/2007	Company CC	06/05/2007

Record: 1 of 10   No Filter   Search

Only five fields of data display in the datasheet.

4. Click the Top Ten Biggest Orders report tab and review the data shown on the report. *Notice that all data fields from the Top Ten Orders by Sales Amount query are displayed in the report except for the Shipped Date. Queries can be used as the basis for creating both forms and reports; however, remember that the data originally comes from tables—queries simply display selected table fields from one or more database tables.*

5. Close all open database objects.

Closing a Database and Exiting Access

Now that you have had a glimpse of the basic elements that make up an Access database, you can close the database and exit Access. The procedures used to perform these tasks are the same as those used to close files and exit other Microsoft Office applications. You can use three techniques to exit Access:

■ Press [Alt]+[F4] from the keyboard.

■ Click the Office button 🗃 →Exit Access.

■ Click the Access 2007 application window Close [x] button.

Because Access databases contain numerous objects, it is always a good idea to close each database properly before exiting Access. This ensures that all objects in the database are put away carefully.

Hands-On 12.8   Close a Database and Exit Access

In this exercise, you will close the Labyrinth Exports database and exit Access.

1. Click 🗃 →Close Database from the Quick Access bar.

2. Click the Access 2007 application window Close [x] button.

Concepts Review

True/False Questions

1. Access databases contain multiple types of objects.   TRUE   FALSE

2. Access databases can hold only one of each object type.   TRUE   FALSE

3. The basic unit of data in a database is referred to as a field.   TRUE   FALSE

4. Access is an object-oriented database program.   TRUE   FALSE

5. All data about one item is referred to as a file.   TRUE   FALSE

6. Records summarize data contained in a database.   TRUE   FALSE

7. Queries, forms, tables, and reports are all object types found in Access databases.   TRUE   FALSE

8. Queries and forms serve as input objects.   TRUE   FALSE

9. Tables hold all other types of database objects.   TRUE   FALSE

10. A datasheet is a row and column layout of data contained in a database.   TRUE   FALSE

Multiple Choice Questions

1. Which Access database object holds the data in a database?
   a. Forms
   b. Queries
   c. Reports
   d. Tables

2. Which of the following statements is true about the relationship between fields and records and databases?
   a. A record is made up of multiple fields.
   b. A field is made up of multiple records.
   c. A database is made up of multiple records.
   d. All of the above

3. The database object used to select specific database records is called what?
   a. Form
   b. Query
   c. Report
   d. Table

4. Which Access object allows users to enter, edit, and view data records onscreen one at the time?
   a. Form
   b. Query
   c. Report
   d. Table

Skill Builders

Skill Builder 12.1 Explore Database Objects

In this exercise, you will open a sample database designed specifically for a medical facility and review the objects contained in the database.

 NOTE! *The Labyrinth Exports database used throughout this lesson focuses on the types of objects common to databases created for businesses that sell products. Other types of businesses would require databases that contain different types of data. Take, for example, a medical facility. Although data for employees and patients would resemble data contained in tables for other types of businesses, some data would be unique.*

1. Launch Access 2007 and use the Open dialog box to open the sb-Valley Hospital database from the Lesson 12 folder on your file storage location.
   Because of security settings, it may, at first, appear that the database failed to open. Notice the filename in the title bar to ensure that the database is open, and then look for the Enable content bar.

2. Enable content and then open the Navigation Pane and expand all database object lists.

Explore Data Tables

Data in a database is stored in tables. Now you will examine some individual tables and learn about the data they contain.

3. Open the Drugs table.

   How many active fields (columns) does the table contain (not counting the Add New Field column)? _____

   How many records (rows) does the table contain? _____

   Are there pieces of information you think should be included in the table that have been omitted? If so, what data is missing?

   _____

4. Open the Employees table.

   How many active fields does the table contain? _____

   How many records does it contain? _____

   What vital data is missing from the table? _____

5. Open the Patient Information table.

   How many active fields does the table contain? _____

   How many records does it contain? _____

   What data from this table is used in another table in the database? _____

   _____

6. Open the Pay Ranks table.

   How many fields does the table contain? _____

   How many records does it contain? _____

   What data from this table is used in another table? _____

Explore Forms

7. Display the Forms list and open the Personnel Records form contained in the database. From which table does the data come? _____

   How many records can you display using this form? _____

   How many fields display for each record? _____

8. Is there a form available for each table in the database? If not, which table has no form?

   _____

Explore a Report

9. Display the Reports list in the database and open the Employees Phone List report. From which table is this report generated?

   _____

10. Now open the Employees table.

    Are all fields from the table displayed in the phone list?_____

    If not, what fields are missing from this report? _____

    Why would the fields be omitted from the report? _____

11. Close each open object, close the database, and exit Access.

Using an Access Database

Most databases are designed and set up by professionals who are database experts. As a result, most company employees are simply required to maintain databases—a task that most people are already accustomed to doing. Consider, for example, the address book you use to store addresses of friends and relatives. Each time someone listed in the address book moves or changes phone numbers, you edit the information in your address book.

The same concept is true of electronic databases. Employees come and go, customers relocate to new addresses, phone numbers change, and websites come online. Updating database data to reflect these changes helps maintain the usefulness of the data. In this lesson, you will learn how to adjust the layout of a database table, add data using database input tools, edit data, delete records, and print database data.

LESSON OBJECTIVES

After studying this lesson, you will be able to:

- Add records to a database using both tables and forms
- Change the layout of a table by adjusting column width, hiding columns, and rearranging column layout
- Locate and update records by sorting, filtering, and using Find and Replace
- Preview and print database data
- Save a database as a new file
- Create a new database using a template

Case Study: Learning to Use Access

Andrew Johnson has just been hired in the data processing department of Labyrinth Exports. Andrew has little experience working with an Access database, but is a proficient typist and a quick learner. He will be updating the Customers table in the database his first day on the job. As he works, he will add new records to the table, adjust the layout of tables, locate and update records, delete records, and print data.

Before adjusting the layout of the table, some columns are so narrow that numbers are hidden and only a portion of some data displays. In addition, some of the empty columns should be moved.

After changing the layout, all numbers appear, all data in all columns displays, and the empty E-mail Address column is repositioned.

Andrew adjusts the column widths and positions of columns shown in the top image so that they appear as shown in the bottom image.

Adding Records and Formatting Datasheet Layout

Two tasks frequently associated with databases include adding records to database tables and formatting the layout of the datasheet to display field data. In many cases, these are two primary tasks of data entry personnel.

Adding Records Using a Table

Many of you will already be acquainted with adding rows to Microsoft Word tables and Microsoft Excel worksheets. Each time you enter text or figures into a new row, the table or worksheet grows to accommodate the new text. The same concept is true of database tables.

The Primacy of Tables

Recall that tables in Access databases hold the raw data. All reports, queries, and forms use table data in different ways. As a result, you must first input—add data to—a table. Access provides two basic input tools for adding data to database tables:

- Typing the data into the datasheet view of the appropriate table.

- Typing data into a form associated with the appropriate table.

 NOTE! *Access automatically saves each record as you complete it when you tab after entering the data into the last field.*

AutoNumbered Fields

Many Access tables contain fields that automatically number records as you add them to a table. As a result, it is unnecessary to type a number in these fields and the numbers are uneditable—the number is

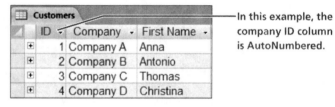

In this example, the company ID column is AutoNumbered.

assigned to the specific record. In addition, if you delete a record from a table, Access never assigns the number to any new records.

QUICK REFERENCE: ADDING A NEW RECORD TO A TABLE	
Task	**Procedure**
Add a new record to a datasheet	■ Open the table in the database to which you want to add a new record.
	■ Click the New Record button to create a new record.
	■ Type data into each field in the row, pressing Tab to move to the next field.
Add a new record using a form	■ Open the form associated with the table in the database to which you want to add a new record.
	■ Click the New Record button to create a new record.
	■ Type data into each field in the form, pressing Tab to move to the next field.

FROM THE KEYBOARD

Ctrl + End to move to the last field in the last record and then press Tab to create a new record

Relaunching Access

As you discovered in Lesson 12, Exploring Access 2007, the first time you launch Access, you often have to navigate through several levels of program menus to launch the program. In addition, the first time you open a database, you use the Open command on the File menu to display the Open dialog box and then navigate to the drive and folder containing the database. After you launch Access the first time, the program appears on the Start menu so that it is much easier to launch. The last nine databases, by default, appear on the Open Recent Database list to make them easier to open.

Hands-On 13.1   Add a Record to a Database Table

In this exercise, you will launch Access, open a database that you have previously not opened, open a table, and add a record to the table using the datasheet.

1. Launch Access and open the Labyrinth Exports database from the Lesson 13 folder in your file storage location.

2. Enable content in the database, and log in as Steven Thorpe.

 NOTE! *There is no particular reason to log in as Steven Thorpe except to ensure that your screens match those shown in this lesson.*

3. Close ⊠ the Home form, open the Navigation Pane, and expand the Tables list.

4. Open the Customers table and follow these steps to create a new record:

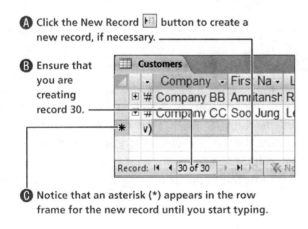

Ⓐ Click the New Record ⊞ button to create a new record, if necessary.

Ⓑ Ensure that you are creating record 30.

Ⓒ Notice that an asterisk (*) appears in the row frame for the new record until you start typing.

5. Type the following data into table columns, pressing ⌷Tab⌷ or ⌷Enter⌷ to move to the next column:

A As you add or edit a record, notice the pencil icon that appears in the row frame.

B Type the data in the columns as shown here.

C Notice, as you start typing the company name, another new record row appears in the table.

D Press the ⌷Tab⌷ key after you fill in this field, and then continue with step 6.

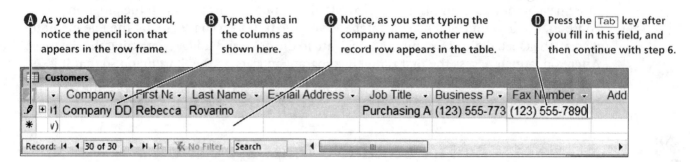

NOTE! *The data you type may appear all misaligned and run together. That's okay for now. You will eventually learn how to format the data so that it appears correctly.*

6. Complete the record for Company DD by typing your data or made-up data into the remaining field columns, as shown.

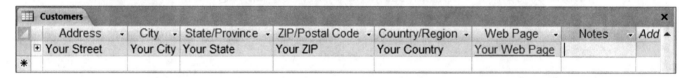

NOTE! *After you press* ⌷Tab⌷ *or* ⌷Enter⌷ *from the Notes column, Access automatically moves to another new record. As long as you leave fields in this record blank, Access will not number the record.*

Formatting a Table Datasheet Layout

Several of the columns in the Customers table are so narrow that the data in the columns appears to be cut off. The data in narrow columns is still there—Access displays only the portion of the data that fits within the column width and *truncates* (stores without displaying) the additional data. You can maximize the Access window to provide more space for the table and close the Navigation Pane to provide even more space for objects you have open. These actions simply allow more columns of data to appear onscreen without affecting the width of each column.

Changing the Width of Columns

You can adjust the width of each column in a datasheet to display all data in the column. Access gives you some useful techniques for changing column width.

- **Drag a column border:** Dragging a column border enables you to make the column on the left of the border wider or narrower.

- **Double-click a column heading border:** Double-clicking a border changes the width of the column on the left to fit the longest data entry in the column or the column heading, whichever is wider.

The data in these columns is truncated because the column widths are too narrow.

First Name	Last Nan	Job Title	Business Phoi
Anna	Bedecs	Owner	(123)555-7891
Antonio	Gratacos S	Owner	(123)555-7892
Thomas	Axen	Purchasing Repr	(123)555-7893
Christina	Lee	Purchasing Mana	(123)555-7894
Martin	O'Donnell	Owner	(123)555-7865
Francisco	Pérez-Olae	Purchasing Mana	(123)555-7883

Widening the column widths prevents truncation.

First Name	Last Name	Job Title
Anna	Bedecs	Owner
Antonio	Gratacos Solsona	Owner
Thomas	Axen	Purchasing Representative
Christina	Lee	Purchasing Manager
Martin	O'Donnell	Owner
Francisco	Pérez-Olaeta	Purchasing Manager

Moving and Hiding Data Columns

In addition, there will be times when you want to reposition a column of data in a table layout or hide some columns so that you can view other field columns. Access contains tools that enable you to rearrange columns and hide columns. When you hide columns, Access temporarily removes them from display. The data, however, remains in the table—it is NOT deleted. When you want to view data in hidden columns, you can unhide the column.

Last Name	E-mail Address	Job Title
Bedecs		Owner
Gratacos Solsona		Owner
Axen		Purchasing Representative

Last Name	Job Title
Bedecs	Owner
Gratacos Solsona	Owner
Axen	Purchasing Representative
Lee	Purchasing Manager

Before and after hiding the E-mail Address column.

Saving a Table Layout

Changing the layout of a table datasheet has no real effect on table data or table structure; however, when you make changes to a table datasheet, Access recognizes the differences between the layout and the structure of the table and prompts you to save the changes to the layout when you close the table. If you abandon the changes you make to the layout, the next time you open the table datasheet, the column widths will return to their original size, the hidden columns will show, and the repositioned columns will occupy their original place in the layout. If you save the changes, the next time you open the table datasheet, Access recalls the layout and displays the datasheet as you formatted it.

FROM THE KEYBOARD

Ctrl+S to save changes to the table layout

 TIP! *The shape and color of the mouse pointer is important when you are adjusting column width and repositioning columns in a table or datasheet layout. Be sure to pay attention to the mouse pointer shape as you work.*

Hands-On 13.2 Format a Table Datasheet Layout

In this exercise, you will adjust the column widths of table datasheet columns, hide columns, and reposition columns.

1. Open the Customers table in the Labyrinth Exports database if it is closed.

2. Follow these steps to change the width of the first table column:

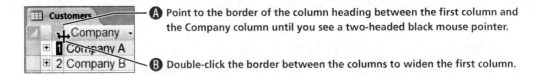

Ⓐ Point to the border of the column heading between the first column and the Company column until you see a two-headed black mouse pointer.

Ⓑ Double-click the border between the columns to widen the first column.

3. Follow these steps to change the width of two columns at the same time:

Ⓐ Point to the column heading First Name, ensuring that you see a black down-pointing arrow, click and drag the pointer to the right toward Last Name to select both columns.

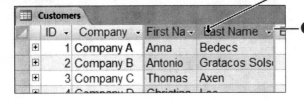

Ⓑ Double-click the right border of the Last Name column, ensuring that your mouse pointer appears as a two-headed black arrow as it did in step 2.

4. Follow these steps to reposition the empty E-mail Address column:

Ⓐ Click the E-mail Address column heading to select the column.

Ⓑ Scroll to the right until the Business Phone and Fax Number columns appear onscreen.

Ⓒ Point to the selected E-mail Address column heading, ensuring that the mouse pointer appears as a white arrow.

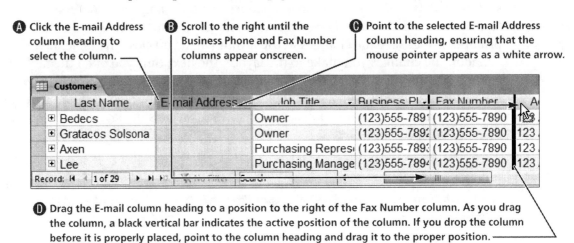

Ⓓ Drag the E-mail column heading to a position to the right of the Fax Number column. As you drag the column, a black vertical bar indicates the active position of the column. If you drop the column before it is properly placed, point to the column heading and drag it to the proper position.

5. Follow these steps to hide the Country/Region column:

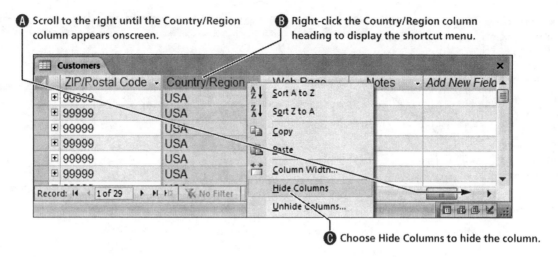

Ⓐ Scroll to the right until the Country/Region column appears onscreen.

Ⓑ Right-click the Country/Region column heading to display the shortcut menu.

Ⓒ Choose Hide Columns to hide the column.

6. Click the Save 🖫 button to save changes to the table layout.

7. Close ☒ the table.

Adding Records Using a Form

As you know, forms are objects that display data onscreen one record at a time and are used to input data into a database. Because of the field layout on most forms, all data contained in a record is normally visible, so it is easier to review all data associated with a record than it is in table datasheet layout. Most forms are also formatted to be more aesthetically pleasing than tables.

Saving the New Record

After you type data into the last field on a form and press the Tab key, Access automatically saves the record into the table.

 Hands-On 13.3   Add a Record to a Database Using a Form

In this exercise, you will use a form to add a new employee to the Employees table.

1. Expand the Forms list in the Navigation Pane and double-click the Employee Details form to open it.

2. Click the New Record 📄 navigation button to create a new blank record.
   Access displays a new blank form.

3. Follow these steps to enter data for a new employee using the form:

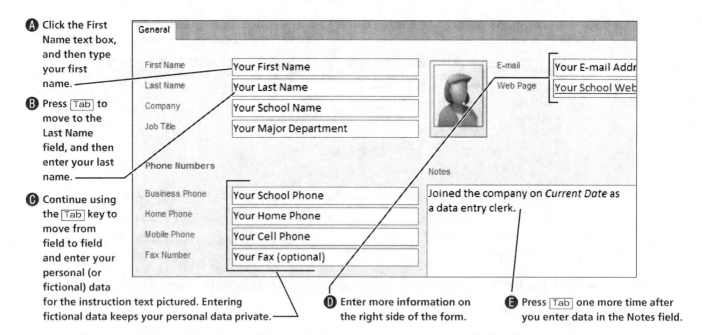

Ⓐ Click the First Name text box, and then type your first name.

Ⓑ Press Tab to move to the Last Name field, and then enter your last name.

Ⓒ Continue using the Tab key to move from field to field and enter your personal (or fictional) data for the instruction text pictured. Entering fictional data keeps your personal data private.

Ⓓ Enter more information on the right side of the form.

Ⓔ Press Tab one more time after you enter data in the Notes field.

4. Close ☒ the form, open the Employees table to ensure that data for the new record appears, and then close the table.

Retrieving Data

The primary purpose of any database is to be able to locate and retrieve data quickly and efficiently. Whether you're processing an order, announcing statistics, or updating records, being able to find the data is important. Access provides three main tools and features for helping locate and retrieve data:

■ Sorting features

■ Filtering tools

■ Find and Replace

Sorting Records

Access automatically sorts records according to the field set up when a table is created and fields are set up. Many times tables are sorted by record number so that as you enter records, Access assigns a number to the record and the records sort in the order in which you enter them. The database sort feature enables you to rearrange table records on the basis of data found in other table columns. Two main sort orders are available:

■ **Sort Ascending:** Arranges data in alphabetical order from A to Z, in numeric order from lowest to highest, or in chronological order from first to last.

■ **Sort Descending:** Arranges data in reverse alphabetical order from Z to A, in numeric order from highest to lowest, or in reverse chronological order from last to first.

Sorting Records Using Tables and Forms

Regardless of whether you are working with a table or a form, the primary procedures for sorting records are the same.

 ## Hands-On 13.4 Sort Records in a Table

In this exercise, you will sort records in both tables and forms and clear all sorts set.

1. Open the Employees table and follow these steps to sort records by last name:

Ⓐ Position the cursor on any record in the Last Name field.

Ⓑ Choose Home→ Sort & Filter→ Ascending on the Ribbon.

2. Follow these steps to set a descending sort order and clear all sorts:

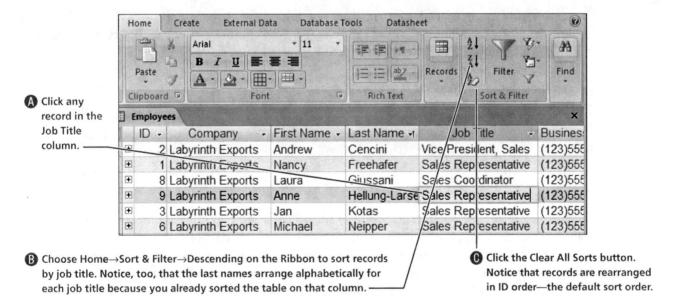

Ⓐ Click any record in the Job Title column.

Ⓑ Choose Home→Sort & Filter→Descending on the Ribbon to sort records by job title. Notice, too, that the last names arrange alphabetically for each job title because you already sorted the table on that column.

Ⓒ Click the Clear All Sorts button. Notice that records are rearranged in ID order—the default sort order.

3. Close ⊠ the table.

   Access displays a prompt asking if you wish to save changes to the table. Because you have changed the sort order a couple of times and then cleared the sorts, Access recognizes that you have changed the layout of the table while it was open. As a result, it prompts you to save changes. If you were to click Yes, the changes would become part of the table design. Instead, choose No and discard the changes.

4. Choose No in response to the prompt to save the changes.

5. Open the Customer Details form and follow these steps to sort the customers:

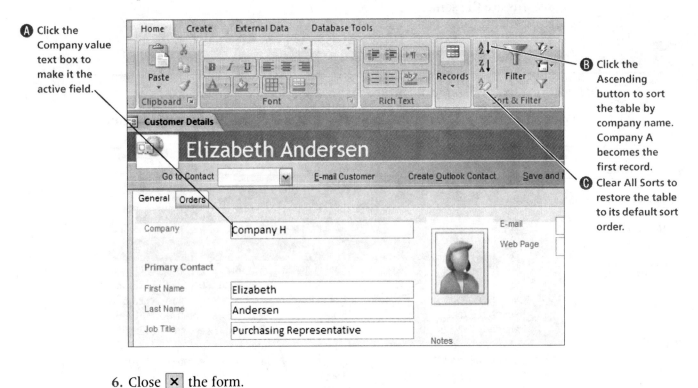

A Click the Company value text box to make it the active field.

B Click the Ascending button to sort the table by company name. Company A becomes the first record.

C Clear All Sorts to restore the table to its default sort order.

6. Close ⊠ the form.

Sorting Records Using Multiple Fields

Data in Access can be sorted on more than one table field at the same time. This can be useful when sorting fields where the value in the first field of more than one record is the same so you want to select a second field on which to organize the records.

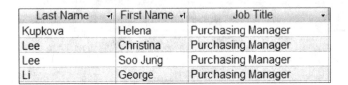

Last Name	First Name	Job Title
Kupkova	Helena	Purchasing Manager
Lee	Christina	Purchasing Manager
Lee	Soo Jung	Purchasing Manager
Li	George	Purchasing Manager

These records are sorted first by Last Name column and then by First Name.

Example

Take, for example, personal names. Many records in a table might contain the same last name value. When this happens, selecting the first name field as a second sort field is often appropriate. Using this example, the last name field would be considered the *primary sort* field, and the first name field is called the *secondary sort* field. The secondary sort field is only considered when multiple records contain the same data in the primary sort field.

How Multiple Column Sorts Work

Access sorts data on multiple fields from left to right. As a result, the columns in a table must appear side by side in the datasheet and the column on the left must be the one you want sorted first (primary sort field). Access will then consider the second column (secondary sort field) only when it finds identical values in the primary sort field. You can perform more complex sorts on multiple fields using the Advanced Filter/Sort options or sort multiple columns by rearranging them in the datasheet so that they appear side by side.

Last Name	First Name	Job Title
Kupkova	Helena	Purchasing Manager
Lee	Christina	Purchasing Manager
Lee	Soo Jung	Purchasing Manager
Li	George	Purchasing Manager

In order to sort the Last Name field first, it had to be moved to the left of the First Name field.

QUICK REFERENCE: SORTING RECORDS

Task	Procedure
Sort Ascending	■ Position the cursor in the field on which you want to sort records. ■ Choose Home→Sort & Filter→Ascending ⬇ on the Ribbon.
Sort Descending	■ Position the cursor in the field on which you want to sort records. ■ Choose Home→Sort & Filter→Descending ⬇ on the Ribbon.
Clear Sorts	■ Choose Home→Sort & Filter→Clear All Sorts ⬇ on the Ribbon.
Sort on Multiple Fields	■ Arrange the fields you want to sort next to each other with the primary field to the left of the secondary field. ■ Select both field column headings and click the sort button for the sort order in which you want to sort the records.

In this exercise, you will sort data in a table on the basis of the values found in two columns.

1. Open the Purchase Orders table in the Labyrinth Exports database.

2. Follow these steps to sort table records on the basis of values contained in multiple fields:

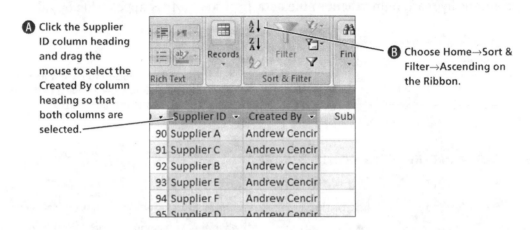

Ⓐ Click the Supplier ID column heading and drag the mouse to select the Created By column heading so that both columns are selected.

Ⓑ Choose Home→Sort & Filter→Ascending on the Ribbon.

3. Review the record sort results.

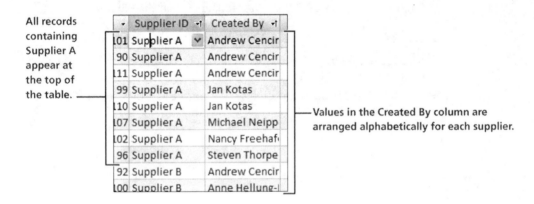

All records containing Supplier A appear at the top of the table.

Values in the Created By column are arranged alphabetically for each supplier.

4. Clear all sort orders and click any value in the Purchase Order ID column to deselect both columns.

5. Follow these steps to sort on the same two columns and obtain different results:

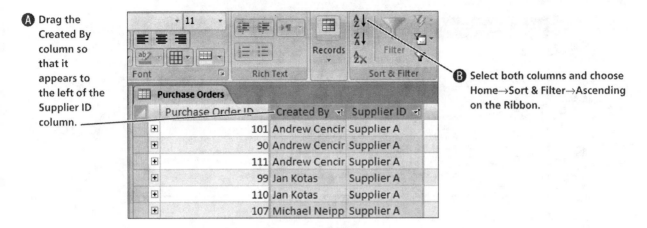

A Drag the Created By column so that it appears to the left of the Supplier ID column.

B Select both columns and choose Home→Sort & Filter→Ascending on the Ribbon.

Notice that the arrangement of all records created by one person with suppliers arranged alphabetically for each person before the next person's records appear.

6. Close ☒ the table. Choose No when prompted to save the changes.

Locating and Deleting Records Using Table Datasheets

The navigation buttons found at the bottom of tables and forms provide an efficient way to move among records when the number of records in a database is relatively few. When a database contains large volumes of data, finding a more efficient way to locate records becomes important. Both tables and forms are the primary objects used to locate records for updating and deleting.

QUICK REFERENCE: DELETING RECORDS

Task	Procedure
Delete a record	Use one of the following procedures to delete a record: ■ Click the record selector button at the left end of the record and press Delete on the keyboard to remove the record. Then choose Yes when warned that you are about to delete a record. ■ Choose Home→Records→Records ▦ on the Ribbon and choose Delete.

Using Find and Replace

The Find and Replace tool in Access improves the efficiency of maintaining a database that constantly changes. Using the tool, you can locate records easily and then delete them or edit them.

The Find feature in Access enables you to locate records containing data that you need to edit or to locate records that you want to delete. The Find page of the Find and Replace dialog box contains a few features similar to those found in other Microsoft applications. Because data stored in a database is somewhat different from the text and data stored in other files, you will find some unique fields as you work in Access.

FROM THE KEYBOARD

Ctrl+F to open the Find page of the Find and Replace dialog box

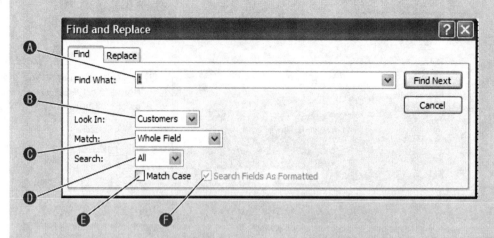

Item	Feature	Description
A	Find What	Contains the text, numbers, dates, and other values you want to locate.
B	Look In	Tells Access where in the data to search for the text. The data in the field that was active when the Find command is issued appears in the Look In box. You can change the location by clicking the down arrow and selecting the table name from the Look In list.
C	Match	Allows you to locate records where the search text appears as the only data in the field (whole field), anywhere in the field value, or at the beginning of the field.
D	Search	Tells Access which direction to search from the active cursor—forward to the end of the table, backward to the beginning of the table, or the whole table.
E	Match Case	Locates data that matches the exact capitalization pattern you type.
F	Search Fields As Formatted	Searches for data as it is displayed in the datasheet rather than as you typed it. For example, if you check the box, you would search for data, such as March 5, 2007, as it appears in the datasheet even though you might have entered the data as 3/5/2007.

Hands-On 13.6   Locate and Delete Records in a Table

In this exercise, you will use Find to locate a record in a table and delete it.

1. Open the Customers table in the Labyrinth Exports database.

2. Follow these steps to find the record to delete:

Ⓐ Choose Home→Find→Find on the Ribbon to display the Find and Replace dialog box.

Ⓑ Enter the values shown in each textbox of the Find page of the dialog box and then click Find Next to start the search.

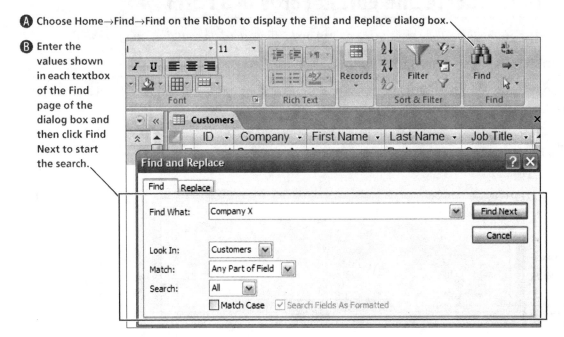

Access finds the record for Company X.

3. Click Cancel to close the Find and Replace dialog box, and then follow these steps to delete the Company X record:

Ⓐ Point to the record selector button at the left end of the record to select the record for Company X and right-click to display the shortcut menu.

Ⓑ Select Delete Record and then click Yes when Access warns you that you are about to delete a record.

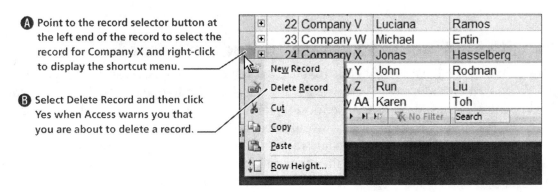

Leave the table open.

Using Forms to Locate and Edit Records

Tables are one type of object you can use to update or delete records from a database. You can also use forms to edit and delete records. The basic procedures required to locate records using a form are the same as those used to locate records in a table.

 Hands-On 13.7   Locate and Edit Records in a Form

In this exercise, you will locate a record using a form and update the data contained in the record.

1. Open the Customer Details form in the Labyrinth Exports database.
2. Choose Home→Find→Find 🔍 on the Ribbon and follow these steps to locate the record to edit:

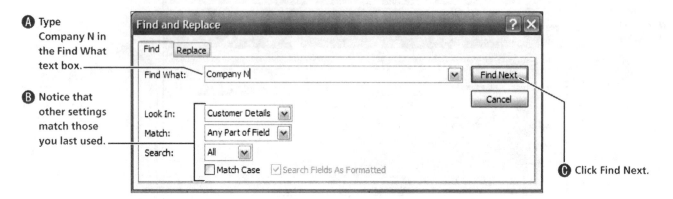

Ⓐ Type Company N in the Find What text box.

Ⓑ Notice that other settings match those you last used.

Ⓒ Click Find Next.

3. Click Cancel to close the Find and Replace dialog box and then type the following new values in the First Name and Last Name fields to replace the current contact name: **Viktor Alonzo.**
4. Close ☒ the form.

Using Find and Replace to Update Records

FROM THE KEYBOARD

Ctrl + H for Find and Replace

When you have specific edits to make to individual records, locating the records and making the edits works well. There are times when you need to update the data in one table field for multiple records with the identical replacement data. For example, when the area code for a city changes, multiple records would need to be updated with the same value. The Replace command enables you to update records in cases such as this by replacing existing data with new data. Because you are already familiar with the options on the Find page of the Find and Replace dialog box, you'll find the Replace page of the dialog box very familiar. The Replace action buttons are used to:

- **Replace:** Replace text for each occurrence of the search text one at a time.
- **Replace All:** Replace all occurrences of the search text with the new text at the same time.

 TIP! In general, the Replace All command should be used with great caution to avoid unexpected results. For example, if you search for a string of characters such as the *and replace those letters with the single character* a *using Replace All, you may find that Access will replace the characters in* their *so that it becomes* air. *Both are valid words.*

Hands-On 13.8   Update Multiple Records Using Find and Replace

In this exercise, you will use the Find and Replace dialog box to update multiple records with the same data.

1. Open the Employees table in the Labyrinth Exports database.

2. Follow these steps to locate and replace text with new values:

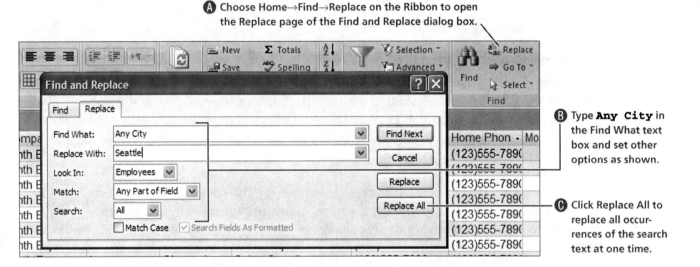

Ⓐ Choose Home→Find→Replace on the Ribbon to open the Replace page of the Find and Replace dialog box.

Ⓑ Type **Any City** in the Find What text box and set other options as shown.

Ⓒ Click Replace All to replace all occurrences of the search text at one time.

Access presents a warning message advising you that you will not be able to undo this action.

3. Choose Yes in response to the warning prompt, click Cancel to close the dialog box, and then scroll to the right to ensure that the value in the City field for all records (except your record) shows Seattle.

4. Close ⊠ the table.

Filtering Records

So far, you have sorted records to place them in an order that they are more easily reviewed, and have used the Find and Replace features to delete and update records. In both cases, you worked with all records contained in the table. When you work with large volumes of table data, there will be times when you want to locate a group of records that contain specific values in specific fields. Filtering enables you to select a subset of records contained in the table to make working with the records more efficient.

Using the Filter Tools

The Filter tool enables you to identify a value in any table field and tell Access to select only those records in the datasheet that contain the same value in the selected field. This process applies a *filter* to the table that hides records when the data in the active field contains different data. For example, if you work with a database that contains thousands of records for consumers across the country, you could apply a filter to identify all the people who live in a specific state.

Access provides two types of methods for filtering records: Filter by Selection and Filter by Form.

- **Filter by Selection:** Selects records on the basis of the value contained in the active field for the active record.

- **Filter by Form:** Selects records on the basis of values or conditions (criteria) that you type in one or more form fields. Again, Access searches only the fields you specify to find the match.

You will explore both techniques in this section.

Filtering Records by Selection

When you filter database records by selection, you have two options. You can instruct Access to select all records containing data that matches the value or selected text in the active field of the selected record. You can also instruct Access to select all records containing any value other than the one selected. Access searches only the active field to find the matches.

Removing a Filter

When you filter records in a table, Access recognizes the change to the display. As a result, if you close the table without removing the filter, Access prompts you to save changes to the table. Many times, you do want to save changes—such as when you widen or hide columns. Normally, filtering data in a table is temporary while you work with the data, so you do not want to save a filtered table. You remove a filter using the Toggle Filter tool.

Using the Toggle Filter Tool

The Toggle Filter ⊻ tool in the Sort & Filter section of the Ribbon serves two purposes:

- After you apply a filter, clicking the Toggle Filter ⊻ button removes the filter and displays all records.

- After removing a filter, clicking the Toggle Filter ⊻ button reapplies the last filter applied.

In addition, when you point to the Toggle Filter button, a ToolTip displays to let you know what action you are performing. For example, when you point to the Toggle Filter button after applying a filter, the ToolTip shows *Remove Filter*. When you point to the Toggle Filter button after removing a filter, the ToolTip shows *Apply Filter*.

Hands-On 13.9   Filter Records by Selection

In this exercise, you will use tables to filter records and review the results before clearing the filter.

1. Open the Products table in the Labyrinth Exports database.

2. Follow these steps to set a filter:

Ⓐ Locate the Supplier IDs field column and select a record that contains the value Supplier D.

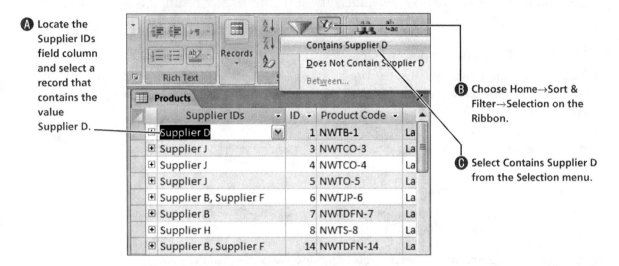

Ⓑ Choose Home→Sort & Filter→Selection on the Ribbon.

Ⓒ Select Contains Supplier D from the Selection menu.

Access applies the filter immediately and displays three records that contain the value.

3. Click the Toggle Filter 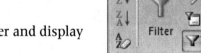 button to remove the filter and display all table records.

4. Follow these steps to display all records in the table that contain values other than Supplier D:

Ⓐ Locate the Supplier IDs field column and select a record that contains the value Supplier D.

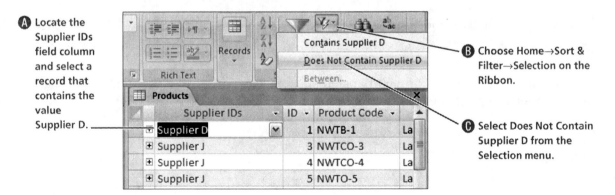

Ⓑ Choose Home→Sort & Filter→Selection on the Ribbon.

Ⓒ Select Does Not Contain Supplier D from the Selection menu.

Access applies the filter immediately and displays 42 records that contain the value.

5. Close ☒ the table. Choose No when prompted to save changes.

Filtering Records by Form

Filtering records by form enables you to set criteria in fields of a blank form. Access then filters the database to select only the records that contain values set in fields on the form.

One advantage to using the Filter By Form feature is that you can select records on the basis of values in multiple fields without rearranging the layout of table fields. Another advantage is that you can use comparison indicators to locate records that fit within a range of values. When you filter by form, Access remembers the sort criteria. As a result, it is important to clear all filters after you apply this filter.

Identifying Logical Operators

When you use the Filter By Form feature in Access, you will often apply comparison operators so that Access can locate records that contain the data you want to find. These operators are identified and described in the following table.

QUICK REFERENCE: DEFINING COMPARISON INDICATORS AND SYMBOLS	
Comparison Symbol	**Description**
=	■ Records in the table must contain a value that matches exactly the value you enter in the form for the field set.
<	■ Records in the table must contain a value less than the value you enter in the form for the field set.
>	■ Records in the table must contain a value greater than the value you enter in the form for the field set.
<>	■ Records in the table must contain a value different from the value you enter in the form for the field set.
<=	■ Records in the table must contain a value less than or equal to the value you set for the field.
>=	■ Records in the table must contain a value greater than or equal to the value you set for the field.

The format of the Filter By Form entry palette depends on whether you are filtering from a table or from a form. If you are filtering from a table, a datasheet palette opens.

Notice that the table name appears in the Filter by Form tab.

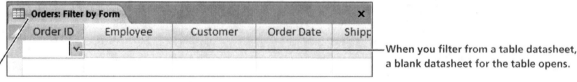

When you filter from a table datasheet, a blank datasheet for the table opens.

Down arrows on active fields enable you to select values on the basis of valid table values.

If you are filtering from a form, a blank form opens.

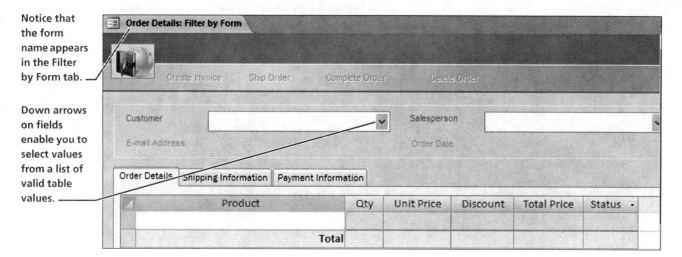

Notice that the form name appears in the Filter by Form tab.

Down arrows on fields enable you to select values from a list of valid table values.

Using Wildcards

Because database users often want to locate records that contain data in a specific field but may also contain additional text or data, Access accepts the use of *wildcards*, such as the asterisk, for setting criteria. Valid wildcards and how Access uses them are identified in the following table.

Wildcard	Example	Description
*		Appears in a position where any number of additional characters may appear in a search string.
	Graham	Locates all records with the string of text *graham* somewhere in the field value. The asterisk allows text and other data characters to appear before the search string as well as after the search text, regardless of how many characters appear.
	Graham*	Locates all records with the string of text *graham* at the beginning of the field value regardless of how many characters follow it.
	*Graham	Locates all records with the string of text *graham* at the end of the field value regardless of how many characters precede it.
	Gra*ham	Locates all records with the string of text beginning *gra* and ending *ham* regardless of how many characters appear between the search strings.
?		Each question mark represents a character and limits the search to a specified number of characters on the basis of the number of question marks that appear.
	Gra?am	Locates all records with the string of text *gra* at the beginning of the field value and *am* at the end of the field value with only one letter between the instances of the letter *a* in the search string.
	Gra???	Locates all records with the string of text *gra* at the beginning of the field value followed by three additional characters.

Hands-On 13.10 Filter Records by Form

In this exercise, you will use both tables and forms to filter records by form.

1. Open the Orders table in the Labyrinth Exports database.

2. Follow these steps to open Filter by Form:

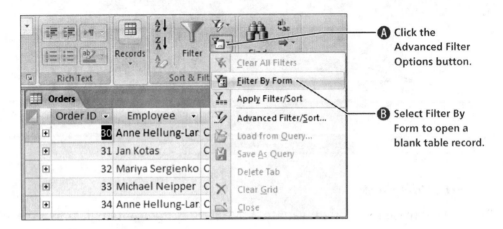

Ⓐ Click the Advanced Filter Options button.

Ⓑ Select Filter By Form to open a blank table record.

3. Follow these steps to filter and select all records in the Orders table that locate orders for one sales rep for a specific company:

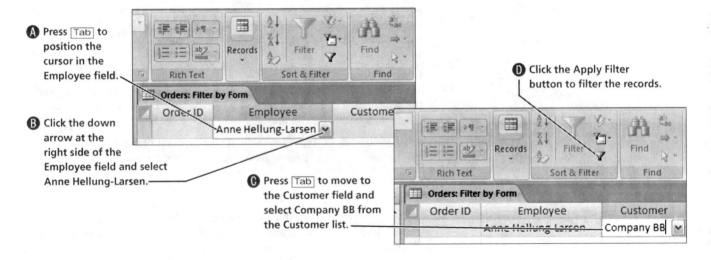

Ⓐ Press Tab to position the cursor in the Employee field.

Ⓑ Click the down arrow at the right side of the Employee field and select Anne Hellung-Larsen.

Ⓒ Press Tab to move to the Customer field and select Company BB from the Customer list.

Ⓓ Click the Apply Filter button to filter the records.

Access locates two records that meet the criteria set and places a filter icon beside each field name for the filter values set.

4. Choose Home→Sort & Filter→Advanced Filter Options ⬛▾ on the Ribbon and select Clear All Filters to display all records and remove criteria from the Filter By Form window.

5. Close ⊠ the Orders table. Choose No when prompted to save the changes.

6. Open the Product Details form.

7. Follow these steps to apply a filter by form to select products from a supplier that cost less than a specified value:

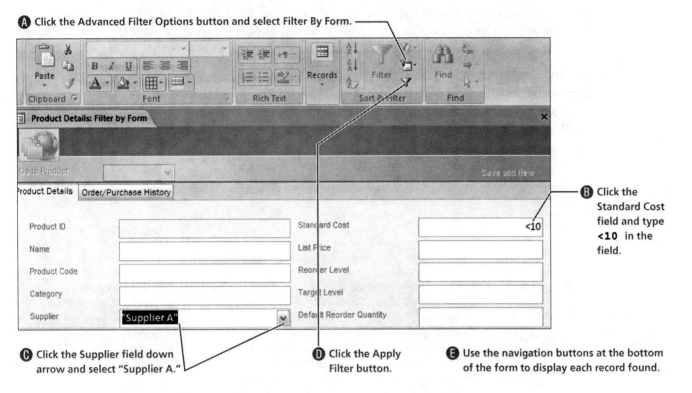

Ⓐ Click the Advanced Filter Options button and select Filter By Form.

Ⓑ Click the Standard Cost field and type **<10** in the field.

Ⓒ Click the Supplier field down arrow and select "Supplier A."

Ⓓ Click the Apply Filter button.

Ⓔ Use the navigation buttons at the bottom of the form to display each record found.

Access locates six records that match the criteria set.

8. Click the Remove Filter ▼ button to remove the filter, and then close ✕ the form.

Previewing and Printing Data

Reports are considered a primary output format for Access databases because they summarize data and display it as meaningful information. There may be times when you want to print raw data contained in a table or query results datasheet, or data contained in specific fields in a database table. You may also want to print a single record within a database in form layout. Access provides tools for printing all of these objects.

Setting Up Data to Print

Earlier in this lesson you learned how to adjust the column layout on a datasheet, how to search for records containing specific data, and how to filter out records that contain data different from the values you want to display. Each of these activities changes the display of data in a datasheet. When you print from a table datasheet, Access prints the data that actually appears in the datasheet when you issue the print command. You can hide columns to prevent them from printing, change the page layout settings to print the datasheet in landscape layout, and change the margins to fit a datasheet on a single sheet of paper.

Examining the Preview Window

Previewing data before you print helps determine adjustments that need to be made to ensure that the datasheet prints on the page as you want it to. You can view multiple pages in print preview to see how columns line up, what columns appear on separate pages, and so forth, so that you can make the necessary adjustments to the datasheet.

Because the layout of database objects differs, options available in the Print dialog box vary depending on what you are printing. However, the basic procedures used to preview and print database objects are the same and are similar to the procedures used to print files in other applications. When you preview an object, the Print Preview tools appear on the Ribbon. These tools are used to change the layout of the page on which you print.

The Print Preview Ribbon contains tools for changing the layout of the printed document.

Preview settings enable you to change the number of pages displayed onscreen at one time.

Close Print Preview restores the access object window.

Navigation buttons enable you to review all pages as they will print.

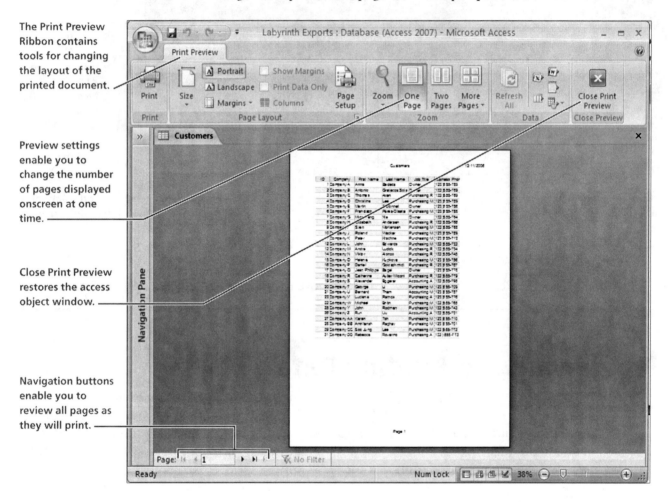

Hands-On 13.11 Preview and Print Data

In this exercise, you will preview and print a database table.

1. Open the Customers table and follow these steps to preview the datasheet:

A Click the Office button.

B Point (don't click) on the Print menu ▶ button. If you click the Print command on the Office list, Access prints without previewing.

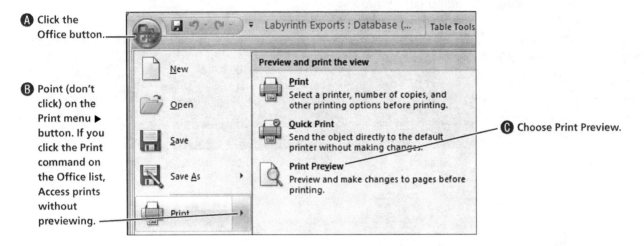

C Choose Print Preview.

2. Follow these steps to view pages that will print:

A Click the Next Page navigation button and review all pages of the document. As long as the Next Page button is active, another page is required to print the datasheet.

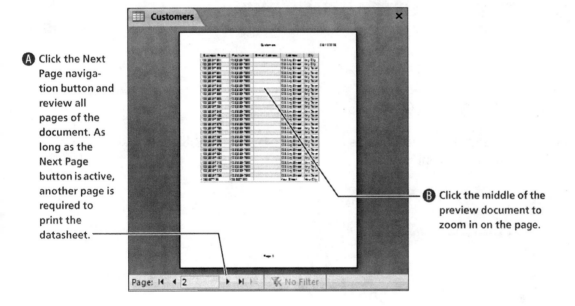

B Click the middle of the preview document to zoom in on the page.

3. Choose Print Preview→Close Preview→Close Print Preview button on the Ribbon as shown to close the preview window.

4. Follow these steps to hide seven fields of data:

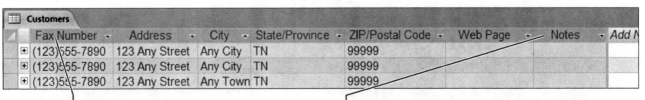

A Click the Fax Number field column heading.

B Hold down the Shift key and click the Notes field column heading to select the two fields and those in between.

5. Right-click one of the selected field column headings and select Hide Columns from the shortcut menu.

6. Adjust the column widths of the remaining columns.

7. Choose Office 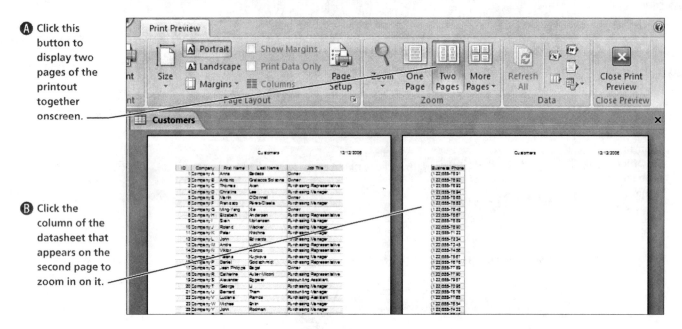→Print menu ▸→Print Preview, and then follow these steps to display multiple pages in the preview window:

Ⓐ Click this button to display two pages of the printout together onscreen.

Ⓑ Click the column of the datasheet that appears on the second page to zoom in on it.

> **!NOTE!** *The appearance of buttons and features on the Ribbon varies depending on screen resolution and size as well as the size of the application window.*

8. Choose Print Preview→Page Layout→Landscape 🅰 on the Ribbon to display the complete datasheet on one page.

Landscape layout displays all columns together on a sheet.

9. Choose Print Preview→Print→Print on the Ribbon to open the Print dialog box.

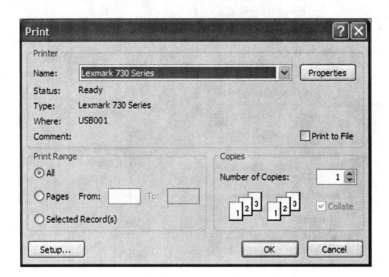

The Print dialog box you see may be different from the one shown here because of the difference in the printer that is active.

10. Select options in the Print dialog box to print one copy of all pages.

11. Close ☒ the table. Choose No when prompted to save changes.

12. Close any other database objects that are open and close the Navigation Pane.

Saving a Database as a New File

Anytime you change a file, you need to save it to prevent unwanted loss of data. Access automatically saves each database record as you enter it and also prompts you to save each object as you modify or change it in any way. As a result, the data stored in a database saves regularly as you work. Existing files often make good files on which to create new files.

Using the Save As Command

2007 new! You can use the Office →Save As menu ▶ command to save an existing database as a new database using a different filename just as you would with any other Microsoft Office application. Saving a database as a new file is not only a good way to quickly create a new database for a different purpose, but it is also a good way to create a backup of your data to protect it. Because many databases contain numerous objects, the Access Save As command also contains options for saving each of the database objects as new objects within the existing database.

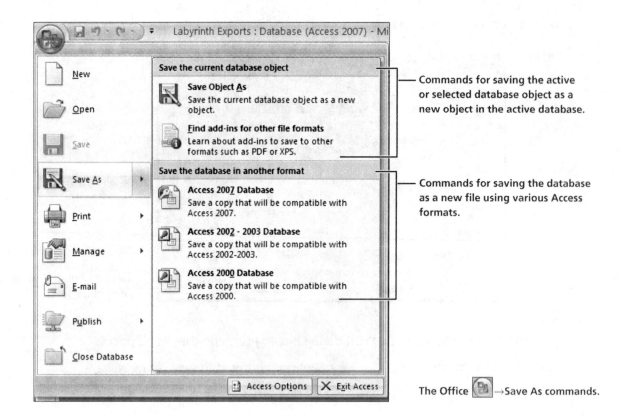

Commands for saving the active or selected database object as a new object in the active database.

Commands for saving the database as a new file using various Access formats.

The Office →Save As commands.

Hands-On 13.12 **Save a Database as a New File**

In this exercise, you will save the Labyrinth Exports database as a new database file.

1. Close all database objects, if you have objects open.

2. Follow these steps to save the file as a new database file:

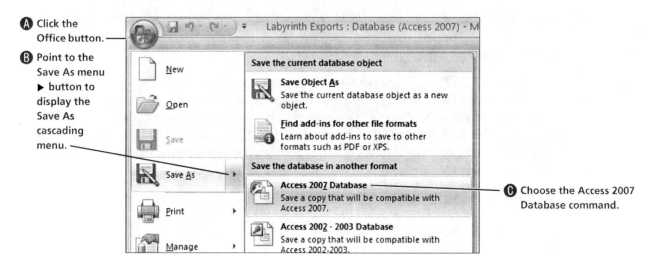

A Click the Office button.

B Point to the Save As menu ▶ button to display the Save As cascading menu.

C Choose the Access 2007 Database command.

Access opens the Save As dialog box.

3. Follow these steps to save your file as a new database file:

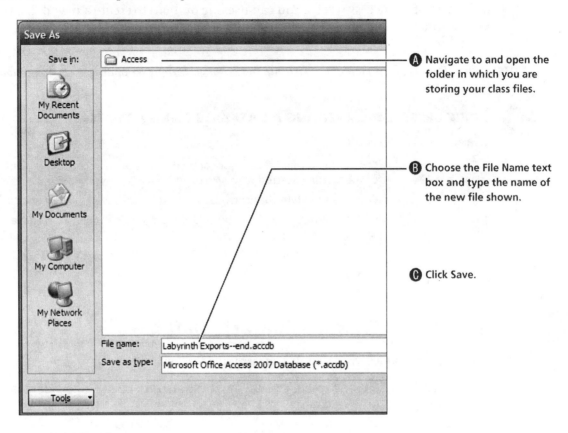

A Navigate to and open the folder in which you are storing your class files.

B Choose the File Name text box and type the name of the new file shown.

C Click Save.

4. Close the database and exit Access.

Creating a New Database Using a Template

2007 new!

Now that you have discovered some of the tools used to work with databases, let's take a look at how easy it is to create a database. Although you could build a database from scratch and outline all the pieces of information and database objects to include in the database, Access 2007 comes with a set of templates for creating some of the most frequently used databases. If you are familiar with Microsoft Word and Excel, you may also be familiar with templates. In Word, templates contain document format and design elements that help you create files that are consistent in their look and design.

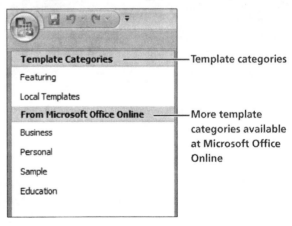

Template categories

More template categories available at Microsoft Office Online

Access templates enable you to create new databases—but in Access, a template is a ready-to-use database that contains all the tables, queries, forms, and reports needed to perform a specific task. When you need to create a database to track expenses or manage contacts, you can create the database using the appropriate template. After you create a database using a template, you can modify it to better meet your needs.

Access comes with a collection of templates that are featured on the Getting Started with Microsoft Office Access screen. You can use one of them to create a new database or connect to Microsoft Office Online and download additional templates.

 NOTE! *The categories of templates in each group may change as more templates become available.*

QUICK REFERENCE: CREATING A DATABASE USING A TEMPLATE

Task	Procedure
Create a Database Using a Template	■ Choose the Template Category or type from the Microsoft Office Online group of the Getting Started with Microsoft Office Access screen.
	■ Click the template that corresponds to the database type you want to create.
	■ Click the Browse button and navigate to the folder in which you want to save the new database.
	■ Type a filename for the database in the File Name text box and click OK.
	■ Choose Download.

Hands-On 13.13 **Create a Contacts Database**

In this exercise, you will create a new database using the Contacts template.

1. Launch Access, if it is closed, and follow these steps to create a new database using a template:

A Choose the Business template group in From Microsoft Office Online.

B Choose the Contacts template.

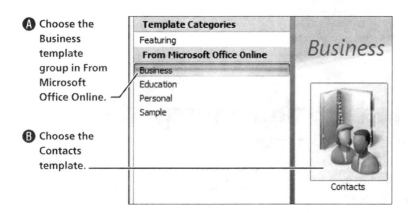

Access displays the Panel on the right that enables you to name the database.

2. Follow these steps to save the new database:

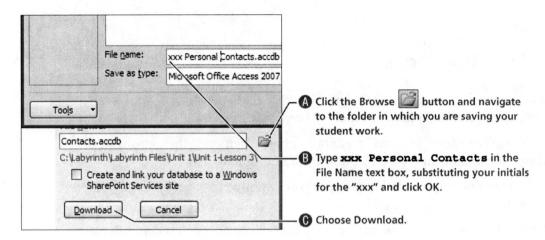

File name: | xxx Personal Contacts.accdb
Save as type: | Microsoft Office Access 2007

Tools

Contacts.accdb
C:\Labyrinth\Labyrinth Files\Unit 1\Unit 1-Lesson 3\
☐ Create and link your database to a Windows SharePoint Services site
Download | Cancel

Ⓐ Click the Browse [icon] button and navigate to the folder in which you are saving your student work.

Ⓑ Type **xxx Personal Contacts** in the File Name text box, substituting your initials for the "xxx" and click OK.

Ⓒ Choose Download.

Access downloads the template, saves it using the filename you assigned, and then opens the database.

Reviewing Database Objects

3. Open the Navigation Pane and display All Access Objects by Object Type.

4. Enable content and open each table, form, query, and report and review the arrangement of data in each object.

5. Close the database and exit [×] Access.

 **Concepts Review**

True/False Questions

1. To locate records containing data for a specific field by selecting a value from a list of data entries, you must use the Filter By Form feature.   TRUE   FALSE

2. When you rearrange columns in a datasheet and then print the datasheet, the printed document shows the columns in their original order.   TRUE   FALSE

3. In the Find and Replace dialog box, you could change the Search setting to tell Access to search the entire table.   TRUE   FALSE

4. The Replace button appears only on the Find tab page of the Find and Replace dialog box.   TRUE   FALSE

5. After you hide a column in a datasheet, there is no way to redisplay the column.   TRUE   FALSE

6. You can use both tables and forms to add records to database tables.   TRUE   FALSE

7. One of the main purposes of a database is to be able to retrieve data quickly and efficiently.   TRUE   FALSE

8. Access contains two tools for locating data in a database: Find and Replace.   TRUE   FALSE

9. Templates in Access hold only the design elements you want to apply to tables, forms, and other database objects.   TRUE   FALSE

10. Filtering helps you narrow down a search for data by displaying only the records that contain values you want to consider.   TRUE   FALSE

Multiple Choice Questions

1. Which Access feature would you use to locate a record containing specific data without hiding any of the records?
   a. Find
   b. Find and Replace
   c. Sort
   d. Filter

2. What happens to a table design (or structure) when you reposition a field in the datasheet?
   a. The field is repositioned in the table design.
   b. Access displays a warning message.
   c. Access deletes the field that originally appeared in the column.
   d. Nothing

3. Which sort order arranges records alphabetically from A to Z?
   a. Sort numerically
   b. Sort alphabetically
   c. Sort ascending
   d. Sort descending

4. What happens to a datasheet when you save it after sorting it?
   a. Nothing
   b. Access resorts it.
   c. The new sort order is saved as part of the datasheet format.
   d. Both b and c

Skill Builders

Skill Builder 13.1   Adjust Datasheet Layout

The sb-Valley Hospital database has been updated to contain additional data in each table. In this exercise, you will adjust the widths of columns in each table to display data appropriately, reposition fields displayed on the datasheet, and hide other fields to obtain a printout of specific data. After you make the changes required, you can print the datasheets.

1. Start Access, and then open the sb-Valley Hospital database from the Lesson 13 folder in your file storage location.

2. Enable content, and choose Office ⬚→Save As→Access 2007 Database.

3. Save the file using the filename **sb-Valley Hospital-end** in the Lesson 13 folder.

Adjust the Datasheet Column Width

4. Open the Patients table and press Ctrl+A to select all fields and data in the datasheet.

5. Point to the border between two of the column headings so the mouse pointer appears as a double-arrow, and then double-click the right column headings border between the column headings to widen all the columns to fit the data.

6. Click the Save 🖫 button to save changes to the table layout.

Enter Data into the Datasheet

7. Click the New Record ⬚ button to create a new blank record and enter the following data to create two additional records:

First Name	Last Name	Street	City	State	ZIP	Telephone	DOB
Alex	KELLY	Olson Avenue	COLUMBUS	OH	43221	6145551024	9/14/1975
Bryan	SANDERS	Quaker Ridge Lane	CHARLESTON	WV	25301		11/22/1946

Now you will hide one of the columns.

8. Right-click the Telephone column heading to display the shortcut menu and select Hide Columns.

Preview and Print the Table

9. Choose Office ⬚→Print menu ▶ button→Print Preview to view the datasheet as it would print and then print the document (optional).

10. Click the Close Print Preview button to close the preview, and then close the table, saving changes if prompted.

Skill Builder 13.2   Locate, Filter, and Print Records

A new record needs to be added to the Employees table in the sb-Valley Hospital—end database. In this exercise—after entering the new record using the Employee Personnel File form—you will locate all records for employees in the department and preview and print a copy of the two forms.

1. Open the sb-Valley Hospital-end database created in Skill Builder 13.1, if necessary, and expand the Forms list in the Navigation Pane.

Create a New Record

2. Open the Employee Personnel File form and click the New (Blank) Record ⊞ to create a new blank form.

3. Type the data shown in the following table to create a new record seven in the database, substituting your name and fictional data in fields indicated.

ID #	First Name	Middle Initial	Last Name	Street Address	City	State	ZIP	Department	Salary Level
EX490	Yours	Yours	Yours	Fictional	Yours	Yours	Yours	Office Adm	O3

Find and Filter Records

4. Choose Home→Find→Find ⚲ on the Ribbon and type **Office Adm** in the Find What text box, select Employees Personnel File from the Look In drop-down list, and then choose Find Next.

5. Click Cancel to close the Find and Replace dialog box.

6. Choose Home→Sort & Filter→Selection ⓥ ▾ on the Ribbon and select the Equals "Office Adm." command to filter the records.
   Access locates only two records that contain the value.

Preview and Print Records

7. Choose Office 🗗→Print menu ▸ →Print Preview to preview the form print page.

8. Choose Print Preview→Print→Print 🖨 on the Ribbon to print the forms.

9. Choose the Pages option in the Print dialog box, enter From **1** to **1** and click OK to print the two records.

10. Close the print preview window and the form.

Skill Builder 13.3   Sort and Print Datasheets and Reports

One of the benefits of storing data in a database is the ease with which you can sort the data. The US Postal Service requires that bulk mail be sorted and arranged by ZIP code before it will be accepted. Businesses, of course, often send letters to their customers and clients. Valley Hospital wants to use the database to organize records by ZIP code before using it to print envelope labels. In this exercise, you will sort the records by ZIP code and save changes to the table settings so that the records will remain organized in this sort order. In addition, because you have added a new employee to the database, you need to print a copy of the Employee Phone List report.

1. Open the sb-Valley Hospital-end database, if necessary, and open the Patients table (not the Patient Information form).

2. Hide the Street column in the datasheet.

Sort Records

3. Place the cursor in the ZIP field for any record.

4. Choose Home→Sort & Filter→Ascending ⏏ on the Ribbon to sort the records.
   Access sorts records so that all records with no data in the ZIP field appear at the top of the datasheet.

5. Press [Ctrl]+[S] to save changes to the table and close it.

6. Open the Patients table again to ensure that the sort order was saved, and then print a copy of the datasheet.

Preview and Print a Report

7. Close the table and open the Employee Phone List report; preview and print the report.

8. Close all open database objects and then close the database.

Unit 4 Assessments

Assessment 4.1   Create a Presentation

In this exercise, you will create a presentation for Classic Cars. Classic Cars is an organization devoted to tracking, categorizing, and preserving classic automobiles. The presentation will be given to members of the Classic Cars organization at the annual Classic Cars convention.

1. Start PowerPoint.
   A new presentation is started for you automatically.

2. Apply the Metro design document theme, as shown in the following illustration.

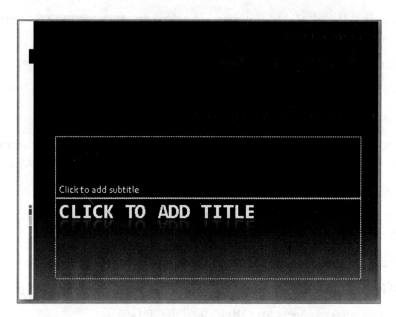

3. Add the following text to the Title slide:
   - **Title: Classic Cars**
   - **Subtitle: 2007 Convention Highlights**

4. Add a second slide with the following text:

Title	Seminar Topics
Bulleted paragraphs	■ Restoration Techniques
	■ Preservation Techniques
	■ Locating Vehicles
	■ Success Stories
	■ Winning Competitions

5. Add a third slide with the following text:

Title	Collections on Display
Bulleted paragraphs	■ James McGee - 1950s Corvettes
	■ Beth Zelinka - Classic Fords
	■ Ricardo Campos - Thunderbirds
	■ Eva Peterson - Corvairs

6. Add a fourth slide and change its layout to a Two Content layout. Add the following text:

Title	Door Prizes
Left bulleted paragraphs	■ Car Care Items
	■ Gift certificates
	■ Floor mats
	■ Waxes and polishes
	■ Magazines
Right bulleted paragraphs	■ Entertainment
	■ Las Vegas vacation
	■ Sporting events
	■ Movie tickets
	■ Dinners

7. Select all but the first bullet in the left text box and increase the list level.

8. Select all but the first bullet in the right text box and increase the list level.
   After you finish, the slide should appear similar to the following illustration.

9. Add a final slide to the presentation and apply the Title and Content layout.

- Title: **The 2007 Convention**
- Text: **Enjoy the Ride…**

10. Save the presentation as **as-Classic Cars** to the Unit 4 Assessments folder on your file storage location.

Assessment 4.2   **Print a Slide**

In this exercise, you will print a slide.

Before You Begin: You must have completed Assessment 4.1 before you can begin this exercise.

1. If necessary, open the as-Classic Cars presentation from the Unit 4 Assessments folder.

2. Select the Door Prizes slide.

3. Using the Grayscale option, print the single slide.

4. Save the changes to the as-Classic Cars presentation.

5. Close the presentation.

Assessment 4.3   Add and Format Clip Art to a Presentation

In this exercise, you will add clip art to the Classic Cars Animation presentation.

1. Open the as-Classic Cars Animation presentation from the Unit 4 Assessments folder.

2. Display the Seminar Topics slide and change its layout to the Two Content layout.

3. Add clip art to the second text box as shown in the illustration. You can locate the picture by doing a search for the keyword phrase **classic cars.** You may want to change your Results Should Be option to include both Clip Art and Photographs. Adjust the size of the picture after inserting it, and adjust the position as shown.

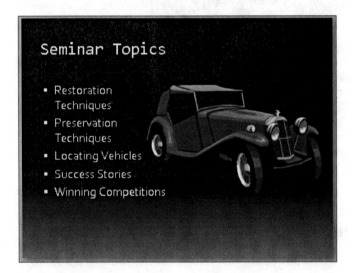

4. Choose the closing slide and change its layout to the Section Header layout, and then change the subtitle from *Enjoy the Ride* to **Enjoy the Road Ahead.** Increase the font size if you like.

5. Use the keyword **highway** to search for clip art that is appropriate for the slide and position the image as shown in the illustration.
   Your clip art selection may differ.

6. Choose the Format tab and apply a Picture Style to your image. The illustration shows the Rounded Diagonal Corner White style applied. Your selection may differ.

7. Save the presentation.

Assessment 4.4   Add Slide Transitions to a Presentation

In this exercise, you will add slide transitions to the Classic Cars Animation presentation.

Before You Begin: The as-Classic Cars Animation presentation from the Unit 4 Assessments folder should be open.

1. Display Slide Sorter view and select all slides in the presentation.

2. Display the Animations tab and select a slide transition to be applied to every slide.

3. Choose Animations→Preview to test your transition. Change the transition effect if you are not happy with your current selection.

4. Save and close the presentation.

5. Exit PowerPoint.

Assessment 4.5   Explore Additional Database Objects

In this exercise, you will explore additional features and objects within the Labyrinth Exports database.

Launch Access, Open, and Log In to a Database

1. Launch Microsoft Office Access 2007 and open the Labyrinth Exports database file listed on the Open Recent Database list.

2. Enable content and log in as Andrew Cencini.

3. Open the Navigation Pane and expand all object lists.

Use Special Features of Forms

4. In the Quick Links section of the Home form, click the View Customers link.

   What object opens? _____

   What object type is it? _____

5. Display the Home form and click the View Purchase Orders link.

   What object opens? _____

   What object type is it? _____

6. Display the Home form again and click the Labyrinth Exports Dried Pears link in the Inventory to Reorder list.

   What happens? _____

   Is it an object? _____ If so, what type?_____

7. Click the Purchase button at the end of the Dried Pears item.

   What does this button do? _____

   What happened to the Dried Pears item on the Restock List?_____

   Why?_____

Compare Queries and Reports

8. Run the Product Sales by Category query and the Product Sales by Category report.

   How do these objects resemble each other? _____

   How do they differ? _____

9. Open the Product Sales Qty by Employee query and the Product Sales Quantity by Employee report.

   How does the arrangement of data in the report differ from the data in the query datasheet? _____

   Are all fields contained in the query datasheet contained in the report?_____

Rearrange Items on the Navigation Pane

10. Display only Tables and Related Views in the Navigation Pane, and then study the arrangement of database objects as they appear in each group of this organization.

11. Change the Navigation Pane to display all object types arranged by object type.

12. Close all database objects, close the Navigation Pane, close the database and exit Access.

Assessment 4.6   Edit Records and Save as a New File

Sales from the Rich Homestead have been doing well; therefore, in this exercise, you will need to update the database to remove records. By first filtering the records by form, you can narrow the list of records displayed to make the update process easier. As you work, you will need to adjust datasheet column widths to fit column contents. You will notice that the data is just raw data; for example, dollar signs have not been added.

1. Launch Access and open the as-Rich Homestead database from the Unit 4 Assessments folder in your file storage location.

2. Enable content, and save the database to the Unit 4 Assessments folder as a new file named **as-Rich Homestead-end** using the current file format.

Format Table Layout and Sort Data

3. Open the Records table, and adjust the column widths of all fields in the table to fit the contents.

4. Scroll to the right side of the table until you see both the Selling Price and Date End field columns, and then move the Date End column and place it just to the left of the Selling Price column.

5. Save changes to the table, and then sort the records alphabetically by the Item Title field.

Filter Records by Form

6. Click the Advanced Filter Options [icon] button and choose Filter By Form to open a blank records form.

7. Type **Decca*** in the Item Title field and **>8/30/07** in the Date End field.

8. Choose Home→Sort & Filter→Apply Filter [icon] on the Ribbon.
   Access locates two records.

Select and Delete Records

9. Click the record selector button for the first record and then press ⬚Shift⬚ and click the second record selector button to select both records.

10. Press ⬚Delete⬚ to delete both records.
    Access prompts you to confirm the deletion.

11. Choose Yes to delete both records.

12. Clear the filter criteria using the Advanced Filter Options shortcut menu.

13. Close the Records table. Choose Yes when prompted to save the table.

Assessment 4.7   Locate and Update Data, and Print Datasheets

New items have been located that need to be added to the Rich Homestead store. They fit into two separate categories, Comics and Collectibles. In addition, the item descriptions of some of the comics and books contain extraneous characters that need to be removed. In this exercise, you will be able to print datasheets that display more uniform data.

1. Open the as-Rich Homestead-end database from the Unit 4 Assessments folder in your file storage location and then open the Comics table.

2. Adjust the field column widths of fields containing truncated data and save changes to the layout.

Add Records

3. Add a new record to the table and type the following data into appropriate fields of the new record. Note that not all fields contain data:

Format	A
Title	Marvel—Spider-Man
Category	4542
Store Category	2961949
Quantity	1
Start Price	5
Duration	7
Selling Price	
Gallery Type	Gallery
Shipping Type	Flat
Shipping Service	9
Shipping Service	5
Dispatch Time Max	2

4. Open the List Collectibles form, create a new blank record in the form, and enter the following data for a new item:

Selling Format	S
Accept Offer	Y
Item Title	Masonic Ceremonial Sword
Starting Price	25
Selling Price	
Postage	15
Insurance	10
Date Listed	07/28/2007
Duration	30
Date End	08/27/2007

5. Close the List Collectibles form, saving changes if prompted.

Locate and Update Records

6. Open the Comics table, sort the table data alphabetically on the Title field, and locate the records at the top of the table that contain multiple asterisks.

7. Select the Title field of each record containing multiple asterisks and remove the asterisks.

 TIP! *If you accidentally delete text other than the asterisks as you update the records, you can reverse the deletion using the Undo command. Simply press* Ctrl + Z *to reverse the deletion.*

8. Repeat the instructions outlined in steps 6 and 7 to sort and remove the asterisks from records in the Books table.

9. Print copies of the datasheets for the following tables: Collectibles, Records, Books, and Comics.

Assessment 4.8 Create a New Database Using a Template

One of the groups of templates available in Access relates to education. In this exercise, you will use the Education templates to create a new database designed to store student data.

1. Launch Access and choose the Education templates group.

2. Create a new database using the Students template, name the database **as-LAU Students-xxx** where xxx represents your initials, and save the file in the folder in which you are storing your student files.

3. Close the Student List form that opens when you create the database, enable content, and then open the Navigation Pane.

4. Review the database tables listed under the Supportive Object Group.
   - What fields would you include in your student database that the Students template did not?
   - What fields did the Students template include that you would not?
   - What objects would you include in your database that the Students template did not?
   - What objects did the Students template include that you would not?

5. Add your name and other data (real or fictional) to the Student List form in the database.

6. Close the form, close the database, and exit Access.

APPENDIX A

Storing Your Exercise Files

This appendix contains an overview for using this book with various file storage media, such as a USB flash drive or hard drive. Detailed instructions for downloading and unzipping the exercise files used with this book appear in exercies for each type of media.

The following topics are addressed in this appendix:

Topic	Description	See Page
Downloading the Student Exercise Files	Retrieving the exercise files and copying them to your file storage location.	432
Using a USB Flash Drive	Storing your work on a USB flash memory drive.	433
Using the Documents Folder	Storing your work in the My Documents folder.	439
Using a Network Folder	Storing your work in a custom folder on a network.	441
Using a Floppy Disk with This Book	Using a floppy disk with this book is not recommended. This topic covers how you can use a floppy with most of the lessons.	442

Downloading the Student Exercise Files

The files needed to complete certain Hands-On, Skill Builder, and unit-level Assessment exercises are available for download at the Labyrinth website. At the end of each media type topic is an exercise with instructions to copy the files to your computer and prepare them for use with this book.

 NOTE! *It is not possible to store all of the unzipped student exercise files on a floppy disk. See the Using a Floppy Disk with This Book section in this appendix for instructions on using a floppy disk to work with student exercise files.*

Using a USB Flash Drive

A USB flash drive stores your data on a flash memory chip. You simply plug it in to a USB port on any computer and Windows immediately recognizes it as an additional disk drive. USB flash drives typically can store 256 megabytes (MB) or more. Large capacity USB flash drives can store 1 gigabyte (GB) or more. Flash drive versatility, capacity, and reliability have made them a popular replacement for the role once filled by the ancient (in computer terms) floppy disk.

Win XP

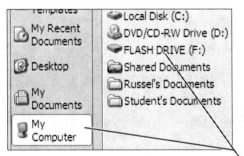

The Word 2007 Open dialog box displays a flash drive in the My Computer view in Windows XP.

Win Vista

The Word 2007 Open dialog box displays a flash drive in the Computer view in Windows Vista.

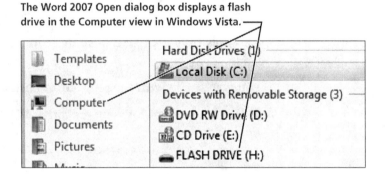

USB Flash Drive Letter

When you plug in a USB flash drive to a Windows computer, Windows automatically assigns it the next available drive letter. Windows uses drive letters to identify each drive connected to the computer. For example, the primary part of the hard drive is always identified as the C drive. A CD/DVD drive is typically the D or E drive. Windows assigns a drive letter to your flash drive when you plug it in. The drive may receive a different drive letter on each computer you use it with.

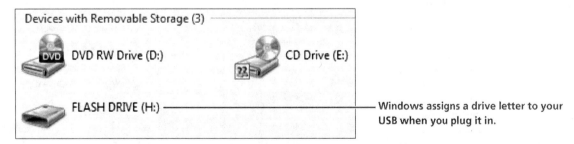

Windows assigns a drive letter to your USB when you plug it in.

Windows lists a USB flash drive as a removable storage device.

 TIP! *Your USB flash drive may receive a different drive letter on different computers. This does not affect any files stored on the drive.*

Hands-On A.1   Download and Unzip the Exercise Files— USB Flash Drive

Follow these steps to download a copy of the student files necessary for this book.

1. Launch Internet Explorer.

2. Enter **labpub.com/learn/oe7b** in the browser's address bar and tap ⌈Enter⌋.

3. Click the Student Exercise Files link below the Downloads heading.
   A prompt to run or save the student exercise files appears.

4. Click the Save button.
   Internet Explorer asks where you wish to save the downloaded file.

5. Carefully plug your USB flash drive into a USB port on the computer.

6. Click the Close ⌈×⌋ (Win XP) / ⌈×⌋ (Win Vista) button if a window appears asking what you want to do with the plugged-in flash drive.

7. Follow these steps for your version of Windows to choose the flash drive as the save destination:

Win XP

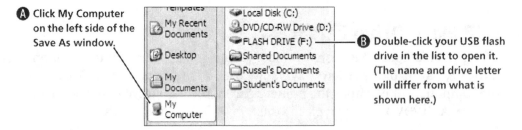

A Click My Computer on the left side of the Save As window.

B Double-click your USB flash drive in the list to open it. (The name and drive letter will differ from what is shown here.)

Win Vista

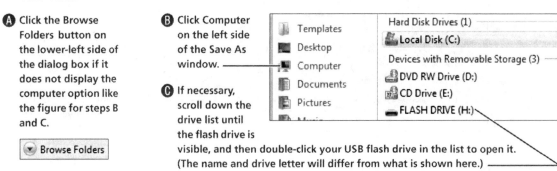

A Click the Browse Folders button on the lower-left side of the dialog box if it does not display the computer option like the figure for steps B and C.

B Click Computer on the left side of the Save As window.

C If necessary, scroll down the drive list until the flash drive is visible, and then double-click your USB flash drive in the list to open it. (The name and drive letter will differ from what is shown here.)

Now that you've shown Windows where to save the file, you are ready to download it.

The rest of the instructions for this exercise apply to both Win XP and Vista.

8. Click the Save button.

After a pause, the exercise file will begin downloading to your computer. Continue with the next step after the download is complete.

NOTE! *If you are downloading the files via a dial-up modem connection, it will take several minutes or more for the download to be completed.*

Unzip the Files

9. Click the Open Folder button on the Download Complete dialog box.

   If the Download Complete dialog box closes after the download is completed, you will need to open a folder window to the USB flash drive you used in step 7:

   ■ **Win XP**: Choose Start→My Computer. Double-click to open your USB flash drive.

   ■ **Win Vista**: Choose Start→Computer. Double-click to open your USB flash drive.

10. Double-click the oe7b_student_files icon, as shown at right.
    Windows may ask if you wish to run the software. This confirmation helps protect your computer from viruses. In this case, you know the file is safe.

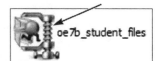

11. Choose Run if Windows asks you if you are sure you want to run this software, otherwise continue with step 14.
    A prompt appears, telling you where the student exercise files will be unzipped.

12. Click the Unzip button.
    The self-extracting archive unzips all of the student exercise files for this book into the new folder. This should take less than one minute to complete.

13. Click OK to acknowledge the successful unzip process.

14. Click the Close button to close the self-extractor window.
    All of the files necessary to use this book are now unzipped to your file storage location. They are located in a new folder named Office 2007 Brief.

    Since the zip file is no longer needed, you will delete it in the next step. (You can always download it again if you need fresh copies of the exercise files in the future.)

15. (Optional) Make sure that the oe7b_student_files zip file is chosen, and then tap the Delete key on the keyboard. Click OK if you are asked to confirm the deletion.

Renaming Your Flash Drive

It may be easier to identify your flash drive on various computer systems if you give it a custom name. For example, you can use your first name, or a generic name such as Flash Drive or Pen Drive. The next exercise shows how you can rename your flash drive on most computer systems.

 NOTE! *Some Windows systems may not give you renaming privileges for drives. This depends on privileges associated with your login name.*

Hands-On A.2   Rename Your USB Flash Drive

You may find it convenient to rename your USB flash drive to make it easier to recognize when you save or open files.

 TIP! *Some Windows systems may not give you renaming privileges for drives.*

1. Plug in the USB flash drive to an available USB port.

2. Click the Close $\boxed{\times}$ / $\boxed{\times}$ button if a window appears asking what you want to do with the plugged-in flash drive.

3. Follow the step for your version of Windows:

   ■ **Win XP**: Choose Start→My Computer.

   ■ **Win Vista**: Choose Start→Computer.

4. Right-click your USB flash drive and choose Rename from the context menu.

 NOTE! *In the next step, Windows may display a prompt indicating that you cannot rename this flash drive. You have not done anything wrong! You can use the drive with its current name. You may also want to try renaming it later using a different login.*

If you have renaming rights, Windows highlights the existing name.

5. Type **Flash Drive** (or any other custom name you wish to use) as the new drive name and tap Enter, or click OK if you receive a prompt that you do not have sufficient rights to perform this operation.
   If you were unable to rename the flash drive, don't worry. Renaming the flash drive is a convenience for recognition and has no other effect.

■

Removing a Flash Drive Safely

Windows XP and Windows Vista allow you to remove a USB flash drive by simply unplugging the drive. However, this method requires you to make sure that no files are active on the drive when you unplug it. For example, if you unplug the drive while a file is being saved, there is a possibility that the file will be corrupted or lost altogether. Normally, if the light is not flashing on the USB flash drive, you can safely remove it. However, if you wish to be *absolutely certain* that the drive is ready for removal, you should use the following procedure.

If you are not sure a USB flash drive is ready to be unplugged, you can use the Safely Remove Hardware command to be certain.

WARNING! *Removing a USB flash drive while files on it are active could result in corruption of the entire drive and the loss of all files on it.*

QUICK REFERENCE: SAFELY REMOVE A USB FLASH DRIVE

Task	Procedure
Remove the flash drive (standard method)	■ Close any program from which you opened files on the USB flash drive. ■ Wait for the light on the drive to stop flashing. ■ Gently unplug the flash drive from its USB port or cable.
Remove the flash drive (careful method)	■ Close any program from which you opened files on the USB flash drive. ■ Click once on the Safely Remove Hardware 🖴 icon in the Notification Area on the Windows taskbar. ■ Choose your USB flash drive from the pop-up list. ■ Gently unplug the flash drive after Windows prompts that you can do so safely. Or, wait to unplug the drive if you see a prompt that the storage device cannot be stopped now.

> **Problem Ejecting USB Mass Storage Device** ☒
>
> ⚠ The device 'Generic volume' cannot be stopped right now. Try stopping the device again later.
>
> [OK]

Hands-On A.3   Use the Safely Remove Hardware Command

In this exercise, you will use the Safely Remove Hardware command to make certain your USB flash drive is ready to be unplugged.

Before You Begin: Skip this exercise if you are not using a USB flash drive.

1. Make sure you have closed any open files on the USB flash drive.

In the following step, the drive letter may differ from the one shown in the figures.

2. Follow these steps to safely unplug the drive:

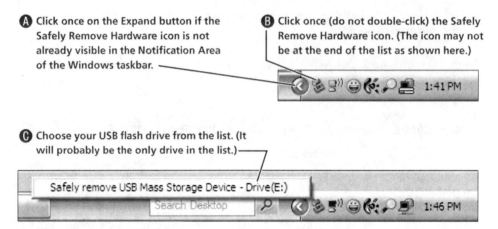

Ⓐ Click once on the Expand button if the Safely Remove Hardware icon is not already visible in the Notification Area of the Windows taskbar.

Ⓑ Click once (do not double-click) the Safely Remove Hardware icon. (The icon may not be at the end of the list as shown here.)

Ⓒ Choose your USB flash drive from the list. (It will probably be the only drive in the list.)

Windows displays a prompt that you can safely remove the drive. Or, you will see a prompt that the drive cannot be removed and that you must wait.

3. Gently unplug the USB flash drive from its port or extension cable.

Using the Documents Folder

NOTE!

Many computer labs do not allow students to use this folder.

Windows creates a unique Documents folder for each login ID. This folder resides on the main system drive (usually the C drive). The Office 2007 application programs provide a Documents navigation link in their Open and Save As dialog boxes for quick navigation to this folder.

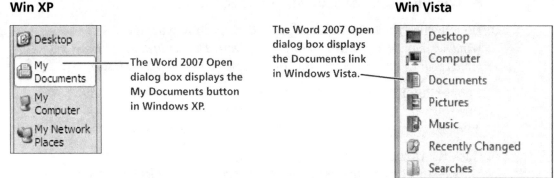

Win XP

The Word 2007 Open dialog box displays the My Documents button in Windows XP.

Win Vista

The Word 2007 Open dialog box displays the Documents link in Windows Vista.

Hands-On A.4 Download and Unzip the Exercise Files— Documents Folder

Follow these steps to download a copy of the student files necessary for this book.

1. Launch Internet Explorer.

2. Enter **labpub.com/learn/oe7b** in the browser's address bar and tap Enter.

3. Click the Student Exercise Files link below the Downloads heading.
   A prompt to run or save the student exercise files appears.

4. Click the Save button.

5. Follow the steps for your version of Windows:
   - **Win XP:** Choose My Documents on the left side of the Save As window.
   - **Win Vista:** If necessary, click the Browse Folders button, and then choose Documents on the left side of the Save As window.

   Now that you've shown Windows where to save the file, you are ready to download it.

6. Click the Save button.
   After a pause, the exercise file will begin downloading to your computer. Continue with the next step after the download is complete.

NOTE! *If you are downloading the files via a dial-up modem connection, it will take several minutes or more for the download to be completed.*

7. Click the Open Folder button on the Download Complete dialog box.

If the Download Complete dialog box closes after the download is completed, follow the step for your version of Windows to open a folder window to the Documents folder you used in step 5.

- **Win XP**: Choose Start→My Documents.
- **Win Vista**: Choose Start→Documents.

8. Double-click the oe7b_student_files icon, as shown at right.
Windows may ask if you wish to run the software. This confirmation helps protect your computer from viruses. In this case, you know the file is safe.

oe7b_student_files

9. Choose Run if Windows asks you if you are sure you want to run this software, otherwise continue with step 10.
A prompt appears, telling you where the student exercise files will be unzipped.

10. Click the Unzip button.
The self-extracting archive unzips all of the student exercise files for this book into the new folder. This should take less than one minute to complete.

11. Click OK to acknowledge the successful unzip process.

12. Click the Close button to close the self-extractor window.
All of the files necessary to use this book are now unzipped to your file storage location. They are located in a new folder named Office 2007 Brief.

Since the zip file is no longer needed, you will delete it in the next step. (You can always download it again if you need fresh copies of the exercise files in the future.)

13. (Optional) Make sure that the oe7b_student_files zip file is chosen, and then tap the [Delete] key on the keyboard. Click OK if you are asked to confirm the deletion.

Using a Network Folder

NOTE!

Your instructor or a computer lab assistant can tell you how to locate a network drive if this is where you are to store your files.

You may use a system connected to a network. There may be a folder on a network server computer in another location that is dedicated to storing your work. Usually, you will find this folder within the (Win XP) *My Network Places* or (Win Vista) *Network* folder of your computer. The Office 2007 application programs provide a Network link in their Open and Save As dialog boxes for quick navigation to this folder. You may have to navigate deeper into the folder to locate your personal network drive folder.

Win XP

In Windows XP, the Word 2007 Open dialog box displays the My Network Places button.

Win Vista

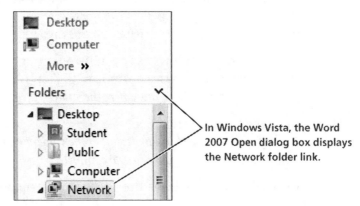

In Windows Vista, the Word 2007 Open dialog box displays the Network folder link.

Hands-On A.5   Download and Unzip the Exercise Files— Network Drive Folder

Follow these steps to download a copy of the student files necessary for this book.

1. Launch Internet Explorer.

2. Enter **labpub.com/learn/oe7b** in the browser's address bar and tap ⌈Enter⌋.

3. Click the Student Exercise Files link below the Downloads heading.
   A prompt to run or save the student exercise files appears.

4. Click the Save button.

5. Follow the steps for your version of Windows:

   ■ **Win XP:** Choose My Network Places on the left side of the Save As window, and then navigate to your network folder.

   ■ **Win Vista**: Click the menu button as shown at right, and then choose Network. Navigate to your network folder.

   Now that you've shown Windows where to save the file, you are ready to download it.

6. Click the Save button.
   The download begins. Continue with the next step after it is complete.

NOTE! *Downloading the files via a dial-up modem connection will take several minutes.*

7. Click the Open Folder button on the Download Complete dialog box.
   If the Download Complete dialog box closes after the download is completed, you will need to open a folder window to the file storage location you used in step 5.

8. Double-click the oe7b_student_files icon, as shown at right.
   Windows may ask if you wish to run the software. This confirmation helps protect your computer from viruses. In this case, you know the file is safe.

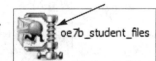
oe7b_student_files

9. Choose Run if Windows asks you if you are sure you want to run this software, otherwise continue with step 10.
   A prompt appears, telling you where the student exercise files will be unzipped.

10. Click the Unzip button.
    The self-extracting archive unzips all of the student exercise files for this book into the new folder. This should take less than one minute to complete.

11. Click OK to acknowledge the successful unzip process.

12. Click the Close button to close the self-extractor window.
    All of the files necessary to use this book are now unzipped to your file storage location. They are located in a new folder named Office 2007 Brief.

    Since the zip file is no longer needed, you will delete it in the next step. (You can always download it again if you need fresh copies of the exercise files in the future.)

13. (Optional) Make sure that the oe7b_student_files zip file is chosen, and then tap the ⌐Delete⌐ key on the keyboard. Click OK if you are asked to confirm the deletion.

Using a Floppy Disk with This Book

It is not recommended that students use floppy disks with this textbook. There are two primary reasons for this:

- Due to the increasing sophistication of files you can create with programs in the Microsoft Office 2007 Suite, it is no longer practical to store all of the exercise files for this book on a floppy disk.

- Many computers no longer feature a floppy drive, and this trend should continue as USB flash drives take over the portable file storage role once filled by floppies.

This section describes how to work around the space limitations of floppy disks for most of the lessons in this book.

Storage Limitations of Floppy Disks

As you work through the exercises in this book, you will create numerous new files that must be saved. A floppy disk will not have enough storage capacity to hold all files created during the course. Thus, you must store your exercise files on a hard drive, and then copy and paste (copy) individual lesson folders between this hard drive and the floppy disk. Use the following instructions to work with this book using a floppy disk.

Hands-On A.6   Using a Floppy Disk with This Book

If you have no choice to use the recommended USB flash drive or other file storage location with this book, use the following procedure to work with the lessons using a floppy disk.

1. Following the instructions in Hands-On A.4, download and unzip the student exercise files for this book to a folder on a computer hard drive or other storage location.

2. Open a folder window to the location where you unzipped the files.

3. Select the folder for the next lesson you will study, and then give the Copy command. (See Lesson 2, Managing Computer Files for details on cutting and pasting files and folders.)

4. Open a window to your floppy disk, and then use the Paste command to paste (move) the folder and its files to the floppy disk.

5. Study the lesson, choosing the $3\frac{1}{2}$ Floppy (A) drive then the lesson folder to open and save files as directed in the exercises.

6. After you complete the lesson, *cut* and paste (do not copy and paste) the lesson folder from the floppy disk back to the same location from which you copied it originally.

   Choose Yes to All if Windows asks if you wish to replace any files with the same name in the destination folder.

7. Repeat steps 2–6 for each lesson.

   If Windows tells you the floppy disk is full, check to make sure that you moved (cut and pasted) the folder in step 6. (The previous folder should no longer be on the floppy disk.)

Glossary of Computer Terms

Antivirus program   Software designed to stop computer viruses from infecting files on the computer (*See also* the Antivirus Software section on page 28)

Example: *Norton Antivirus*

Application program   Software designed to help you get work done (*See also* the Application Programs section on page 27)

Example: *Microsoft Word, Outlook Express*

Broadband   A generic term for a high-speed Internet connection

Example: *cable, DSL, T1*

Byte   Single character of data; it is composed of 8 bits in a specific order

Example: *A, B, C, etc.*

Cable modem   Device designed to send and receive digital data over television cable system wiring (*See also* the Modems section on page 21)

Cathode ray tube (CRT)   The technology used by large, television-style monitors; CRT monitors have largely been replaced by thinner, more efficient LCD panels

Default   A setting that a computer program assumes you will use unless you specify a different setting

Dots per inch (DPI)   Measure of the sharpness of a printer's output; the higher the dots per inch, the sharper the print will appear on the page

Example: *1,200 DPI (laser printer), 4,800 DPI (scanner)*

DSL   Short for digital subscriber line; a popular form of high-speed Internet connection

Ergonomics   Science of creating work environments and furnishings well-tuned to the shape and function of the human body

Example: *Natural (split) keyboards*

File   Group of computer data with a common purpose

Example: *A letter you have typed, a program*

File Format   A technique for storing information in a computer file; application programs normally have a special file format that they use by default

Example: *docx (Word), xlsx (Excel)*

Firewall   Software and hardware designed to prevent attacks on a computer from an external operator

Gigabyte   Approximately one billion bytes of data (*See also* the Defining Units of Measure section on page 8)

Example: *About 3,000 books*

Gigahertz (GHz)   One billion pulses of electricity in an electrical circuit in a single second; the speed of most microprocessors sold today is measured in gigahertz (*See also* the Clock Speed section on page 10)

Example: *3.2 GHz Pentium 4*

Hardware   Physical components of a computer system

Example: *Disk drive, monitor, microprocessor*

Kilobyte (KB)   Approximately one thousand bytes of data (*See also* the Defining Units of Measure section on page 8)

Example: *One single-spaced page of text*

JPEG   A popular file format for storing photos

LCD Panel   Monitor that uses liquid crystal display technology, rather than a cathode ray tube (CRT) as in earlier monitors, to create screen images (*See also* the Purchasing an LCD Monitor section on page 16)

Malware   A generic term for malicious software viruses that can damage a computer system

Example: *love bug*

Megabyte (MB)   Approximately one million bytes of data (*See also* the Defining Units of Measure section on page 8)

Example: *three average-length novels*

Microprocessor   One single silicon chip containing the complete circuitry of a computer (*See also* the The Microprocessor section on page 10)

Example: *Intel Core™ Duo, AMD Athlon™ 64 X2*

Modem   Device that lets a computer communicate digital data to other computers over a non-digital communication line, such as a telephone line or TV cable (*See also* the Types of Modems section on page 21)

Example: *56K modem, cable modem*

Monitor   The computer screen (*See also* the Computer Video section on page 15)

Example: *17" CRT monitor, 15" flat panel*

MP3   Acronym for Moving Picture Experts Group Layer-3 Audio; first popular format for highly compressed music files

Example: *A music file*

Peripherals   Hardware components outside the system unit

Example: *Monitor, keyboard*

Phishing Message   A bogus email message that asks you to submit personal information to a hoax website

Pixel   A single dot of light on a computer monitor (*See also* the Computer Video section on page 15)

Port   A place (usually at the back of the computer) to plug in a cable (*See also* the Ports section on page 18)

Example: *USB port, parallel port*

RAM   Short for random access memory; computer chip designed to temporarily store data to be processed (*See also* the Random Access Memory section on page 11)

Example: *512 MB RAM*

Resolution   Measure of the sharpness of a computer monitor display or a printout (*See also* the Printer Performance section on page 23)

Example: *1024 × 768 (monitor), 600 DPI (ink-jet printer)*

Scanner   Device that turns photographs and other images into computer files

Example: *HP Scanjet 4750c*

Software   Logical component of a computer system; composed of digital code stored in the form of files; some software exists as programs to help you get work done; also stores work

Example: *Windows XP, Internet Explorer, a document file*

Spam   Junk email

Spyware   Software installed on the computer without your knowledge; can steal personal information

System unit   Main box that contains the primary components of the computer

USB port   Short for Universal Serial Bus port; a single USB port can connect several devices simultaneously, including keyboards, scanners, modems, cameras, and more; USB 2.0 ports transfer data about forty times faster than the original USB 1.0 port (*See also* the USB Ports section on page 19)

Example: *Printer cable plugged into a USB port*

Virus   Program that invisibly "infects" files and disrupts operation of a computer in some way

Example: *Michelangelo, Good News*

Zip Archive   A file into which other files are compressed for faster and easier transmission

Example: *The student exercise files for this book are downloaded in a zip archive*

Index